DATE DUE

JUN 06 2008			
JUN 03 2009			

DEMCO 38-296

Landscape Estimating Methods

Fourth Edition

Sylvia H. Fee

RSMeans

Landscape Estimating Methods

Fourth Edition

Sylvia H. Fee

RSMeans

Copyright 2002
Construction Publishers & Consultants
63 Smiths Lane
Kingston, MA 02364-0800
(781) 422-5000

The editors for this book were Mary Greene, Barbara Balboni, and Andrea Keenan. The production manager was Michael Kokernak. The production coordinator was Marion Schofield. The electronic publishing specialist was Paula Reale-Camelio. The proofreader was Robin Richardson. The book and cover were designed by Norman R. Forgit.

Printed in the United States of America

10 9 8 7 6 5

Library of Congress Catalog Number 2002511405

ISBN 0-87629-663-0

 Reed Construction Data

Table of Contents

Foreword

This new fourth edition of *Means Landscape Estimating Methods* details the process of landscape estimating from start to finish—with tips on the best techniques for saving money and winning jobs. It enables the landscape professional or facility manager to produce accurate, reliable estimates. The author, a landscape contractor and designer for over 25 years, takes you through the process of estimating step-by-step—showing you how to analyze the project, cost it out, and produce both a reliable estimate and a bid that will win the job *and* make a profit.

Basically, this is a book about standards and procedures in landscape construction estimating. The author is closely acquainted with these procedures because she has worked with estimating, bidding and job planning on projects ranging from patios to parks to power plants. Also, the author's years of experience as a course instructor for landscape professionals has demonstrated that many students are not thoroughly skilled in using logical methods in sequence. It is important for the landscape professional to be aware of the most suitable materials and equipment, know the capability and capacity of workers and machinery, and establish an operating system that is known and accepted by *all* responsible parties in the organization. This book demonstrates how to create a logical, methodical system for estimating the jobs and then scheduling and doing the actual work.

Step-by-step, an overview of the estimating process is provided—from the invitation to bid through job planning once the contract is signed. Included are the project analysis site visit, the quantity takeoff, estimating costs for material and labor, calculating overhead and profit, and bidding and scheduling. Following the completely updated sample estimate are detailed explanations of how to use the annual cost reference *Means Site Work and Landscape Cost Data*, from which most costs in this book are taken. For over 60 years, R. S. Means Company has been researching and publishing cost data for the building industry.

Acknowledgments

The author wishes to express her appreciation for the creative and practical guidance she received from many design professionals, nurserymen, landscape contractors, clients and students with whom she has been privileged to work in the dynamic and creative landscape industry. Professional firms, trade associations, commercial organizations and research facilities have contributed references and graphic examples found in this book. Many companies and organizations have made specific contributions to this book, and are acknowledged as their contributions appear. They include the Agricultural Research Service of USDA, American Nursery and Landscape Association, The Associated General Contractors of America, Brick Industry Association, Center for Irrigation Technology, Coffin & Coffin—Landscape Architects and Urban Designers, Hunter Industries Incorporated, Landscape Forms, Inc., Neenah Foundry Company, and Quick Crete Products Corporation.

In addition the author expresses a special thanks to the staff of professionals at R.S. Means. The staff of editors and construction and engineering professionals have provided the authoritative and timely construction cost data found here.

Introduction

The landscape industry of today is dealing with changing uses of outdoor spaces, and new technologies as well. To meet these challenges we must utilize past experience, new methods and materials, and creativity to develop effective solutions.

Within the landscape industry, contractors, designers, facilities managers and suppliers contribute to each project. Each of these professionals has his or her own perspective and role in the industry. Yet, they all help in developing answers to the ever-changing requirements of the landscape industry.

Landscape project management, and especially estimating, is one area that may be approached in many different ways. Yet among these diverse methods, there are certain sound estimating techniques that have proven most successful. The methods and examples presented in the following chapters will guide you through the steps of producing accurate estimates. The latest computer technology offers new possibilities, but it is still organization that is the key to efficiency and profit.

The source material for *Means Landscape Estimating Methods* comes from the author's 25 years experience in the landscape industry. The cost and productivity information in this book has been assembled by the experienced staff of construction professionals at R.S. Means Company, Inc.

Chapter 1

A View of
the Landscape
Industry

Chapter One

A View of the Landscape Industry

Landscape design and construction is both an art and a business that is commanding an increasing share of attention and profit within the construction industry. Today, landscaping is integral to real estate development. Zoning laws often require that trees and green, open spaces be incorporated into plans for new projects. Yet even when landscaping is not a legal requirement, real estate developers now see that outdoor spaces that are functional and eye-catching appeal to prospective buyers or tenants.

Landscape construction has become a major industry with customers ranging from metropolitan transportation projects... to neighborhood parks... to private residences. It has also proven to be an investment that provides significant returns. As the president of a large New England construction company defines landscaping, it is "the 3% of the construction job that makes a 30% difference."

In landscaping, the needs of the client define the job. The criteria for each project are established by:

* The aesthetic effect desired.
* Practical requirements of the client.
* Resolution of site problems.
* Adequate access for pedestrians and vehicles.
* Appropriate distancing between people and undesirable conditions and activities.

Clients are interested not only in handsome spaces around structures, but also in open areas for recreation. Whether the client is a town government seeking a street tree planting—or a homeowner wanting a new lawn—attractive, functional, economical green spaces are the goal.

Figure 1.1, "The Development of a Landscaping Plan," shows how existing features, "people use" planning and environmental factors all contribute to development of a residential landscaping plan. The planning process is shown, as are the design solutions.

With the specialized skills and tremendous range of materials that are available today, the solutions offered by landscape professionals are limitless. However, success in the landscaping industry also requires good planning, expert performance, and familiarity with these new materials and methods. Up-to-date

DEVELOPMENT OF
A LANDSCAPING PLAN

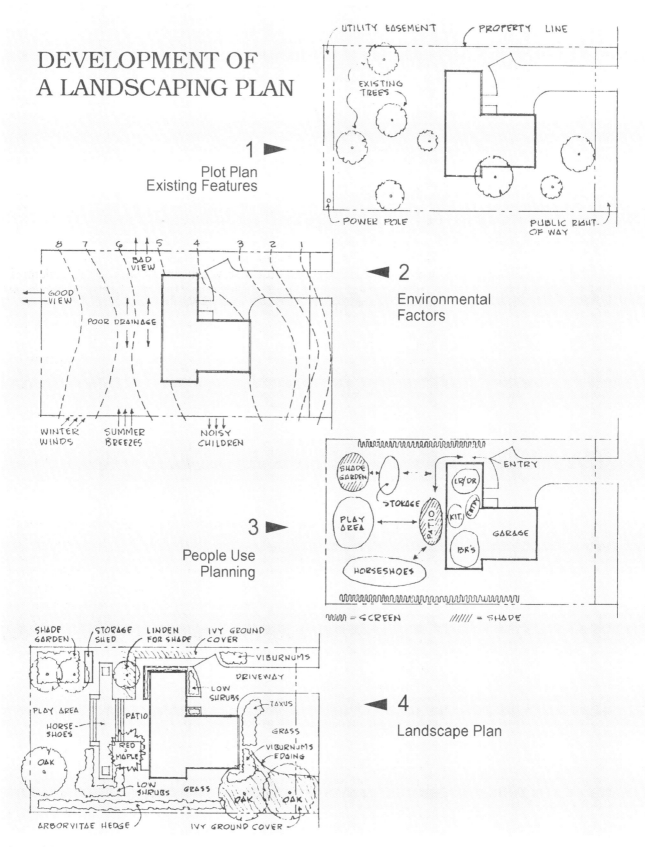

1 ▶
Plot Plan
Existing Features

◀ 2
Environmental
Factors

3 ▶
People Use
Planning

◀ 4
Landscape Plan

Figure 1.1

knowledge of industry costs and values is critical to effective estimating and business management. The sources of reliable cost information are discussed in detail in Chapter 5.

Divisions of Landscape Jobs

Landscape construction involves many construction disciplines. The jobs required for a typical project fit into five general categories:

- Site Work
- Hard Construction
- Planting
- Specialties
- Landscape Maintenance

Site Work

Site Work includes clearing the land of excess trees and brush, digging utilities trenches, creating or leveling banks and slopes, grading, excavating and filling, and providing for proper drainage. This work includes the preservation of designated areas in conformance with local, state and federal regulations. Such work calls for decisions on the use of heavy equipment and is typically performed by the general contractor. This is a high cost item that must be effectively managed in order to keep project costs under control.

This work establishes spot elevations and creates a bare setting for "people use" of the project. Access and circulation of vehicles and people, aesthetics and expected usages are all considered in creating the project's terrain. Information on suitability, productivity and costs of equipment utilized in the site work are all compared and analyzed. A wide range of site work materials, methods and systems for drainage, erosion control, paving, retaining walls and more are provided in the Appendix.

The scope of site work for a landscape contractor is usually separated from the site work of a general contractor. That is to say, the landscape contractor may typically perform finish grade work.

Hard Construction

This category covers both the practical needs and the aesthetic requirements of a landscaping project. Included in this category is the construction of walls, steps, driveways and walks, decks, fences, and other work needed for the safe access and comfort of people. Designers and builders strive to combine beauty with utility while also responding to environmental concerns and regulations. A well-placed wall, for example, serves as a sound barrier as well as a physical barrier. It may also control erosion of slopes and support flowering vines for screening and beauty. Likewise, a circular roadway can provide an elegant design feature, while serving as a practical access route for emergency vehicles. When effectively planned, hard construction resolves problems while it enhances the use of the land. Common landscape construction materials are defined in Chapter 2, "Materials and Methods."

Plantings

Planting is performed for both practical and aesthetic reasons. Trees, shrubs, and hedges may control erosion, guide pedestrians and vehicles, provide shade in summer and shelter from the wind in winter. Plantings also act as architectural design features, and of course, beautify. Since aesthetic concerns are so important to landscape construction, beautification belongs high on the list of

concerns for planting, as it does for site work and hard construction. Some standards for plant materials are provided in Figure 2.15 "Trees and Plants by Environment & Purpose" in Chapter 2. More detailed reference information is included in the Appendix.

Specialties

Specialties make up an ever-expanding category of landscape construction that calls upon many different skills including landscape maintenance, irrigation, retail sales of items such as site amenities, the installation of play equipment, and seasonal services such as snow removal. The need for outdoor lighting, recreational facilities, street furniture, gardening, property design, and a host of other elements may call upon the skills of specialty subcontractors. Debate continues, however, on whether it is more economical for landscape contractors to perform these kinds of specialties as part of their own in-house services, or to delegate them to outside suppliers and tradesmen.

The creative latitude and independent decision-making permitted to the landscape architect and contractor varies with the size, characteristics, and management of a given project. In any case, it is the landscape specialist's knowledge and professional excellence that provide a workable solution for the optimum use of the site.

The Landscape Professional and Project Management

A great percentage of landscape work is for private residences. In most of these cases, the owner is the only party to be served by the work contract. Generally, the limited scope of a residential project calls for only one design professional or contractor to arrange and complete the work. It is on these relatively smaller, residential projects that the landscape architect or contractor is more likely to exercise total control and to take responsibility for most of the key decisions.

Unlike residential projects, commercial and industrial landscape projects usually involve the combined efforts of a group. Foremost in that group is the owner, who is to be either the principal user of the project or a representative of its tenants. It is the owner or developer who oversees matters of property acquisition and title, proposed land use, and finances for the project under discussion. Working closely with the owner are the architect and the landscape architect, jointly termed "design professionals," and the contractor. The design professionals conceive and prepare the plans of the project, and the contractor builds it.

The amount of responsibility that the owner delegates to designers, contractors or facility managers varies greatly. For large commercial or industrial projects, the management picture can be complex, with the general contractor serving as manager of numerous subcontractors—the landscape contractor among them. At a school campus or sprawling office or research facility, it may be the *facility manager* who determines the selection of contractors as well as the type of work to be done. On a smaller job, the landscape contractor might fulfill the contract under the direct supervision of the owner or the design professionals. No matter how the management of a project is delegated, contractors should have a clear agreement with the principal party for whom the work is being performed.

Before work begins on a project, each responsible party is called upon to handle certain preliminary arrangements and negotiations. These responsibilities entail meetings with businesses, governing boards, and other authorities whose consent or contribution is needed if the project is to proceed. Be aware that the consent and contributions of other parties may be critical for the fulfillment

of your contractural obligation. Figure 1.2 shows the areas of involvement for each of the responsible parties in a typical commercial project. The complex nature of building codes, securing the required permits and timely scheduling of inspections are of key importance to all parties and the subsequent success of the project.

The goals of the *owner* or *facilities manager* determine the character and scope of the project. As Figure 1.2 illustrates, it is the responsibility of the owner to handle all legal and monetary matters involved in obtaining the property and financing its development. The owner may be working with bankers, realtors, and financiers in this phase of the project.

The *design professionals*, as the originators of the project's plans and specifications, produce a landscape plan that "fits" the ground, not one that "twists" the ground to fit the plan. Their experience makes them aware of the problems likely to be encountered as development gets under way. These professionals may be called upon to meet with planning boards, zoning boards, conservation commissions, and other local or national regulatory agencies. It is also the responsibility of design professionals to consult and coordinate with interior planners, structural and mechanical engineers, and product manufacturers who are expected to participate in the project. Before plans are drawn, it is essential for the architect and landscape architect to familiarize themselves with the building codes and by-laws of the host community. Wasted moves in the planning stage can add thousands of dollars to project costs.

General contractors are problem solvers. It is their business to know which methods, materials, and equipment can be used most effectively to solve difficulties posed in the preparation and use of the land, to keep costs under control, and to bring the designer's concepts to reality. It is the contractor who seeks and procures building permits, negotiates with trade unions, carries out transactions with product manufacturers and suppliers, and arranges for utility hookups with local suppliers. The contractor also secures the services of craftsmen/subcontractors and oversees their performance of the work.

Above all other contractors, the landscaper deals with living materials and bio-systems. These unique conditions make every project a learning experience. Through skillful application of the trade, the landscape contractor can quickly become a very visible asset to a project's general contractor, and a credit to the developer. As the landscape contractor becomes increasingly familiar with new methods and materials, the probability increases of obtaining desirable and profitable future contracts.

Building Your Business

Staying up-to-date and working effectively with a general contractor are important aspects of landscape construction. Competitive bidding, however, calls for more than a sound reputation and the goodwill of the construction industry. It is a discipline in itself and involves experience, exhaustive research, planning, calculation, and a measure of good, intuitive judgment. Chapter 7 of this book is devoted to a detailed description of the bidding process. It includes an explanation of proper procedures and shows bid forms for an example proposal.

Landscape contracts are secured by negotiation or by competitive bid. The bid is your proposal to complete a project for a stated sum. Before bids are accepted, however, the client may insist on knowing the qualifications of all prospective bidders. Landscape contractors who hope to compete must be prepared to provide owners and/or general contractors with all of the required information.

THE PARTIES IN A TYPICAL COMMERCIAL LANDSCAPE PROJECT: THEIR INTERACTIONS AND RESPONSIBILITIES

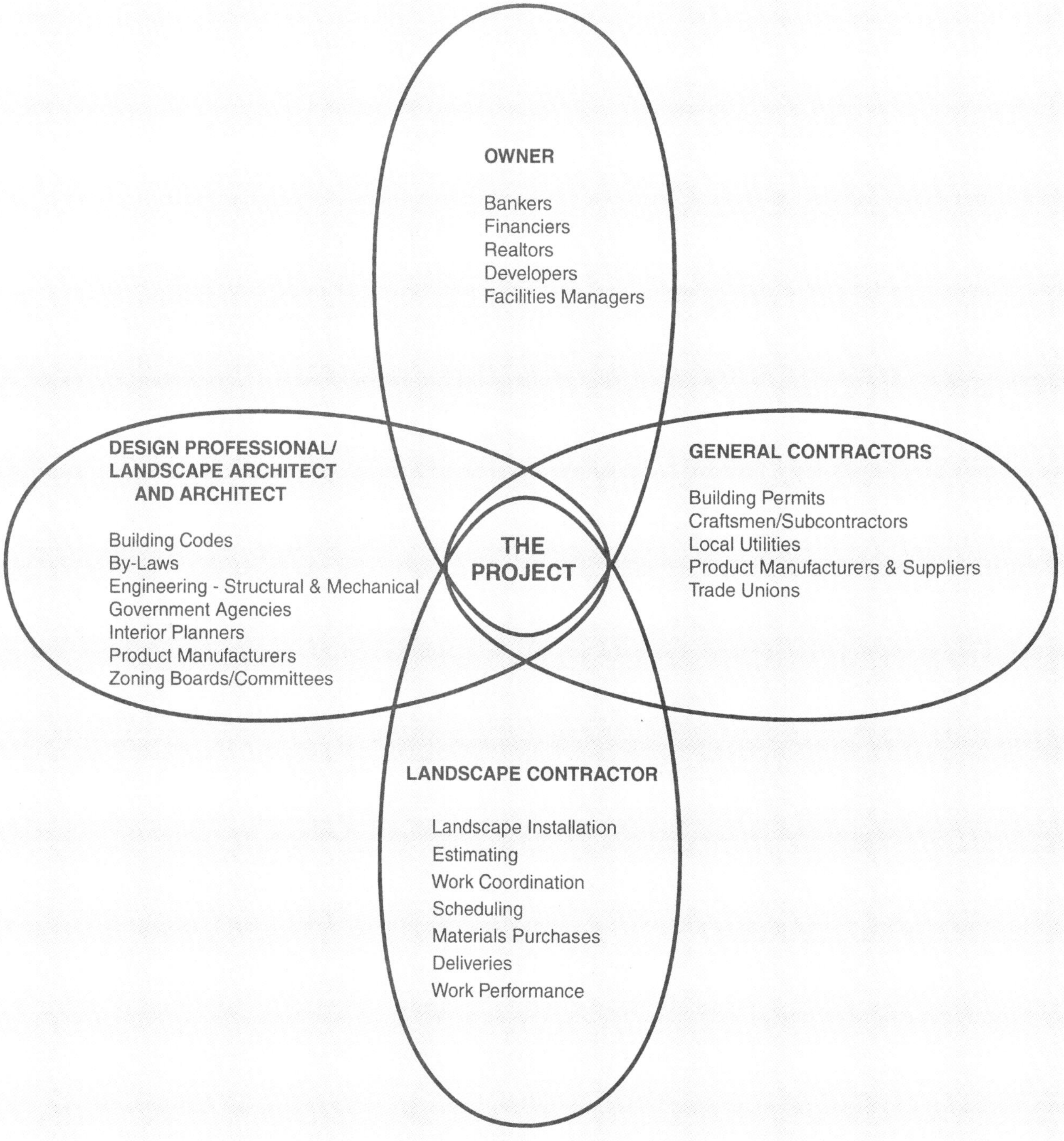

OWNER

Bankers
Financiers
Realtors
Developers
Facilities Managers

**DESIGN PROFESSIONAL/
LANDSCAPE ARCHITECT
AND ARCHITECT**

Building Codes
By-Laws
Engineering - Structural & Mechanical
Government Agencies
Interior Planners
Product Manufacturers
Zoning Boards/Committees

THE PROJECT

GENERAL CONTRACTORS

Building Permits
Craftsmen/Subcontractors
Local Utilities
Product Manufacturers & Suppliers
Trade Unions

LANDSCAPE CONTRACTOR

Landscape Installation
Estimating
Work Coordination
Scheduling
Materials Purchases
Deliveries
Work Performance

Figure 1.2

To assess contractors' qualifications, clients may need to know the following:

- Type of landscape firm (corporation, partnership, sole proprietorship)
- How long in business
- Net worth (financial statement)
- Dollar volume (last three years)
- Bank references
- Certificate of insurance
- Bonding capacity
- Name of bonding company
- Licenses
- Trade affiliations
- References from clients for whom the company has completed work

In addition, the landscaping firm may be required to give information or to submit affidavits to prove that it is an equal opportunity employer and that it has complied with affirmative action programs established by the state and federal governments. Some projects also require a bid bond, which is a guarantee that a landscape contractor will sign a contract on the basis of the bid submitted.

Most established firms doing commercial work are familiar with the process of submitting credentials. A promotional package is usually sent to clients, with pamphlets and advertising materials which emphasize the company's experience and highlight their specialties, along with a letter tailored specifically to the job.

Successfully completed projects are the most compelling advertisements for your landscaping business. They let prospective clients see for themselves how well-planned and well-executed outdoor spaces can conserve and beautify property while expanding its use.

Your marketing materials should be directed towards the person who is authorized to award the landscape construction services contract. Seek the person in charge of selecting subcontractors and address your information package to that person. In residential projects, this is frequently the property owner or an appointed representative. In other instances, the general contractor, construction manager, or the owner's architect is responsible for awarding the contract.

Another way to track down new work is to scan newspapers and trade publications that list starting dates of construction, new proposals, and invitations to bid. The law usually requires that public projects be advertised, giving all competitors a fair chance. Government projects are also open to all qualified companies and are almost always awarded to the low bidder, a consideration which challenges the aggressive young company to exercise shrewd judgment and planning skills in preparation of the bid.

By contrast, private clients often choose bidders from a selected list of qualified companies. Contracts do not necessarily go to the lowest bidder, but are awarded at the owner's discretion. Architects and construction companies often choose bidders from their own select list of qualified applicants. By complying with the highest standards of the trade, establishing a reputation for quality and goodwill, and advertising that fact, a landscaping company can establish a reliable reputation in the community and greatly improve its chance of winning a place on a list of select bidders.

Arrangements of this sort need not discourage the qualified newcomer; indeed, they can be a welcome challenge. There are always opportunities within the bidding process to remain competitive. For example, certain bid invitations encourage bidders to suggest changes and additions. This approach gives the landscape contractor an opportunity to show a measure of knowledge, skill, and creativity that may earn special consideration. In addition, projects that are large enough for competitive bidding usually enter a phase of negotiations between management and the chosen bidder. Here again, the landscape contractor has a chance to win the confidence of the client.

The growth of a landscape-related business requires both creative and business skills. Site work, hard construction, planting, and specialties comprise the general categories on a typical landscape project; experience in these essential areas is the cornerstone for growth and profit in the competitive landscape industry. Success also depends upon good planning, knowledge, and management.

Design professionals and contractors who want to expand their businesses should also develop marketing strategies. Selling one's skills is a new task for design pros and tradesmen alike. Formal and/or professional training often does not include marketing and accounting. Look for assistance in these areas from the many industry member organizations. (See listing at the end of this chapter and in the Appendix.) Take advantage of these information sources to learn, grow, and prosper.

Planning the Landscape Proposal

Landscape architects and contractors must conduct extensive studies of all newly proposed projects before they are able to submit an appropriate proposal for the work. Architects use the term "program" to put a job into focus on a human scale. Their program defines who will use the newly created space and what activities the users will perform there. The requirements may be as down-to-earth as a playground or a baseball diamond for a housing project, or as abstract and dignified as the desire of a company to improve its corporate image. In either case, design professionals follow a carefully charted sequence of activities to determine the needs of the client and how those needs are best served.

Survey of the project site is the first step. The design professional's survey encompasses more than the physical conditions of the site. Traffic studies, historical preservation values and ecological systems may also be considered. The landscape architect should determine what work will be needed to prepare the site for the proposed uses. For example, soil tests, pits, or earth borings may be required. Will the parcel support the work from an ecological standpoint? Does water need to be retained or diverted? How much grading and excavation will be required? The survey gathers together all of the physical, environmental, and historical information that will come to bear on the project.

Analysis of all the survey information reveals both the advantages as well as the problems of the site. These must then be incorporated into the designer's plan—mitigating the difficulties and highlighting the good features. The landscape architect examines the owner's needs versus existing conditions for the proposed development. Consideration is given to such details as the time frame, the budget, building codes, and all zoning mandates, requirements, and restrictions. The scope of the project determines the degree of detail to be studied and included in further negotiations with the client.

A **Proposal** to the client is based on the site survey and analysis of all restrictions, requirements and codes that affect the site. Once the landscape designer or contractor has completed these steps, he or she is finally able to submit a proposal to the client, stating the details of the services and/or work to be performed, and the total project cost. The proposal may be presented in direct negotiations with the owner, as is customary for smaller residential projects, or it may be submitted as a competitive bid, as part of a formal bidding procedure. In any event, the landscape professional should seek out the party authorized to award the contract and, if possible, negotiate directly with that person.

When the job is estimated, bid and won, you can get on your way to building a functional and handsome landscape—that 3% of the job that makes a 30% difference.

National Landscaping Organizations

Landscape construction is a rapidly growing and changing industry. High quality work, adherence to local codes, accepted trade practices, and competitive bidding all play a part in making your landscaping business a continuing success. Yet to stay on top, landscapers must also keep up with the latest technological developments and confront challenging new demands within their field. It is here that they find strength in numbers.

National landscape trade and professional organizations exist to keep members informed of new materials and methods, as well as ways to cut costs, boost profits, and improve their practices. Among the many advantages provided by association memberships are: trade publications that offer up-to-date advice and information on every specialty, continuing education in seminars and workshops, representation in government, and conferences where members meet to share useful new ideas and developments in the field.

The best-known national associations are the *American Society of Landscape Architects*, *American Nursery and Landscape Association*, and *Associated Landscape Contractors of America*. Members include landscape architects, landscape contractors, and businesses that supply products and services to the industry. Also on the membership rolls are educators, technicians, and private citizens devoted to preservation and beautification of the land.

Professional groups provide and sponsor technical reports and monitor technical advances. They also publish manuals on industry practices, and trade journals filled with ideas to promote growth, profit, and savings in the landscaping industry. Conferences, symposia, and exhibits are among the services performed by the national associations.

In an age of urban sprawl and vanishing countryside, beautifying the landscape can be a battle. National landscape organizations are dedicated to this cause. The leaders of these groups are active in political lobbies and on industry awareness committees, where they remain alert to proposed laws that will affect the interests of the landscape business. Acting to promote what is best for the industry, they often exert a strong influence on the decisions reached by lawmakers.

Trade and professional organizations within the landscaping industry cooperate with local communities by encouraging their own high standards. Shows and exhibitions for design, building, and service trades bring new products and services to the attention of the entire landscape contracting industry. Each year, the national associations recognize citizens who underwrite outstanding

landscaping projects and present awards to the professionals who design and perform the work.

Local and regional chapters of landscape organizations carry on the work of the national groups within the community. They are known to have a positive influence on towns and cities, winning the confidence of town boards and regulatory commissions by keeping standards high among all landscaping contractors practicing in the area.

For a complete list of landscaping trade associations in your area, contact these organizations at their national headquarters.

American Society of Landscape Architects (202) 898-2444
636 I Street, NW
Washington, DC 20001-3736

American Nursery and Landscape Association (202) 789-2900
1250 I Street, NW, Suite 500
Washington, DC 20005

Associated Landscape Contractors of America (703) 736-9666
150 Elden Street, Suite 270
Herndon, VA 20170

Association of Professional Landscape Designers (717) 238-9780
1924 North Second Street
Harrisburg, PA 17102

Chapter 2

Materials and Methods

Chapter Two
Materials and Methods

Working with highly vulnerable plant materials under ever-changing weather conditions at very different sites challenges the ingenuity and skills of even the most experienced landscape professionals. The variety of landscape materials and equipment they can utilize is ever-increasing and seemingly inexhaustible. The challenge lies in how to use these resources most efficiently and effectively. The startling impact of 20' trees planted within one day often brings the delighted response, "it's like magic," but the designers and installers responsible are no magicians. Their "magic" results from a thorough knowledge of design possibilities and installation methods, along with a keen understanding of the capacity, and character of power equipment, tools, materials and supplies.

Site Work

Site analysis and design issues are best handled by professionals such as landscape architects, civil engineers and qualified contractors. Otherwise, the potential of a site may never be realized. Maximum utilization of any site is obtained by careful analysis and preconstruction evaluation by design professionals. Both upside and downside features need to be analyzed for their potential. Opportunities and challenges abound as all physical, biological, social, cultural, environmental and regulatory constraints are brought into focus and addressed for the solution needed by the client.

Preliminary explorations such as subsurface investigations are necessary. Site clearing and cut and fill operations may create vistas and screen other areas. A sequence of work is planned to minimize the impact of cut and fill operations. Essential to the earthwork portion of any job is the careful selection of cost-effective equipment, which is examined in Chapter 3, "Equipment". The impact of weather on production may be dramatic, and create significant delays or necessitate rescheduling completely. Figure 2.1 gives a clear reminder of that.

For the landscape contractor, site work consists primarily of earthwork, but can also include paving, drainage, and piping. Attention to surface water problems at driveways and walkways may be anticipated and resolved at lesser cost by doing the work at the time paving is installed. Drainage systems such as trench drains are too often a remedial application. Further information on typical trench drains is shown in Figure 2.27 at the end of this chapter.

Erosion control is increasingly relevant for the landscape contractor. Common sense and environmental concerns have brought useful solutions that may be required by local or state authorities. Hydro applications such as air seeding with tackifiers and mulches are well known to landscapers. Other systems include erosion control blankets, silt control fabrics, gabions, the use of plants

Weather Data and Design Conditions

City	Latitude (1) °	Latitude (1) 1'	Winter Temperatures (1) Med. of Annual Extremes	Winter Temperatures (1) 99%	Winter Temperatures (1) 97½%	Winter Degree Days (2)	Summer (Design Dry Bulb) Temperatures and Relative Humidity 1%	Summer (Design Dry Bulb) Temperatures and Relative Humidity 2½%	Summer (Design Dry Bulb) Temperatures and Relative Humidity 5%
UNITED STATES									
Albuquerque, NM	35	0	5.1	12	16	4,400	96/61	94/61	92/61
Atlanta, GA	33	4	11.9	17	22	3,000	94/74	92/74	90/73
Baltimore, MD	39	2	7	14	17	4,600	94/75	91/75	89/74
Birmingham, AL	33	3	13	17	21	2,600	96/74	94/75	92/74
Bismarck, ND	46	5	-32	-23	-19	8,800	95/68	91/68	88/67
Boise, ID	43	3	1	3	10	5,800	96/65	94/64	91/64
Boston, MA	42	2	-1	6	9	5,600	91/73	88/71	85/70
Burlington, VT	44	3	-17	-12	-7	8,200	88/72	85/70	82/69
Charleston, WV	38	2	3	7	11	4,400	92/74	90/73	87/72
Charlotte, NC	35	1	13	18	22	3,200	95/74	93/74	91/74
Casper, WY	42	5	-21	-11	-5	7,400	92/58	90/57	87/57
Chicago, IL	41	5	-8	-3	2	6,600	94/75	91/74	88/73
Cincinnati, OH	39	1	0	1	6	4,400	92/73	90/72	88/72
Cleveland, OH	41	2	-3	1	5	6,400	91/73	88/72	86/71
Columbia, SC	34	0	16	20	24	2,400	97/76	95/75	93/75
Dallas, TX	32	5	14	18	22	2,400	102/75	100/75	97/75
Denver, CO	39	5	-10	-5	1	6,200	93/59	91/59	89/59
Des Moines, IA	41	3	-14	-10	-5	6,600	94/75	91/74	88/73
Detroit, MI	42	2	-3	3	6	6,200	91/73	88/72	86/71
Great Falls, MT	47	3	-25	-21	-15	7,800	91/60	88/60	85/59
Hartford, CT	41	5	-4	3	7	6,200	91/74	88/73	85/72
Houston, TX	29	5	24	28	33	1,400	97/77	95/77	93/77
Indianapolis, IN	39	4	-7	-2	2	5,600	92/74	90/74	87/73
Jackson, MS	32	2	16	21	25	2,200	97/76	95/76	93/76
Kansas City, MO	39	1	4	2	6	4,800	99/75	96/74	93/74
Las Vegas, NV	36	1	18	25	28	2,800	108/66	106/65	104/65
Lexington, KY	38	0	-1	3	8	4,600	93/73	91/73	88/72
Little Rock, AR	34	4	11	15	20	3,200	99/76	96/77	94/77
Los Angeles, CA	34	0	36	41	43	2,000	93/70	89/70	86/69
Memphis, TN	35	0	10	13	18	3,200	98/77	95/76	93/76
Miami, FL	25	5	39	44	47	200	91/77	90/77	89/77
Milwaukee, WI	43	0	-11	-8	-4	7,600	90/74	87/73	84/71
Minneapolis, MN	44	5	-22	-16	-12	8,400	92/75	89/73	86/71
New Orleans, LA	30	0	28	29	33	1,400	93/78	92/77	90/77
New York, NY	40	5	6	11	15	5,000	92/74	89/73	87/72
Norfolk, VA	36	5	15	20	22	3,400	93/77	91/76	89/76
Oklahoma City, OK	35	2	4	9	13	3,200	100/74	97/74	95/73
Omaha, NE	41	2	-13	-8	-3	6,600	94/76	91/75	88/74
Philadelphia, PA	39	5	6	10	14	4,400	93/75	90/74	87/72
Phoenix, AZ	33	3	27	31	34	1,800	109/71	107/71	105/71
Pittsburgh, PA	40	3	-1	3	7	6,000	91/72	88/71	86/70
Portland, ME	43	4	-10	-6	-1	7,600	87/72	84/71	81/69
Portland, OR	45	4	18	17	23	4,600	89/68	85/67	81/65
Portsmouth, NH	43	1	-8	-2	2	7,200	89/73	85/71	83/70
Providence, RI	41	4	-1	5	9	6,000	89/73	86/72	83/70
Rochester, NY	43	1	-5	1	5	6,800	91/73	88/71	85/70
Salt Lake City, UT	40	5	0	3	8	6,000	97/62	95/62	92/61
San Francisco, CA	37	5	36	38	40	3,000	74/63	71/62	69/61
Seattle, WA	47	4	22	22	27	5,200	85/68	82/66	78/65
Sioux Falls, SD	43	4	-21	-15	-11	7,800	94/73	91/72	88/71
St. Louis, MO	38	4	-3	3	8	5,000	98/75	94/75	91/75
Tampa, FL	28	0	32	36	40	680	92/77	91/77	90/76
Trenton, NJ	40	1	4	11	14	5,000	91/75	88/74	85/73
Washington, DC	38	5	7	14	17	4,200	93/75	91/74	89/74
Wichita, KS	37	4	-3	3	7	4,600	101/72	98/73	96/73
Wilmington, DE	39	4	5	10	14	5,000	92/74	89/74	87/73
ALASKA									
Anchorage	61	1	-29	-23	-18	10,800	71/59	68/58	66/56
Fairbanks	64	5	-59	-51	-47	14,280	82/62	78/60	75/59
CANADA									
Edmonton, Alta.	53	3	-30	-29	-25	11,000	85/66	82/65	79/63
Halifax, N.S.	44	4	-4	1	5	8,000	79/66	76/65	74/64
Montreal, Que.	45	3	-20	-16	-10	9,000	88/73	85/72	83/71
Saskatoon, Sask.	52	1	-35	-35	-31	11,000	89/68	86/66	83/65
St. John, Nwf.	47	4	1	3	7	8,600	77/66	75/65	73/64
Saint John, N.B.	45	2	-15	-12	-8	8,200	80/67	77/65	75/64
Toronto, Ont.	43	4	-10	-5	-1	7,000	90/73	87/72	85/71
Vancouver, B.C.	49	1	13	15	19	6,000	79/67	77/66	74/65
Winnipeg, Man.	49	5	-31	-30	-27	10,800	89/73	86/71	84/70

(1) Handbook of Fundamentals, ASHRAE, Inc., NY 1989
(2) Local Climatological Annual Survey, USDC Env. Science Services Administration, Asheville, NC

(from *Means Assemblies Cost Data* 1999)

Figure 2.1

(bio-engineering) and others. Some are illustrated at the end of this chapter in Figures 2.28 and 2.29a & b. Site utilities and drainage involve the additional cost of pipe bedding, manholes, and catch basins. Electrical cables and ducts, although installed in the site work area, are more properly the work of others. The various kinds of site work may require specific types of equipment (see the Appendix for illustrations).

Hard Construction

Hard construction includes a wide variety of materials and methods. Selecting the proper materials while balancing aesthetics and cost effectiveness requires skill and ingenuity. Paving materials, for example, offer many options of shape, form, and cost. Various types can be coordinated. Concrete can be cast in place or used in the form of precast paver units; it can be used on its own or in combination with other materials. The American Society for Testing and Materials (ASTM) establishes standards for these materials, as well as thousands of others. Further information on this organization may be found in the Appendix.

Bricks, blocks, and tiles are available in a wide range of sizes, colors, shapes, and textures. Other materials, such as water and earth, are not listed as "materials," but are instead defined as items like pools and fountains, or berms and mounds. Installation of these items may require work in the categories of both site work and construction. Much landscape construction involves paving for outdoor floor surfaces. There are specialized pavings for various recreational uses. Such special uses (playgrounds, ball fields, etc.) typically conform to agency and landscape architects' specifications and drawings. Within the landscape industry, many proprietary paving products are available. The most commonly used materials include: **asphalt, brick, concrete, stone, tile** and **wood**. See Figures 2.30a & b at the end of this chapter for comparison and appearance of brick, concrete and stone paving, as well as labor-hour data.

Bituminous Paving

Asphaltic concrete, or bituminous concrete material, incorporates a number of methods and systems for the installation of walks, roadways, and parking lots. Bituminous concrete is composed of carefully graded coarse and fine aggregates, bound together with asphaltic cement. Figure 2.2 shows area costs based on large volume work for bituminous and other sidewalks from *Means Site Work & Landscape Cost Data*.

Brick

Brick is a material that has been used for paving for centuries. It is made from kiln-fired clay or shale. It is popular as a paving material because it is easy to produce and readily available in a wide range of sizes, shapes, colors, and textures. Brick textures vary from smooth to glazed and highly finished to mottled surfaces. Highly distinctive, decorative surfaces are made for ornamental and special purposes. Brick is graded by weather resistance, a measure of porosity. Manufacturers also claim slip resistance for certain brick finishes. Most paving brick is suitable as a facing material, but many types of face brick are not appropriate for paving in northern climates. Continuous freeze-thaw cycles and heavy abrasion can damage brick that is not made for paving.

Pavers are a type of brick made specifically for outdoor walkway and floor surfaces. They are sized to permit a wide variety of paving patterns, as shown in Figure 2.3. Their thicknesses range from 1-1/8″ to 2-1/4″. Thin pavers are a cost-effective choice when specifications call for brick walks to be set in a mortar bed.

02775 | **Sidewalks**	CREW	DAILY OUTPUT	LABOR-HOURS	UNIT	2002 BARE COSTS				TOTAL INCL O&P
					MAT.	LABOR	EQUIP.	TOTAL	
275 0010 **SIDEWALKS, DRIVEWAYS, & PATIOS** No base									275
0020 Asphaltic concrete, 2" thick	B-37	720	.067	S.Y.	3.71	1.66	.16	5.53	6.80
0100 2-1/2" thick	"	660	.073	"	4.70	1.81	.18	6.69	8.15
0110 Bedding for brick or stone, mortar, 1" thick	D-1	300	.053	S.F.	.32	1.44		1.76	2.56
0120 2" thick	"	200	.080		.80	2.16		2.96	4.19
0130 Sand, 2" thick	B-18	8,000	.003		.13	.07	.01	.21	.27
0140 4" thick	"	4,000	.006	▼	.27	.14	.01	.42	.54
0300 Concrete, 3000 psi, CIP, 6 x 6 - W1.4 x W1.4 mesh,									
0310 broomed finish, no base, 4" thick	B-24	600	.040	S.F.	1.15	1.10		2.25	2.95
0350 5" thick		545	.044		1.53	1.21		2.74	3.54
0400 6" thick	▼	510	.047	▼	1.79	1.29		3.08	3.94
0440 For other finishes, see Div. 033-450									
0450 For bank run gravel base, 4" thick, add	B-18	2,500	.010	S.F.	.37	.23	.02	.62	.79
0520 8" thick, add	"	1,600	.015		.74	.36	.03	1.13	1.42
0550 Exposed aggregate finish, add to above, minimum	B-24	1,875	.013		.07	.35		.42	.62
0600 Maximum		455	.053		.23	1.44		1.67	2.47
0700 Patterned surface, add to above min.		1,200	.020			.55		.55	.84
0710 Maximum	▼	500	.048	▼		1.31		1.31	2.01
0800 For integral colors, see Div. 03310-220									
0850 Splash block, precast concrete	1 Clab	150	.053	Ea.	5.20	1.25		6.45	7.65
0950 Concrete tree grate, 5' square	B-6	25	.960		265	24.50	7.15	296.65	340
0960 Cast iron tree grate with frame, 2 piece, round, 5' diameter		25	.960		730	24.50	7.15	761.65	845
0980 Square, 5' side	▼	25	.960	▼	750	24.50	7.15	781.65	870
1000 Crushed stone, 1" thick, white marble	2 Clab	1,700	.009	S.F.	.22	.22		.44	.58
1050 Bluestone		1,700	.009		.20	.22		.42	.56
1070 Granite chips	▼	1,700	.009		.19	.22		.41	.55
1200 For 2" asphaltic conc base and tack coat, add to above	B-37	7,200	.007		.42	.17	.02	.61	.75
1660 Limestone pavers, 3" thick	D-1	72	.222		6.20	6		12.20	16
1670 4" thick		70	.229		8.20	6.15		14.35	18.50
1680 5" thick	▼	68	.235		10.30	6.35		16.65	21
1700 Redwood, prefabricated, 4' x 4' sections	2 Carp	316	.051		7.15	1.52		8.67	10.20
1750 Redwood planks, 1" thick, on sleepers	"	240	.067		4.99	2		6.99	8.60
1830 1-1/2" thick	B-28	167	.144		3.50	4		7.50	10.05
1840 2" thick		167	.144		4.50	4		8.50	11.15
1850 3" thick		150	.160		6.65	4.45		11.10	14.25
1860 4" thick		150	.160		8.70	4.45		13.15	16.55
1870 5" thick	▼	150	.160	▼	11.05	4.45		15.50	19.15
2100 River or beach stone, stock	B-1	18	1.333	Ton	25	32		57	77.50
2150 Quarried	"	18	1.333	"	44	32		76	98
2160 Load, dump, and spread stone with skid steer, 100' haul	B-62	24	1	C.Y.		25.50	5.45	30.95	45.50
2165 200' haul		18	1.333			34	7.25	41.25	60.50
2168 300' haul	▼	12	2	▼		51	10.90	61.90	90.50
2170 Shale paver, 2-1/4" thick	D-1	200	.080	S.F.	2.50	2.16		4.66	6.05
2200 Coarse washed sand bed, 1"	B-62	1,350	.018	S.Y.	1.03	.45	.10	1.58	1.94
2250 Stone dust, 4" thick	"	900	.027	"	2.42	.68	.15	3.25	3.87
2300 Tile thinset pavers, 3/8" thick	D-1	300	.053	S.F.	2.75	1.44		4.19	5.25
2350 3/4" thick	"	280	.057	"	4.39	1.54		5.93	7.20
2400 Wood rounds, cypress	B-1	175	.137	Ea.	8	3.31		11.31	13.95

(from *Means Site Work & Landscape Cost Data 2002*)

Figure 2.2

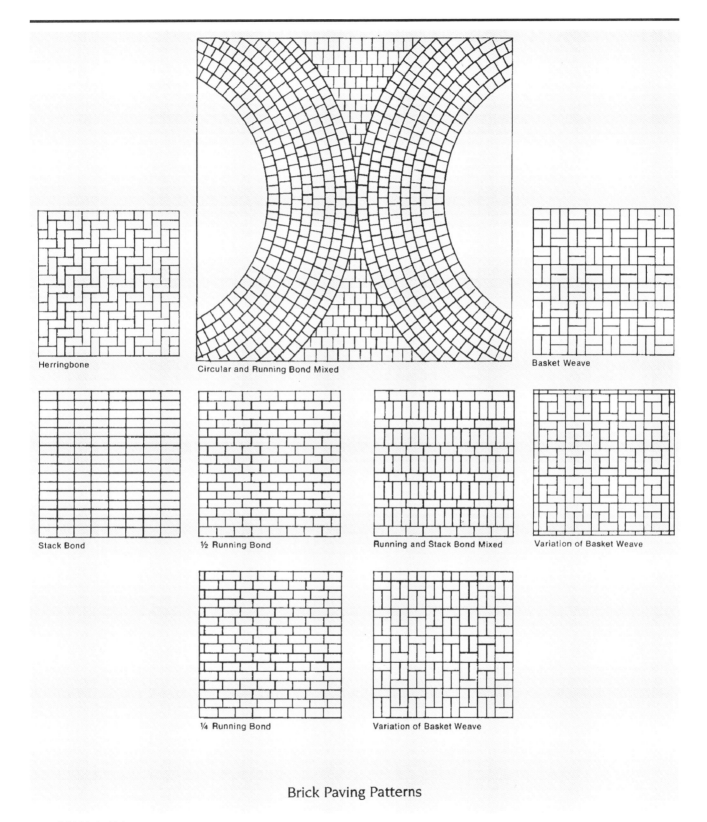

Herringbone

Circular and Running Bond Mixed

Basket Weave

Stack Bond

½ Running Bond

Running and Stack Bond Mixed

Variation of Basket Weave

¼ Running Bond

Variation of Basket Weave

Brick Paving Patterns

(courtesy Brick Industry Association)

Figure 2.3

Brick has many other applications in landscaping beyond its use for paving. The most obvious of these is its use for many types of walls and stairs. Examples of brick stair and ramp configurations are shown in Figure 2.4. Although brick is long-lasting, other materials are cheaper to purchase and apply. Brick does offer other advantages, such as the fact that it is easy to work with in small areas and can often be used in combination with other paving materials. It can also "match" brick buildings. In large areas, however, brick is costly to install and bulk materials such as concrete or asphalt paving are considerably less expensive. Figure 2.5, from *Means Site Work & Landscape Cost Data*, shows the cost variation for different types of paving materials.

The terminology for brick surfaces, positions, and courses is illustrated in Figures 2.6 and 2.7. A table listing the dimensions of available brick sizes can be found in the Appendix.

Other masonry units have gained the interest and approval of designers and builders. Among the more popular types are building and paving blocks of concrete, adobe, and glass. Concrete block is functional for a range of uses—from rugged walls to lacy wall screens. *Turf blocks*, a type of concrete paver with openings or slots for growing grass turf, are popular in appropriate climates and conditions. Glass block is available in a range of styles and functions. Adobe, a kind of mud brick, is also a good choice for decorative use or special effect walls and structures in appropriate climates. Manufacturers of these products may provide illustrations, literature, and samples. Trade shows are forums for these products.

Concrete

Concrete is a composite material. It consists essentially of a binding medium called cement, combined with sand, aggregate, and sufficient water to make the mixture workable. When cured, concrete attains a hardness not unlike stone. It is usually specified and ordered in the minimum compressive strength required (after curing for 28 days), varying from 2,500 psi to 6,000 or even 7,000 psi. A rule of thumb for field-mixed 3,000 psi concrete is one part cement, two parts sand, four parts stone, and no more than six gallons of water per 100 lbs. of cement. An air entrainment additive is advised for exposed exterior concrete. Concrete is a good compressive material, but usually requires steel or glass fiber reinforcing to function in tension.

Concrete is a very versatile material. It may be mixed in bulk and placed in forms of wood, steel, aluminum, or glass fiber to achieve any desired shape or surface. Concrete is also available in a great variety of precast units. The exposed surface may be finished with techniques such as steel trowel, wood float, or broom, and the hardened concrete surface may be sandblasted or bush hammered to achieve various textures. Partially set concrete may be carved to achieve a sculpted effect.

Many concrete materials can be used for paving and other landscape applications. Concrete toppings or coatings are presented by manufacturers as solutions to problems generated by certain uses or conditions of paved surfaces. Patterned concrete may be cast in place by a number of proprietary systems used in the industry. Concrete masonry units (CMUs) are manufactured in all manner of sizes and finishes and in a dazzling array of colors. Manufactured paver stones can be formed in a wide range of textures and finishes. Interlocking concrete pavers find wide application and allow designers to use an arrangement other than parallel lines. Figure 2.8 is a concrete sidewalk system from *Means Site Work*

Brick Step and Ramp Configurations

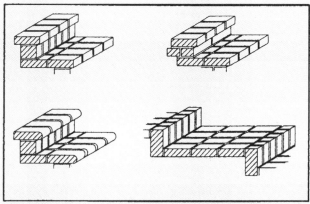

Step Configurations

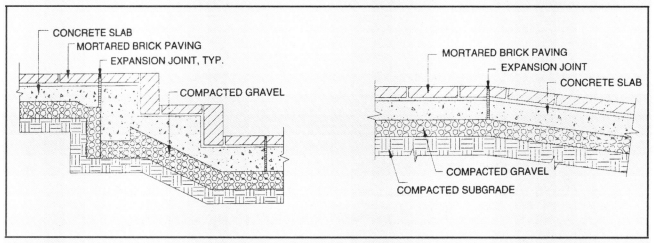

Stair and Ramp Sections

(courtesy *Brick Industry Association*)

Figure 2.4

G2030 Pedestrian Paving

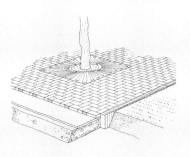

The Plaza Systems listed include several brick and tile paving surfaces on three different bases: gravel, slab on grade and suspended slab. The system cost includes this base cost with the exception of the suspended slab. The type of bedding for the pavers depends on the base being used, and alternate bedding may be desirable. Also included in the paving costs are edging and precast grating costs and where concrete bases are involved, expansion joints.

System Components	QUANTITY	UNIT	COST PER S.F.		
			MAT.	INST.	TOTAL
SYSTEM G2030 310 2050					
PLAZA, BRICK PAVERS, 4″ X 8″ X 1-1/2″, GRAVEL BASE, STONE DUST BED					
Compact subgrade, static roller, 4 passes	.111	S.Y.		.03	.03
Bank gravel, 2 mi haul, dozer spread	.012	C.Y.	.20	.06	.26
Compact gravel bedding or base, vibrating plate	.012	C.Y.		.03	.03
Grading fine grade, 3 passes with grader	.111	S.Y.		.32	.32
Stone dust, 1″ thick, skid steer loader spread	.003	C.Y.	.06	.05	.11
Brick paver, 4″ x 8″ x 1-3/4″	4.150	Ea.	2.57	2.76	5.33
Brick edging, stood on end, 6 per L.F.	.060	L.F.	.24	.41	.65
Precast concrete tree grating, 1 per 250 S.F.	.004	Ea.	1.14	.18	1.32
TOTAL			4.21	3.84	8.05

G2030 310	Brick & Tile Plazas	COST PER S.F.		
		MAT.	INST.	TOTAL
1050	Plaza, asphalt pavers, 6″ x 12″ x 1-1/4″, gravel base, asphalt bedding	5.50	7.10	12.60
1100	Slab on grade, asphalt bedding	7.25	7.65	14.90
1150	Suspended slab, insulated & mastic bedding	8.70	9.45	18.15
1300	6″ x 12″ x 3″, gravel base, asphalt, bedding	7.45	7.30	14.75
1350	Slab on grade, asphalt bedding	8.95	7.85	16.80
1400	Suspended slab, insulated & mastic bedding	10.40	9.60	20
2050	Brick pavers, 4″ x 8″ x 2-1/4″, aggregate base, course washed sand bedding	4.21	3.84	8.05
2100	Slab on grade, asphalt bedding	5.60	5.50	11.10
2150	Suspended slab, insulated & no bedding	7.10	7.30	14.40
2300	4″ x 8″ x 2-1/4″, gravel base, stone dust bedding	4.73	3.83	8.56
2350	Slab on grade, asphalt bedding	6.10	5.50	11.60
2400	Suspended slab, insulated & no bedding	7.60	7.30	14.90
2550	Shale pavers, 4″ x 8″ x 2-1/4″, gravel base, stone dust bedding	4.39	4.38	8.77
2600	Slab on grade, asphalt bedding	5.80	6.05	11.85
2650	Suspended slab, insulated & no bedding	3.73	5.10	8.83
3050	Thin set tile, 4″ x 4″ x 3/8″, slab on grade	6	6.15	12.15
3300	4″ x 4″ x 3/4″, slab on grade	7.45	4.10	11.55
3550	Concrete paving stone, 4″ x 8″ x 2-1/2″, gravel base, sand bedding	2.90	2.69	5.59
3600	Slab on grade, asphalt bedding	4.06	4.04	8.10
3650	Suspended slab, insulated & no bedding	2.01	3.05	5.06
3800	4″ x 8″ x 3-1/4″, gravel base, sand bedding	2.90	2.69	5.59
3850	Slab on grade, asphalt bedding	3.71	3.12	6.83
3900	Suspended slab, insulated & no bedding	2.01	3.05	5.06
4050	Concrete patio blocks, 8″ x 16″ x 2″, gravel base, sand bedding	2.82	3.51	6.33
4100	Slab on grade, asphalt bedding	4.14	5.10	9.24
4150	Suspended slab, insulated & no bedding	1.93	3.87	5.80

(from *Means Site Work & Landscape Cost Data* 2002)

Figure 2.5

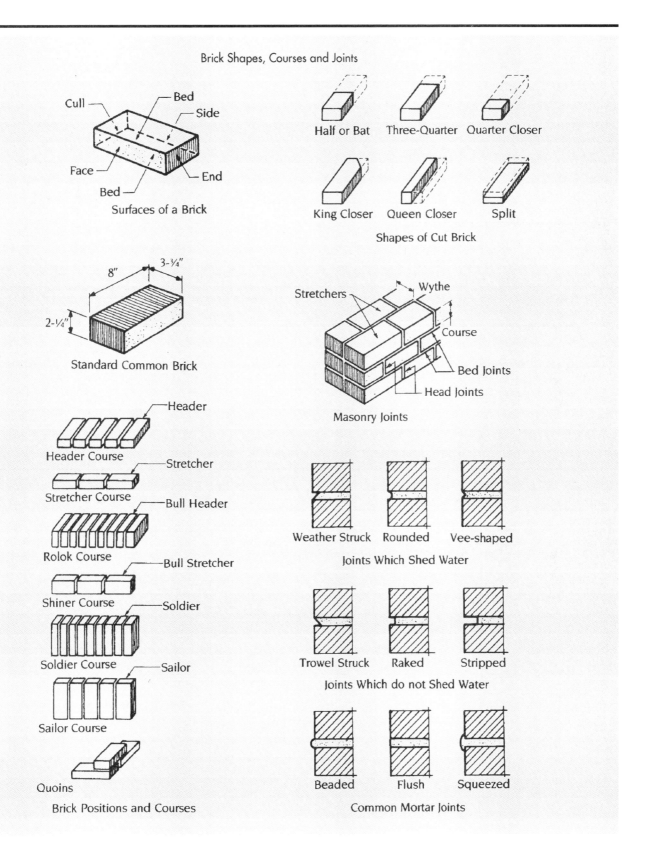

Brick Shapes, Courses and Joints

Surfaces of a Brick
Cull, Bed, Side, Face, Bed, End

Shapes of Cut Brick
Half or Bat, Three-Quarter, Quarter Closer, King Closer, Queen Closer, Split

Standard Common Brick
8″, 3-¾″, 2-¼″

Brick Positions and Courses
Header Course — Header
Stretcher Course — Stretcher
Rolok Course — Bull Header
Shiner Course — Bull Stretcher
Soldier Course — Soldier
Sailor Course — Sailor
Quoins

Masonry Joints
Stretchers, Wythe, Course, Bed Joints, Head Joints

Joints Which Shed Water
Weather Struck, Rounded, Vee-shaped

Joints Which do not Shed Water
Trowel Struck, Raked, Stripped

Common Mortar Joints
Beaded, Flush, Squeezed

Figure 2.6

Running or Stretcher Bond	The face brick are all stretchers and are tied to the backing by metal or reinforcing. Waste – 5%.
Common or American Bond	Every sixth course of stretcher bond is usually a header course. Waste – 4%.
Flemish Bond	Each course has alternate headers and stretchers with the alternate headers centered over the stretcher. Waste – 3 to 5%.
English Bond	Consists of alternate headers and stretchers with the vertical joints in the header and stretcher aligning or breaking over each other. Waste – 8 to 15%.
Stack Bond	Has no overlapping of units since all vertical joints are aligned. Usually this pattern is bonded to the backing with rigid steel ties. Waste – 3%.
English Cross or Dutch Bond	Built up of interlocking crosses. This wall consists of two headers and a stretcher forming a cross. Waste – 8%.

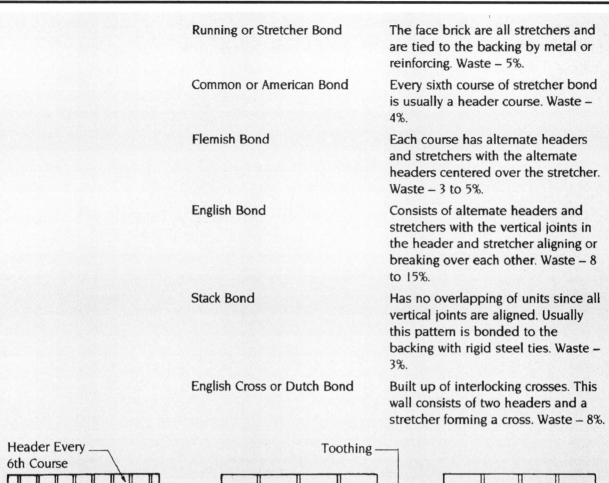

Header Every 6th Course

Common Bond
(Running Bond if no Headers)

Toothing

1/3 Running Bond

Stack Bond
(A Pattern Bond)

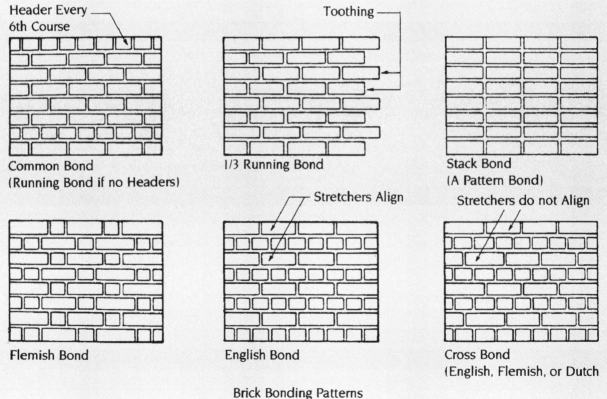

Flemish Bond

Stretchers Align

English Bond

Stretchers do not Align

Cross Bond
(English, Flemish, or Dutch

Brick Bonding Patterns

Figure 2.7

G2030 Pedestrian Paving

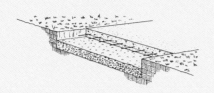

The Concrete Sidewalk System includes: excavation; compacted gravel base (hand graded); forms; welded wire fabric; and 3,000 p.s.i. air-entrained concrete (broom finish).

The Expanded System Listing shows Concrete Sidewalk systems with wearing course depths ranging from 4″ to 6″. The gravel base ranges from 4″ to 8″. Sidewalk widths are shown ranging from 3′ to 5′. Costs are on a linear foot basis.

System Components	QUANTITY	UNIT	COST PER L.F.		
			MAT.	INST.	TOTAL
SYSTEM G2030 240 1580					
CONCRETE, SIDEWALK 4″ THICK, 4″ GRAVEL BASE, 3′ WIDE					
Excavation, box out with dozer	.100	C.Y.		.15	.15
Gravel base, haul 2 miles, spread with dozer	.037	C.Y.	.59	.19	.78
Compaction with vibrating plate	.037	C.Y.		.06	.06
Fine grade by hand	.333	S.Y.		2	2
Concrete in place including forms and reinforcing	.037	C.Y.	3.81	5.04	8.85
Backfill edges by hand	.010	C.Y.		.21	.21
TOTAL			4.40	7.65	12.05

G2030 240	Concrete Sidewalks	COST PER L.F.		
		MAT.	INST.	TOTAL
1580	Concrete sidewalk, 4″ thick, 4″ gravel base, 3′ wide	4.40	7.65	12.05
1600	4′ wide	5.85	9.45	15.30
1620	5′ wide	7.35	11.25	18.60
1640	6″ gravel base, 3′ wide	4.70	7.80	12.50
1660	4′ wide	6.25	9.65	15.90
1680	5′ wide	7.80	11.55	19.35
1700	8″ gravel base, 3′ wide	4.98	7.95	12.93
1720	4′ wide	6.65	9.85	16.50
1740	5′ wide	8.30	11.75	20.05
1800	5″ thick concrete, 4″ gravel base, 3′ wide	5.65	8.30	13.95
1820	4′ wide	7.55	10.25	17.80
1840	5′ wide	9.45	12.25	21.70
1860	6″ gravel base, 3′ wide	5.95	8.45	14.40
1900	5′ wide	9.90	12.10	22
1920	8″ gravel base, 3′ wide	6.25	8.60	14.85
1940	4′ wide	8.35	11.20	19.55
1960	5′ wide	10.40	12.35	22.75
2120	6″ thick concrete, 4″ gravel base, 3′ wide	6.50	8.75	15.25
2140	4′ wide	8.65	10.80	19.45
2160	5′ wide	10.85	12.95	23.80
2180	6″ gravel base, 3′ wide	6.80	8.90	15.70
2200	4′ wide	9.05	11	20.05

(from *Means Site Work & Landscape Cost Data* 2002)

Figure 2.8

& Landscape Cost Data. Note information such as haul distance and backfill by hand, the kinds of costs too often overlooked by hurried estimators.

Materials Recycling

Recycling is one of many environmental issues and regulations that affect the landscape industry. Recycling of pavement materials, particularly asphaltic concrete and concrete, is standard for material quantities weighing one ton or more. Disposal and storage of materials as required by regulations are standard business practices that are routinely monitored within the profession. Horticultural materials that can be re-used as compost, mulch or for other uses, can be of special value.

Stone

Stone is nature's most enduring material. Stone pavers are available as blocks and modules. Because of its beauty and durability, stone is often used for stair treads, borders, and coping. Stone is well suited to irregular floor patterns that can utilize *quarry run* irregular lines. Stone for paving is graded by:

- Hardness (U.S. Government Standards)
- Porosity
- Abrasion resistance

Stone is used cut or uncut, and the varieties and applications of each type are many. See Figure 2.9 for some examples of stone face types. Uncut (rubble) stone is available with rough or smoothly worn surfaces. Examples are roughly broken quarry stone and smooth river rock stone. Both are usually measured and priced by weight (ton). Rubble stone is used for uncoursed work and often for fillings; river rock may be prized for Japanese garden effects. Cut stone is available in varieties ranging from roughly squared blocks to uniform ashlar; the latter may be laid like brick in walls or used for elegant paving. Ashlar may be squared and dressed in various finishes. Facing (veneer) applications are also common for costly finish stone. Fully trimmed ashlar is measured by the surface face in square feet or square yards. It is priced on these measurements as well as by its thickness. Stone block may be sold by unit price. Stone quarries and dealers may offer stone cut to measure, and can recommend sizes and corresponding thickness for paving. Unit price stone costs and a variety of stonework systems are included in *Means Site Work & Landscape Cost Data*. An example, a stone retaining wall system, is shown in Figure 2.10.

Synthetic stone has many economical applications. Many products made of concrete mixtures are often so like stone that most stone yards promote their cost- and labor-saving qualities. The relatively light weight of synthetic stone veneers is a great economy feature as well. Imitation stone block resembles natural stone, costs much less, and is available in a variety of shapes, colors, and textures.

Tile

Tiles are baked clay units of various shapes, and can be glazed or unglazed. They are available in a wide range of colors, shapes, and finishes, including skid-resistant finishes. The nonporous quality of glazed tile makes it very useful for certain kinds of applications. Small units, while labor intensive, are easy to handle and to work with in areas where space is limited. Tile has an ornamental character and is sometimes used as a decorative material. Like brick, it is graded for weather resistance.

TYPES OF STONEWORK

Rubble Stone — Random

Rubble Stone — Coursed

Ashlar Stone — Roughly Squared, Random

Ashlar Stone — Trimmed, Random

Ashlar Stone — Coursed, Narrow

Ashlar Stone — Coursed

Ashlar Stone — Cut, Stacked Joints

Ashlar Stone — Cut, Broken Joints

Figure 2.9

The Stone Retaining Wall System is constructed of one of four types of stone. Each of the four types is listed in terms of cost per ton. Construction is either dry set or mortar set. System elements include excavation; concrete base; crushed stone; underdrain; and backfill.

The Expanded System Listing shows five heights above grade for each type, ranging from 3' above grade to 12' above grade.

System Components	QUANTITY	UNIT	COST PER L.F.		
			MAT.	INST.	TOTAL
SYSTEM G2040 260 2400					
STONE RETAINING WALL, DRY SET, STONE AT $16.00/TON, 3' ABOVE GRADE					
Excavation, trench, hyd backhoe	.880	C.Y.		4	4
Concrete in place incl. forms and reinf. strip footings, 36" x 12"	.111	C.Y.	11.88	9.07	20.95
Stone, wall material, type 1	6.550	C.F.	7.15		7.15
Setting stone wall, dry	6.550	C.F.		43.56	43.56
Stone borrow, delivered, 3/8", machine spread	.320	C.Y.	4.46	1.64	6.10
Piping, subdrainage, perforated PVC, 4" diameter	1.000	L.F.	1.57	2.65	4.22
Backfill with dozer, trench, up to 300' haul, no compaction	1.019	C.Y.		1.62	1.62
TOTAL			25.06	62.54	87.60

G2040 260	Stone Retaining Walls		COST PER L.F.		
			MAT.	INST.	TOTAL
2400	Stone retaining wall, dry set, stone at $16.00/ton, height above grade 3'		25	62.50	87.50
2420	Height above grade 4'		27.50	74.50	102
2440	Height above grade 6'		31.50	99.50	131
2460	Height above grade 8'		40	156	196
2480	Height above grade 10'		47	204	251
2500	Height above grade 12'		54.50	255	309.50
2600	$32.00/ton stone, height above grade 3'		32	62.50	94.50
2620	Height above grade 4'		36.50	74.50	111
2640	Height above grade 6'		45	99.50	144.50
2660	Height above grade 8'		60	156	216
2680	Height above grade 10'		74.50	204	278.50
2700	Height above grade 12'		89.50	255	344.50
2800	$48.00/ton stone, height above grade 3'		39.50	62.50	102
2820	Height above grade 4'		46	74.50	120.50
2840	Height above grade 6'		58.50	99.50	158
2860	Height above grade 8'		80.50	156	236.50
2880	Height above grade 10'		101	204	305
2900	Height above grade 12'		124	255	379
3000	$64.00/ton stone, height above grade 3'		46.50	62.50	109
3020	Height above grade 4'		55.50	74.50	130

(from *Means Site Work & Landscape Cost Data* 2002)

Figure 2.10

Wood

Wood and wood products are used in the construction of many outdoor floors, walks, fences, and steps. Wood is a strong and durable material for its weight. Pressure-treated wood or that which has specific decay-, insect-, and weather-resistant qualities, is most often specified for landscape construction. Plywood is a wood product that may be used for outdoor projects. Depending on the application, exterior or marine grade plywood may be required. Hardboard, often called HDO or MDO (high or medium density overlay), is another wood product with many outdoor applications. It is tempered to resist moisture and weather in outdoor use, and is commonly used for highway signage, both for traffic and advertising.

Figure 2.11 is a chart showing a broad classification of commonly used domestic woods according to their characteristics and properties. Many lumber species will provide good service in a wood deck. Still, some are better suited for the purpose than others. Usual wood characteristics necessary for decking and other outdoor applications include: high decay resistance, non-splintering grain, good stiffness, strength, wear-resistance, and freedom from warping. Woods with many of these characteristics include: cypress, white oak, locust, Douglas fir, western larch, redwood, cedar, and southern pine.

Landscape timbers and railroad ties are sold by the unit. Lumber is priced and sold by the board foot. A board 1″ thick by 12″ wide and 12″ long equals one board foot. To find the number of board feet in a piece of lumber, multiply thickness in inches times width in inches, times length in feet. Then divide by twelve. For example, a 2 × 8 board that is 10 feet long has 13.3 board feet: 2″ × 8″ × 10′ = 160 ÷ 12 = 13.3 board feet. Figure 2.12 is a chart of dimensional lumber converted to board feet.

Perhaps the most prevalent use of wood in landscape construction today is for decks. Figure 2.13 shows an illustrated wood deck system from *Means Site Work & Landscape Cost Data.*

Further data on the uses of wood can be obtained from many wood trade associations, universities, and wood research laboratories; some of these organizations and their addresses are listed in the Appendix.

Earthen Materials

The type of earthen materials, such as sand, topsoil, and gravel, as well as site conditions will be large factors in equipment selection. The other major factors are the work to be done, i.e., the quantity and area of excavation, the appropriate equipment for a particular site, and the distance of hauling. Characteristics such as weight and comparative volume of excavated material vary depending on moisture content and compaction. Soil volume is determined by its state in the earth-moving process. The three measures of soil volume are:

BCY – Bank Cubic Yard: one cubic yard of material as it lies undisturbed in the natural state.

LCY – Loose Cubic Yard: one cubic yard of material that has been disturbed and has swelled as a result of excavation.

CCY – Compacted Cubic Yard: one cubic yard of material that has been compacted and has thereby decreased in volume.

The illustration in Figure 2.14 shows comparative volumes for common earth. The tables show characteristics of various soil types. Additional charts on materials and measures can be found in the Appendix.

	Broad Classification of Woods According to Characteristics and Properties[1]										
	Working and Behavior Characteristics							Strength Properties			
Kind of Wood	Hardness	Freedom from Warping	Ease of Working	Paint Holding	Nail Holding	Decay Resistance of Heartwood	Proportion of Heartwood	Bending Strength	Stiffness	Strength as a Post	Freedom from Pitch
Ash	A	B	C	C	A	C	C	A	A	A	A
Western Red Cedar	C	A	A	A	C	A	A	C	C	B	A
Cypress	B	B	B	A	B	A	B	B	B	B	A
Douglas-fir, Larch	B	B	B-C	C	A	B	A	A	A	A	B
Gum	B	C	B	C	A	B	B	B	A	B	A
Hemlock, White Fir[2]	B-C	B	B	C	C	C	C	B	A	B	A
Soft Pine[3]	C	A	A	A	C	C	B	C	C	C	B
Southern Pine	B	B	B	C	A	B	C	A	A	A	C
Poplar	C	A	B	A	B	C	B	B	B	B	A
Redwood	B	A	B	A	B	A	A	B	B	A	A
Spruce	C	A-B	B	B	B	C	C	B	B	B	A

[1]A — among the woods relatively high in the particular respect listed; B — among woods intermediate in that respect; C — among woods relatively low in that respect. Letters do not refer to lumber grades.

[2]Includes west coast and eastern hemlocks.

[3]Includes the western and northeastern pines.

(courtesy U.S. Dept. of Agriculture)

Figure 2.11

Crushed stone and gravel are measured and sold on the same basis as earthen materials, that is, by weight (ton) or by volume (cubic yard). Costs for loading and hauling earthen material are provided annually in *Means Site Work & Landscape Cost Data.*

Horticultural Materials

Plantings are among the first materials the landscape professional considers. The selection of the right plant for the right place is both a technical and an aesthetic issue. Much horticultural information and many services are provided to the landscape industry from both public and private sources. Public information and services exist on a federal, state, and local level. The wise professional in the field keeps up to date with local agencies such as county offices of the U.S. Department of Agriculture, and with state university cooperative extension services and publications.

Board Feet & Measure	
Nominal Dimension	**Board Feet**
1 x 1	.08
1 x 2	.17
1 x 3	.25
1 x 4	.33
1 x 6	.50
1 x 8	.67
1 x 10	.83
1 x 12	1.00
2 x 2	.33
2 x 4	.67
2 x 6	1.00
2 x 8	1.33
2 x 10	1.67
2 x 12	2.00
3 x 2	.50
3 x 4	1.00
3 x 6	1.50
3 x 8	2.00
3 x 10	2.50
3 x 12	3.00
3 x 16	4.00
4 x 2	.67
4 x 4	1.33
4 x 6	2.00
4 x 8	2.67
4 x 10	3.33
4 x 12	4.00
6 x 6	3.00
6 x 8	4.00
8 x 8	5.34

Figure 2.12

G2040 Site Development

Wood Deck Systems are either constructed of pressure treated lumber or redwood lumber. The system includes: the deck, joists (16″ or 24″ on-center), girders, posts (8′ on-center) and railings. Decking is constructed of either 1″ x 4″ or 2″ x 6″ stock. Joists range from 2″ x 8″ to 2″ x 10″ depending on the size of the system. The size ranges hold true for both pressure treated lumber and redwood systems.

Costs are on a square foot basis.

System Components			COST PER S.F.		
	QUANTITY	UNIT	MAT.	INST.	TOTAL
SYSTEM G2040 910 1000					
WOOD DECK, TREATED LUMBER, 2″X8″ JOISTS @ 16″ O.C., 2″X6″ DECKING					
Decking, planks, fir 2″ x 6″ treated	2.080	B.F.	2.55	3.12	5.67
Framing, joists, fir 2″ x 8″ treated	1.330	B.F.	1.60	1.66	3.26
Framing, beams, fir 2″ x 10″ treated	.133	B.F.	.16	.15	.31
Framing, post, 4″ x 4″, treated	.333	B.F.	.40	.41	.81
Framing, railing, 2″ x 4″ lumber, treated	.667	B.F.	.55	1.39	1.94
Excavating pits by hand, heavy soil or clay	.002	C.Y.		.22	.22
Spread footing, concrete	.002	C.Y.	.22	.26	.48
TOTAL			5.48	7.21	12.69

G2040 910	Wood Decks	COST PER S.F.		
		MAT.	INST.	TOTAL
1000	Wood deck, treated lumber, 2″ x 8″ joists @ 16″ O.C., 2″ x 6″ decking	5.50	7.20	12.70
1004	2″ x 4″ decking	4.82	8.85	13.67
1008	1″ x 6″ decking	5.55	5.70	11.25
1012	1″ x 4″ decking	5.30	5.55	10.85
1500	2″ x 10″ joists @ 16″ O.C., 2″ x 6″ decking	5.90	7.65	13.55
1504	2″ x 4″ decking	5.20	9.30	14.50
1508	1″ x 6″ decking	5.95	6.15	12.10
1512	1″ x 4″ decking	5.70	6	11.70
1560	2″ x 10″ joists @ 24″ O.C., 2″ x 6″ decking	5.50	7.20	12.70
1564	2″ x 4″ decking	4.82	8.85	13.67
1568	1″ x 6″ decking	5.55	5.70	11.25
1572	1″ x 4″ decking	5.30	5.55	10.85
4000	Redwood lumber, 2″ x 8″ joists @ 16″ O.C., 2″ x 6″ decking	9	3.65	12.65
4004	2″ x 4″ decking	9.35	3.79	13.14
4008	1″ x 6″ decking	10.10	4.22	14.32
4012	1″ x 4″ decking	10	4.15	14.15
4500	2″ x 10″ joists @ 16″ O.C., 2″ x 6″ decking	10.90	3.98	14.88
4504	2″ x 4″ decking	11.20	3.77	14.97
4508	1″ x 6″ decking	10.90	4.39	15.29
4512	1″ x 4″ decking	10.75	4.32	15.07

(from *Means Site Work & Landscape Cost Data* 2002)

Figure 2.13

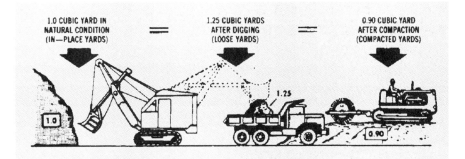

Approximate Material Characteristics*

Material	Loose (lb/cu yd)	Bank (lb/cu yd)	Swell (%)	Load Factor
Clay, dry	2,100	2,650	26	0.79
Clay, wet	2,700	3,575	32	0.76
Clay and gravel, dry	2,400	2,800	17	0.85
Clay and gravel, wet	2,600	3,100	17	0.85
Earth, dry	2,215	2,850	29	0.78
Earth, moist	2,410	3,080	28	0.78
Earth, wet	2,750	3,380	23	0.81
Gravel, dry	2,780	3,140	13	0.88
Gravel, wet	3,090	3,620	17	0.85
Sand, dry	2,600	2,920	12	0.89
Sand, wet	3,100	3,520	13	0.88
Sand and gravel, dry	2,900	3,250	12	0.89
Sand and gravel, wet	3,400	3,750	10	0.91

*Exact values will vary with grain size, moisture content, compaction, etc. Test to determine exact values for specific soils.

Typical Soil Volume Conversion Factors

Soil Type	Initial Soil Condition	Bank	Converted to: Loose	Converted to: Compacted
Clay	Bank	1.00	1.27	0.90
	Loose	0.79	1.00	0.71
	Compacted	1.11	1.41	1.00
Common earth	Bank	1.00	1.25	0.90
	Loose	0.80	1.00	0.72
	Compacted	1.11	1.39	1.00
Rock (blasted)	Bank	1.00	1.50	1.30
	Loose	0.67	1.00	0.87
	Compacted	0.77	1.15	1.00
Sand	Bank	1.00	1.12	0.95
	Loose	0.89	1.00	0.85
	Compacted	1.05	1.18	1.00

Figure 2.14

An extensive array of products that facilitate working with plantings are now manufactured for the landscape industry. Soil amendments, edgings, landscape fabrics, tree guys/ties, mulches, hydro seed, and grass sod are some of the most common items. Catalogs and information are available from manufacturers.

Ornamental plants chosen for landscaping must also pass horticultural requirements and fit specific site conditions and climate restrictions. Fortunately, the ornamental plant-growing industries have their own information and promotion campaigns, and rely greatly on the needs and approval of the landscape industry. In addition, there are many excellent guides and references to the selection, use, function, and installation of plants; a list of recommended sources is given in the Appendix. Also consider advice from your local nursery, landscape architect, or landscape gardener. Some nursery catalogues are widely used as references within the industry. A selection of these catalogues is included in the above-mentioned reference list. The most accurate and relevant of all sources are local suppliers. Figure 2.15 suggests trees and plants for specific purposes and local conditions.

The nursery industry generally conforms to certain industry-wide classifications. One uniform classification is "plant hardiness," generally referred to in terms of annual average minimum temperature zones. Based on the USDA Plant Hardiness Zone Map, Figure 2.16, growers classify their plants by the northernmost zone where the plant may be expected to survive with vigor. The lower the zone number, the hardier the plant. Figures 2.17a, b, c & d, a chart of major and minor trees and shrubs, indicates the appropriate hardiness zone for each tree and shrub. The chart also shows tree shape and expected height at 10 years, mature height and spread, leaf color, Latin name, and recommendations for use in street planting.

Regional climate has the greatest impact on the use of specific plants. Many fine books and gardening encyclopedias are available on the characteristics and culture of plants. No attempt will be made in this book to adequately cover this subject. Indeed, "horticulture is a very large field." A basic introduction for the non-landscape professional to types of plantings follows. General categories of plant types may be listed as:

- Trees – evergreen or deciduous
- Shrubs – evergreen or deciduous
- Herbaceous Plants, such as perennial and annual flowers
- Ground Covers and Vines, which may be evergreen, deciduous, or herbaceous

The fact that plants are growing and changing over time gives them dramatic and unique characteristics that we may label and put into categories. Examples of these characteristics are described below.

Evergreen Plants

This category may include trees, shrubs, flowers, and vines. The term *evergreen* is merely a broad definition meaning that leaves remain on the plant in a green condition throughout the year. Some are called *narrow-leaved*, such as pines, and some are called *broad-leaved*, such as boxwood (Buxus species) and many types of rhododendron. Some plants will be evergreen in the South, but lose their leaves in the winter in the North. In addition, many low ground covers are evergreen in the North, as are some succulent plants in all climates.

Trees and Plants by Environment and Purposes

Dry, Windy, Exposed Areas
Barberry
Junipers, all varieties
Locust
Maple
Oak
Pines, all varieties
Poplar, Hybrid
Privet
Spruce, all varieties
Sumac, Staghorn

Lightly Wooded Areas
Dogwood
Hemlock
Larch
Pine, White
Rhododendron
Spruce, Norway
Redbud

Total Shade Areas
Hemlock
Ivy, English
Myrtle
Pachysandra
Privet
Spice Bush
Yews, Japanese

Cold Temperatures of Northern U.S. and Canada
Arborvitae, American
Birch, White
Dogwood, Silky
Fir, Balsam
Fir, Douglas
Hemlock
Juniper, Andorra
Juniper, Blue Rug
Linden, Little Leaf
Maple, Sugar
Mountain Ash
Myrtle
Olive, Russian

Pine, Mugho
Pine, Ponderosa
Pine, Red
Pine, Scotch
Poplar, Hybrid
Privet
Rosa Rugosa
Spruce, Dwarf Alberta
Spruce, Black Hills
Spruce, Blue
Spruce, Norway
Spruce, White, Engelman
Yellow Wood

Wet, Swampy Areas
American Arborvitae
Birch, White
Black Gum
Hemlock
Maple, Red
Pine, White
Willow

Poor, Dry, Rocky Soil
Barberry
Crownvetch
Eastern Red Cedar
Juniper, Virginiana
Locust, Black
Locust, Bristly
Locust, Honey
Olive, Russian
Pines, all varieties
Privet
Rosa Rugosa
Sumac, Staghorn

Seashore Planting
Arborvitae, American
Juniper, Tamarix
Locust, Black
Oak, White
Olive, Russian
Pine, Austrian
Pine, Japanese Black

Pine, Mugho
Pine, Scotch
Privet, Amur River
Rosa Rugosa
Yew, Japanese

City Planting
Barberry
Fir, Concolor
Forsythia
Hemlock
Holly, Japanese
Ivy, English
Juniper, Andorra
Linden, Little Leaf
Locust, Honey
Maple, Norway, Silver
Oak, Pin, Red
Olive, Russian
Pachysandra
Pine, Austrian
Pine, White
Privet
Rosa Rugosa
Sumac, Staghorn
Yew, Japanese

Bonsai Planting
Azaleas
Birch, White
Ginkgo
Junipers
Pine, Bristlecone
Pine, Mugho
Spruce, Engleman
Spruce, Dwarf Alberta

Street Planting
Linden, Little Leaf
Oak, Pin
Ginkgo

Fast Growth
Birch, White

Crownvetch
Dogwood, Silky
Fir, Douglas
Juniper, Blue Pfitzer
Juniper, Blue Rug
Maple, Silver
Olive, Autumn
Pines, Austrian, Ponderosa, Red
   Scotch and White
Poplar, Hybrid
Privet
Spruce, Norway
Spruce, Serbian
Taxus, Cuspidata, Hicksi
Willow

Dense, Impenetrable Hedges
Field Plantings:
   Locust, Bristly,
   Olive, Autumn
   Sumac

Residential Areas:
   Barberry, Red or Green
   Juniper, Blue Pfitzer
   Rosa Rugosa

Food for Birds
Ash, Mountain
Barberry
Bittersweet
Cherry, Manchu
Dogwood, Silky
Honeysuckle, Rem Red
Hawthorn
Oaks
Olive, Autumn, Russian
Privet
Rosa Rugosa
Sumac

Erosion Control
Crownvetch
Locust, Bristly
Willow

Figure 2.15

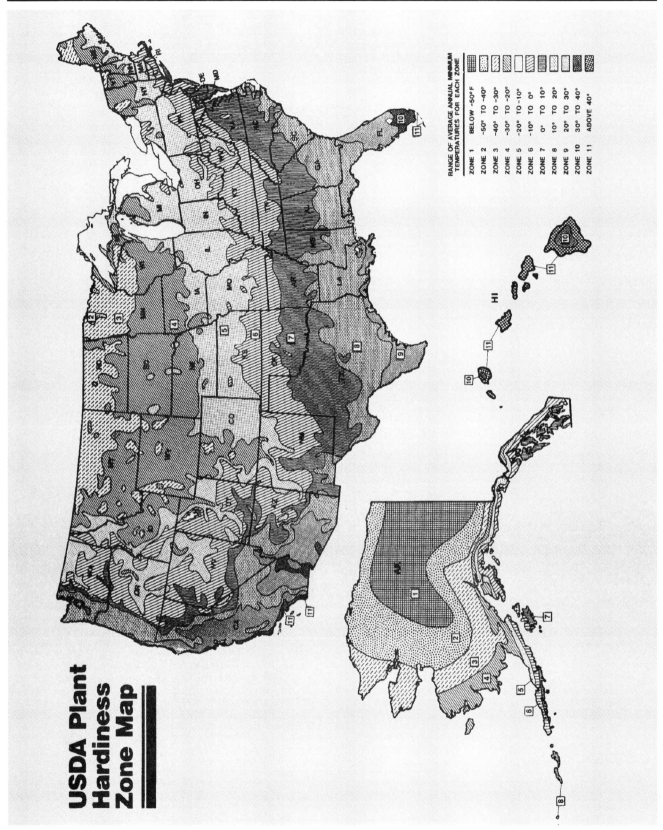

USDA Plant Hardiness Zone Map

RANGE OF AVERAGE ANNUAL MINIMUM
TEMPERATURES FOR EACH ZONE

ZONE 1   BELOW -50°F
ZONE 2   -50° TO -40°
ZONE 3   -40° TO -30°
ZONE 4   -30° TO -20°
ZONE 5   -20° TO -10°
ZONE 6   -10° TO 0°
ZONE 7   0° TO 10°
ZONE 8   10° TO 20°
ZONE 9   20° TO 30°
ZONE 10   30° TO 40°
ZONE 11   ABOVE 40°

(courtesy *Agricultural Research Service*, USDA)

Figure 2.16

MAJOR TREES

Silhouettes indicate specimens of natural form, but varieties or forced forms possessing compact, spreading, columnar or pyramidal characteristics are available. The height at the ten year stage of development is given as an architectural design factor to be considered in the selection of tree sizes.

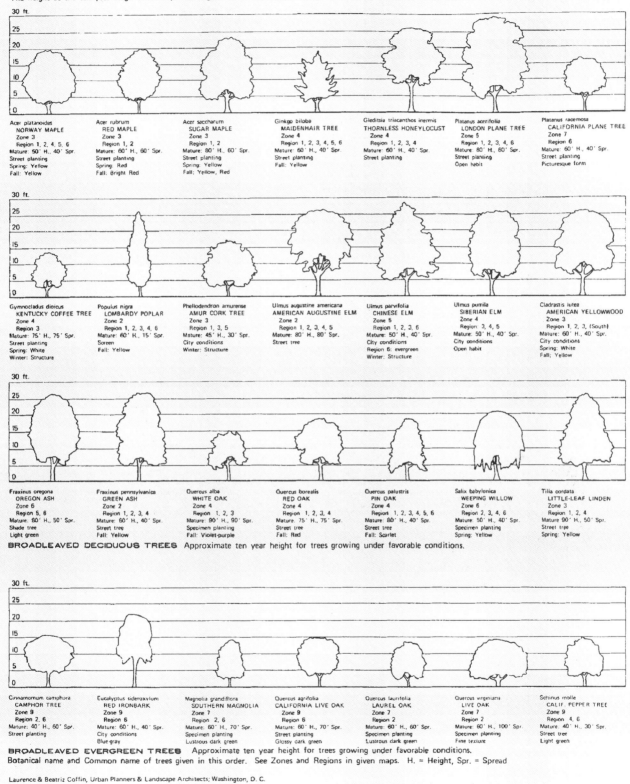

BROADLEAVED DECIDUOUS TREES Approximate ten year height for trees growing under favorable conditions.

BROADLEAVED EVERGREEN TREES Approximate ten year height for trees growing under favorable conditions.
Botanical name and Common name of trees given in this order. See Zones and Regions in given maps. H. = Height, Spr. = Spread

Laurence & Beatriz Coffin, Urban Planners & Landscape Architects; Washington, D. C.

Figure 2.17a

MAJOR TREES

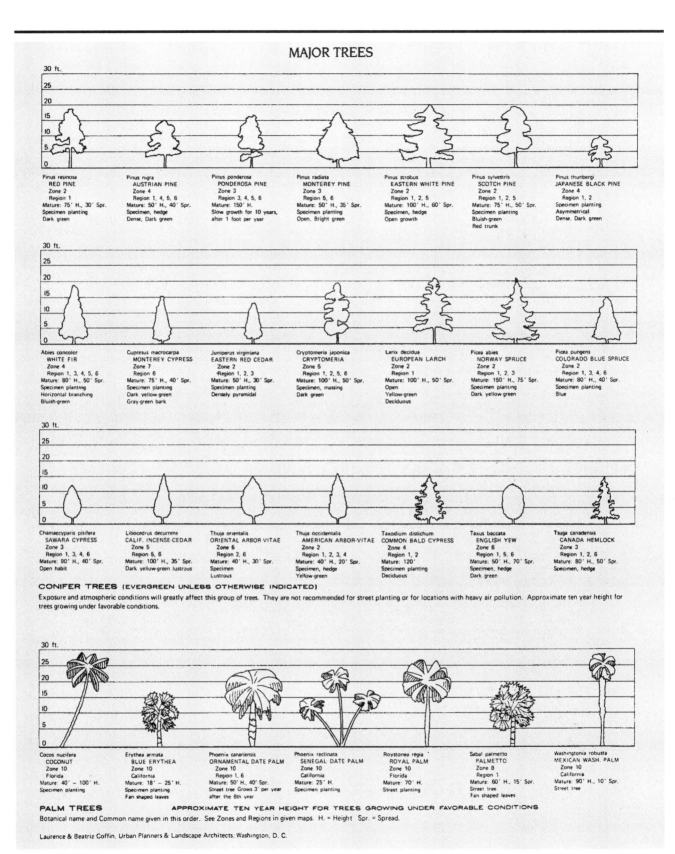

Pinus resinosa
RED PINE
Zone 2
Region 1
Mature: 75' H., 30' Spr.
Specimen planting
Dark green

Pinus nigra
AUSTRIAN PINE
Zone 4
Region 1, 4, 5, 6
Mature: 50' H., 40' Spr.
Specimen, hedge
Dense, Dark green

Pinus ponderosa
PONDEROSA PINE
Zone 3
Region 3, 4, 5, 6
Mature: 150' H.
Slow growth for 10 years,
after 1 foot per year

Pinus radiata
MONTEREY PINE
Zone 3
Region 5, 6
Mature: 50' H., 35' Spr.
Specimen planting
Open, Bright green

Pinus strobus
EASTERN WHITE PINE
Zone 2
Region 1, 2, 5
Mature: 100' H., 60' Spr.
Specimen, hedge
Open growth

Pinus sylvestris
SCOTCH PINE
Zone 2
Region 1, 2, 5
Mature: 75' H., 50' Spr.
Specimen planting
Bluish-green
Red trunk

Pinus thunbergi
JAPANESE BLACK PINE
Zone 4
Region 1, 2
Specimen planting
Asymmetrical
Dense, Dark green

Abies concolor
WHITE FIR
Zone 4
Region 1, 3, 4, 5, 6
Mature: 80' H., 50' Spr.
Specimen planting
Horizontal branching
Bluish-green

Cupresus macrocarpa
MONTEREY CYPRESS
Zone 7
Region 6
Mature: 75' H., 40' Spr.
Specimen planting
Dark yellow-green
Gray-green bark

Juniperus virginiana
EASTERN RED CEDAR
Zone 2
Region 1, 2, 3
Mature: 50' H., 30' Spr.
Specimen planting
Densely pyramidal

Cryptomeria japonica
CRYPTOMERIA
Zone 5
Region 1, 2, 5, 6
Mature: 100' H., 50' Spr.
Specimen, massing
Dark green

Larix decidua
EUROPEAN LARCH
Zone 2
Region 1
Mature: 100' H., 50' Spr.
Open
Yellow-green
Deciduous

Picea abies
NORWAY SPRUCE
Zone 2
Region 1, 2, 3
Mature: 150' H., 75' Spr.
Specimen planting
Dark yellow green

Picea pungens
COLORADO BLUE SPRUCE
Zone 2
Region 1, 3, 4, 6
Mature: 80' H., 40' Spr.
Specimen planting
Blue

Chamaecyparis pisifera
SAWARA CYPRESS
Zone 3
Region 1, 3, 4, 6
Mature: 90' H., 40' Spr.
Open habit

Libocedrus decurrens
CALIF. INCENSE-CEDAR
Zone 5
Region 5, 6
Mature: 100' H., 35' Spr.
Dark yellow-green lustrous

Thuja orientalis
ORIENTAL ARBOR-VITAE
Zone 6
Region 2, 6
Mature: 40' H., 30' Spr.
Specimen
Lustrous

Thuja occidentalis
AMERICAN ARBOR-VITAE
Zone 2
Region 1, 2, 3, 4
Mature: 40' H., 20' Spr.
Specimen, hedge
Yellow-green

Taxodium distichum
COMMON BALD CYPRESS
Zone 4
Region 1, 2
Mature: 120'
Specimen planting
Deciduous

Taxus baccata
ENGLISH YEW
Zone 6
Region 1, 5, 6
Mature: 50' H., 70' Spr.
Specimen, hedge
Dark green

Tsuga canadensis
CANADA HEMLOCK
Zone 3
Region 1, 3, 4, 6
Mature: 80' H., 50' Spr.
Specimen, hedge

CONIFER TREES (EVERGREEN UNLESS OTHERWISE INDICATED)

Exposure and atmospheric conditions will greatly affect this group of trees. They are not recommended for street planting or for locations with heavy air pollution. Approximate ten year height for trees growing under favorable conditions.

Cocos nucifera
COCONUT
Zone 10
Florida
Mature: 40' – 100' H.
Specimen planting

Erythea armata
BLUE ERYTHEA
Zone 10
California
Mature: 18' – 25' H.
Specimen planting
Fan shaped leaves

Phoenix canariensis
ORNAMENTAL DATE PALM
Zone 10
Region 1, 6
Mature: 50' H., 40' Spr.
Street tree Grows 3' per year
after the 6th year

Phoenix reclinata
SENEGAL DATE PALM
Zone 10
California
Mature: 25' H.
Specimen planting

Roystonea regia
ROYAL PALM
Zone 10
Florida
Mature: 70' H.
Street planting

Sabal palmetto
PALMETTO
Zone 8
Region 1
Mature: 60' H., 15' Spr.
Street tree
Fan shaped leaves

Washingtonia robusta
MEXICAN WASH. PALM
Zone 10
California
Mature: 90' H., 10' Spr.
Street tree

PALM TREES   APPROXIMATE TEN YEAR HEIGHT FOR TREES GROWING UNDER FAVORABLE CONDITIONS

Botanical name and Common name given in this order. See Zones and Regions in given maps. H. = Height Spr. = Spread.

Laurence & Beatriz Coffin, Urban Planners & Landscape Architects; Washington, D. C.

(courtesy *Laurence & Beatriz Coffin, Urban Planners & Landscape Architects, Washington, DC*)

Figure 2.17b

MINOR TREES AND SHRUBS

| Betula populifolia
GREY BIRCH
Zone 2
Region 1, 2, 3, 4, 5
Mature: 30' H., 20' Spr.
White bark
Fall: Yellow | Cornus florida
FLOWERING DOGWOOD
Zone 4
Region 1, 2, 3(East)
Mature: 20' H., 25' Spr.
Spring: White or Pink
Fall: Red | Cornus nutalli
PACIFIC DOGWOOD
Zone 7
Region 5, 6
Mature: 30' H., 30' Spr.
Spring: White
Fall: Scarlet and Yellow | Cercis canadensis
EASTERN REDBUD
Zone 4
Region 1, 2, 4
Mature: 30' H., 30' Spr.
Spring: Purplish Pink
Fall: Yellow | Crataegus phaenopyrum
WASHINGTON HAWTHORN
Zone 4
Region 1, 2
Mature: 30' H., 30' Spr.
Spring: White
Fall: Orange | Ilex opaca
AMERICAN HOLLY
Zone 5
Region 1, 2
Mature: 40' H., 25' Spr.
Dark green, Red fruit
Evergreen | Lagerstroemia indica
CRAPE MYRTLE
Zone 7
Region 2, 6
Mature: 20' H., 20' Spr.
Spring: Pink, Bluish
Dense |

| Acer palmatum
JAPANESE MAPLE
Zone 5
Region 1, 2, 6
Mature: 20' H., 20' Spr.
Spring: Red
Fall: Red | Delonix regia
FLAME TREE
Zone 10
Florida
Mature: 40' H., 40' Spr.
Summer: Red flowers
Fern-like foliage | Myrica californica
CALIFORNIA BAYBERRY
Zone 7
Region 5, 6
Mature: 30' H., 15' Spr.
Bronze colored
Evergreen | Magnolia soulangeana
SAUCER MAGNOLIA
Zone 5
Region 1, 2, 6
Mature: 25' H., 25' Spr.
Spring: White · Pink
Coarse texture | Malus (species)
FLOWERING CRAB
Zone 4
Region 1, 2, 4
Mature: 20' H., 25' Spr.
Spring: White, Pink, Red
Dense | Prunus serrulata
ORIENTAL CHERRY
Zone 5, 6
Region 1, 2, 5, 6
Mature: 25' H., 25' Spr.
Spring: White, Pink
Glossy bark | Photinia serrulata
CHINESE PHOTINIA
Zone 7
Region 2, 6
Mature: 36' H., 25' Spr.
Spring: New growth Red
Lustrous evergreen |

Botanical name and Common name of trees and shrubs given in this order. See Zones and Regions in given maps.
H. = Height   Spr. = Spread
MINOR TREES—ADAPTED TO CITY CONDITIONS, DECIDUOUS UNLESS OTHERWISE SPECIFIED.

SIZE	DECIDUOUS SHRUBS—WITHSTANDING CITY CONDITIONS				EVERGREEN SHRUBS—WITHSTANDING CITY CONDITIONS		
10' to 15' HIGH Scale 1" = 30'	Cornus racemosa GRAY DOGWOOD Zone 4 Region 1, 2 Red stalks Hedge	Hamamelis virginiana COMMON WITCH HAZEL Zone 4 Region 1, 2, 3 Fall: Yellow	Ligustrum amurense AMUR PRIVET Zone 3 Region 1, 2, 3, 5, 6 Nearly evergreen Hedge or specimen	Syringa vulgaris COMMON LILAC Zone 3 Region 1, 4, 5 Spring: Lilac Massing	Juniperus chinensus columnaris CHINESE JUNIPER Zone 4 Region 1, 2, 3 Hedge specimen	Taxus cupidata capitata JAPANESE YEW Zone 4 Region 1, 2, 3, 4, 5, 6 Specimen Dark green	Rhododendron maximum ROSEBAY RHODODENDRON Zone 3 Region 1, 2, 5 Spring: Pink Dark green, dense
6' to 10' HIGH Scale 1" = 20'	Aronia arbutifolia RED CHOKEBERRY Zone 5 Region 1, 2 Spring: White Fall: Red	Fremontia californica FLANNEL BUSH Zone 7 California Spring: Yellow Massing	Spirea prunifolia plena BRIDALWREATH SPIREA Zone 4 Region 1, 2, 3 Spring: White	Vibornum tomentosum DOUBLEFILE VIBURNUM Zone 2 Region 1, 2, 3, 4, 5, 6 Spring: White Massing	Taxus cuspidata JAPANESE YEW Zone 4 Region 1, 2, 3, 4, 5, 6 Hedge Dark green	Myrtus communis MYRTLE Zone 8–9 Region 2, 6 Hedge, Specimen Massing	Nerium oleander NERIUM Zone 7–8 Region 2, 3, 4, 6 Bamboo-like Light green—white flower
2' to 6' HIGH Scale 1" = 20'	Berberis thunbergi JAPANESE BARBERRY Zone 5 Region 1, 2, 3, 4, 5, 6 Fall: Scarlet Hedge	Forsythia intermediaspetabilis SHOWY BORDER FORSYTHIA Zone 5 Region 1, 2, 3, 4, 5, 6 Spring: Yellow Massing	Euonymus alata WINGED EUONYMUS Zone 3 Region 1, 2, 3, 5, 6 Fall: Scarlet Hedge: Massing	Rosa rugosa RUGOSA ROSE Zone 2 Region 1, 2 Fall: Orange Hedge	Juniperus chinensis pfitzeriana PFITZER'S JUNIPER Zone 4 Region 1, 2 Feathery texture	Buxus suffruticosa DWARF BOX Zone 5 Region 2, 3, 6 Dark lustrous	Pinus mugo mughus MUGO PINE Zone 2 Region 1, 2, 4, 5, 6 Bright green Specimen, Massing
6" to 24" HIGH Used as ground cover	Cotoneaster horizontalis ROCK SPRAY Zone 4 Region 1, 2, 3, 4, 5, 6	Cytisus albus PORTUGUESE BROOM Zone 5 Region 1, 5 White flowers	Euonymus fortunei WINTER CREEPER Zone 2 Region 1, 2, 3, 4, 5, 6	Juniperus sabina tamariscifolia TAMARIX JUNIPER Zone 4 Region 3, 4, 5, 6	Juniperus chinensis sargenti SARGENT JUNIPER Zone 4 Region 1, 2	Hedera helix vars. ENGLISH IVY Zone 4 Region 1, 2	Pachistima cambyi CAMBYI PACHISTIMA Zone 5 Region 1, 2 Fall: Bronze

Silhouettes indicate specimens of natural form. Shrubs are adaptable to different height and forms by pruning. A wide range of varieties and exotic shrubs can be found throughout the plant regions. A few shrubs commonly used are listed here.

Laurence & Beatriz Coffin, Urban Planners & Landscape Architects; Washington, D. C.

(courtesy *Laurence & Beatriz Coffin, Urban Planners & Landscape Architects, Washington, DC*)

Figure 2.17c

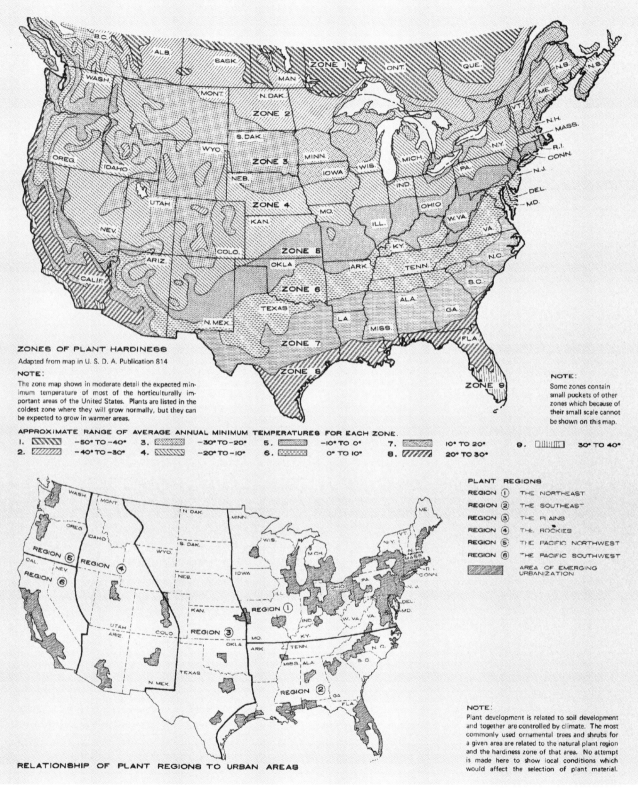

ZONES OF PLANT HARDINESS

Adapted from map in U. S. D. A. Publication 814

NOTE:

The zone map shows in moderate detail the expected minimum temperature of most of the horticulturally important areas of the United States. Plants are listed in the coldest zone where they will grow normally, but they can be expected to grow in warmer areas.

NOTE:

Some zones contain small pockets of other zones which because of their small scale cannot be shown on this map.

APPROXIMATE RANGE OF AVERAGE ANNUAL MINIMUM TEMPERATURES FOR EACH ZONE.

1. $-50°$ TO $-40°$ 3. $-30°$ TO $-20°$ 5. $-10°$ TO $0°$ 7. $10°$ TO $20°$ 9. $30°$ TO $40°$
2. $-40°$ TO $-30°$ 4. $-20°$ TO $-10°$ 6. $0°$ TO $10°$ 8. $20°$ TO $30°$

PLANT REGIONS

REGION ① THE NORTHEAST
REGION ② THE SOUTHEAST
REGION ③ THE PLAINS
REGION ④ THE ROCKIES
REGION ⑤ THE PACIFIC NORTHWEST
REGION ⑥ THE PACIFIC SOUTHWEST
AREA OF EMERGING URBANIZATION

NOTE:

Plant development is related to soil development and together are controlled by climate. The most commonly used ornamental trees and shrubs for a given area are related to the natural plant region and the hardiness zone of that area. No attempt is made here to show local conditions which would affect the selection of plant material.

RELATIONSHIP OF PLANT REGIONS TO URBAN AREAS

(courtesy *Laurence & Beatriz Coffin, Urban Planners & Landscape Architects, Washington, DC*)

Figure 2.17d

Deciduous Plants

Deciduous plants have leaves that fall; they do not remain on the plant throughout the year. Examples are maple trees, lilac shrubs, and grapevines. Many useful lists of plants for special situations have been drawn up by horticulturists. Figures 2.17a, b, c & d are good examples. A list of other references is included in the Appendix.

Once the design has been created, certain standards are used as a basis for selecting and purchasing plant materials. The measurement of plants involves several approaches. For example, field-grown plants are measured differently than those grown in containers. Field-grown plants are specified by landscape architects as *balled and burlapped* (B&B) and are dug from growing fields with their roots intact in an earthen ball. The ball is then protected and packaged with wire, ropes, and cloth as appropriate. Such B&B plants are measured by their height or width or a combination of both, exclusive of the earthen ball. For example, a juniper of upright growth habit is measured by its height, while a juniper of spreading growth is measured by its width. Some plants are measured by both dimensions, such as a rhododendron 3' high and 2-1/2' wide.

Container-grown plants are sometimes graded (measured) by the size or volume of the container. However, shrubs and trees grown in containers are also measured by the height and width of the plant. Consult nursery catalogs for their standards. The American Nursery and Landscape Association has set many standards that are widely accepted in the nursery industry. See the Appendix for more information on industry associations and publications.

Trees are measured by the thickness of their trunks. The figure representing the tree trunk diameter is called a *caliper* measure. Trees of 1-1/2" to 4" caliper are measured 6" above the ground, and trees over 4" in caliper are measured 12" above ground.

Professional growers and landscape architects also urge the listing of color and use of proper Latin names for plants. A cross-reference list of common and Latin plant names is provided in the Appendix.

Lawns

Lawns and grasses and other ground covers are often a significant part of any landscape. Here again, the characteristics of the site, climate, and soils, as well as the desires of the client, dictate the selection of products and method of installation. Maintenance of lawn areas and all landscaped areas is a consideration the wise designer programs into the landscape proposal. Comparisons of average production rates and costs for some lawns, grasses and ground covers is shown in Figures 2.18a & b.

Within the landscape industry, a separate lawn care industry has been established. These specialists manage golf courses, parks, and places where lawns are significant. A great deal of materials and methods research, as well as the practice of lawn care, are supported by university, government, and private research. A lawn system from *Means Site Work & Landscape Cost Data* is illustrated in Figure 2.19.

Specialties

New trends in the landscape industry are reflected in a diverse group of products, applications, and systems, that are known as *specialties*. Specialties range from flagpoles to elaborate water features and street furnishings. Outdoor lighting for practical and ornamental purposes is now requested by residential as well as commercial clients. Water features are increasingly popular. Street furniture, planters, tree guards and grates, recreational and playground items, benches,

02900 | Planting

		02920	Lawns & Grasses	CREW	DAILY OUTPUT	LABOR-HOURS	UNIT	2002 BARE COSTS				TOTAL INCL O&P	
								MAT.	LABOR	EQUIP.	TOTAL		
340	6250		6" deep	A-1	750	.011	S.Y.		.25	.08	.33	.48	340
510	0010		**SEEDING** Athletic field mix, 8#/M.S.F., push spreader R02920 -500	1 Clab	8	1	M.S.F.	16.60	23.50		40.10	55	510
	0100		Tractor spreader	B-66	52	.154		16.60	4.58	3	24.18	28.50	
	0200		Hydro or air seeding, with mulch & fertil.	B-81	80	.300		18.25	7.95	6.75	32.95	39.50	
	0400		Birdsfoot trefoil, .45#/M.S.F., push spreader	1.Clab	8	1		6.85	23.50		30.35	44	
	0500		Tractor spreader	B-66	52	.154		6.85	4.58	3	14.43	17.80	
	0600		Hydro or air seeding,with mulch & fertil.	B-81	80	.300		13.20	7.95	6.75	27.90	34	
	0800		Bluegrass, 4#/M.S.F., common, push spreader	1 Clab	8	1		14.40	23.50		37.90	52.50	
	0900		Tractor spreader	B-66	52	.154		14.40	4.58	3	21.98	26	
	1000		Hydro or air seeding, with mulch & fertil.	B-81	80	.300		24	7.95	6.75	38.70	45.50	
	1100		Baron, push spreader	1 Clab	8	1		19.05	23.50		42.55	57.50	
	1200		Tractor spreader	B-66	52	.154		19.05	4.58	3	26.63	31.50	
	1300		Hydro or air seeding, with mulch & fertil.	B-81	80	.300		26	7.95	6.75	40.70	48.50	
	1500		Clover, 0.67#/M.S.F., white, push spreader	1 Clab	8	1		1.25	23.50		24.75	38	
	1600		Tractor spreader	B-66	52	.154		1.25	4.58	3	8.83	11.65	
	1700		Hydro or air seeding, with mulch and fertil.	B-81	80	.300		6.90	7.95	6.75	21.60	27	
	1800		Ladino, push spreader	1 Clab	8	1		4.94	23.50		28.44	42	
	1900		Tractor spreader	B-66	52	.154		4.94	4.58	3	12.52	15.70	
	2000		Hydro or air seeding, with mulch and fertil.	B-81	80	.300		21.50	7.95	6.75	36.20	43.50	
	2200		Fescue 5.5#/M.S.F., tall, push spreader	1 Clab	8	1		9.80	23.50		33.30	47.50	
	2300		Tractor spreader	B-66	52	.154		9.80	4.58	3	17.38	21	
	2400		Hydro or air seeding, with mulch and fertilizer	B-81	80	.300		32.50	7.95	6.75	47.20	55	
	2500		Chewing, push spreader	1 Clab	8	1		9.80	23.50		33.30	47.50	
	2600		Tractor spreader	B-66	52	.154		9.80	4.58	3	17.38	21	
	2700		Hydro or air seeding, with mulch and fertil.	B-81	80	.300		32.50	7.95	6.75	47.20	55	
	2800		Creeping, push spreader	1 Clab	8	1		7.55	23.50		31.05	45	
	2810		Tractor spreader	B-66	26	.308		7.55	9.15	6	22.70	29	
	2820		Hydro or air seeding, with mulch and fertilizer	B-81	80	.300		25	7.95	6.75	39.70	47	
	2900		Crown vetch, 4#/M.S.F., push spreader	1 Clab	8	1		36	23.50		59.50	76	
	3000		Tractor spreader	B-66	52	.154		36	4.58	3	43.58	50	
	3100		Hydro or air seeding, with mulch and fertilizer	B-81	80	.300		49.50	7.95	6.75	64.20	74	
	3300		Rye, 10#/M.S.F., annual, push spreader	1 Clab	8	1		4.78	23.50		28.28	42	
	3400		Tractor spreader	B-66	52	.154		4.78	4.58	3	12.36	15.50	
	3500		Hydro or air seeding, with mulch and fertilizer	B-81	80	.300		10.50	7.95	6.75	25.20	31	
	3600		Fine textured, push spreader	1 Clab	8	1		7	23.50		30.50	44	
	3700		Tractor spreader	B-66	52	.154		7	4.58	3	14.58	17.95	
	3800		Hydro or air seeding, with mulch and fertilizer	B-81	80	.300		15.40	7.95	6.75	30.10	36.50	
	4000		Shade mix, 6#/M.S.F., push spreader	1 Clab	8	1		9.40	23.50		32.90	47	
	4100		Tractor spreader	B-66	52	.154		9.40	4.58	3	16.98	20.50	
	4200		Hydro or air seeding, with mulch and fertilizer	B-81	80	.300		20.50	7.95	6.75	35.20	42.50	
	4400		Slope mix, 6#/M.S.F., push spreader	1 Clab	8	1		9.40	23.50		32.90	47	
	4500		Tractor spreader	B-66	52	.154		9.40	4.58	3	16.98	20.50	
	4600		Hydro or air seeding, with mulch and fertilizer	B-81	80	.300		23.50	7.95	6.75	38.20	45.50	
	4800		Turf mix, 4#/M.S.F., push spreader	1 Clab	8	1		6.30	23.50		29.80	43.50	
	4900		Tractor spreader	B-66	52	.154		6.30	4.58	3	13.88	17.15	
	5000		Hydro or air seeding, with mulch and fertilizer	B-81	80	.300		15.70	7.95	6.75	30.40	37	
	5200		Utility mix, 7#/M.S.F., push spreader	1 Clab	8	1		11	23.50		34.50	48.50	
	5300		Tractor spreader	B-66	52	.154		11	4.58	3	18.58	22.50	
	5400		Hydro or air seeidng, with mulch and fertilizer	B-81	80	.300		41	7.95	6.75	55.70	65	
	5600		Wildflower, .10#/M.S.F., push spreader	1 Clab	8	1		3.85	23.50		27.35	40.50	
	5700		Tractor spreader	B-66	52	.154		3.85	4.58	3	11.43	14.50	

(from *Means Site Work & Landscape Cost Data 2002*)

Figure 2.18a

02920 | Lawns & Grasses

		CREW	DAILY OUTPUT	LABOR-HOURS	UNIT	2002 BARE COSTS				TOTAL INCL O&P	
						MAT.	LABOR	EQUIP.	TOTAL		
510	7060	Limestone, mechanical spread [R02920-500]	A-1	1.74	4.598	Acre	3.33	108	35	146.33	210	510
	7100	Apply mulch, see div. 02910-500										
600	0010	SODDING 1" deep, bluegrass sod, on level ground, over 8 M.S.F.	B-63	22	1.818	M.S.F.	215	45	5.95	265.95	315	600
	0200	4 M.S.F.		17	2.353		237	58	7.70	302.70	360	
	0300	1000 S.F.		3.50	11.429		258	283	37.50	578.50	760	
	0500	Sloped ground, over 8 M.S.F.		6	6.667		215	165	22	402	515	
	0600	4 M.S.F.		5	8		237	198	26	461	595	
	0700	1000 S.F.		4	10		258	247	32.50	537.50	700	
	1000	Bent grass sod, on level ground, over 6 M.S.F.		20	2		470	49.50	6.55	526.05	605	
	1100	3 M.S.F.		18	2.222		505	55	7.25	567.25	655	
	1200	Sodding 1000 S.F. or less		14	2.857		570	70.50	9.35	649.85	745	
	1500	Sloped ground, over 6 M.S.F.		15	2.667		470	66	8.70	544.70	630	
	1600	3 M.S.F.		13.50	2.963		505	73	9.70	587.70	685	
	1700	1000 S.F.		12	3.333		570	82.50	10.90	663.40	765	
700	0010	STOLENS, SPRIGGING										700
	0100	6" O.C., by hand	1 Clab	4	2	M.S.F.	13	47		60	87.50	
	0110	Walk behind sprig planter	"	80	.100		13	2.35		15.35	17.95	
	0120	Towed sprig planter	B-66	350	.023		13	.68	.45	14.13	15.80	
	0130	9" O.C., by hand	1 Clab	5.20	1.538		9.55	36		45.55	66.50	
	0140	Walk behind sprig planter	"	92	.087		9.55	2.04		11.59	13.65	
	0150	Towed sprig planter	B-66	420	.019		9.55	.57	.37	10.49	11.75	
	0160	12" O.C., by hand	1 Clab	6	1.333		6.10	31.50		37.60	55	
	0170	Walk behind sprig planter	"	110	.073		6.10	1.71		7.81	9.35	
	0180	Towed sprig planter	B-66	500	.016		6.10	.48	.31	6.89	7.75	
	0200	Broadcast, by hand, 2 Bu per M.S.F.	1 Clab	15	.533		5.30	12.50		17.80	25.50	
	0210	4 Bu. per M.S.F.		10	.800		10.60	18.75		29.35	40.50	
	0220	6 Bu. per M.S.F.		6.50	1.231		15.90	29		44.90	62.50	
	0300	Hydro planter, 6 Bu. per M.S.F.	B-64	100	.160		15.90	3.82	2.70	22.42	26.50	
	0320	Manure spreader planting 6 Bu. per M.S.F.	B-66	200	.040		15.90	1.19	.78	17.87	20	

02930 | Exterior Plants

		CREW	DAILY OUTPUT	LABOR-HOURS	UNIT	MAT.	LABOR	EQUIP.	TOTAL	TOTAL INCL O&P	
680	0010	PLANT BED PREPARATION										680
	0100	Backfill planting pit, by hand, on site topsoil	2 Clab	18	.889	C.Y.		21		21	32.50	
	0200	Prepared planting mix	"	24	.667			15.65		15.65	24.50	
	0300	Skid steer loader, on site topsoil	B-62	340	.071			1.81	.38	2.19	3.20	
	0400	Prepared planting mix	"	410	.059			1.50	.32	1.82	2.65	
	1000	Excavate planting pit, by hand, sandy soil	2 Clab	16	1			23.50		23.50	36.50	
	1100	Heavy soil or clay	"	8	2			47		47	73	
	1200	1/2 C.Y. backhoe, sandy soil	B-11C	150	.107			2.92	1.19	4.11	5.75	
	1300	Heavy soil or clay	"	115	.139			3.80	1.55	5.35	7.50	
	2000	Mix planting soil, incl. loam, manure, peat, by hand	2 Clab	60	.267		19.55	6.25		25.80	31.50	
	2100	Skid steer loader	B-62	150	.160		19.55	4.09	.87	24.51	29	
	3000	Pile sod, skid steer loader	"	2,800	.009	S.Y.		.22	.05	.27	.39	
	3100	By hand	2 Clab	400	.040			.94		.94	1.46	
	4000	Remove sod, F.E. loader	B-10S	2,000	.006			.17	.14	.31	.41	
	4100	Sod cutter	B-12K	3,200	.005			.15	.27	.42	.52	
	4200	By hand	2 Clab	240	.067			1.56		1.56	2.43	
	6000	For planting bed edging, see div. 02945-310										
820	0010	SHRUBS, temperate zones 2 - 6										820
	1000	Abelia grandiflora, (Abelia), Z6, cont										

(from *Means Site Work & Landscape Cost Data 2002*)

Figure 2.18b

G2050 Landscaping

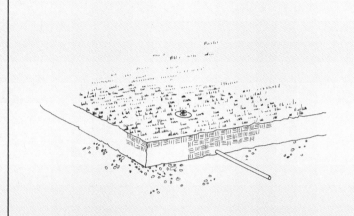

The Lawn Systems listed include different types of seeding, sodding and ground covers for flat and sloped areas. Costs are given per thousand square feet for different size jobs; residential, small commercial and large commercial. The size of the job relates to the type and productivity of the equipment being used. Components include furnishing and spreading screened loam, spreading fertilizer and limestone and mulching planted and seeded surfaces. Sloped surfaces include jute mesh or staking depending on the type of cover.

System Components	QUANTITY	UNIT	COST PER M.S.F. MAT.	COST PER M.S.F. INST.	COST PER M.S.F. TOTAL
SYSTEM G2050 410 1000					
LAWN, FLAT AREA, SEEDED, TURF MIX, RESIDENTIAL					
Scarify subsoil, residential, skid steer loader	1.000	M.S.F.		16.60	16.60
Root raking, residential, no boulders	1.000	M.S.F.		21.39	21.39
Spread topsoil, skid steer loader	18.500	C.Y.	227.55	74.56	302.11
Spread ground limestone, push spreader	110.000	S.Y.	9.90	2.20	12.10
Spread fertilizer, push spreader	110.000	S.Y.	7.70	2.20	9.90
Till topsoil, 26" rototiller	110.000	S.Y.		39.60	39.60
Rake topsoil, screened loam	1.000	M.S.F.		19.45	19.45
Roll topsoil, push roller	18.500	C.Y.		1.67	1.67
Seeding, turf mix, push spreader	1.000	M.S.F.	6.90	36.50	43.40
Straw, mulch	110.000	S.Y.	36.30	67.10	103.40
TOTAL			288.35	281.27	569.62

G2050 410	Lawns & Ground Cover	COST PER M.S.F. MAT.	COST PER M.S.F. INST.	COST PER M.S.F. TOTAL
1000	Lawn, flat area, seeded, turf mix, residential	288	282	570
1040	Small commercial	292	305	597
1080	Large commercial	300	260	560
1200	Shade mix, residential	292	282	574
1240	Small commercial	295	305	600
1280	Large commercial	310	260	570
1400	Utility mix, residential	294	282	576
1440	Small commercial	297	305	602
1480	Large commercial	330	260	590
2000	Sod, bluegrass, residential	530	655	1,185
2040	Small commercial	510	390	900
2080	Large commercial	485	315	800
2200	Bentgrass, residential	870	297	1,167
2240	Small commercial	810	385	1,195
2280	Large commercial	770	320	1,090
2400	Ground cover, english ivy, residential	1,050	735	1,785

(from *Means Site Work & Landscape Cost Data 2002*)

Figure 2.19

and bollards (short stone or concrete posts used to prevent vehicular access) are generally prefabricated products. Examples are shown in Figures 2.20, 2.21 and 2.22. Specialties may be installed on the site by the landscape contractor or others. Lighting and swimming pools are examples of specialties that may be installed by subcontractors. Product manufacturers often provide technical information (as well as current prices) for the application and installation of their products.

Historic Landscape Preservation

Renewed appreciation for "lost places" and concern for preserving and/or restoring historic sites has inspired design professionals, landscape contractors and manufacturers. New manufacturing technologies are producing reproductions, custom materials, faux finishes and many more related products. A focus on antique styles has generated increased sales of specialty fixtures and furnishings.

An historic landscape preservation site checklist includes special considerations very different from other projects. These might include the priorities of historians, archeologists and other specialists. A team of experts focused on the historic value of a site may clash with contemporary building codes and local restrictions. Questions such as "What is to be preserved?" and "What is to be restored or recreated?" set guidelines for the project. Historic landscape preservation and restoration work has created an industry manufacturing products that imitate styles and materials from past eras.

Removal of work that is inconsistent with preservation goals is often a very costly budget item. Particularly high costs are associated with excavations, demolitions and repairs. Projects with environmental impacts as great as restoration of a river have been accomplished. Such large scale projects are typically supported by public funds. The U.S. National Park Service presently maintains the Olmstead Center for Landscape Preservation at the F. L. Olmstead National Historic Site in Brookline, MA.

Professional associations for historic landscape preservation and restoration include the following organizations:

Historic Landscape Preservation Committee (202) 898-2444
American Society of Landscape Architects
636 I Street, NW
Washington, DC 20001-3736

National Trust for Historic Preservation (202) 588-6000
1785 Massachusetts Ave. NW
Washington, DC 20036

Irrigation

While irrigation is considered a specialty in some regions, it is intrinsic to landscape development in arid regions. Applications are designed for the varied needs of residences, commercial developments, golf courses, agriculture, public parks and sports facilities. Figure 2.23 is an illustration of irrigation plans for baseball fields.

Mandates for developers to provide open and green spaces require infrastructure to support and maintain those systems. Yet at the same time, local ordinances and codes restrict landscape water use. Advances in water conservation technology have created sophisticated controllers and application devices for all imaginable scenarios.

Benches

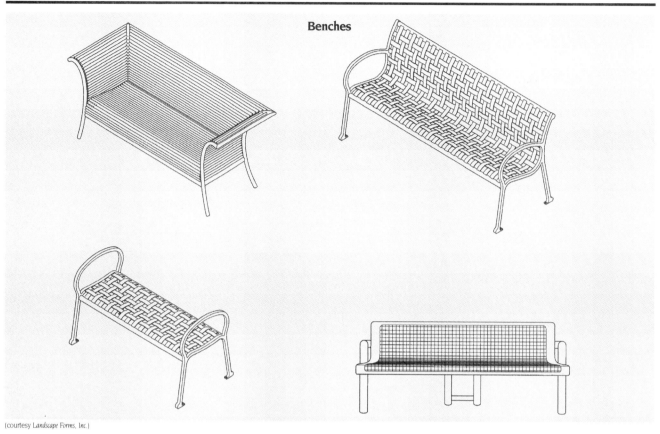

(courtesy *Landscape Forms, Inc.*)

Figure 2.20

Bollards

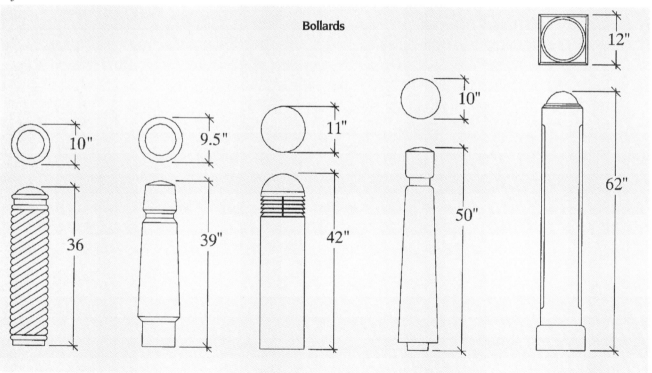

(courtesy *Quick Crete Products, Corp.*)

Figure 2.21

Tree Guards and Grates

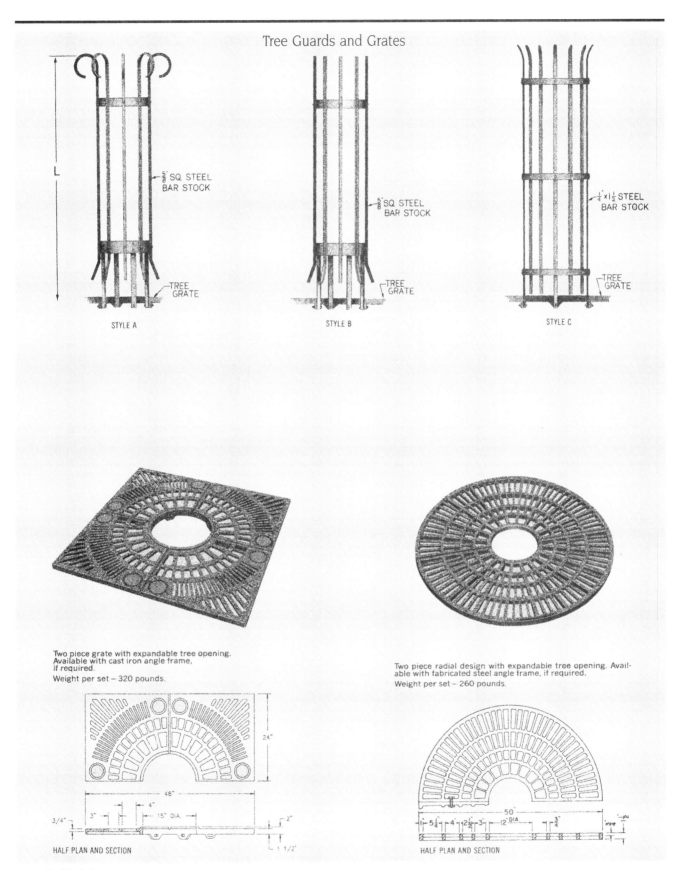

STYLE A

5/8" SQ STEEL BAR STOCK

TREE GRATE

L

STYLE B

5/8" SQ STEEL BAR STOCK

TREE GRATE

STYLE C

1/4" x 1 1/2" STEEL BAR STOCK

TREE GRATE

Two piece grate with expandable tree opening. Available with cast iron angle frame, if required.
Weight per set – 320 pounds.

24"
48"
15" DIA.
3" 4"
3/4"
2"
1 1/2"

HALF PLAN AND SECTION

Two piece radial design with expandable tree opening. Available with fabricated steel angle frame, if required.
Weight per set – 260 pounds.

50"
12" DIA.
5 1/4" 4" 2 1/2" 3" 3/4"

HALF PLAN AND SECTION

(courtesy *Neenah Foundry Company*)

Figure 2.22

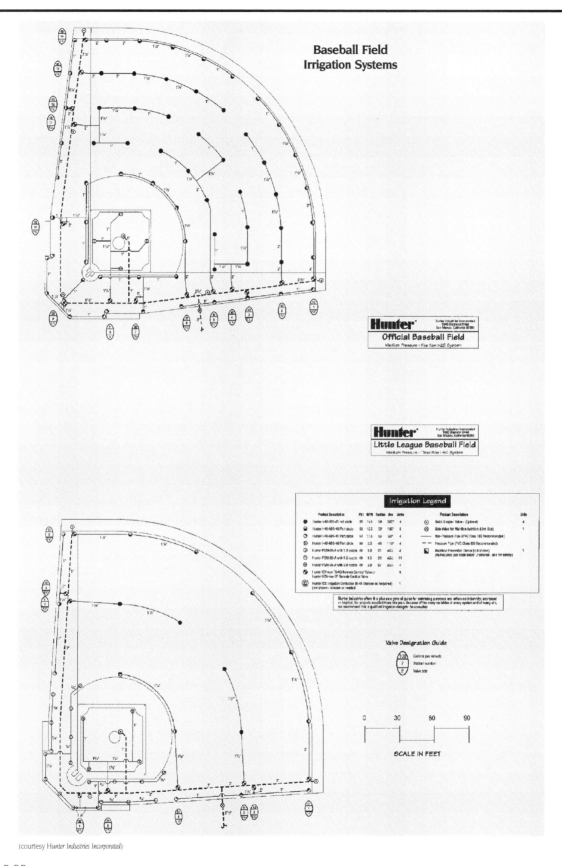

(courtesy Hunter Industries Incorporated)

Figure 2.23

Manufacturers of irrigation equipment provide detailed plans and technical assistance with their products. Professional organizations provide information, member support and industry guidelines. See the Appendix for listings. Two prominent irrigation organizations are: The Irrigation Association (IA) of Fairfax, VA, which conducts regional education seminars; and The Center for Irrigation Technology (CIT), located at California State University at Fresno. CIT is an independent testing and research center that is dedicated to the efficient use of water for irrigation. Some examples of test results for verification of manufacturer's literature follow. Figure 2.24 is a table of test results on a drip emitter that shows the relationship between water pressure PSI (pounds per square inch) and delivery of GPH (gallons per hour) with deviations noted. The chart dramatizes the relationship of PSI to GPH. Figure 2.25 reports a sample turf sprinkler's inches per hour of water delivered at different radii of throw under control conditions. Test results such as these illustrate the many factors that influence selection and installation of efficient and cost-effective irrigation equipment.

The Irrigation Association (703) 536-7080
6540 Arlington Boulevard
Falls Church, VA 22042-6638

Center for Irrigation Technology (559) 278-2066
California State University, Fresno
5370 North Chestnut Ave. M/S 18
Fresno, CA 93740-0018

Playground Equipment

Landscape designers and contractors have become actively involved in the design, sale and installation of playground equipment. A broad range of specialized equipment and materials for recreation and safety have been developed in response to the age and abilities of proposed users. See Figure 2.26 for examples of play structures as listed in *Means Site Work & Landscape Cost Data*. The Americans with Disabilities Act (ADA) has established Act Guidelines (ADAAG) for recreational spaces. To obtain a copy of this material, or for more information, call the ADA Technical Assistance Center at 800-949-4232.

Seasonal Specialties

Case histories of entrepreneurship in the landscape industry are often featured in trade journals. The design, sales and servicing of holiday items, especially Christmas displays, has boosted profits for an increasing number of landscape companies. What was once seasonal down time has now become a busy and lucrative time for many landscape businesses.

The more information and ingenuity the landscape contractor has, the greater his/her ability to solve problems and generate a dependable year-round income. Experience, combined with knowledge of materials, can generate greater creativity and innovation in landscape construction, and make the landscape designer more effective in both bringing a design concept to reality and increasing the size of his or her business.

Drip Emitter Evaluation

Emitter Description:	NON-COMPENSATING EMITTER
Manufacturer:	SAMPLE
Supplier:	SAMPLE
Test Date:	2/28/95
Number Tested:	25

Pressure (PSI)	Temp (°F)	Mean Flow (GPH)	Std. Dev (GPH)	Mfg's Cv	EU (%)	CU (%)	Emitter Constant	Emitter Exponent
5.0	67.5	0.23	0.01	0.024	97	98		
10.0	70.0	0.34	0.01	0.023	97	98	0.096	0.550
15.0	69.3	0.42	0.01	0.021	97	98	0.097	0.541
20.0	68.2	0.49	0.01	0.023	97	98	0.103	0.524
25.0	66.2	0.55	0.01	0.021	97	98	0.120	0.471
30.0	70.0	0.60	0.01	0.023	97	98	0.111	0.494
35.0	69.9	0.65	0.02	0.023	97	98	0.112	0.494
40.0	66.8	0.69	0.02	0.022	97	98	0.112	0.492
50.0	69.8	0.77	0.02	0.023	97	98	0.102	0.518
60.0	70.0	0.85	0.02	0.024	97	98		

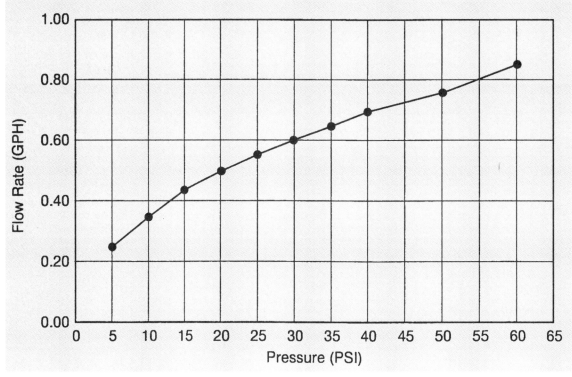

(courtesy *Center for Irrigation Technology, Fresno, CA*)

Figure 2.24

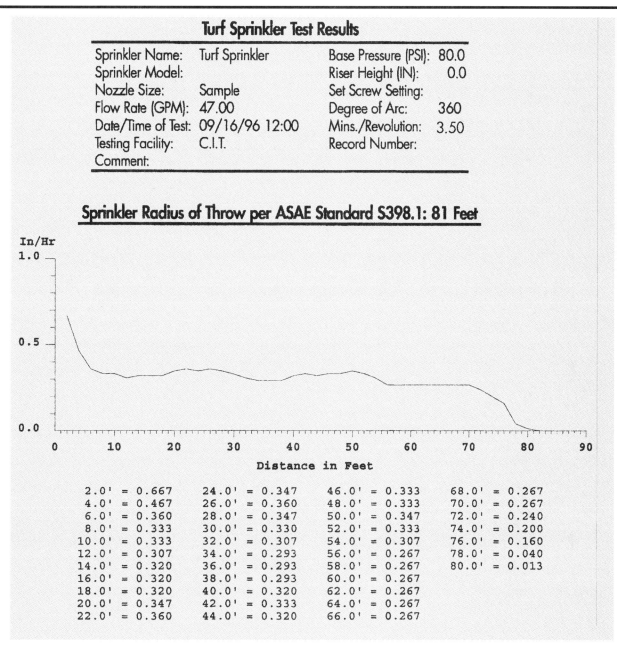

Turf Sprinkler Test Results

Sprinkler Name:	Turf Sprinkler	Base Pressure (PSI):	80.0
Sprinkler Model:		Riser Height (IN):	0.0
Nozzle Size:	Sample	Set Screw Setting:	
Flow Rate (GPM):	47.00	Degree of Arc:	360
Date/Time of Test:	09/16/96 12:00	Mins./Revolution:	3.50
Testing Facility:	C.I.T.	Record Number:	
Comment:			

Sprinkler Radius of Throw per ASAE Standard S398.1: 81 Feet

In/Hr

Distance in Feet

2.0' = 0.667	24.0' = 0.347	46.0' = 0.333	68.0' = 0.267
4.0' = 0.467	26.0' = 0.360	48.0' = 0.333	70.0' = 0.267
6.0' = 0.360	28.0' = 0.347	50.0' = 0.347	72.0' = 0.240
8.0' = 0.333	30.0' = 0.330	52.0' = 0.333	74.0' = 0.200
10.0' = 0.333	32.0' = 0.307	54.0' = 0.307	76.0' = 0.160
12.0' = 0.307	34.0' = 0.293	56.0' = 0.267	78.0' = 0.040
14.0' = 0.320	36.0' = 0.293	58.0' = 0.267	80.0' = 0.013
16.0' = 0.320	38.0' = 0.293	60.0' = 0.267	
18.0' = 0.320	40.0' = 0.320	62.0' = 0.267	
20.0' = 0.347	42.0' = 0.333	64.0' = 0.267	
22.0' = 0.360	44.0' = 0.320	66.0' = 0.267	

(courtesy *Center for Irrigation Technology*, Fresno, CA)

Figure 2.25

		02880	**Playfield Equipment**	CREW	DAILY OUTPUT	LABOR-HOURS	UNIT	2002 BARE COSTS				TOTAL INCL O&P	
								MAT.	LABOR	EQUIP.	TOTAL		
225	0300		Football, convertible to soccer	B-1	1.50	16	Pr.	1,850	385		2,235	2,650	**225**
	0500		Soccer, regulation	↓	2	12	↓	1,475	289		1,764	2,075	
700	0010		**PLAYGROUND EQUIPMENT** See also individual items										**700**
	0200		Bike rack, 10' long, permanent	B-1	12	2	Ea.	395	48		443	510	
	0240		Climber, arch, 6' high, 12' long, 5' wide		4	6		605	145		750	890	
	0260		Fitness trail, with signs, 9 to 10 stations, treated pine, minimum		.25	96		3,275	2,325		5,600	7,225	
	0270		Maximum		.17	141		6,700	3,400		10,100	12,700	
	0280		Metal, minimum		.25	96		3,375	2,325		5,700	7,300	
	0285		Maximum		.17	141		5,100	3,400		8,500	10,900	
	0300		Redwood, minimum		.25	96		9,950	2,325		12,275	14,500	
	0310		Maximum		.17	141		6,700	3,400		10,100	12,700	
	0320		16 to 20 station, treated pine, minimum		.17	141		4,825	3,400		8,225	10,600	
	0330		Maximum		.13	184		4,875	4,450		9,325	12,300	
	0340		Metal, minimum		.17	141		11,200	3,400		14,600	17,600	
	0350		Maximum		.13	184		13,400	4,450		17,850	21,700	
	0360		Redwood, minimum		.17	141		6,000	3,400		9,400	11,900	
	0370		Maximum		.13	184		14,500	4,450		18,950	22,900	
	0400		Horizontal monkey ladder, 14' long, 6' high		4	6		530	145		675	810	
	0590		Parallel bars, 10' long		4	6		229	145		374	475	
	0600		Posts, tether ball set, 2-3/8" O.D.		12	2	▼	147	48		195	237	
	0800		Poles, multiple purpose, 10'-6" long		12	2	Pr.	110	48		158	196	
	1000		Ground socket for movable posts, 2-3/8" post		10	2.400		76.50	58		134.50	174	
	1100		3-1/2" post		10	2.400	▼	106	58		164	207	
	1300		See-saw, spring, steel, 2 units		6	4	Ea.	765	96.50		861.50	995	
	1400		4 units		4	6		970	145		1,115	1,300	
	1500		6 units		3	8		1,950	193		2,143	2,450	
	1700		Shelter, fiberglass golf tee, 3 person		4.60	5.217		2,150	126		2,276	2,575	
	1900		Slides, stainless steel bed, 12' long, 6' high		3	8		1,900	193		2,093	2,400	
	2000		20' long, 10' high		2	12		2,800	289		3,089	3,525	
	2200		Swings, plain seats, 8' high, 4 seats		2	12		855	289		1,144	1,400	
	2300		8 seats		1.30	18.462		1,550	445		1,995	2,425	
	2500		12' high, 4 seats		2	12		1,000	289		1,289	1,550	
	2600		8 seats		1.30	18.462		1,500	445		1,945	2,350	
	2800		Whirlers, 8' diameter		3	8		2,100	193		2,293	2,625	
	2900		10' diameter	▼	3	8	▼	2,550	193		2,743	3,125	
710	0010		**MODULAR PLAYGROUND** Basic components										**710**
	0100		Deck, square, steel, 48" x 48"	B-1	1	24	Ea.	575	580		1,155	1,525	
	0110		Recycled polyurethane		1	24	↓	530	580		1,110	1,475	
	0120		Triangular, steel, 48" side		1	24	↓	420	580		1,000	1,350	
	0130		Post, steel, 5" square		18	1.333	L.F.	19.50	32		51.50	71.50	
	0140		Aluminum, 2-3/8" square		20	1.200		17.50	29		46.50	64.50	
	0150		5" square		18	1.333	▼	23.50	32		55.50	76	
	0160		Roof, square poly, 54" side		18	1.333	Ea.	825	32		857	960	
	0170		Wheelchair transfer module, for 3' high deck		3	8	"	1,925	193		2,118	2,400	
	0180		Guardrail, pipe, 36" high		60	.400	L.F.	215	9.65		224.65	252	
	0190		Steps, deck-to-deck, 3 - 8" steps		8	3	Ea.	1,075	72.50		1,147.50	1,300	
	0200		Activity panel, crawl through panel		2	12		330	289		619	810	
	0210		Alphabet/spelling panel		2	12		675	289		964	1,200	
	0360		With guardrails		3	8		1,775	193		1,968	2,250	
	0370		Crawl tunnel, straight, 56" long		4	6		1,000	145		1,145	1,325	
	0380		90°, 4' long		4	6		1,250	145		1,395	1,600	

(from *Means Site Work & Landscape Cost Data* 2002)

Figure 2.26

TRENCH DRAINS

Trench drains are used to remove surface water and to serve as a linear boundary to retain surface drainage. Situations where trench drains may be called for include: a sloped driveway entering a building, a stairway intersecting a plaza, or a sloping landscape where surface water may collect. Trench drains are often constructed from formed concrete with a cast iron grating cover, but other natural and man-made materials may also be used.

Trench drains are designed for open-channel flow. The cover of the drain is recessed to the level of the surrounding grade to allow for unobstructed crossing by foot or wheeled traffic. The cover can be manufactured from light- or heavy-duty material, depending on the amount of support required by the expected traffic flow. A framing angle is embedded into the perimeter of the trench to receive the cover.

Prefabricated concrete trench drains can be installed much faster than poured-in-place concrete drains. One type, for example, is manufactured from polymer concrete with sections that snap together for relatively easy and quick installation. The polymer concrete material used in the drain also resists chemicals and is not affected by the freeze-thaw cycle. Modular catch basins are also available with this prefabricated drainage system.

Materials other than concrete are used occasionally to create trench drains in lawns and/or other landscaped or site areas where concrete drains are not desired for aesthetic or other reasons. One alternative method of trench drain installation is to place drainage stone in an envelope of geotextile fabric, usually 4- to 6-ounce nonwoven polyester. The fabric is unrolled into an open trench, filled with the stone, and then overlapped. Additional stone or suitable landscaping materials may then be used to cover the drain.

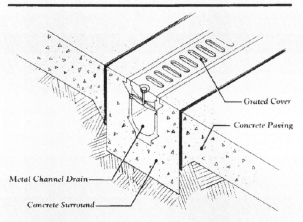

Embedded Trench Drain

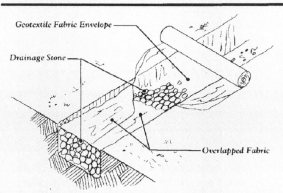

Stone Trench Drain

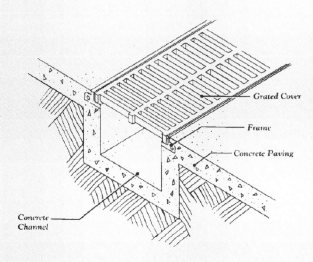

Man-hours

Description	m/hr	Unit
Trench Forms		
1 Use	.200	sfca
4 Uses	.173	sfca
Reinforcing	15.240	ton
Concrete		
Direct Chute	.320	cu yd
Pumped	.492	cu yd
With Crane and Bucket	.533	cu yd
Trench Cover, Including Angle Frame		
To 18" Wide	.400	lf
Cover Frame Only		
For 1" Grating	.178	lf
For 2" Grating	.229	lf
Geotextile Fabric in Trench		
Ideal Conditions	.007	sq yd
Adverse Conditions	.010	sq yd
Drainage Stone		
3/4"	.092	cu yd
Pea Stone	.092	cu yd

(from *Means Graphic Construction Standards*)

Figure 2.27

Sewage and drainage usually flow by gravity from the source of collection, through service lines, into mains, and eventually to a point of treatment. However, force mains are not uncommonly substituted for gravity mains in sewage systems in which the fluid head must be augmented with pumping stations to assist the drainage flow. Manholes are spaced at regular intervals along the main lines to provide access for repair and maintenance. Sewage and drainage systems operate in the same manner, but their components vary in the types of materials used, because their functions are different.

Sewage-collection systems conduct biological waste to a treatment facility. Gravity sewer mains are usually manufactured from reinforced concrete, but plastic piping can also be used. Asbestos cement piping, at one time the most commonly used form of main piping material, has declined in use due to the hazards of handling asbestos. Force sewer mains (under pressure) are usually manufactured from ductile iron or reinforced plastic pipe. Service lines to individual users consist of vitrified clay or plastic piping. The fittings used in tying the service lines into the main should be made of the same material as that of the service line.

Drainage systems are used to collect stormwater and surface drainage from roadways and parking areas and to conduct the flow away to a suitable outfall. Drainage piping is usually manufactured from reinforced concrete or corrugated metal, although plastic piping has become increasingly popular. Catch basins, which are located at the sump, or low point, of the area to be drained, are sized to handle the maximum volume of rainfall for that area. A catch basin is protected from clogging by a cast iron grating that is removed for maintaining and periodic cleaning. Because the basin outlet pipe is located several feet above the lowest level of the basin, silt and debris settle and accumulate at the bottom of the structure. This material must be cleaned out at regular intervals to prevent buildup and the eventual clogging of the outlet pipe.

Although manholes may require the installation of steps, and may differ from catch basins in function, size, and type of cover, both structures are commonly constructed in the same way and of the same materials. Both structures are fabricated from brick, concrete blocks, c.i.p. concrete or precast concrete sections that are assembled on a poured-in-place concrete slab or on a precast base. A typical manhole or catch basin is a cylinder 4' ± in diameter and 6' high (internal dimensions) at the lower section. The cylinder tapers into an upper section, 2' in diameter by 2' high, that receives the cover. The cover, and the frame, range from 4" to 10" in depth and may be adjusted to grade with brick.

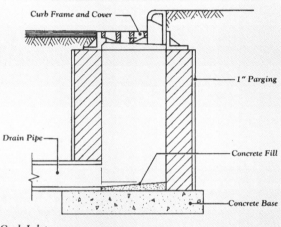

Curb Inlet

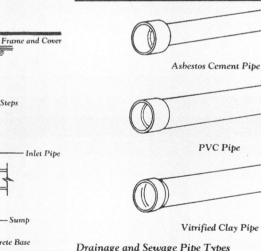

Drainage and Sewage Pipe Types

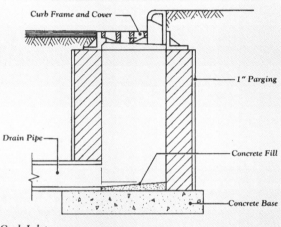

Catch Basin

(from *Means Graphic Construction Standards*))

Figure 2.28

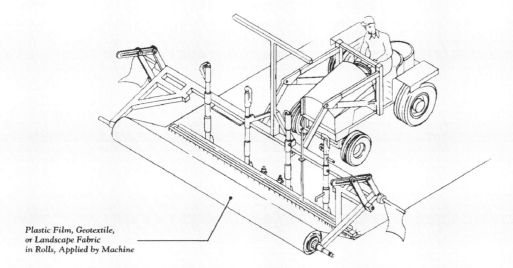

Plastic Film, Geotextile,
or Landscape Fabric
in Rolls, Applied by Machine

Erosion control may be used when top soil, subsoil, or fill tends to run off with the rapid flow of water down a sloped surface. The type of erosion control selected varies for different situations and is determined by the size and severity of the erosion problem, the amount of time available to establish the control system, cost factors, and the final landscaping design of the site. Natural controls, mulches of all types, fiber grids, and rip rap stone are among the many erosion control materials used to keep soil in place.

For moderate slopes and swales, the planting of natural materials may serve as an adequate method for slowing runoff. The root systems of shrubbery, ground cover, and, especially, grass provide a constantly growing and expanding source of natural erosion control. This method of control, however, often takes a long time to establish and may require regular maintenance of mowing and pruning after the vegetation takes root. More immediate controls, even if they are temporary, can be implemented to hold the soil in place while grass or other vegetation gets established.

Included among these faster methods of erosion control are many different types of organic and stone mulches which can be spread over large areas to control runoff. Most organic mulches are relatively inexpensive and can be easily distributed by wheelbarrow or light-duty loader. Wood chips, often a by-product of site clearing, can be placed to a depth of 1" to 2". Straw can be placed by itself or as a cover to protect seeded banks. Blankets of excelsior, held together with biodegradable plastic netting, can be unrolled and stapled into place on the slope. For rapid installation, mulch may also be applied by the hydro-spraying method from a distribution truck. This slurry consists of water and wood cellulose alone or mixed with grass seed and fertilizer. Expensive organic mulches, which include peat and bark in shreaded or nugget form, should be installed where the aesthetic impact of the site is a prime consideration.

Stone mulches provide permanent protection against slope erosion, but they are harder to install and more expensive than most organic erosion control materials. Quarry stone is the most economical type of stone mulch, but other types of decorative stone are available at costs of ten to thirty times that of quarry stone. The size of stone mulch ranges from pea stone to boulders.

To control weeds and other unwanted growth which may establish themselves beneath and between the mulch, several methods may be employed. For example, two mil black plastic film can be installed on the slope prior to the spreading of the mulch. Geotextile and landscaping fabric can be substituted for the plastic film if a porous material is needed to allow water penetration into the slope. Lightweight polypropylene fabric can be installed prior to the placing of small stone mulch, but heavier stones may require a heavier fabric or a light fabric with a granular bedding layer.

Several types of organic and synthetic fiber grids, nettings, and fabric materials may also be used alone or in conjunction with mulches or with ground covers and plantings to control slope erosion. Recycled tobacco cloth, which is used for shading tobacco fields, is available from landscaping wholesalers in many parts of the country. Jute mesh and woven polyethylene mesh cost a little more than tobacco cloth, but they can serve as an adequate substitute in areas where tobacco cloth is not available. Polypropylene, which is often used in the manufacture of geotextiles, has been adapted for use in erosion control as a flat, loosely bonded film that allows air and moisture to pass freely while inhibiting weed growth. Flexible three-dimensional matting, which is fabricated from bonded vinyl, nylon, or polypropylene filaments, becomes permanently interlocked in vegetation growth after it has been placed.

(from *Means Graphic Construction Standards*)

Figure 2.29a

For more severe erosion control situations, such as shorelines, the banks of channels, and very steep slopes, heavier materials are required. Rip rap stone, which ranges in size from 8″ to 1/3 of a cubic yard and larger, can be installed by a variety of methods. Small rip rap may be distributed by truck or loader and then spread or placed by hand or machine. Large rip rap must be placed a stone at a time, often with a crane. The stone may be set in a gravel bedding or a geotextile base, grouted in place with concrete, or dry grouted by filling voids with smaller stone.

Several other materials and methods besides rip rap can be employed for severe erosion control. Precast interlocking concrete blocks, which are installed like rip rap, can be employed as a heavy-duty paving material on eroded slopes. A unique concrete forming system for interconnected modular blocks is also available. This system consists of a heavy fabric which can be unrolled in place and then pumped full of concrete. Gabion revetment mats can be set on banks, filled with stone, and then coated with an asphaltic slurry.

A final method of severe erosion control includes the installation of a barrier or a series of barriers set at right angles to the direction of flow to interrupt the runoff. These barriers consist of materials which filter out and retain the sediment in the runoff but allow the water to pass. Hay bales supported by wood stakes comprise the most commonly installed barrier of this type. Another type of barrier, called a silt fence, is constructed from sections of woven polypropylene strip fabric that are reinforced and drawn between posts located at intervals of 8′ to 10′.

(from *Means Graphic Construction Standards*)

Man-hours

Description	m/hr	Unit
Mulch		
Hand Spread		
Wood Chips, 2″ Deep	.004	sf
Oat Straw, 1″ Deep	.002	sf
Excelsior w/Netting	.001	sf
Polyethylene Film	.001	sf
Shredded Bark, 3″ Deep	.009	sf
Pea Stone	.643	cu yd
Marble Chips	2.400	cu yd
Polypropylene Fabric	.001	sf
Jute Mesh	.001	sf
Machine Spread		
Wood Chips, 2″ Deep	1.970	MSF
Oat Straw, 1″ Deep	.089	MSF
Shreded Bark, 3″ Deep	2.960	MSF
Pea Stone	.047	cu yd
Hydraulic Spraying		
Wood Cellulose	.200	MSF
Rip Rap		
Filter Stone, Machine Placed	.258	cu yd
1/3 cu yd Pieces, Crane Set Grouted	.700	sq yd
18″ Thick, Crane Set, Not Grouted	1.060	sq yd
Gabion Revetment Mats, Stone Filled, 12″ Deep	.366	sq yd
Precast Interlocking Concrete Block Pavers	.078	sf

Figure 2.29b

BRICK, STONE AND CONCRETE PAVING

Brick and stone provide durable, weather-resistant surfaces for exterior pavements. Many types of hard brick and stone are available to meet the practical and cosmetic needs of a given surface. The patterns in which the brick or stone is placed should be determined according to the surface's use and its desired appearance.

Both brick and stone may be set in a sand or concrete bed and grouted with mortar or watered and tamped sand. Regardless of the type of bed material, the subbase must first be leveled and thoroughly compacted to prevent cracking and settling of the finished surface. Wire mesh reinforcing may be required in concrete beds that are large in area or subjected to heavy traffic.

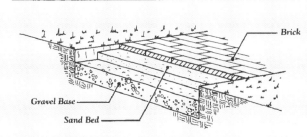

Brick Sidewalk

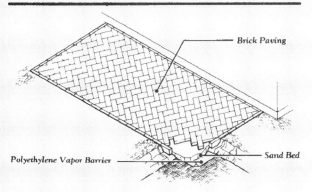

Brick Paving on Sand Bed

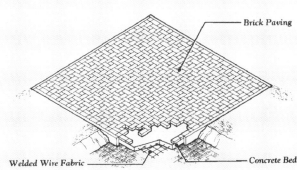

Brick Paving on Concrete Bed

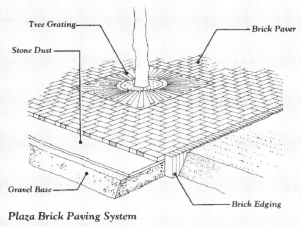

Plaza Brick Paving System

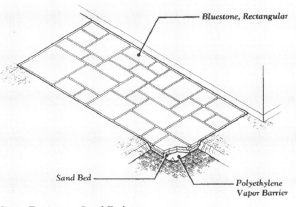

Stone Paving on Sand Bed

(from *Means Graphic Construction Standards*)

Figure 2.30a

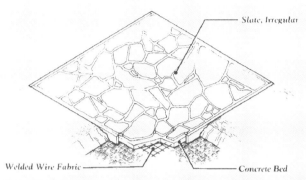

Stone Paving on Concrete Bed

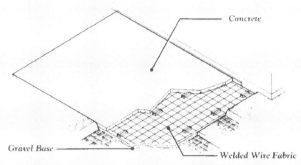

Concrete Paving

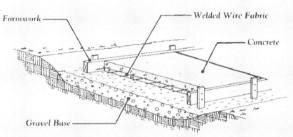

Concrete Sidewalk

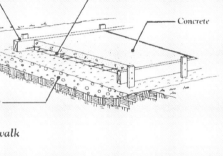

Concrete Stairs

Man-hours

Description	m/hr	Unit
Brick Paving without Joints (4.5 Brick/sf)	.145	sf
Grouted, 3/8" Joints (3.9 Brick/sf)	.178	sf
Sidewalks		
Brick on 4" Sand Bed		
Laid on Edge (7.2/sf)	.229	sf
Flagging		
Bluestone, Irregular, 1" Thick	.198	sf
Snapped Randon Rectangular 1" Thick	.174	sf
1-1/2" Thick	.188	sf
2" Thick	.193	sf
Slate		
Natural Cleft, Irregular, 3/4" Thick	.174	sf
Random Rectangular, Gauged, 1/2" Thick	.152	sf
Random Rectangular, Butt Joint, Gauged,		
1/4" Thick	.107	sf
Granite Blocks, 3-1/2" x 3-1/2" x 3-1/2"	.174	sf
4" to 12" Long, 3" to 5" Wide, 3" to 5" Thick	.163	sf
6" to 15" Long, 3" to 6" Wide, 3" to 5" Thick	.152	sf

(from *Means Graphic Construction Standards*)

Figure 2.30b

Chapter 3

Equipment

Chapter Three
Equipment

Equipment Investments

The pressures of competition, environmental regulations and the need to make a profit require a streamlined, cost-effective company. Equipment such as trucks, backhoes, and riding mowers are capital investments and an important component in cost-effective management. A large portion of business profits may be invested or designated toward major equipment purchase. Before a decision is made to acquire new equipment, there must be careful consideration of the allocation of present and future cash assets to cover equipment costs. The options for obtaining the equipment needed to perform planned work includes subcontractor-provided, rental, lease or outright purchase. The volume of work and financial strength of a company may determine its options.

Other factors should be carefully considered before a specific equipment choice is made. Selecting the most suitable size and power of a piece of equipment has a significant impact on productivity. Chapter 2, "Materials and Methods," and Chapter 5, "How to Take Off Quantities," provide examples of the factors influencing appropriate equipment selection.

The scope of work each business performs determines which machines are most suitable for that company. Experienced owners focus on contracts that are most profitable and base purchasing decisions on known productivity of machines they operate. Other sources of information on equipment productivity are manufacturers, trade associations (see Appendix), and Means annual cost data books. The Means cost data books provide suggested daily outputs under varying conditions.

In exploring the subject of equipment, we will first look at the rental or subcontracting of equipment as applied to a landscape estimate. Then, we will examine the economics of purchase and leasing.

Equipment Rental and Subcontracting

It may not be worth purchasing machines that a business uses only occasionally. In this situation, the options are equipment rental or subcontracting the work. Either way, any work that requires use of that machine (possibly on more than one job) should be coordinated so it can be accomplished at the same time.

Figure 3.1 is a listing of national average rental rates and operating costs of typical site work equipment and accessories from *Means Site Work & Landscape Cost Data*. The rental rates shown here pertain to late model, high quality machines in excellent working condition, rented from equipment dealers. Rental rates from contractors may be substantially lower than those of equipment dealers, depending on economic conditions. Contractor rentals can include the skilled operator of the machine and its transportation. For a more detailed explanation of Means format, cost, and productivity figures, see Chapter 10, "How to Use *Means Site Work & Landscape Cost Data*".

The selection of earthwork equipment depends on the type and quantity of materials being worked, as well as site conditions and available access. The hauling distance, the type and condition of the road, as well as the time allowed and the availability of equipment are other important considerations. Short-haul cut-and-fill operations may require light duty equipment only, while another

01590 | Equipment Rental

			UNIT	HOURLY OPER. COST	RENT PER DAY	RENT PER WEEK	RENT PER MONTH	CREW EQUIPMENT COST/DAY	
200	2900	Rake, spring tooth, with tractor	R01590 -100	Ea.	1.14	190	571	1,725	123.30	**200**
	3000	Roller, tandem, gas, 3 to 5 ton			5.15	127	380	1,150	117.20	
	3050	Diesel, 8 to 12 ton	R02315 -400		4.30	223	670	2,000	168.40	
	3100	Towed type, vibratory, gas 12.5 H.P., 2 ton			2.70	255	765	2,300	174.60	
	3150	Sheepsfoot, double 60" x 60"	R02315 -450		.85	110	330	990	72.80	
	3200	Pneumatic tire diesel roller, 12 ton			6.10	315	945	2,825	237.80	
	3250	21 to 25 ton			10.25	590	1,775	5,325	437	
	3300	Sheepsfoot roller, self-propelled, 4 wheel, 130 H.P.			29.80	875	2,630	7,900	764.40	
	3320	300 H.P.			41.55	975	2,930	8,800	918.40	
	3350	Vibratory steel drum & pneumatic tire, diesel, 18,000 lb.			11.30	355	1,065	3,200	303.40	
	3400	29,000 lb.			18.95	470	1,415	4,250	434.60	
	3410	Rotary mower, brush, 60", with tractor			7.15	237	710	2,125	199.20	
	3450	Scrapers, towed type, 9 to 12 C.Y. capacity			3.37	161	482	1,450	123.35	
	3500	12 to 17 C.Y. capacity			3.58	214	643	1,925	157.25	
	3550	Scrapers, self-propelled, 4 x 4 drive, 2 engine, 14 C.Y. capacity			69.40	1,450	4,320	13,000	1,419	
	3600	2 engine, 24 C.Y. capacity			101.35	2,275	6,815	20,400	2,174	
	3650	Self-loading, 11 C.Y. capacity			31.35	825	2,470	7,400	744.80	
	3700	22 C.Y. capacity			61.35	1,475	4,410	13,200	1,373	
	3710	Screening plant 110 hp. w / 5' x 10'screen			15.85	370	1,115	3,350	349.80	
	3720	5' x 16' screen			17.20	475	1,420	4,250	421.60	
	3850	Shovels, see Cranes division 01590-600								
	3860	Shovel/backhoe bucket, 1/2 C.Y.		Ea.	.85	53.50	160	480	38.80	
	3870	3/4 C.Y.			.85	61.50	185	555	43.80	
	3880	1 C.Y.			.90	71.50	215	645	50.20	
	3890	1-1/2 C.Y.			1	170	510	1,525	110	
	3910	3 C.Y.			1.15	305	920	2,750	193.20	
	3950	Stump chipper, 18" deep, 30 H.P.			3.08	185	555	1,675	135.65	
	4110	Tractor, crawler, with bulldozer, torque converter, diesel 75 H.P.			12.15	325	970	2,900	291.20	
	4150	105 H.P.			17.20	490	1,475	4,425	432.60	
	4200	140 H.P.			19.80	510	1,530	4,600	464.40	
	4260	200 H.P.			29.80	975	2,925	8,775	823.40	
	4310	300 H.P.			39.20	1,200	3,600	10,800	1,034	
	4360	410 H.P.			53.65	1,575	4,725	14,200	1,374	
	4380	700 H.P.			109.65	3,400	10,235	30,700	2,924	
	4400	Loader, crawler, torque conv., diesel, 1-1/2 C.Y., 80 H.P.			9.70	310	930	2,800	263.60	
	4450	1-1/2 to 1-3/4 C.Y., 95 H.P.			11.70	380	1,145	3,425	322.60	
	4510	1-3/4 to 2-1/4 C.Y., 130 H.P.			16.05	615	1,850	5,550	498.40	
	4530	2-1/2 to 3-1/4 C.Y., 190 H.P.			23.20	840	2,525	7,575	690.60	
	4560	3-1/2 to 5 C.Y., 275 H.P.			31.15	1,200	3,610	10,800	971.20	
	4610	Tractor loader, wheel, torque conv., 4 x 4, 1 to 1-1/4 C.Y., 65 H.P.			10.05	223	670	2,000	214.40	
	4620	1-1/2 to 1-3/4 C.Y., 80 H.P.			11.05	315	940	2,825	276.40	
	4650	1-3/4 to 2 C.Y., 100 H.P.			11.55	335	1,000	3,000	292.40	
	4710	2-1/2 to 3-1/2 C.Y., 130 H.P.			14.55	425	1,270	3,800	370.40	
	4730	3 to 4-1/2 C.Y., 170 H.P.			18.10	565	1,700	5,100	484.80	
	4760	5-1/4 to 5-3/4 C.Y., 270 H.P.			32.95	855	2,570	7,700	777.60	
	4810	7 to 8 C.Y., 375 H.P.			50.20	1,100	3,305	9,925	1,063	
	4870	12-1/2 C.Y., 690 H.P.			93.50	2,350	7,015	21,000	2,151	
	4880	Wheeled, skid steer, 10 C.F., 30 H.P. gas			5.85	140	420	1,250	130.80	
	4890	1 C.Y., 78 H.P., diesel			7.60	223	670	2,000	194.80	
	4891	Attachments for all skid steer loaders								
	4892	Auger		Ea.	.46	77.50	232	695	50.10	
	4893	Backhoe			.64	107	320	960	69.10	
	4894	Broom			.66	110	331	995	71.50	
	4895	Forks			.21	34.50	104	310	22.50	

(from *Means Site Work & Landscape Cost Data 2002*)

Figure 3.1

operation may call for excavators, a fleet of trucks, and spreading and compaction equipment.

Factors influencing excavation, and examples of excavating and hauling equipment are shown in Figure 3.2 (from *Means Site Work & Landscape Cost Data*). Charts that show equipment capacity, volume per hour, and haul distance, can be matched with the number and size of trucks for hauling to ensure that all equipment is continuously in use, with no waiting or down time.

In creating earthwork systems or "assemblies," Means has matched various excavating operations equipment with the most efficient size and quantity of equipment. A comparison of dozer sizes and hauling distance is shown in Figure 3.3 from *Means Site Work & Landscape Cost Data*. (See Chapter 10 for details on using assemblies in an estimate.)

The Economics of Purchase and Leasing

Analyzing Equipment Costs Before Making an Investment

Before you purchase any major unit of equipment, you will probably want to determine whether it is more cost efficient than continuing to get by with old equipment. To perform this analysis you need to collect and compare information on the old machine versus a new one. Figure 3.4 shows a useful comparison method. Factors to be considered include:

- Price of new vs. resale value of old
- Projected loss of value in the next year from use and depreciation
- Operating costs per hour, based on the projected life cycle (or hours of use)
- Other factors, such as projected repairs and down time which are covered in detail later in this chapter

The example in Figure 3.4 demonstrates that productive capacity of new versus old is the determining factor. A change in any of the data could produce a different result.

The allocation of cash assets for the purchase or lease of equipment is best guided by professional tax advisors familiar with the company's business plan. Figure 3.5 illustrates a lease-versus-buy example. This example assumes all five years are *profitable*, and suggests purchase would be the best choice based on the present value of a series of monthly net outlays over five years.

A thorough analysis of equipment costs requires consideration of **life cycle costs** based on the projected life of the unit. To make cost-effective purchases, you need to list expected costs in a projected life cycle of the item. In Figure 3.5 a life cycle of 5 years is projected. Figure 3.4 examines the projected costs of a machine to be used 2000 hours annually. Hours of use is the standard measure of life cycles. A major factor in the annual usage schedule of some types of equipment is climate. In some regions, the growing season and therefore landscape work may last for nearly an entire year, while in other locations snow removal equipment may be all that is needed in winter months.

Life Cycle Costs

An essential part of financial operations is planning cash flow for equipment. When deciding how to allocate limited budgets, managers need to invest wisely in capital equipment. Your purpose in projecting costs before purchase is to achieve the lowest cost of ownership of a piece of equipment over the life of that unit. For that purpose, a record is created listing the projected life of the unit.

R02315-400   Excavating

The selection of equipment used for structural excavation and bulk excavation or for grading is determined by the following factors.

1. Quantity of material.
2. Type of material.
3. Depth or height of cut.
4. Length of haul.
5. Condition of haul road.
6. Accessibility of site.
7. Moisture content and dewatering requirements.
8. Availability of excavating and hauling equipment.

Some additional costs must be allowed for hand trimming the sides and bottom of concrete pours and other excavation below the general excavation.

When planning excavation and fill, the following should also be considered.

1. Swell factor.
2. Compaction factor.
3. Moisture content.
4. Density requirements.

A typical example for scheduling and estimating the cost of excavation of a 15' deep basement on a dry site when the material must be hauled off the site, is outlined below.

Assumptions:

1. Swell factor, 18%.
2. No mobilization or demobilization.
3. Allowance included for idle time and moving on job.
4. No dewatering, sheeting, or bracing.
5. No truck spotter or hand trimming.

Number of B.C.Y. per truck = 1.5 C.Y. bucket x 8 passes = 12 loose C.Y.

$$= 12 \times \frac{100}{118} = 10.2 \text{ B.C.Y. per truck}$$

Truck Haul Cycle:

Load truck 8 passes	=	4 minutes
Haul distance 1 mile	=	9 minutes
Dump time	=	2 minutes
Return 1 mile	=	7 minutes
Spot under machine	=	1 minute
		23 minute cycle

Fleet Haul Production per day in B.C.Y.

$$4 \text{ trucks} \times \frac{50 \text{ min. hour}}{23 \text{ min. haul cycle}} \times 8 \text{ hrs.} \times 10.2 \text{ B.C.Y.}$$

$$= 4 \times 2.2 \times 8 \times 10.2 = 718 \text{ B.C.Y./day}$$

Excavating Cost with a 1-1/2 C.Y. Hydraulic Excavator 15' Deep, 2 Mile Round Trip Haul			L.H./Day	Hourly Cost	Daily Cost	Subtotal	Unit Price
1	Equipment Operator		8	$32.35	$ 258.80		
1	Oiler		8	26.65	213.20		
4	Truck Drivers		32	25.00	800.00	$1,272.00	$1.77
1	Hydraulic Excavator				593.20		
4	Dump Trucks				1,931.20	2,524.40	$3.51
Bare Total for 720 B.C.Y.					$3,796.40	$3,796.40	$5.28

Description		1-1/2 C.Y. Hyd. Backhoe 15' Deep		1-1/2 C.Y. Power Shovel 7' Bank		1-1/2 C.Y. Dragline 7' Deep		2-1/2 C.Y. Trackloader Stockpile
Operator (and Oiler, if required)		$ 472.00		$ 472.00		$ 472.00		$ 472.00
Truck Drivers	3 Ea.	600.00	4 Ea.	800.00	3 Ea.	600.00	4 Ea.	800.00
Equipment Rental		593.20		850.20		921.00		770.00
20 C.Y. Trailer Dump Trucks	3 Ea.	1,448.40	4 Ea.	1,931.20	3 Ea.	1,448.40	4 Ea.	1,931.20
Bare Total Cost per Day		$3,113.60		$4,053.40		$3,441.40		$3,973.20
Daily Production, C.Y. Bank Measure		720.00		960.00		640.00		1000.00
Bare Cost per C.Y.		$ 4.32		$ 4.22		$ 5.38		$ 3.97

Add the mobilization and demobilization costs to the total excavation costs. When equipment is rented for more than three days, there is often no mobilization charge by the equipment dealer. On larger jobs outside of urban areas, scrapers can move earth economically provided a dump site or fill area and adequate haul roads are available. Excavation within sheeting bracing or cofferdam bracing is usually done with a clamshell and production is low, since the clamshell may have to be guided by hand between the bracing. When excavating or filling an area enclosed with a wellpoint system, add 10% to 15% to the cost to allow for restricted access. When estimating earth excavation quantities for structures, allow work space outside the building footprint for construction of the foundation, and a slope of 1:1 unless sheeting is used.

(from *Means Site Work & Landscape Cost Data* 2002)

Figure 3.2

G1030 Site Earthwork

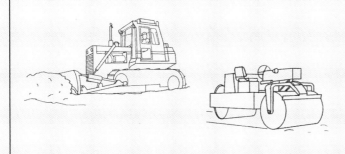

The Cut and Fill Common Earth System includes: moving common earth cut from an area above the specified grade to an area below the specified grade utilizing a bulldozer and/or scraper, with the addition of compaction equipment, plus a water wagon to adjust the moisture content of the soil.

The Expanded System Listing shows Cut and Fill operations with hauling distances that vary from 50′ to 5000′. Lifts for compaction in the filled area vary from 4″ to 8″. There is no waste included in the assumptions.

System Components	QUANTITY	UNIT	COST PER C.Y.		
			EQUIP.	LABOR	TOTAL
SYSTEM G1030 115 1000					
EARTH CUT & FILL, 75 HP DOZER & COMPACTOR, 50′ HAUL, 4″ LIFT, 2 PASSES					
Excavating, bulk, dozer & compactor, 50′ haul, common earth	1.000	C.Y.	.80	1.31	2.11
Water wagon, rent per day	.004	Hr.	.25	.15	.40
Backfill dozer, from existing stockpile, 75 H.P., 50′ haul	1.000	C.Y.	.33	.54	.87
Compaction, roller, 4″ lifts, 2 passes	1.000	C.Y.	.56	2.29	2.85
Total			1.94	4.29	6.23

G1030 115	Cut & Fill Common Earth	COST PER C.Y.		
		EQUIP.	LABOR	TOTAL
1000	Earth cut & fill, 75HP dozer & roller compact, 50′ haul, 4″ lift, 2 passes	1.94	4.29	6.23
1050	4 passes	2.76	6.75	9.51
1100	8″ lift, 2 passes	1.55	3.11	4.66
1150	4 passes	1.94	4.29	6.23
1200	150′ haul, 4″ lift, 2 passes	3.06	6.15	9.21
1250	4 passes	3.88	8.60	12.48
1300	8″ lift, 2 passes	2.67	4.95	7.62
1350	4 passes	3.06	6.15	9.21
1400	300′ haul, 4″ lift, 2 passes	4.98	9.30	14.28
1450	4 passes	5.80	11.75	17.55
1500	8″ lift, 2 passes	4.59	8.10	12.69
1550	4 passes	4.98	9.30	14.28
1600	105 H.P. dozer and roller compactor, 50′ haul, 4″ lift, 2 passes	1.98	3.73	5.71
1650	4 passes	2.80	6.20	9
1700	8″ lift, 2 passes	1.59	2.55	4.14
1750	4 passes	1.98	3.73	5.71
1800	150′ haul, 4″ lift, 2 passes	3.35	5.25	8.60
1850	4 passes	4.17	7.70	11.87
1900	8″ lift, 2 passes	2.96	4.06	7.02
1950	4 passes	3.35	5.25	8.60
2000	300′ haul, 4″ lift, 2 passes	5.95	8.05	14
2050	4 passes	6.75	10.50	17.25
2100	8″ lift, 2 passes	5.55	6.90	12.45
2150	4 passes	5.95	8.05	14

(from *Means Site Work & Landscape Cost Data 2002*)

Figure 3.3

Old	Data	New
$10,000	Resale Value and Price	$110,000
20%	% Loss of Value Next Year	25%
$30	Operating Cost/Hour	$15
1	Relative Productive Capacity*	1.3
15%	Down Time	5%
$1,500	Other Fixed Cost/Year	$10,000

(*Model improvements in new machines – greater horsepower or other efficiencies – translate into higher capacities)

$	Calculations	$
$0.2 \times 10,000 = 2,000$	Loss of resale value	$.25 \times 110,000 = 27,500$
$1,789^* \times 30 = 53,700$	Operating costs, assuming 2,000 hours for new, hence, $ {}^*\left(\dfrac{85\% \text{ Uptime for Old}}{95\% \text{ Uptime for New}}\right) \times 2,000 \text{ hrs.}$	$2,000 \times 15 = 30,000$
1,500	Other fixed	10,000
57,200	**Total Cost Next Year**	**67,500**
57,200 for A units	Cost per unit (LF, CY, etc.); if the old machine will produce A units in 2,000 hrs., the new one must produce more due to greater up time and greater capacity/hr.	$\dfrac{67,500}{\dfrac{.95}{.85} \times 1.3A} = 46,500$ for A units

Note that although the new machine will cost more next year as a total, its *unit* cost is lower.

Conclusion: *Buy now* if you anticipate working 2,000 hours. The calculations can be made for any number of hours.

"Make Do" vs. "Get New" Example

(from *Means Heavy Construction Handbook*)

Figure 3.4

Initial outlay: $50,000 + $1,200 (freight) + $2,000 (sales tax) = $53,200

Depreciable amount: $51,200

Year (n)	1	2	3	4	5
Depreciation	5/15	4/15	3/15	2/15	1/15
Depreciation amount	$17,067	$13,653	$10,240	$6,827	$3,413
(Note: These add up to $51,200)					
35% of rollback on depreciation	$5,974	$4,779	$3,584	$2,389	$1,194
35% of sales tax ($2,000)	$ 700				
Rollback totals	$6,674	$4,779	$3,584	$2,389	$1,194
Reduce to present value *	$6,007 +	$3,950 +	$2,693 +	$1,632 +	$ 741 = $15,023

(Net Effective Cost Today: $53,200 (−) $15,023 = $38,177)

Lease: R = $1,500/mo.

$1,500 × $.35 = $525 rollback

$$1,500 - \left[525 \left(1 + \frac{.10}{2} \right) \right] = 1,500 - 551 = \$949 \text{ net}$$

*Divide by $(1 + i^n)$ where i = interest [0.10]

**Every year the firm pays $1,500/mo. 12 times. When the firm gets 12 × $525 back (in effect) from the IRS, it will have lost interest on each payment from 10% on the first to 0% on the last, or an average of i/2.

The present value of a series of monthly net outlays over 5 years is $47.06 × R. In this case:

$ 949 × $47.06 = $44,660

$38,177 < $44,660 so BUY

This also assumes "0" salvage value at the end of 5 years.

Lease vs. Buy Example

(from *Means Heavy Construction Handbook*)

Figure 3.5

It would begin with the year of purchase and extend to the last year of use. In this manner a life cycle cost is similar to a cash flow diagram.

Life cycle costs include:

- Initial purchase cost
- Operating and associated expenses
- Maintenance and repair costs

Initial Purchase Cost (including all one-time costs such as sales tax and freight) must be recovered by the utilization of the machine. Initial purchase cost (along with operating and associated costs, and anticipated maintenance and repair costs) are divided by the projected life of the machine to determine the amount that must be charged for each hour the machine will be used.

Operating and Associated Costs include fuel, routine maintenance, license, insurance, etc. These costs are distributed over the projected life of the machine and adjusted for cost differences over time.

Maintenance Costs such as machine parts and tires and major **repairs** are difficult to estimate, while at the same time inevitable. It is important to allocate an amount for this item based on experience. The repair history of a machine you already own serves as a guideline for future performance, as well as a check on the reality of prior estimates.

For the purposes of this example, we will assume a unit is purchased. The first step in determining the unit's life cycle cost is to create a cash flow diagram beginning with the year of purchase and extending to the last projected year of use. Figure 3.6 is a simplified example with an initial investment cost of $1,000. Since four years are the projected life of the unit, a time schedule line is set for four years. Note the assumption of an annual increase in usage cost due to anticipated increase in frequency and level of needed repairs, and rise in the cost of fuel and replacement parts. Other associated costs are licenses, taxes and insurances, etc.

Both usage and associated costs are shown to increase each year, based on expected increases over time. Finally the unit is suggested to have a salvage value of $50. Anticipating costs that will occur is a step in budgeting for future years. In this example, the costs are shown as positive, and the payback of the salvage value is shown as negative.

Data compiled from equipment records and cash flow charts show the true cost of an initial capital investment over a given period of time. Such information includes the cost of maintenance, repairs, operation and usage, less its resale value. This technique of life cycle costing assumes knowledge of the basics of *compounding, discounting, present value* and *uniform annual value.*

Compounding is the adding of interest to an amount over a period of time, in the same way a bank pays interest on a savings account. Interest is added to accrued interest as well as to the principal sum.

Discounting is a technique for converting future cash expenditures to equivalent present value amounts. Figure 3.7 shows $1000 cash both compounding and discounting at the rate of 10%. It can be seen that if one had to pay out $1611 in 5 years, or $2594 in 10 years, the initial amount needed to be invested now at 10% interest would be $1000. Today's $1000 is the present value of a future amount of $1611 in 5 years; and today's $1000 is the present value of $2594 in 10 years, and so on as shown in the illustration. These calculations are made by *discounting* a future value in a specific year at a given rate of interest.

Present Value is the value of a future cost in today's (present value) dollars. This amount is determined by discounting the effect of interest to convert future dollars to current dollars.

Tracking Costs

Once you have made an equipment investment, you will need to track the true costs of the equipment by documenting hours of use and costs. An individual record must be made for every capital investment. Begin by listing each individual unit with the date purchased, year of manufacture, serial number, make and model. Include all information relevant to warranties and life expectancy, and any former repair history. Create a column for each projected year of use. The initial cost is divided over projected years of use. The rest of the record should document:

1. Hours of use
2. Maintenance and repairs
3. License, insurance, etc.
4. Usage costs

The total maintenance and operation history of a particular piece of equipment is important for budget, insurance and tax purposes. Documenting the costs and hours of use is also necessary to assess the cost efficiency of your equipment. Depreciation schedules may also be listed on the equipment record, providing useful information for your tax records. Major repairs may be capitalized for

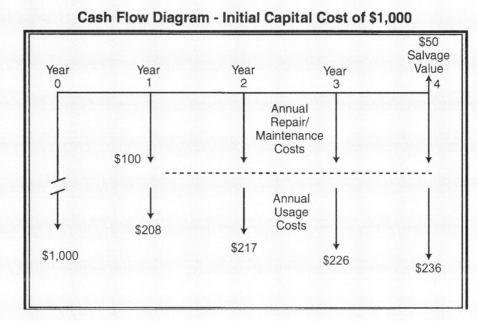

Cash Flow Diagram - Initial Capital Cost of $1,000

(from *Means Facilities Maintenance & Repair Cost Data 2002*)

Figure 3.6

tax purposes and added to the original cost. If used units are sold, detailed records that document compliance with manufacturer-recommended maintenance can be helpful in selling the item.

Minimizing Down Time

It is necessary to achieve balance between hours of use for a piece of equipment and needed down time for service and repair. Strictly following manufacturer-recommended service intervals is one step you can take. In areas that have seasonal equipment needs, it is wise to use the summer to service plows and sanders, and use the winter months to bring grass-mowing, trimming and edging equipment into good repair.

We can see from Figure 3.8 that as equipment ages, operating costs go up. Repair costs are not easy to estimate, but might be expected to increase over the years. The graphs in Figure 3.9 illustrate ideal versus typical repair cost records. Although some years will have few repairs and other years will have more

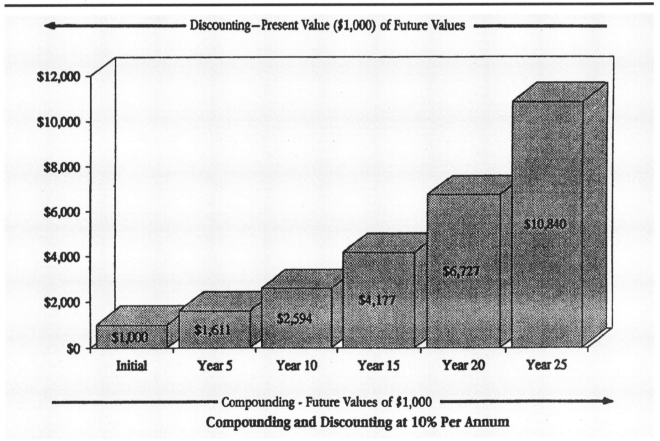

(from *Means Facilities Maintenance & Repair Cost Data*)

Figure 3.7

frequent repairs at greater expense, the eventual outcome may be a similar curve. This information enables the careful manager to make a fairly accurate prediction of the overall repair budget.

Equipment Life Expectancy

Calculating the life expectancy of all equipment at the time it is put into service and then tracking repairs will help you plan for its eventual repair and replacement. Tracking repairs on a unit will help you determine the point at which the equipment becomes more costly to keep operating with repairs, than it would be to replace it. A detailed record also provides valuable information on the effectiveness and efficiency of a particular model.

Another advantage of knowing the costs over the life of capital equipment is to be able to plan future equipment purchases, and budget for the cash required. Typically contractors keep a unit until it is no longer profitable. One large contractor declares when the repair value is greater than half the value of the unit, it is time to get rid of the machine. Whether repairs are done in-house, or sent out to dealers, down time can be a significant cost factor. Scheduling maintenance according to the manufacturer's suggestions is a necessity, despite the associated down time, but can usually be scheduled to minimize disruption.

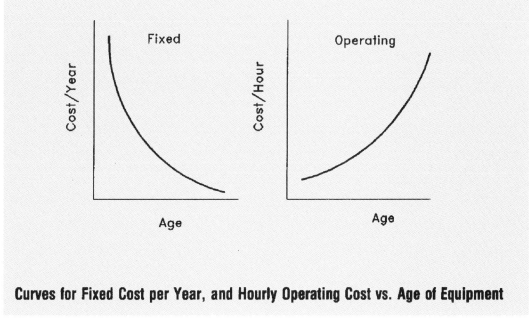

Curves for Fixed Cost per Year, and Hourly Operating Cost vs. Age of Equipment

(from *Means Heavy Construction Handbook*)

Figure 3.8

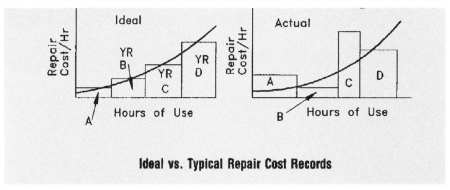

Ideal vs. Typical Repair Cost Records

(from *Means Heavy Construction Handbook*)

Figure 3.9

How to Estimate

Chapter Four

How to Estimate

Initial interest in bidding a landscape contract is based on various factors. First of all, an analysis of all aspects of the proposed job is necessary to reveal the special conditions or features that could influence the landscape contractor's ability to do the contract work. If the work is especially suited to your capabilities and conveniently located, you may want to "go for it". So will your competitors. However, not all jobs should be bid by every landscape contractor.

Many landscaping companies fit the definition of small businesses. Owner/foremen are typical in the business, and many larger companies have evolved from the hands-on labor of their owners. In the competitive landscape business, it is the practical cost estimator who survives. Often this successful survivor has concentrated on the work he is best equipped to perform and the work on which the greatest profit can be made.

To Bid or Not to Bid

The decision whether or not to bid a project is always carefully considered by the experienced contractor. Before spending a lot of time estimating, it is wise to analyze the project objectively, looking at negative as well as positive aspects. Not all landscape projects in the vicinity will prove to be profitable or even manageable for your firm. Factors to consider may include:

- Current job commitments
- Location of the job
- Employee expertise
- Labor restrictions
- Government regulations
- Need for work

Once the decision is made to bid or price the job, the estimating process begins. The landscape contractor may estimate and bid from plans and/or written specifications prepared by others. In other cases, the landscape bidder may be actively involved in the design proposal, and may submit a design with details, along with a price for the work. In *both* situations, it is critical that the entire scope of all the work be clearly defined. This complete definition of the project serves as a base, and enables the contractor to make informed decisions regarding bidding and estimating. Suggested procedures for analysis and estimating are described here and in the following chapters. Many of the steps are explained with the help of examples, charts, forms, and diagrams.

Establishing a consistent routine for project analysis and estimating procedures and techniques is important. One advantage of a pre-established format is that everyone involved with the project can easily use and evaluate recorded information. Data compiled using familiar methods can be checked and traced easily.

The wise landscape contractor bases estimating decisions on an accumulated knowledge of prior works. While it may vary for each contractor, this knowledge base can generally be divided into three categories. These are **Information, Capability**, and **Capacity**.

Information

- Accepted trade practices
- Knowledge of materials
- Operating expenses/overhead costs
- Labor force (including subcontractors) required for a job
- Local conditions
- Constraints and incentives of a potential project

Capability

- Experience
- Skill
- Labor productivity
- Type of equipment available
- Mobilization capability

Capacity

- Labor force availability
- Amount of equipment available
- Purchasing power
- Time of year (seasonal limitations)

The landscape contractor relies on this knowledge base in making the decision to bid or perform the job.

Information

The Information categories can be further defined as follows:

Accepted Trade Practices are standards or norms within the industry. These standards are often determined from an analysis of the best overall results among different materials and methods over a wide range of conditions. Many of these results are published by product manufacturers, trade journals, and associations. In practice, some materials and methods are typical, or historically used for certain applications. The estimator must be familiar with these practices to ensure a complete and proper estimate.

Knowledge of Materials means knowing how and what items to use for specific applications and solutions; for example, knowing which plants will survive drought or other kinds of temperature or weather extremes. Knowing the full range, versatility, and appropriate application of all types of landscaping materials adds tremendously to the capability of the designer or contractor. Chapter 2, "Materials and Methods," describes the kinds of materials used in the landscaping industry and explains their standards of measure. The American Society for Testing and Materials (ASTM) establishes industry-accepted standards for thousands of materials. Further information on this organization may be found in the Appendix.

Operating Expenses, or **Overhead**, is the cost of doing business. Such costs do not contribute directly to the physical costs of a project, but are necessary for securing and completing contracts. They include items such as management salaries, office and vehicle expenses, insurance, and advertising—numerous costly but necessary items that are the costs of maintaining a business. These

expenses must be paid out of the income generated from the work of the landscape business and must, therefore, be included in the fees or estimated cost of the project. Overhead can be determined as the total annual cost of running the business, exclusive of direct project costs, i.e., field or materials expenses. One way to estimate and recover these overhead costs is to distribute them over the total available work hours (your **capacity**), establishing an hourly rate that includes overhead. A detailed analysis and explanation of overhead costs are included in Chapter 6.

Labor Force information is needed to project your gross weekly payroll and to determine such items as project capacity. The complete labor burden is based on salary rates, estimated hours, and the following considerations:

- Workers' Compensation and liability insurance
- Employer's contributions for Social Security and Medicare
- State Unemployment Tax
- Federal Unemployment Tax
- Fringe benefits

Subcontractors are a segment of the labor force requiring separate consideration. Subcontracting for special skills has become an accepted and desirable way of responding to the need for these skills on a part-time basis. The mason who specializes in stone walls or bluestone set in stone dust can provide quality work that is also cost effective. *Manageability* of subcontractors is crucial for successful job performance. Even if extremely talented and skillful, a subcontractor who is unable to meet the schedule can be detrimental to the project.

Local Conditions are important factors. Among these considerations are prevailing wages and the ability to procure an adequate number of workers. The availability of materials and supplies must also be known. These important, specific conditions override any printed and suggested costs found in manuals. Local government regulations can also have a significant impact, not only on the design, but on the implementation of a project. The contractor (and designer) must be aware of applicable codes and zoning requirements.

Constraints and Incentives must also be considered in analyzing a landscape project. Past experience and present need will help you to reach a conclusion. Some judgment considerations are listed below.

- Location (travel distance)
- Character of project (simple or complex)
- Quality of drawings and specs
- Quality of supervision
- Quality of workers
- Expected level of cooperation between landscape architect and general contractor
- Allowed completion time (ample or tight)
- Subcontractor availability
- Need for work
- Economic conditions

Capability

Capability translates easily into production, or the work a company is able to accomplish. The amount of skill and experience of designers, managers, foremen,

and crew is a good indicator of overall capability. The availability of manpower and equipment also affects the contractor's ability to efficiently and effectively perform the job.

Experienced management not only increases employee production, but can also be a teaching tool, training employees for future responsibilities. Skill comes from practice and becomes more finely tuned with use. An accumulation of experience and skill increases the capability of apprentices. Everyone knows that "It's hard to get good help these days," and landscape contractors, like other good business managers, try to keep good, experienced workers. This aim can, however, be difficult to carry out due to the seasonal character of landscape work. Keeping workers through the winter can be an expensive proposition, but such a practice might pay off in the long run. By retaining a good work force, the contractor can be assured of higher productivity, and the estimator has a more reliable base from which to determine labor costs.

Determining the best equipment to have available requires careful, cost-effective analysis. Is it best to own certain equipment, or more cost effective to lease on a job-by-job basis? Such a decision is often based on how quickly a piece of equipment may become "needed" on projects. If equipment is often required on a moment's notice, ownership might be more practical. As with all cost questions, associated expenses such as licenses, insurance, depreciation, storage, and maintenance must be entered into the basic (life) cost of equipment.

Mobilization capability is the ability to respond with appropriate manpower and equipment—in other words, all available manpower and equipment that can be placed on a job at a scheduled time. If the contractor does not have a well-established mobilization capability, bidding certain jobs may not be feasible. Some work contracts may carry penalties for delayed or late performance.

Capacity

In addition to the capability, or productivity, of the available work force and equipment, the contractor (and estimator) must also know the *capacity* of the company's resources. Capacity involves the availability of resources, in the quantities needed. The availability of manpower is greatly dependent on regional economics. On a case-by-case basis, labor availability may be the crucial factor in deciding whether to bid a specific project, or certain types of projects. **Labor Capacity** is a measurable resource that can be assessed for not only long-range planning, but specific task productivity as well.

Capacity also refers to the number of working hours or work days that are available for carrying out the required work in a project. A sample work force capacity chart, as shown in Figure 4.1, can help to anticipate available work hours. In this hypothetical case, the chart covers the period from March 15 to the middle of December and takes place in the Northeast U.S. The chart is based on a six-day week with holidays off, and compensates for a certain percentage of loss time for any reason, including weather. Eight hours are suggested as the average working time per day. For help in determining anticipated loss time, always list weather conditions in a daily work diary. This sample chart suggests that for this hypothetical example, the total number of working hours in a typical season for a full-time employee is 1600. This number times the number of full-time employees represents the total available work hours for the year. A similar chart could be created for equipment.

Labor Productivity varies with the skill and experience of foreman and crew. Daily work order forms give records of task accomplishment and rates of

production, and therefore serve as valuable historic data for pricing and bidding future work.

Distributing labor, trucks, equipment, and tools effectively and choosing the most productive equipment to own, hire, or rent has a dramatic impact on productivity and costs. Examples of the relationship between equipment and production are shown in Chapter 3, Figures 3.1 and 3.2. The purchasing power of a company may be assessed by its insurers, banks, and clients as well as by company management. Profitable business expansion is more likely to be sustained when it is properly and effectively planned.

Timing, within a project or over the course of a year, is an essential element in all business endeavors. This statement may have an even stronger meaning in the landscape industry, where many operations are restricted by weather and climate. In the New England region, for example, landscape contractors may postpone optional or nonessential tree removals until winter, when few other landscape operations can be done. Timing may also be essential to the finances of a business. Large investments or expenditures may be tied in to seasonal cash flow. If certain work (such as the tree removal mentioned above) is postponed for seasonal reasons, payments for that work may also be postponed. This possibility should be figured into the cash flow analysis of the company. In addition, the estimator must anticipate and include any incurred costs for such restrictions when preparing a proposal.

	Available Work Hours		
	Number of Work Days	Loss Time	Work Time
March	14	2	12
April	26	4	22
May	26	4	22
June	27	4	23
July	26	4	23
August	26	4	22
September	26	4	22
October	27	4	21
November	25	4	21
December	13	2	11
	236	36 days	200 days
Average number of hours per work day			8 hrs./day
Total available work hours (per worker)			1600 hrs.

Figure 4.1

Subcontractors and Vendors

Finally, a word should be said about subcontractors and vendors, a critical element in a contractor's capability *and* capacity. To insure reliability and quality work, the contractor must establish good relationships with these vital participants in the project.

Before Starting the Estimate

To begin, every job proposal must receive a critical review. Ask questions to obtain a clear understanding of the total job. The landscape architect may refer to this understanding as the **scope of work**. The complete scope of the work should be clear, based on the plans and written specifications. A landscape checklist form can help both planners and contractors to assemble all necessary information, and confirm that nothing is left out. It provides a good starting place for the estimating process. A sample of such a form, a "Landscape Project Analysis" form, appears later in this chapter.

Carefully look over the site plans and written specifications. A chart listing plant materials and their sizes frequently appears directly on landscape plans. Drawings may note such items as fences and paving that may or may not be furnished and installed by others. Requirements may be listed for tests, samples, methods of delivery, and storage. Methods of installation may be referenced as standards, for example, "according to standards of the American Nursery and Landscape Association." The estimator should be familiar with or reference any such information in order to properly estimate the project.

Be alert to the state of progress on the job. Find out when work can begin on the site and if the complete site is accessible for inspection. Is the estimate being done at a conceptual stage? If so, considerable variation from the original project requirements should be anticipated. These changes may greatly alter the final landscape proposal. All of this information gathering will serve as a knowledge base for your cost estimate.

Accuracy in estimating depends on several factors as we have already discussed. Reliable sources of cost information, the availability of specific design details, and knowledge of proper methods and materials are all crucial elements. Another factor affecting estimating accuracy is finding adequate time to do the estimate. This is often a problem. When preparing an estimate for bidding, time must be allowed so that the project may be thoroughly reviewed. Be alert for omissions, ambiguities, or other defects in the drawings or specifications. Requests for clarification may result in an addendum to all bidders issued prior to the bidding. Contract documents often contain a paragraph stating the manner in which such addenda and interpretations must be handled.

Be sure to visit the site to confirm the data provided and to obtain additional information that may not appear in the plans or specifications. Sometimes plans, detail drawings, and written specs do not adequately highlight certain work components. Existing site conditions are not often detailed on plans. A checklist such as the "Landscape Project Analysis" form (Figures 4.2–4.6) can be very helpful in assuring that all pertinent information is obtained. Note additional information such as travel time to the job and access for machinery if it is needed. At the site, compare actual conditions to the drawings. This procedure includes reading contour lines that show existing and proposed grades and learning if soil tests or borings have revealed any useful information. Most sites change a great deal during building construction and before landscape operations begin, but the existing vegetation and site conditions can give you valuable information nonetheless.

For large jobs that have more paperwork and involve many subcontractors, a checklist such as the one following can be helpful.

Job Checklist

1. Obtain plans and specs (including enough copies for subcontractors and vendors).
2. Check instructions to bidders for:
   a. Bid date, time, and place
   b. Bid security required
   c. Pre-bid conference with owner, if any

Mark dates on wall calendar to minimize conflicting job requirements. Be alert to the vital and unbendable guidelines regarding bid date, time, and place. Public works bids that miss a deadline even by minutes are rejected and not considered. Likewise, required bid security must also be documented as required, or the bid may be invalidated. Pre-bid conferences with owners may explain or interpret specs and shed a new light on costs and requirements.

3. Examine the General and Special Conditions sections for completion time, liquidated damage dates and amounts, scope of the work, installation of owner-supplied items, allowances, alternates, retainage percentage and date of release, and any unusual payment requirements.
4. Make a special list of any questionable items for further clarification by owner or architect.
5. Estimate alternates separately from the primary scope of work.

Alternates are separate prices, or "subquotes," submitted for additional work or variations of the specified work. The owner or architect will often request alternates. They may want to compare costs of different components for a particular project's requirements, or analyze the cost differences between bidders. For example, the landscape architect may feel that the landscape contractor knows more about the availability of specimen ornamental plants and may request suggestions for specific applications, along with the resulting cost variations. Watch for appropriate listing place for alternate items. Check if alternate is to be listed in grand total or listed as a separate item.

The successful bidder/negotiator depends on the complete and accurate interpretation of plans and specifications. A careful review of documents, a site inspection, and if necessary, written clarification from the landscape architect and others are essential elements in an accurate estimation of costs.

The Landscape Project Analysis Form

A project analysis form may be used as an information gathering tool and a systematic checklist. It can provide a format for listing all specified products and work. As a checklist, the form can ensure that all requirements (even those that may not be directly stated in the plans and specifications) are included. When the form is filled out, notes should be made of all relevant factors, using additional sheets as required. If the project is large or has unusual features, using this kind of form may reveal the need for cost contingencies. It may also be used as an on-site inspection checklist for the bidder to verify an estimate.

The **site investigation** accomplishes the following:

- Allows a comparison of drawings and specs to the facts and the actual existing conditions.

- Provides new information that may explain (or contradict) that shown on the drawings and specs.
- Creates a space and dimension realization that may not be easily imagined from scaled drawings (the impact of slopes and obstacles, for example).

For the contractor, the project analysis form may help in deciding whether or not to bid the project. It may provide a format for recording and evaluating factors such as the suitability of equipment, the location and access of the project, and the expectations of both the prime contractor and the landscape architect or owner. The project analysis form can also be helpful with the scheduling of various work phases. For the planner, this form can serve as a detailed checklist for the specifications and drawings that are intended and required for a project. Both contractors and planners can use the form to ensure that all items affecting the project's costs are considered and included. An example project analysis form is shown in the following pages, Figures 4.2 through 4.6.

For projects with complete plans and specifications, cost estimating begins with a detailed quantity takeoff. This procedure is described in the following chapter. A sample takeoff also appears in Chapter 7, where it is completed as part of the example estimate.

Types of Estimates

Estimating takes time and skill, and both are costly. The degree of accuracy required in the estimate must be balanced against the cost of creating it. The best, or most appropriate kind of estimate is determined by its purpose and just how much specific design detail is available when the estimate is done. For example, "around an acre or so" could vary two or three thousand square feet or more. There is no point in proposing exact figures when only an approximation of site measurements is possible. The estimator must analyze various factors in order to choose the most appropriate estimating method.

The choice of estimating method is determined by several factors. Among these considerations are the amount and detail of the information given to the estimator, the amount of time available to complete the estimate, and the purpose of the estimate (e.g., project budget, construction bid, etc.). Whatever method the estimator uses, all costs are derived from an established information base, using sources that are as accurate and relevant to the project as possible. Sources of cost information are discussed in Chapter 6.

No matter what the method, the estimating process involves breaking the landscape project down into various stages of detail. When the scope of the work is completely identified, the job categories, such as masonry, planting, and machine work should be listed separately and in as much detail as possible (or as necessary). By determining the quantities involved and the cost of each item, the estimator is able to complete a cost estimate.

Variables in both the estimating process and individual landscape project requirements are responsible for the spread in estimates. The two basic types of estimates that are most commonly used are:

- Systems, or "Assemblies" Estimates
- Unit Price Estimates

A third type, Square Foot Estimates, may also be used, usually for budgetary or cross-checking purposes.

LANDSCAPE PROJECT ANALYSIS FORM

Date _____

Travel Time From _____ To _____

Travel Minutes _____ Travel Miles _____

Project _____ **Location** _____

Owner _____ **Project Manager** _____

Landscape Architect _____

Contractor, General _____

Building Type _____
Quality: _____ Economy _____ Average _____ Custom _____ Luxury

Describe _____

Size: _____
    Ground floor area of building _____ S.F.
    Outdoor surface parking _____ S.F.
    Number of parking spaces required _____
    Lawn area _____ S.F.
    Landscape planting area _____ S.F.
    Other area _____ S.F.

Zoning: _____ Residential _____ Commercial _____ Industrial _____ None _____ Other
Zoning Requirements _____

ESTIMATE DATA

Budget due: _____ _____
Schematic estimate due: _____ _____
Preliminary estimate due: _____ _____
Bid/Final estimate due: _____ _____ , _____ a.m./p.m.
Working drawings _____

LABOR MARKET _____ Highly competitive _____ Normal _____ Union _____ Nonunion

Describe _____

TAXES Tax Exempt: ____ No ____ Yes ____ % State ____ % County ____ % City ____ % Other

BOND _____ Not required _____ Required Type _____ Amount _____

BIDDING DATE _____ Start date _____ Construction duration _____
_____ Open competitive _____ Selected committee _____ Negotiated _____ Filed bids

CONTRACT _____ Single _____ Multiple Describe _____
Multiple type assigned to general contractor _____ No _____ Yes

Figure 4.2

SITE WORK, EARTHWORK, AND DRAINAGE

Date _____ Location _____

Project _____

DEMOLITION: _____ No _____ Yes Allowance _____ _____ Separate contract

Removal from site: _____ No _____ Yes Dump location _____ _____ Separate contract

TOPOGRAPHY: _____ Level _____ Moderate grades _____ Steep grades

Describe _____

SUBSURFACE EXPLORATION: _____ Borings _____ Test pits _____ USDA maps _____ Other

SITE AREA: Total _____ Acres to clear _____ Acres to thin _____ Acres open _____

CLEARING & GRUBBING: _____ No _____ Light _____ Medium _____ Heavy

TOPSOIL: _____ No _____ Strip _____ Stockpile _____ Dispose on site

_____ Dispose off site _____ miles

_____ Furnish: ·

Existing: _____ inches deep Final depth: _____ inches

Describe _____

SOIL TYPE: _____ Gravel _____ Sand _____ Clay _____ Silt _____ Rock _____ Peat _____ Other

Describe _____

Rock expected: _____ No _____ Ledge _____ Boulders _____ Hardpan

Describe _____

How paid _____

GROUND WATER EXPECTED: _____ No _____ Yes Depth or elevation _____

Disposal of _____ by _____

Figure 4.3a

SITE WORK, EARTHWORK, AND DRAINAGE (cont.)

EXCAVATION: _____ Grade and fill on site _____ Dispose off site _____ miles

_____ Borrow expected _____ miles

Quantity involved: Disposal _____ Borrow _____

BACKFILL:

Paving area _____ No _____ Yes

Area _____

Material _____ Inches deep _____ % Compaction _____

Landscape area _____ No _____ Yes

Area _____

Material _____ Inches deep _____ % Compaction _____

Source of materials _____

TERMITE CONTROL: _____

WATER CONTROL: Describe _____

STORM DRAINS: _____ No _____ Yes Type _____

Headwall: _____ No _____ Yes Type _____

Catch basins: _____ No _____ Yes _____ Block _____ Brick

_____ Concrete _____ Precast

Size _____ Number _____

FRENCH DRAINS: _____ No _____ Yes Describe _____

RIP RAP: _____ No _____ Yes Describe _____

SPECIAL CONSIDERATIONS: _____

_____

_____

Figure 4.3b

UTILITIES,
ROADS, AND WALKS

WATER SUPPLY: Existing Main   _____ No   _____ Yes   Location _____   Size _____

Service Piping   _____ By utility   _____ By others   _____ This contract

Water Pumping Station   _____ No   _____ Yes   Type _____

SPECIAL CONSIDERATIONS: _____

_____

DRIVEWAYS: _____ No   _____ Yes   _____ By others _____

_____ Bituminous   _____ Concrete   _____ Gravel   Thickness _____

PARKING AREA: _____ No   _____ Yes   _____ By others _____

_____ Bituminous   _____ Concrete   _____ Gravel   Thickness _____

Base Course: _____ No   _____ Yes   _____ By others   _____ Gravel   _____ Stone

CURBS: _____ No   _____ Yes   _____ By others

_____ Bituminous   _____ Concrete   _____ Granite

PARKING BUMPERS: _____ No   _____ Yes   _____ By others

_____ Concrete   _____ Timber

PAINTING LINES: _____ No   _____ Yes   _____ By others

_____ Paint   _____ Thermoplastic   _____ Traffic lines   _____ Stalls

GUARD RAIL: _____ No   _____ Yes   _____ By others

_____ Cable   _____ Steel   _____ Timber

SIDEWALKS: _____ No   _____ Yes   _____ By others

_____ Bituminous   _____ Concrete   _____ Brick   _____ Stone

Width _____   Thickness _____

STEPS: _____ No   _____ Yes   _____ Brick   _____ Concrete   _____ Stone   _____ Timber

SIGNAGE: _____ No   _____ Yes   _____ By others

SPECIAL CONSIDERATIONS: _____

_____

_____

Figure 4.4

SITE IMPROVEMENTS
AND SPECIALTIES

ARTWORK: _____ No _____ Yes _____ By others

CARPENTRY: _____ No _____ Yes _____ By others

FENCING: _____ No _____ Yes _____ By others

_____ Chain link _____ Aluminum _____ Steel   Other _____

Height _____ Length _____ Gates _____

FLAGPOLES: _____ No _____ Yes _____ By others

FOUNTAINS: _____ No _____ Yes _____ By others

**INTERIOR
LANDSCAPING:** _____ No _____ Yes _____ By others

**PATIOS
AND TERRACES:** _____ No _____ Yes _____ By others

PLANTERS: _____ No _____ Yes _____ By others   Type _____

EQUIPMENT: _____ No _____ Yes _____ By others

_____ Benches   _____ Bleachers   _____ Bike rack   _____ Goal posts
_____ Posts   _____ Running track   _____ Seesaw   _____ Shelters
_____ Slides   _____ Swings

**PLAYGROUND
SURFACE:** _____ No _____ Yes _____ By others

Surface Type _____ Area _____

**PLAYING
FIELD:** _____ No _____ Yes _____ By others

**RETAINING
WALLS:** _____ No _____ Yes _____ By others

_____ CIP   _____ Unit Masonry   _____ Brick   _____ Stone   _____ Timber
Other _____ Height _____ Length _____

STRUCTURES:

Benches   _____ No _____ Yes _____ By others
Garden house _____ No _____ Yes _____ By others
Greenhouse   _____ No _____ Yes _____ By others
Other   _____ No _____ Yes _____ By others

POOLS: _____ No _____ Yes _____ By others _____Swimming _____ Other

**IRRIGATION
SYSTEM:** _____ No _____ Yes _____ By others

**TENNIS
COURTS:** _____ No _____ Yes _____ By others Surface Type _____
                                               Number _____

**TRASH
ENCLOSURES:** _____ No _____ Yes _____ By others

Figure 4.5

LAWNS AND PLANTING

TOPSOIL: ____ No ____ Yes ____ By others

            Depth _____ inches Source _____

SHRUBS: ____ No ____ Yes ____ By others

            Number _____ Size Range: _____ Small ____ Medium _____ Large

TREES: ____ No ____ Yes ____ By others

            Number Conifer _____ _____ Small ____ Medium _____ Large

            Number Deciduous _____ _____ Small ____ Medium _____ Large

Tree Plazas: ____ No ____ Yes ____ By others

Describe _____

SEEDING: ____ No ____ Yes ____ By others S.F. Area _____

Describe _____

SOD: ____ No ____ Yes S.F. Area _____

GROUND COVER: Type _____ S.F. Area _____

EDGING: Type _____ L.F. Area _____

WEED BARRIER: _____ Physical _____ Chemical

Describe _____

MULCHING: Material _____ Thickness _____

MAINTENANCE: ____ No ____ Yes ____ By others

Describe _____

SPECIAL CONSIDERATIONS: _____

Figure 4.6

Systems Estimates

In systems estimating, various components of a landscape installation are grouped together in an assembly. For example, Figure 4.7, from *Means Site Work & Landscape Cost Data*, illustrates tree pit "assemblies." Different tasks, which could be estimated separately, are combined into one cost. Note that in this case, the tree is not included. Time is saved using assemblies costs because much of the detail work is eliminated. Figures 4.8 and 4.9 illustrate two other typical systems: lawns and site irrigation. In these cases, assemblies costs in *Means Site Work & Landscape Cost Data* include overhead and profit. A full explanation of the derivation and use of Means cost information is included in Chapter 10.

Unit Price Estimates

Unit price estimates involve a careful breakdown of all the elements that go into the landscape project. In order to successfully perform a unit price estimate, detailed drawings and explicit specifications are necessary. This type of estimate is assembled item by item within each major category. Each component and associated unit price is matched to a specific quantity. To maintain accuracy, "ballparking" should not be used. In order to complete a unit price estimate, you need to know the specified or required unit prices for all material, equipment, and labor. Unit price estimates can provide the highest degree of accuracy, but require the most time, and therefore the greatest expense, to complete. For this reason, unit price estimates are typically performed on projects that are being competitively bid. Public works contracts, for example, sometimes require a unit price estimate. Unless written unit prices are required on a bid, the landscape contractor's best choice might be a lump sum bid. Unit prices may be more useful as an accurate estimating method important for landscape contractors to understand, rather than a method for them to regularly use in their own bidding. This method is usually not cost effective for preliminary budget or design development pricing.

Square Foot Estimates

Square foot estimates primarily involve an overall project cost and should be based on experience as well as past, similar projects. Square foot estimates are useful for establishing rough budget costs, usually before design development. Certain considerations should be taken into account when using square foot estimates: these include variations from the initial project requirements, and differences that occur from one project to another.

Square foot estimates are based on the concept that many jobs and small items involved in planting, hard construction, and landscape specialties can be grouped together into total project costs for "typical" installations. Care must be taken in using cost data from more than one source when preparing a square foot estimate. Be aware that a lawn that costs 36 cents per square foot to install under good working conditions may be considerably more costly under adverse conditions, such as steep slopes, or locations that require extensive watering. Cost information taken from several sources should be applied only to jobs that are essentially identical to those used as the source of information.

In summary, each estimator should have a reliable estimating system that accommodates his/her business and the bidding requirements of potential clients. Project analysis and estimating is a thoughtful process. After deciding to bid, it is important to gather as much information as possible on the job's requirements. No amount of drawings and documents can take the place of

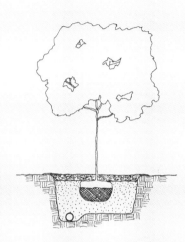

The Tree Pit Systems are listed for different heights of deciduous and evergreen trees, from 4' to 18'. Costs are given showing the pit size to accommodate the soil ball and the type of soil being excavated. In clay soils drainage tile has been included in addition to gravel drainage. Woven drainage fabric is applied before bark mulch is spread, assuming runoff is not harmful to roots.

System Components	QUANTITY	UNIT	COST EA.		
			MAT.	INST.	TOTAL
SYSTEM G2050 910 1220					
TREE PIT, 5' TO 6' TREE, DECIDUOUS, 2' X 1-1/4' DEEP PIT, CLAY SOIL					
Excavate planting pit, backhoe, clay soil	.262	C.Y.		19.13	19.13
Fill in pit, screened gravel, 3/4" to 1/2"	.050	C.Y.	.79	1.26	2.05
Drain tile 4"	3.000	L.F.	6.24	6.96	13.20
Mix planting soil, by hand, incl. loam, peat & manure	.304	C.Y.	6.54	2.96	9.50
Backfill planting pit, by hand, prepared mix	.304	C.Y.		7.45	7.45
Drainage fabric, woven	.500	S.Y.	.69	.12	.81
Bark mulch, hand spread, 3"	.346	C.Y.	.89	1.01	1.90
TOTAL			15.15	38.89	54.04

G2050 910	Tree Pits	COST EACH		
		MAT.	INST.	TOTAL
1000	Tree pit, 4' to 5' tree, evergreen, 2-1/2' x 1-1/2' deep pit, sandy soil	21	44	65
1020	Clay soil	24.50	50	74.50
1200	5' to 6' tree, deciduous, 2' x 1-1/4' deep pit, sandy soil	11.55	22.50	34.05
1220	Clay soil	15.15	39	54.15
1300	Evergreen, 3' x 1-3/4' deep pit, sandy soil	34.50	67	101.50
1320	Clay soil	36.50	78.50	115
1360	3-1/2' x 1-3/4' deep pit, sandy soil	44	83.50	127.50
1380	Clay soil	45.50	90.50	136
1400	6' to 7' tree, evergreen, 4' x 1-3/4' deep pit, sandy soil	53	97.50	150.50
1420	Clay soil	55	105	160
1600	7' to 9' tree, deciduous, 2-1/2' x 1-1/2' deep pit, sandy soil	21	55	76
1620	Clay soil	24.50	50	74.50
1800	8' to 10' tree, deciduous, 3' x 1-3/4' deep pit, sandy soil	34.50	67	101.50
1820	Clay soil	36.50	78.50	115

(from *Means Site Work & Landscape Cost Data 2002*)

Figure 4.7

G2050 Landscaping

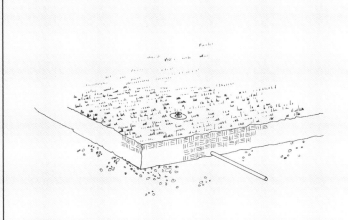

The Lawn Systems listed include different types of seeding, sodding and ground covers for flat and sloped areas. Costs are given per thousand square feet for different size jobs; residential, small commercial and large commercial. The size of the job relates to the type and productivity of the equipment being used. Components include furnishing and spreading screened loam, spreading fertilizer and limestone and mulching planted and seeded surfaces. Sloped surfaces include jute mesh or staking depending on the type of cover.

System Components	QUANTITY	UNIT	COST PER M.S.F. MAT.	COST PER M.S.F. INST.	COST PER M.S.F. TOTAL
SYSTEM G2050 410 1000					
LAWN, FLAT AREA, SEEDED, TURF MIX, RESIDENTIAL					
Scarify subsoil, residential, skid steer loader	1.000	M.S.F.		16.60	16.60
Root raking, residential, no boulders	1.000	M.S.F.		21.39	21.39
Spread topsoil, skid steer loader	18.500	C.Y.	227.55	74.56	302.11
Spread ground limestone, push spreader	110.000	S.Y.	9.90	2.20	12.10
Spread fertilizer, push spreader	110.000	S.Y.	7.70	2.20	9.90
Till topsoil, 26″ rototiller	110.000	S.Y.		39.60	39.60
Rake topsoil, screened loam	1.000	M.S.F.		19.45	19.45
Roll topsoil, push roller	18.500	C.Y.		1.67	1.67
Seeding, turf mix, push spreader	1.000	M.S.F.	6.90	36.50	43.40
Straw, mulch	110.000	S.Y.	36.30	67.10	103.40
TOTAL			288.35	281.27	569.62

G2050 410		Lawns & Ground Cover	COST PER M.S.F. MAT.	COST PER M.S.F. INST.	COST PER M.S.F. TOTAL
1000	Lawn, flat area, seeded, turf mix, residential		288	282	570
1040		Small commercial	292	305	597
1080		Large commercial	300	260	560
1200		Shade mix, residential	292	282	574
1240		Small commercial	295	305	600
1280		Large commercial	310	260	570
1400		Utility mix, residential	294	282	576
1440		Small commercial	297	305	602
1480		Large commercial	330	260	590
2000	Sod, bluegrass, residential		530	655	1,185
2040		Small commercial	510	390	900
2080		Large commercial	485	315	800
2200		Bentgrass, residential	870	297	1,167
2240		Small commercial	810	385	1,195
2280		Large commercial	770	320	1,090
2400	Ground cover, english ivy, residential		1,050	735	1,785

(from *Means Site Work & Landscape Cost Data* 2002)

Figure 4.8

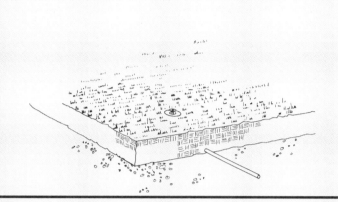

There are three basic types of Site Irrigation Systems: pop-up, riser mounted and quick coupling. Sprinkler heads are spray, impact or gear driven. Each system includes: the hardware for spraying the water; the pipe and fittings needed to deliver the water; and all other accessory equipment such as valves, couplings, nipples, and nozzles. Excavation heads and backfill costs are also included in the system.

The Expanded System Listing shows a wide variety of Site Irrigation Systems.

System Components	QUANTITY	UNIT	COST PER S.F.		
			MAT.	INST.	TOTAL
SYSTEM G2050 710 1000					
SITE IRRIGATION, POP UP SPRAY, PLASTIC, 10' RADIUS, 1000 S.F., PVC PIPE					
Excavation, chain trencher	54.000	L.F.		30.78	30.78
Pipe, fittings & nipples, PVC Schedule 40, 1" dia	5.000	Ea.	30.20	932.69	962.89
Tees, PVC plastic, high pressure schedule, 40, 1" diameter	5.000	Ea.	15.35	262.50	277.85
Couplings PVC plastic, high pressure, 1" diameter	5.000	Ea.	2.25	86.75	89
Valves, bronze, globe, 125 lb. rising stem, threaded, 1" diameter	1.000	Ea.	76.50	23	99.50
Head & nozzle, pop-up spray, PVC plastic	5.000	Ea.	17.35	64.50	81.85
Backfill by hand with compaction	54.000	L.F.		24.30	24.30
Total/M.S.F.			141.65	1,424.52	1,566.17
Total/S.F.			.14	1.42	1.57

G2050 710	Site Irrigation	COST PER S.F.		
		MAT.	INST.	TOTAL
1000	Site irrigation, pop up spray, plastic, 10' radius, 1000 S.F.,PVC pipe	.14	1.43	1.57
1100	Polyethylene pipe	.15	.50	.65
1200	14' radius, 8000 S.F., PVC pipe	.05	.26	.31
1300	Polyethylene pipe	.05	.23	.28
1400	18' square, 1000 S.F. PVC pipe	.13	.41	.54
1500	Polyethylene pipe	.12	.33	.45
1600	24' square, 8000 S.F., PVC pipe	.04	.16	.20
1700	Polyethylene pipe	.04	.15	.19
1800	4' x 30' strip, 200 S.F., PVC pipe	.55	1.71	2.26
1900	Polyethylene pipe	.54	1.54	2.08
2000	6' x 40' strip, 800 S.F., PVC pipe	.16	.57	.73
2100	Polyethylene pipe	.15	.51	.66
2200	Economy brass, 11' radius, 1000 S.F., PVC pipe	.16	.57	.73
2300	Polyethylene pipe	.16	.50	.66
2400	14' radius, 8000 S.F., PVC pipe	.06	.26	.32
2500	Polyethylene pipe	.06	.23	.29
2600	3' x 28' strip, 200 S.F., PVC pipe	.60	1.71	2.31
2700	Polyethylene pipe	.59	1.54	2.13

(from *Means Site Work & Landscape Cost Data 2002*)

Figure 4.9

an inspection of the actual site. Landscape construction estimates commonly represent a combination of approaches. For example, trees and shrubs may be estimated using unit prices, while lawns, paving, some hard construction, and such specialties as irrigation may be estimated using the assemblies method.

Whatever method is used by the estimator, costs should be derived from an established information base, using sources and resources that are as accurate and relevant to the circumstances as possible. Be methodical. Many helpful forms and records follow in Chapters 5 and 6.

How to Take Off Quantities

Chapter Five

How to Take Off Quantities

After the decision to "go for" a job is made, the work of getting the job begins. Once all details on the project have been assembled, the quantity takeoff is the next step. A **quantity takeoff** is a detailed list of the amounts of materials, labor-hours, and equipment needed for a particular project. The takeoff step should not be confused with pricing. The takeoff is a list of items and quantities. Costs for material and labor will be added at a later date during the pricing stage.

During the takeoff process, a systematic list is developed of the amounts of materials, the number of labor-hours and the equipment required. In order to take off certain quantities, and to be sure that all items are included, the estimator must have an overall concept of how the job will be constructed. This is best achieved by visualizing the construction process and planning the work as the estimate is done.

A good form to use to list quantities is seen in Figure 5.1. Use a separate sheet for each category of work, such as site work, planting, and hard construction. You will consolidate your lists when you are ready for pricing.

Some quantities which can easily be overlooked involve items that require costs for labor only, such as pruning and thinning of trees. A takeoff list of items includes not only amounts of materials and measurements of time (labor-hours) but also should include equipment usage. Unusual conditions and special requirements that may abnormally influence materials, labor, or equipment are also noted, so that quantities (thus costs) may be adjusted accordingly. For example, traffic restrictions at the site of the project could adversely affect a normal project schedule, and therefore increase the costs. Another example is a tree installation project that is to be started in the fall and completed the following spring. Such a schedule should alert the estimator to divided work segments and the possibility of price changes from one year to the next.

The analysis recorded during the site visit can serve as a checklist to guard against oversights. Keep in mind how conditions can significantly affect costs and profitability. The estimator must consider all sorts of factors from travel time to equipment access. The analysis form can also help to identify and note items for pricing that might otherwise be overlooked.

When working with plans, try to approach each segment of a project in the same logical manner. For example, one might begin with the plant list from the plans. Lists that place plants in categories beginning with all deciduous trees, then conifer trees, deciduous shrubs, evergreen shrubs, flowers, and ground covers are organized in the same manner in which the materials will be purchased. It makes sense to take off and list the plants similarly on the takeoff

Means° Forms

QUANTITY SHEET

PROJECT			SHEET NO.	
LOCATION		ARCHITECT	DATE	
TAKEOFF BY		EXTENSIONS BY	CHECKED BY	

DESCRIPTION	NO.	DIMENSIONS			UNIT		UNIT		UNIT	

Figure 5.1

sheet. Putting individual species within these groups in alphabetical order allows for handy and immediate reference to any particular plant.

As with all steps of the estimating process, it is very important to be consistent when it comes to plant list codes and keys. Examples of the use of codes in a landscape plan can be seen in Chapter 7, Figure 7.1, the landscape plan for the sample estimate. In addition to keys of abbreviated plant names, landscape architects also use many symbols and graphics on drawings and plans to provide information. A chart of typical symbols is found in Figure 5.2. Different designers may use different symbols for the same items. It is important to review each set of plans individually and carefully.

Experienced estimators often use preprinted forms to list all of the costs involved in a project and to note the probable impact of particular working conditions. A standard form such as that shown in Chapter 6, Figure 6.2 will work well for many sections of the takeoff. Some materials or work may, however, require a different or custom-made takeoff format. A custom summary sheet such as one for planting may also serve as a reminder to include the costs of items that are normally included whether they are listed for a particular project or not.

Preprinted forms can reduce errors and make reviews and corrections easier. Figure 5.1 is a form specifically designed for a quantity takeoff. The different columns allow for different quantities to be derived from the same dimensions. The form in Figure 5.3 combines takeoff and pricing on one sheet. This feature provides easy reference to data and helps to eliminate errors of transposition. (These and all of the forms shown in this book are available in either *Means Forms for Contractors*, or *Means Forms for Building Construction Professionals*. Both are three-ring binders containing removable, reproducible forms, to help in managing both projects and business needs.)

Preprinted forms are among the many resources the estimator uses to be sure that all items for a particular project are included in the estimate. The most reliable of all resources are experience and common sense. The estimator should visualize the step-by-step completion of the project while making a mental comparison to past projects. This is a good way to be sure that all requirements are included.

Mathematical errors are discovered and corrected with a simple review and calculation check of the estimate. However, errors due to omissions of items are much harder to remedy. In dealing with unfamiliar items, the estimator may rely on other sources. For example, one such source could be the Assemblies section of *Means Site Work & Landscape Cost Data*. Figures 5.4 and 5.5 show systems for a brick tree plaza and a retaining wall. Note that for each, all of the components (primary and associated) typically found in each type of construction are listed, along with required quantities. A quick review of such assemblies provides the estimator with another checklist to be sure that all required items are included.

Guidelines for the Takeoff

The following guidelines are recommended to help organize the quantity takeoff. Most are common sense suggestions. However, in the haste of the estimating process, some of these steps may be overlooked. The use of these guidelines will help reduce errors and assure that all required items are included.

- **Use preprinted forms** for an orderly sequence of descriptions, dimensions, quantities, extensions, totals, etc. (See examples in Chapter 6.)

Landscape Systems and Graphics

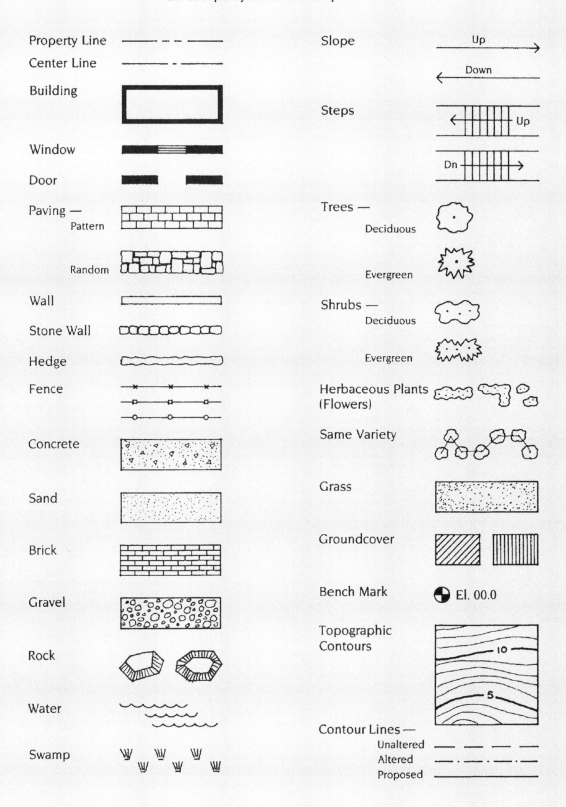

Figure 5.2

Means Forms

**CONSOLIDATED
ESTIMATE**

SHEET NO. _____

PROJECT _____ ESTIMATE NO. _____

ARCHITECT _____ DATE _____

TAKE OFF BY	QUANTITIES BY	PRICES BY	EXTENSIONS BY	CHECKED BY

DESCRIPTION	NO.	DIMENSIONS			QUANTITIES						MATERIAL		LABOR	
						UNIT			UNIT	UNIT COST	TOTAL	UNIT COST	TOTAL

Figure 5.3

G2030 Pedestrian Paving

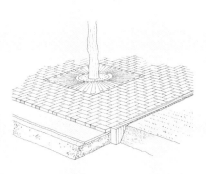

The Plaza Systems listed include several brick and tile paving surfaces on three different bases: gravel, slab on grade and suspended slab. The system cost includes this base cost with the exception of the suspended slab. The type of bedding for the pavers depends on the base being used, and alternate bedding may be desirable. Also included in the paving costs are edging and precast grating costs and where concrete bases are involved, expansion joints.

System Components	QUANTITY	UNIT	COST PER S.F. MAT.	COST PER S.F. INST.	COST PER S.F. TOTAL
SYSTEM G2030 310 2050					
PLAZA, BRICK PAVERS, 4" X 8" X 1-1/2", GRAVEL BASE, STONE DUST BED					
Compact subgrade, static roller, 4 passes	.111	S.Y.		.03	.03
Bank gravel, 2 mi haul, dozer spread	.012	C.Y.	.20	.06	.26
Compact gravel bedding or base, vibrating plate	.012	C.Y.		.03	.03
Grading fine grade, 3 passes with grader	.111	S.Y.		.32	.32
Stone dust, 1" thick, skid steer loader spread	.003	C.Y.	.06	.05	.11
Brick paver, 4" x 8" x 1-3/4"	4.150	Ea.	2.57	2.76	5.33
Brick edging, stood on end, 6 per L.F.	.060	L.F.	.24	.41	.65
Precast concrete tree grating, 1 per 250 S.F.	.004	Ea.	1.14	.18	1.32
TOTAL			4.21	3.84	8.05

G2030 310	Brick & Tile Plazas	COST PER S.F. MAT.	COST PER S.F. INST.	COST PER S.F. TOTAL
1050	Plaza, asphalt pavers, 6" x 12" x 1-1/4", gravel base, asphalt bedding	5.50	7.10	12.60
1100	Slab on grade, asphalt bedding	7.25	7.65	14.90
1150	Suspended slab, insulated & mastic bedding	8.70	9.45	18.15
1300	6" x 12" x 3", gravel base, asphalt, bedding	7.45	7.30	14.75
1350	Slab on grade, asphalt bedding	8.95	7.85	16.80
1400	Suspended slab, insulated & mastic bedding	10.40	9.60	20
2050	Brick pavers, 4" x 8" x 2-1/4", aggregate base, course washed sand bedding	4.21	3.84	8.05
2100	Slab on grade, asphalt bedding	5.60	5.50	11.10
2150	Suspended slab, insulated & no bedding	7.10	7.30	14.40
2300	4" x 8" x 2-1/4", gravel base, stone dust bedding	4.73	3.83	8.56
2350	Slab on grade, asphalt bedding	6.10	5.50	11.60
2400	Suspended slab, insulated & no bedding	7.60	7.30	14.90
2550	Shale pavers, 4" x 8" x 2-1/4", gravel base, stone dust bedding	4.39	4.38	8.77
2600	Slab on grade, asphalt bedding	5.80	6.05	11.85
2650	Suspended slab, insulated & no bedding	3.73	5.10	8.83
3050	Thin set tile, 4" x 4" x 3/8", slab on grade	6	6.15	12.15
3300	4" x 4" x 3/4", slab on grade	7.45	4.10	11.55
3550	Concrete paving stone, 4" x 8" x 2-1/2", gravel base, sand bedding	2.90	2.69	5.59
3600	Slab on grade, asphalt bedding	4.06	4.04	8.10
3650	Suspended slab, insulated & no bedding	2.01	3.05	5.06

(from *Means Site Work & Landscape Cost Data 2002*)

Figure 5.4

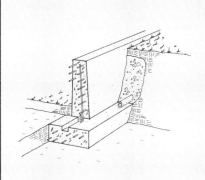

There are four basic types of Concrete Retaining Wall Systems: reinforced concrete with level backfill; reinforced concrete with sloped backfill or surcharge; unreinforced with level backfill; and unreinforced with sloped backfill or surcharge. System elements include: all necessary forms (4 uses); 3,000 p.s.i. concrete with an 8″ chute; all necessary reinforcing steel; and underdrain. Exposed concrete is patched and rubbed.

The Expanded System Listing shows walls that range in thickness from 10″ to 18″ for reinforced concrete walls with level backfill and 12″ to 24″ for reinforced walls with sloped backfill. Walls range from a height of 4′ to 20′. Unreinforced level and sloped backfill walls range from a height of 3′ to 10′.

System Components	QUANTITY	UNIT	COST PER L.F.		
			MAT.	INST.	TOTAL
SYSTEM G2040 210 1000					
CONC.RETAIN. WALL REINFORCED, LEVEL BACKFILL 4′ HIGH					
Forms in place, cont. wall footing & keyway, 4 uses	2.000	S.F.	1.62	5.82	7.44
Forms in place, retaining wall forms, battered to 8′ high, 4 uses	8.000	SFCA	4.08	44.80	48.88
Reinforcing in place, walls, #3 to #7	.004	Ton	2.34	2.46	4.80
Concrete ready mix, regular weight, 3000 psi	.204	C.Y.	15.50		15.50
Placing concrete and vibrating footing con., shallow direct chute	.074	C.Y.		1.17	1.17
Placing concrete and vibrating walls, 8″ thick, direct chute	.130	C.Y.		2.78	2.78
Pipe bedding, crushed or screened bank run gravel	1.000	L.F.	2.18	.83	3.01
Pipe, subdrainage, corrugated plastic, 4″ diameter	1.000	L.F.	.63	.49	1.12
Finish walls and break ties, patch walls	4.000	S.F.	.12	2.52	2.64
TOTAL			26.47	60.87	87.34

G2040 210	Concrete Retaining Walls	COST PER L.F.		
		MAT.	INST.	TOTAL
1000	Conc.retain.wall, reinforced, level backfill, 4′ high x 2′-2″ base,10″thick	26.50	61	87.50
1200	6′ high x 3′-3″ base, 10″ thick	38.50	88.50	127
1400	8′ high x 4′-3″ base, 10″ thick	50.50	116	166.50
1600	10′ high x 5′-4″ base, 13″ thick	66.50	170	236.50
1800	12′ high x 6′-6″ base, 14″ thick	82.50	203	285.50
2200	16′ high x 8′-6″ base, 16″ thick	124	276	400
2600	20′ high x 10′-5″ base, 18″ thick	180	355	535
3000	Sloped backfill, 4′ high x 3′-2″ base, 12″ thick	32	63.50	95.50
3200	6′ high x 4′-6″ base, 12″ thick	46	90.50	136.50
3400	8′ high x 5′-11″ base, 12″ thick	61	120	181
3600	10′ high x 7′-5″ base, 16″ thick	87.50	178	265.50
3800	12′ high x 8′-10″ base, 18″ thick	114	217	331
4200	16′ high x 11′-10″ base, 21″ thick	188	305	493
4600	20′ high x 15′-0″ base, 24″ thick	289	415	704
5000	Unreinforced, level backfill, 3′-0″ high x 1′-6″ base	15	41	56
5200	4′-0″ high x 2′-0″ base	23	54.50	77.50
5400	6′-0″ high x 3′-0″ base	43	84	127
5600	8′-0″ high x 4′-0″ base	68.50	112	180.50
5800	10′-0″ high x 5′-0″ base	102	174	276
7000	Sloped backfill, 3′-0″ high x 2′-0″ base	17.90	42.50	60.40

(from *Means Site Work & Landscape Cost Data 2002*)

Figure 5.5

- **Be consistent** when listing dimensions, for example, always describing length × width × height in the same sequence.
- **Use printed dimensions where given.** Since portions of a landscape plan may be schematic and/or curvilinear, it may be difficult to scale drawings in order to determine accurate quantities.
- **Convert** feet and inch measurements to decimal feet when you list them. A plant bed of 4'-6" should convert to 4.5 feet. Otherwise, dimensions in feet can be confused with dimensions in inches. The chart shown in Figure 5.6 can be used to convert inches to decimal fractions of a foot. For further measurement references, see the Appendix.

The Takeoff Process

What follows is an overview of the quantity takeoff process, using a few pertinent examples. More detailed information is included in the sample estimate in Chapter 7. Armed with site drawings, specifications, and information collected on site, it is time to begin the takeoff. This process will include a systematic listing of all materials and work needed to complete the project. A great deal of information may already have been noted about amounts and types of materials from plant lists on plans or in the written specifications. Such data could be in the form of a project analysis (See Chapter 4).

Begin the takeoff using standard forms (See Figure 5.1 for an example), listing each broad category separately, such as site clearing, grading, retaining walls, etc. For each category, begin systematically listing materials that are noted or indicated on the plans. Give yourself plenty of space; use extra lines as needed. Don't crowd information that you may refer to many times. Frequent reference to the other data sources, specs, project analysis, and checklist forms will be necessary. When doing a takeoff from a plan, read and make notations in a planned sequence. For example, one method is to always begin at the upper right quarter of a plan, listing the plants in this part of the drawing.

Continue, working around the drawing in a consistent pattern, e.g., clockwise. Complete the takeoff for each group or category of materials by making separate searches around the plan. Be methodical. A typical sequence may proceed as follows: locate all lawn seed areas, then all sod areas, followed by all paved walkway areas of similar materials. Note each item on the plan when listed to prevent duplication or omissions. A different color pencil might be used for each category. Always use the same "path" through the plan that was followed in listing the other categories. Keep in mind that the "low-ball" bidder may often be the one who left out an item.

For takeoff purposes, dimensions may appear in notations on the drawing or in detail drawings that accompany landscape plans. Unfortunately, landscape drawings are often sparsely dimensioned and sometimes not to scale. Be aware of the risks of measuring the length of a planting bed by "scaling" off a building. If quantities are difficult to determine, the contractor may qualify the estimate by stating certain assumed dimensions. In the contract bid, for example, "42,000 square feet of sod installed" may be stated, rather than simply, "grass sod installed." Field verification of measurements will be helpful, and is recommended if possible.

Many items that are mentioned briefly on the plans or in the specifications (or perhaps not mentioned, but required) may imply many different tasks and types of work. "Finish grade" is a typical specification for landscape contractors. The necessary methods are, however, rarely specified. Finish grade might be

achieved by hand work, by York rake, or may require a significant amount of earthwork. The methods and the amount of work needed to achieve each specified portion of the project (and cleanup) must be determined and listed. This information will clearly have an impact on the estimate.

Wrapping Up the Takeoff

As the takeoff progresses, look over all of the quantities and compare the quantity sheets that you have collected. Many items are a "natural check" against each other. For example, if specifications call for 3 inches of topsoil under grass sod, the relationship between square feet of sod and cubic yards of topsoil must be known for purposes of comparison. Mulch may need to be similarly calculated, based on the square footage of planting beds. There are many relationships between materials, work areas, and equipment and installation costs; and these are cross-referenced by the experienced estimator.

When estimating alternates, both at the takeoff and pricing stages, it is best to first list all of the items that are in the basic bid. Then figure the alternates separately. In this way, positive numbers are compared in both cases. Confusion is more likely when adds and deducts are both used. If any "outs," or exclusions are necessary, they should be *distinctly* noted so that it is clear that they should be deducted instead of added.

When figuring the time requirements for equipment, the estimator must plan how best to coordinate its use. This is especially true for extensive or heavy site work equipment, an expensive component in a landscape installation. The information in *Means Site Work & Landscape Cost Data* can be used to determine the most cost effective use of equipment for various kinds of earthwork. See the examples in Chapter 3, Figure 3.2.

When the quantity takeoff is complete and all material, labor, and equipment items have been identified and listed, the next step is to extend and summarize

Conversion of Inches to Decimal Parts per Foot												
	0	1″	2″	3″	4″	5″	6″	7″	8″	9″	10″	11″
0	0	.08	.17	.25	.33	.42	.50	.58	.67	.75	.83	.92
1/8″	.01	.09	.18	.26	.34	.43	.51	.59	.68	.76	.84	.93
1/4″	.02	.10	.19	.27	.35	.44	.52	.60	.69	.77	.85	.94
3/8″	.03	.11	.20	.28	.36	.45	.53	.61	.70	.78	.86	.95
1/2″	.04	.12	.21	.29	.37	.46	.54	.62	.71	.79	.87	.96
5/8″	.05	.14	.22	30	.39	.47	.55	.64	.72	.80	.89	.97
3/4″	.06	.15	.23	.31	.40	.48	.56	.65	.73	.81	.90	.98
7/8″	.07	.16	.24	.32	.41	.49	.57	.66	.74	.82	.91	.99

Figure 5.6

the quantities and price the estimate. Takeoff units should be converted to pricing units. For example, requirements for depths of topsoil or mulch over a given area can be converted to cubic yards (or cubic feet) of material—those units in which the material will be priced and purchased. The chart in Figure 5.7 is an example of a chart used for converting measurements for a few specific items. Each estimator should develop or become familiar with these kinds of references which facilitate the estimating process. Quantities of similar items from different areas of the plan should be totaled and summarized. Only then are prices applied and overhead and profit added to arrive at the final estimated cost. At completion of this quantity takeoff, a "picture" of the project is clear to the estimator. A discussion of pricing follows in Chapter 6.

Conversion Chart for Loam, Baled Peat, and Mulch			
Loam Requirements		Mulch Requirements (Bulk Peat, Crushed Stone, Shredded Bark, Wood Chips)	
Depth per 10,000 S.F.	Cubic yards required	Depth per 1,000 S.F.	Cubic yards required
2 inches	70	1 inch	3-1/2
4 "	140	2 inches	7
6 "	210	3 "	10-1/2
		4 "	14
Per 1,000 S.F.		Per 100 S.F.	
2 inches	7	1 inch	1/3
4 "	14	2 inches	2/3
6 "	21	3 "	1
		4 "	1-1/3
Baled (or Compressed) Peat			
Per 100 S.F.		Bales Required	
1 inch		one 4 cubic foot bale	
2 inches		two 4 cubic foot bales	
3 "		two 6 cubic foot bales	
4 "		one 4 cubic foot bales and two 6 cubic foot bales	

Note: Opened and spread, peat from bales will be about 2-1/2 times the volume of the unopened bale.

Figure 5.7

The Skill of Pricing

Chapter Six

The Skill of Pricing

After the quantity takeoff is completed, a clear picture of the project emerges and the pricing of the estimate may begin. With all the quantities of material, equipment, and labor determined, the next task is recording the costs of every item and category. This process involves first listing all items with their prices on cost analysis sheets (Figure 6.1), then summarizing this information on an estimate form. An example of an estimate form for landscape work is shown in Figure 6.2. Here again the widsom of listing by categories is seen.

Grouping the Items

Begin by entering or listing all of the categories that apply to the job (from the takeoff sheets). The breakdown and sequence should be the same as that used for the quantity takeoff. Such a routine and consistent pattern makes it easier to spot duplications, errors, or omissions. The list below provides an example of how this approach might be used in the order of work on the site.

1. Demolition, clearing and grubbing
2. Excavation and backfill
3. Drainage
4. Utilities
5. Roads and walks
6. Site improvements
7. Planting

This approach helps to determine the types of equipment required and the sequence in which the work should be performed. Each type of plant material has its own installation requirements and methods, and these may vary depending upon the seasons. Special conditions such as temperature, typical rainfall, soil types, site grades, and access may also have a great influence on material, labor, and equipment costs. An experienced estimator takes all of these factors into consideration and makes notations on the takeoff sheets. All items must be priced—from tree wrap to backhoe.

The planting category may be further broken down. Plant materials are typically priced on a separate sheet and summarized in groups such as trees, shrubs, grass, sod, etc. (See Chapter 7, Figure 7.16 for an example.)

As it is, some categories will become assemblies developed from a unit price basis. For example, a retaining wall may be figured by putting all components together to develop an assemblies price. Illustrated in Figure 6.3 is a retaining wall assembly which provides a cost per linear foot based on the quantities and costs of the individual components. Assemblies such as this from *Means Site Work & Landscape Cost Data* may be developed for many other category items.

Means Forms
COST ANALYSIS

PROJECT

LOCATION

TAKE OFF BY

QUANTITIES BY

CLASSIFICATION

ARCHITECT

PRICES BY

EXTENSIONS BY

SHEET NO.

ESTIMATE NO.

DATE

CHECKED BY

DESCRIPTION	SOURCE/DIMENSIONS		QUANTITY	UNIT	MATERIAL		LABOR		EQUIPMENT		SUBCONTRACT		TOTAL	
					UNIT COST	TOTAL	UNIT COST	TOTAL	UNIT COST	TOTAL	UNIT COST	TOTAL	UNIT COST	TOTAL

Figure 6.1

110

Means® Forms

LANDSCAPE ESTIMATE SHEET

DATE _____

PROJECT _____

LOCATION _____

LANDSCAPE ARCHITECT _____

SHEET NO. _____

ESTIMATE NO. _____

OWNER _____

TAKEOFF BY	EXTENSIONS BY		CHECKED BY		
CATEGORY	DESCRIPTION	QUAN.	PRICE	EXTENSION	TOTAL
Plants					
Trees					
Shrubs					
Flowers					
Ground Cover					
Other					
Tax					
Subtotal					
Horticultural Material					
Mulch for Trees					
Mulch					
Soil Conditioner					
Fertilizer					
Other					
Tax					
Subtotal					
Hardware					
Gravel & Boulders					
Landscape Timbers					
Soil					
Sod					
Lawn Seeding					
Other Materials					
Labor					
Tools & Equipment					
Equipment on Job					
Rental Equipment					
Other					
Freight					
Dump Charges					
Maintenance Program					
Grand Total					

Figure 6.2

G2040 Site Development

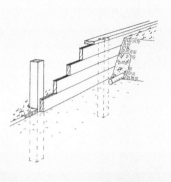

A Post and Board Retaining Wall System is constructed of one of four types of lumber: redwood, cedar, creosoted wood or pressure-treated lumber. The system includes all the elements that must go into a wall that resists lateral pressure. System elements include: posts and boards; cap; underdrain; and deadman where required.

The Expanded System Listing shows a wide variety of wall configurations with each type of lumber. The spacing of the deadman in the wall is indicated for each wall system. Wall heights vary from 3′ to 10′.

System Components			COST PER L.F.		
	QUANTITY	UNIT	MAT.	INST.	TOTAL
SYSTEM G2040 240 1000					
POST & BOARD RETAINING WALL, 2″ PLANKS, 4 X 4 POSTS, 3′ HIGH					
Redwood post, 4″ x 4″	2.000	B.F.	4.80	2.85	7.65
Redwood joist and cap, 2″ x 10″	7.000	B.F.	18.40	3.40	21.80
Pipe bedding, crushed or screened bank run gravel	1.000	L.F.	1.09	.42	1.51
Pipe, subdrainage, corrugated plastic, 4″ diameter	1.000	L.F.	.63	.49	1.12
TOTAL			24.92	7.16	32.08

G2040 240	Post & Board Retaining Walls	COST PER L.F.		
		MAT.	INST.	TOTAL
1000	Post & board retaining wall,2″ planking,redwood,4 x 4 post,4′spacing,3′high	25	7.15	32.15
1200	2′ spacing, 4′ high	36	12.30	48.30
1400	6 x 6 post, 4′ spacing, 5′ high	53.50	15.20	68.70
1600	3′ spacing, 6′ high	74.50	21.50	96
1800	6 x 6 post with deadman, 3′ spacing, 8′ high	97.50	28.50	126
2000	8 x 8 post, 2′ spacing, 8′ high	217	56.50	273.50
2200	8 x 8 post with deadman, 2′ spacing, 9′ high	249	62.50	311.50
2400	Cedar, 4 x 4 post, 4′ spacing, 3′ high	19.90	7.50	27.40
2600	4 x 4 post with deadman, 2′ spacing, 4′ high	34	13.30	47.30
2800	6 x 6 post, 4′ spacing, 4′ high	33	13.05	46.05
3000	3′ spacing, 5′ high	43.50	18.70	62.20
3200	2′ spacing, 6′ high	64	29.50	93.50
3400	6 x 6 post with deadman, 3′ spacing, 6′ high	54.50	23	77.50
3600	8 x 8 post with deadman, 2′ spacing, 8′ high	151	58	209
3800	Pressure treated, 4 x 4 post, 4′ spacing, 3′ high	12.70	13.90	26.60
4000	3′ spacing, 4′ high	18.65	19.85	38.50
4200	4 x 4 post with deadman, 2′ spacing, 5′ high	31.50	27	58.50
4400	6 x 6 post, 3′ spacing, 6′ high	67	45	112
4600	2′ spacing, 7′ high	53.50	46	99.50
4800	6 x 6 post with deadman, 3′ spacing, 8′ high	53.50	44.50	98
5000	8 x 8 post with deadman, 2′ spacing, 10′ high	159	101	260
5200	Creosoted, 4 x 4 post, 4′ spacing, 3′ high	12.70	13.90	26.60

(from *Means Site Work & Landscape Cost Data* 2002)

Figure 6.3

For an estimate to be well organized, it must have a clear direction from the start. The various items to be priced should be transferred from the takeoff sheets to the pricing sheets. This can be done using the contractor's own forms and methods, or in the same general sequence as the work will take place. Examples are shown in Figures 6.1 and 6.2. Figure 6.1 is a generic form that can be tailored to each particular project. Figure 6.2 is a custom-made form that would be appropriate for planting. Examples of the use of such forms are illustrated in Chapter 7. Most firms would find it useful to develop custom forms that fit the type of work and methods familiar to their particular company.

Sources of Cost Information

One of the most difficult parts of the estimator's job is determining accurate and reliable bare cost data. Sources for such data are varied, but can be categorized in terms of their relative reliability. The most reliable source of any cost information is the accurate, up-to-date, well-kept records of the estimator's own company. There is no better cost for a particular construction item than the actual cost to the contractor of that item from another recent job, modified (if necessary) to meet the requirements of the project being estimated. Preprinted forms, such as those shown in Figures 6.4, Daily Time Sheet, 6.5, Material Cost Record, and 6.6, Labor Cost Record, can simplify this kind of record keeping.

Bids from responsible subcontractors are the second most reliable source of cost data. A subcontract bid is a known, fixed cost, prior to the project. Whether the price is "right" or "wrong" does not matter (as long as it is a responsible bid with no gross errors). The bid provides the estimator with the cost of a designated portion of the work. No further estimating is required, except for possible verification of the quote. When pricing from a subcontractor's bid, it is essential to have a clear agreement between the parties on the complete scope of the work, and confidence that the subcontractor will be able to perform at the required time. Obtain the bid in writing or see Figure 6.7 for a form that may assist in obtaining all pertinent information and details from subcontractors.

Quotations by nurseries or other suppliers for material costs are, for the same reasons, as reliable as subcontract bids. For these materials, the estimator must apply estimated labor costs. Thus the installed price for a particular item may be variable. Be sure the supplier's price will be good at the time of actual purchase. Whenever possible, all price quotations from vendors or subcontractors should be obtained in writing. Qualifications and exclusions should be clearly stated. Quoted prices should be checked to be sure that they are complete and as specified. One way to assure these requirements is to prepare a form on which all subcontractors and vendors must submit quotations. This form can ask all appropriate questions, such as "Is the price delivered or FOB?" or "Is sales tax included?"

The above procedures are ideal, but often in the more realistic haste of estimating and bidding, quotations are received verbally—in person or by telephone. The importance of gathering all pertinent information is heightened because omissions are more likely. A preprinted form, such as the one shown in Figure 6.7, can be extremely useful to assure that all required information and qualifications are obtained and understood. How often has the subcontractor stated, "I didn't know that I was supposed to include that?" With the help of such forms, the appropriate questions are asked and answered.

If the estimator has no cost records for a particular item and is unable to obtain a quotation, then the next most reliable source of price information is a

Means® Forms

DAILY TIME SHEET

PROJECT

FOREMAN

WEATHER CONDITIONS

TEMPERATURE

DATE

SHEET NO.

NO.	NAME		DESCRIPTION OF WORK									TOTALS		RATES		OUTPUT	
												REG-ULAR	OVER-TIME	REG-ULAR	OVER-TIME		
		HOURS															
		UNITS															
		HOURS															
		UNITS															
		HOURS															
		UNITS															
		HOURS															
		UNITS															
		HOURS															
		UNITS															
		HOURS															
		UNITS															
		HOURS															
		UNITS															
		HOURS															
		UNITS															
		HOURS															
		UNITS															
		HOURS															
		UNITS															
		HOURS															
		UNITS															
		HOURS															
		UNITS															
		HOURS															
		UNITS															
		HOURS															
		UNITS															
		HOURS															
		UNITS															
	TOTALS	HOURS															
	EQUIPMENT	UNITS															

Figure 6.4

Means° Forms

**MATERIAL
COST RECORD**

SHEET NO. _____

DATE FROM _____

PROJECT _____

DATE TO _____

LOCATION _____

BY _____

DATE	P.O. NUMBER	VENDOR/DESCRIPTION	QTY.	UNIT PRICE	TOTAL			DATE DUE	DATE REC'D	COMMENTS

Figure 6.5

Means® Forms

**LABOR
COST RECORD**

SHEET NO.

DATE FROM:

PROJECT

DATE TO:

LOCATION

BY:

DATE	CHARGE NO.	DESCRIPTION	HOURS	RATE	AMOUNT	HOURS	RATE	AMOUNT	HOURS	RATE	AMOUNT

Figure 6.6

Means° Forms

**TELEPHONE
QUOTATION**

DATE _____

PROJECT _____   TIME _____

FIRM QUOTING _____   PHONE (__) _____

ADDRESS _____   BY _____

ITEM QUOTED _____   RECEIVED BY _____

WORK INCLUDED	AMOUNT OF QUOTATION

DELIVERY TIME	TOTAL BID

DOES QUOTATION INCLUDE THE FOLLOWING:			If ☐ NO is checked, determine the following:	
STATE & LOCAL SALES TAXES	☐ YES	☐ NO	MATERIAL VALUE	
DELIVERY TO THE JOB SITE	☐ YES	☐ NO	WEIGHT	
COMPLETE INSTALLATION	☐ YES	☐ NO	QUANTITY	
COMPLETE SECTION AS PER PLANS & SPECIFICATIONS	☐ YES	☐ NO	DESCRIBE BELOW	

EXCLUSIONS AND QUALIFICATIONS	

ADDENDA ACKNOWLEDGEMENT	TOTAL ADJUSTMENTS
	ADJUSTED TOTAL BID

ALTERNATES	
ALTERNATE NO.	
ALTERNATE NO.	
ALTERNATE NO.	
ALTERNATE NO.	
ALTERNATE NO.	
ALTERNATE NO.	
ALTERNATE NO.	

Figure 6.7

current cost book such as *Means Site Work & Landscape Cost Data*. Means presents all such data in the form of national averages. These figures must be adjusted to local conditions, a procedure explained in Chapter 10. In addition to being a source of primary costs, such books can be useful as a reference or crosscheck for verifying costs obtained elsewhere. For example, a quote from a subcontractor for an unfamiliar item can be checked to assure that the bid is "in the ballpark."

Lacking cost information from any of the above-mentioned sources, the estimator may have to rely on data from old books or adjusted records from old projects. While these types of costs may not be very accurate, they may be better than the final alternative—guesswork.

No matter which source of cost information is used, the system and sequence of pricing should be the same as that used for the quantity takeoff. This consistent approach should continue through both accounting and cost control during construction of the project.

Types of Costs

For accurate pricing, the landscape project should first be broken down into categories and then into components within each category. Depending on the type of estimate and the amount of detail involved, each item can be broken down further into material, labor, and equipment. Each of these categories involves different kinds of costs. Examples of these follow in Chapter 7.

All costs included in a landscape estimate can be classified as direct or indirect. Direct costs are those directly linked to the physical construction of a project: such as work crew, plant material, and sod. The material, labor, and equipment costs mentioned above, as well as subcontract costs, are all direct costs. These may also be referred to as *bare* costs.

Indirect costs are usually added to the estimate at the summary stage and are most often calculated as a percentage of the direct costs. They include such items as administrative wages, overhead, profit, and contingencies. It is the indirect costs that may account for a large variation in estimating. Methods for determining indirect costs are included later in this chapter.

Types of Costs in a Construction Estimate

Direct Costs	Indirect Costs
Material	Taxes
Labor	Overhead
Equipment	Profit
Subcontractors	Contingencies
Project Overhead	

Direct Costs

In the preceding list, **Project Overhead** is classified as a direct cost. Project Overhead represents those costs of a construction project that are usually included in Division One–General Requirements. Typical items are the job site office trailer, supervisory labor costs, daily and final cleanup, and temporary water. While these items may not be directly part of the "installed" work, the project could not be completed without them. Project overhead, like all other direct costs, can be separated into material, labor, and equipment components.

Material: When quantities have been carefully taken off, estimates of material costs can be very accurate. In order to maintain a high level of accuracy, the unit prices for materials must be reliable and current. The most reliable source of material costs is a quotation from a familiar local nursery, lumberyard, or gravel

pit for the particular job in question. Ideally, the vendor should have access to the plans and specifications for verification of quantities and specified products. Current catalogs (e.g., for plant materials) may not account for actual availability in an industry that is often dependent on uncontrollable factors such as weather.

Material pricing appears relatively simple and straightforward. There are, however, certain considerations that the estimator must address when analyzing material quotations. The reputation of the vendor is a significant factor. Can the vendor "deliver," both figuratively and literally? Often estimators may choose not to rely on a "competitive" lower price from an unknown vendor, but will instead use a slightly higher price from a known, reliable vendor. Experience is the best judge for such decisions.

There are many questions that the estimator should ask. How long is the price guaranteed? How long are the plant materials guaranteed? At the end of the period, is there an escalation clause? Does the price include delivery or sales tax, if required? Some of these questions are addressed on the form in Figure 6.7. But more information should be obtained to assure that a quoted price is accurate and competitive. Secure a written quote if possible.

The estimator must be sure that the quotation or obtained price is for the materials as per plans and specifications. Are the tree caliper sizes correct? Designers may write into the specifications that:

    a. the particular type of material or brand of product must be used *exactly* as specified, with no substitution,

    b. the particular type of material is recommended, but alternate materials or brands may be accepted *upon approval*, or

    c. no particular type or brand is specified.

Depending upon the options, the estimator may be able to find an acceptable, less expensive alternative. In some cases, these substitutions can substantially lower the cost of a project.

When the estimator has received material quotations, there are still other considerations which have a bearing on the final choice of a vendor. Lead time —the amount of time between order and delivery—must be determined and considered. It does not matter how competitive or low a quote is if the nursery cannot deliver the plant material to the job site on time. If a delivery date is promised, is there a guarantee, or a penalty clause for late delivery?

The estimator should also determine if there are any unusual payment requirements. Cash flow for a company can be severely affected if a large material purchase thought to be payable in 30 days is delivered C.O.D. Truck drivers may not allow unloading until payment has been received. Such requirements must be determined during the estimating stage so that the cost of borrowing money, if necessary, can be included. If unable to obtain the quotation of a vendor from whom the material would be purchased, the estimator has other sources for obtaining material prices. These include, in order of reliability:

    1. Current price lists from manufacturer's catalogs. Be sure to check that the list is for "contractor prices."

    2. Cost records from previous jobs. Historical costs must be updated for present conditions.

3. Reputable and current, annual, unit-price cost books, such as *Means Site Work & Landscape Cost Data*. Such books usually represent national averages and must be factored to local markets.

No matter which price source is used, the estimator must be sure to include any costs (e.g., delivery, tax) over the actual cost of the material.

Labor: In order to determine the labor cost for each unit of construction, the estimator must know the following: first, the labor rate (hourly wage or salary) of the work classification, and second, how much work the crews can produce or install in a given time period—in other words, the output or productivity. Wage rates are known going into a project, but productivity may be very difficult to determine. The best source of labor productivity (and therefore labor costs) is the estimator's well-kept records from previous projects. If no accurate labor cost records are available, the estimator has two basic alternatives for determining labor costs. Get a firm quote from a subcontractor experienced and qualified to perform such tasks. The second alternative is to consult published data. Cost data books, such as *Means Site Work & Landscape Cost Data*, provide national averages. Figure 6.8 shows national average *union* rates for the construction industry (based on January 1, 2002). Figure 6.9 lists national average *nonunion* rates, again based on January 1, 2002. These figures do include average fixed overhead costs, such as fringe benefits, Workers' Compensation, unemployment, Social Security, and liability insurance, which must be paid by the employer.

If more accurate rates are required, the estimator has alternate sources. Union locals can provide rates (as well as negotiated increases) for a particular location. This source requires the estimator to call the union hall for each trade. Employer bargaining groups can usually provide labor cost data, but this data may not be continually updated. Means publishes *Labor Rates for the Construction Industry* on an annual basis. This book lists the union labor rates by trade for over 300 U.S. and Canadian cities.

Determination of other specific pay rates is much more difficult. In some larger cities, there are organizations that represent nonunion contractors. These groups may be a source of local pay scales, but ultimately the wage rates are determined by each contractor.

Productivity reference books, such as *Means Productivity Standards for Construction*, can be helpful. Included with the listing for each individual construction item is the designation of typical crew makeup, together with the productivity or output—the amount of work that the crew will produce. Figure 6.10, a typical page from *Means Productivity Standards for Construction*, includes this data and indicates the required number of labor-hours for each unit of work for the appropriate task. The estimator can apply local, known labor rates to determine unit costs for labor. With known labor rates and proposed schedules (See Chapter 9 for a discussion of scheduling), the estimator can also develop weekly payroll estimates. This process will help to anticipate costs and the work crew that will be needed. In this way, the scheduled projects can be planned to meet budget and cash flow requirements. Weekly payroll estimates can then be compared to actual costs, and reliable productivity records can be made. An example of a weekly payroll estimate is shown in Figure 6.11.

The estimator who has neither company records nor the published sources described takes the remaining alternative—judgment based on experience. In this case, the estimator must put together the appropriate crews and determine the expected output or productivity. This type of estimating should only be

R01100-070 Contractor's Overhead & Profit

Below are the **average** installing contractor's percentage mark-ups applied to base labor rates to arrive at typical billing rates.

Column A: Labor rates are based on union wages averaged for 30 major U.S. cities. Base rates including fringe benefits are listed hourly and daily. These figures are the sum of the wage rate and employer-paid fringe benefits such as vacation pay, employer-paid health and welfare costs, pension costs, plus appropriate training and industry advancement funds costs.

Column B: Workers' Compensation rates are the national average of state rates established for each trade.

Column C: Column C lists average fixed overhead figures for all trades. Included are Federal and State Unemployment costs set at 7.0%; Social Security Taxes (FICA) set at 7.65%; Builder's Risk Insurance costs set at 0.34%; and Public Liability costs set at 1.55%. All the percentages except those for Social Security Taxes vary from state to state as well as from company to company.

Columns D and E: Percentages in Columns D and E are based on the presumption that the installing contractor has annual billing of $1,500,000 and up. Overhead percentages may increase with smaller annual billing. The overhead percentages for any given contractor may vary greatly and depend on a number of factors, such as the contractor's annual volume, engineering and logistical support costs, and staff requirements. The figures for overhead and profit will also vary depending on the type of job, the job location, and the prevailing economic conditions. All factors should be examined very carefully for each job.

Column F: Column F lists the total of Columns B, C, D, and E.

Column G: Column G is Column A (hourly base labor rate) multiplied by the percentage in Column F (O&P percentage).

Column H: Column H is the total of Column A (hourly base labor rate) plus Column G (Total O&P).

Column I: Column I is Column H multiplied by eight hours.

Abbr.	Trade	A Base Rate Incl. Fringes Hourly	A Daily	B Workers' Comp. Ins.	C Average Fixed Overhead	D Overhead	E Profit	F Total Overhead & Profit %	G Amount	H Rate with O&P Hourly	I Daily
Skwk	Skilled Workers Average (35 trades)	$30.95	$247.60	16.8%	16.5%	13.0%	10.0%	56.3%	$17.40	$48.35	$386.80
	Helpers Average (5 trades)	22.75	182.00	18.5		11.0		56.0	$12.75	35.50	284.00
	Foreman Average, Inside ($0.50 over trade)	31.45	251.60	16.8		13.0		56.3	17.70	49.15	393.20
	Foreman Average, Outside ($2.00 over trade)	32.95	263.60	16.8		13.0		56.3	18.55	51.50	412.00
Clab	Common Building Laborers	23.45	187.60	18.1		11.0		55.6	13.05	36.50	292.00
Asbe	Asbestos/Insulation Workers/Pipe Coverers	33.45	267.60	16.2		16.0		58.7	19.65	53.10	424.80
Boil	Boilermakers	36.25	290.00	14.7		16.0		57.2	20.75	57.00	456.00
Bric	Bricklayers	30.50	244.00	16.0		11.0		53.5	16.30	46.80	374.40
Brhe	Bricklayer Helpers	23.50	188.00	16.0		11.0		53.5	12.55	36.05	288.40
Carp	Carpenters	30.00	240.00	18.1		11.0		55.6	16.70	46.70	373.60
Cefi	Cement Finishers	28.70	229.60	10.6		11.0		48.1	13.80	42.50	340.00
Elec	Electricians	35.45	283.60	6.7		16.0		49.2	17.45	52.90	423.20
Elev	Elevator Constructors	37.10	296.80	7.7		16.0		50.2	18.60	55.70	445.60
Eqhv	Equipment Operators, Crane or Shovel	32.35	258.80	10.6		14.0		51.1	16.55	48.90	391.20
Eqmd	Equipment Operators, Medium Equipment	31.20	249.60	10.6		14.0		51.1	15.95	47.15	377.20
Eqlt	Equipment Operators, Light Equipment	29.80	238.40	10.6		14.0		51.1	15.25	45.05	360.40
Eqol	Equipment Operators, Oilers	26.65	213.20	10.6		14.0		51.1	13.60	40.25	322.00
Eqmm	Equipment Operators, Master Mechanics	32.80	262.40	10.6		14.0		51.1	16.75	49.55	396.40
Glaz	Glaziers	30.00	240.00	13.8		11.0		51.3	15.40	45.40	363.20
Lath	Lathers	28.75	230.00	11.1		11.0		48.6	13.95	42.70	341.60
Marb	Marble Setters	30.10	240.80	16.0		11.0		53.5	16.10	46.20	369.60
Mill	Millwrights	31.75	254.00	10.6		11.0		48.1	15.25	47.00	376.00
Mstz	Mosaic and Terrazzo Workers	29.25	234.00	9.8		11.0		47.3	13.85	43.10	344.80
Pord	Painters, Ordinary	27.15	217.20	13.8		11.0		51.3	13.95	41.10	328.80
Psst	Painters, Structural Steel	27.90	223.20	48.4		11.0		85.9	23.95	51.85	414.80
Pape	Paper Hangers	27.10	216.80	13.8		11.0		51.3	13.90	41.00	328.00
Pile	Pile Drivers	29.80	238.40	24.9		16.0		67.4	20.10	49.90	399.20
Plas	Plasterers	28.10	224.80	15.8		11.0		53.3	15.00	43.10	344.80
Plah	Plasterer Helpers	23.70	189.60	15.8		11.0		53.3	12.65	36.35	290.80
Plum	Plumbers	35.95	287.60	8.3		16.0		50.8	18.25	54.20	433.60
Rodm	Rodmen (Reinforcing)	34.25	274.00	28.3		14.0		68.8	23.55	57.80	462.40
Rofc	Roofers, Composition	26.60	212.80	32.6		11.0		70.1	18.65	45.25	362.00
Rots	Roofers, Tile and Slate	26.75	214.00	32.6		11.0		70.1	18.75	45.50	364.00
Rohe	Roofer Helpers (Composition)	19.80	158.40	32.6		11.0		70.1	13.90	33.70	269.60
Shee	Sheet Metal Workers	35.10	280.80	11.7		16.0		54.2	19.00	54.10	432.80
Spri	Sprinkler Installers	36.20	289.60	8.7		16.0		51.2	18.55	54.75	438.00
Stpi	Steamfitters or Pipefitters	36.20	289.60	8.3		16.0		50.8	18.40	54.60	436.80
Ston	Stone Masons	30.65	245.20	16.0		11.0		53.5	16.40	47.05	376.40
Sswk	Structural Steel Workers	34.25	274.00	39.8		14.0		80.3	27.50	61.75	494.00
Tilf	Tile Layers	29.15	233.20	9.8		11.0		47.3	13.80	42.95	343.60
Tilh	Tile Layer Helpers	23.35	186.80	9.8		11.0		47.3	11.05	34.40	275.20
Trlt	Truck Drivers, Light	24.30	194.40	14.9		11.0		52.4	12.75	37.05	296.40
Trhv	Truck Drivers, Heavy	25.00	200.00	14.9		11.0		52.4	13.10	38.10	304.80
Sswl	Welders, Structural Steel	34.25	274.00	39.8		14.0		80.3	27.50	61.75	494.00
Wrck	*Wrecking	23.45	187.60	41.2	▼	11.0	▼	78.7	18.45	41.90	335.20

*Not included in Averages.

(from *Means Site Work & Landscape Cost Data* 2002)

Figure 6.8

RO1100-070 Contractor's Overhead & Profit

Below are the **average** installing contractor's percentage mark-ups applied to base labor rates to arrive at typical billing rates.

Column A: Labor rates are based on average open shop wages for 7 major U.S. regions. Base rates including fringe benefits are listed hourly and daily. These figures are the sum of the wage rate and employer-paid fringe benefits such as vacation pay, and employer-paid health costs.

Column B: Workers' Compensation rates are the national average of state rates established for each trade.

Column C: Column C lists average fixed overhead figures for all trades. Included are Federal and State Unemployment costs set at 7.0%; Social Security Taxes (FICA) set at 7.65%; Builder's Risk Insurance costs set at .34%; and Public Liability costs set at 1.55%. All the percentages except those for Social Security Taxes vary from state to state as well as from company to company.

Columns D and E: Percentages in Columns D and E are based on the presumption that the installing contractor has annual billing of $1,000,000 and up. Overhead percentages may increase with smaller annual billing. The overhead percentages for any give such as the contractor's annual volume, engineering and logistical support costs, and staff requirements. The figures for overhead and profit will also vary depending on the type of job, the job location, and the prevailing economic conditions. All factors should be examined very carefully for each job.

Column F: Column F lists the total of Columns B, C, D, and E.

Column G: Column G is Column A (hourly base labor rate) multiplied by the percentage in Column F (O&P percentage).

Column H: Column H is the total of Column A (hourly base labor rate) plus Column G (Total O&P).

Column I: Column I is Column H multiplied by eight hours.

Abbr.	Trade	A Base Rate Incl. Fringes Hourly	A Daily	B Workers' Comp. Ins.	C Average Fixed Overhead	D Overhead	E Profit	F Total Overhead & Profit %	G Amount	H Rate with O & P Hourly	I Daily
Skwk	Skilled Workers Average (35 trades)	$21.25	$170.00	16.8%	16.5%	27.0%	10.0%	70.3%	$14.95	$36.20	$289.60
	Helpers Average (5 trades)	15.65	125.20	18.5		25.0		70.0	$10.95	26.60	212.80
	Foreman Average, Inside ($.50 over trade)	21.75	174.00	16.8		27.0		70.3	15.30	37.05	296.40
	Foreman Average, Outside ($2.00 over trade)	23.25	186.00	16.8		27.0		70.3	16.35	39.60	316.80
Clab	Common Building Laborers	15.25	122.00	18.1		25.0		69.6	10.60	25.85	206.80
Asbe	Asbestos Workers	22.10	176.80	16.2		30.0		72.7	16.05	38.15	305.20
Boil	Boilermakers	23.95	191.60	14.7		30.0		71.2	17.05	41.00	328.00
Bric	Bricklayers	21.35	170.80	16.0		25.0		67.5	14.40	35.75	286.00
Brhe	Bricklayer Helpers	16.45	131.60	16.0		25.0		67.5	11.10	27.55	220.40
Carp	Carpenters	21.00	168.00	18.1		25.0		69.6	14.60	35.60	284.80
Cefi	Cement Finishers	20.10	160.80	10.6		25.0		62.1	12.50	32.60	260.80
Elec	Electricians	23.75	190.00	6.7		30.0		63.2	15.00	38.75	310.00
Elev	Elevator Constructors	24.85	198.80	7.7		30.0		64.2	15.95	40.80	326.40
Eqhv	Equipment Operators, Crane or Shovel	22.30	178.40	10.6		28.0		65.1	14.50	36.80	294.40
Eqmd	Equipment Operators, Medium Equipment	21.55	172.40	10.6		28.0		65.1	14.05	35.60	284.80
Eqlt	Equipment Operators, Light Equipment	20.55	164.40	10.6		28.0		65.1	13.40	33.95	271.60
Eqol	Equipment Operators, Oilers	18.40	147.20	10.6		28.0		65.1	12.00	30.40	243.20
Eqmm	Equipment Operators, Master Mechanics	22.65	181.20	10.6		28.0		65.1	14.75	37.40	299.20
Glaz	Glaziers	21.30	170.40	13.8		25.0		65.3	13.90	35.20	281.60
Lath	Lathers	20.15	161.20	11.1		25.0		62.6	12.60	32.75	262.00
Marb	Marble Setters	21.05	168.40	16.0		25.0		67.5	14.20	35.25	282.00
Mill	Millwrights	22.25	178.00	10.6		25.0		62.1	13.80	36.05	288.40
Mstz	Mosaic and Terrazzo Workers	20.50	164.00	9.8		25.0		61.3	12.55	33.05	264.40
Pord	Painters, Ordinary	19.30	154.40	13.8		25.0		65.3	12.60	31.90	255.20
Psst	Painters, Structural Steel	19.80	158.40	48.4		25.0		99.9	19.80	39.60	316.80
Pape	Paper Hangers	19.25	154.00	13.8		25.0		65.3	12.55	31.80	254.40
Pile	Pile Drivers	20.85	166.80	24.9		30.0		81.4	16.95	37.80	302.40
Plas	Plasterers	19.65	157.20	15.8		25.0		67.3	13.20	32.85	262.80
Plah	Plasterer Helpers	16.60	132.80	15.8		25.0		67.3	11.15	27.75	222.00
Plum	Plumbers	23.75	190.00	8.3		30.0		64.8	15.40	39.15	313.20
Rodm	Rodmen (Reinforcing)	22.95	183.60	28.3		28.0		82.8	19.00	41.95	335.60
Rofc	Roofers, Composition	18.35	146.80	32.6		25.0		84.1	15.45	33.80	270.40
Rots	Roofers, Tile and Slate	18.45	147.60	32.6		25.0		84.1	15.50	33.95	271.60
Rohe	Roofer Helpers (Composition)	13.65	109.20	32.6		25.0		84.1	11.50	25.15	201.20
Shee	Sheet Metal Workers	23.15	185.20	11.7		30.0		68.2	15.80	38.95	311.60
Spri	Sprinkler Installers	23.90	191.20	8.7		30.0		65.2	15.60	39.50	316.00
Stpi	Steamfitters or Pipefitters	23.90	191.20	8.3		30.0		64.8	15.50	39.40	315.20
Ston	Stone Masons	20.85	166.80	16.0		25.0		67.5	14.05	34.90	279.20
Sswk	Structural Steel Workers	22.95	183.60	39.8		28.0		94.3	21.65	44.60	356.80
Tilf	Tile Layers (Floor)	20.40	163.20	9.8		25.0		61.3	12.50	32.90	263.20
Tilh	Tile Layer Helpers	16.35	130.80	9.8		25.0		61.3	10.00	26.35	210.80
Trlt	Truck Drivers, Light	17.25	138.00	14.9		25.0		66.4	11.45	28.70	229.60
Trhv	Truck Drivers, Heavy	17.75	142.00	14.9		25.0		66.4	11.80	29.55	236.40
Sswl	Welders, Structural Steel	22.95	183.60	39.8		28.0		94.3	21.65	44.60	356.80
Wrck	*Wrecking	15.70	125.60	41.2	▼	25.0	▼	92.7	14.55	30.25	242.00

*Not included in Averages.

(from *Means Open Shop Cost Data 2002*)

Figure 6.9

		029 500 | Trees/Plants/Grnd Cover	CREW	MAKEUP	DAILY OUTPUT	LABOR HOURS	UNIT	
516	0950	Tractor spreader	B-66	1 Equip. Oper. (light) 1 Backhoe Ldr. w/Attchmt.	700	.011	M.S.F.	516
	1000	Polyethylene film, 6 mil.	2 Clab	2 Common Building Laborers	2,000	.008	S.Y.	
	1100	Redwood nuggets, 3" deep, hand spread	1 Clab	1 Common Building Laborer	150	.053	S.Y.	
	1150	Skid steer loader	B-63	4 Laborers 1 Equip. Oper. (light) 1 Loader, Skid Steer	13.50	2.963	M.S.F.	
	1200	Stone mulch, hand spread, ceramic chips, economy	B-14	1 Labor Foreman (outside) 4 Laborers 1 Equip. Oper. (light) 1 Backhoe Loader, 48 H.P.	125	.384	S.Y.	
	1250	Deluxe	"	"	95	.505	S.Y.	
	1300	Granite chips	B-1	1 Labor Foreman (outside) 2 Laborers	10	2.400	C.Y.	
	1400	Marble chips			10	2.400	C.Y.	
	1500	Onyx gemstone			10	2.400	C.Y.	
	1600	Pea gravel			28	.857	C.Y.	
	1700	Quartz	↓		10	2.400	C.Y.	
	1800	Tar paper, 15 Lb. felt	1 Clab	1 Common Building Laborer	800	.010	S.Y.	
	1900	Wood chips, 2" deep, hand spread	"	"	220	.036	S.Y.	
	1950	Skid steer loader	B-63	4 Laborers 1 Equip. Oper. (light) 1 Loader, Skid Steer	20.30	1.970	M.S.F.	
520	0010	PLANTING Moving shrubs on site, 12" ball	B-1	1 Labor Foreman (outside) 2 Laborers	28	.857	Ea.	520
	0100	24" ball	"	"	22	1.091	Ea.	
	0300	Moving trees on site, 36" ball	B-6	2 Laborers 1 Equip. Oper. (light) 1 Backhoe Loader, 48 H.P.	3.75	6.400	Ea.	
	0400	60" ball	"	"	1	24	Ea.	
521	0010	PLANTING Trees, shrubs and ground cover						521
	0100	Light soil						
	0110	Bare root seedlings, 3" to 5"	1 Clab	1 Common Building Laborer	960	.008	Ea.	
	0120	6" to 10"			520	.015	Ea.	
	0200	Potted, 2-1/4" diameter			840	.010	Ea.	
	0210	3" diameter	↓	↓	700	.011	Ea.	
	0300	Container, 1 gallon	2 Clab	2 Common Building Laborers	84	.190	Ea.	
	0330	5 gallon			29	.552	Ea.	
	0400	Bagged and burlapped, 12" diameter ball, by hand			19	.842	Ea.	
	0420	18" diameter by hand	↓	↓	12	1.333	Ea.	
	0550	Medium soil						
	0560	Bare root seedlings, 3" to 5"	1 Clab	1 Common Building Laborer	672	.012	Ea.	
	0561	6" to 10"			364	.022	Ea.	
	0570	Potted, 2-1/4" diameter			590	.014	Ea.	
	0572	3" diameter	↓	↓	490	.016	Ea.	
	0590	Container, 1 gallon	2 Clab	2 Common Building Laborers	59	.271	Ea.	
	0595	5 gallon			20	.800	Ea.	
	0600	Bagged and burlapped, 12" diameter ball, by hand			13	1.231	Ea.	
	0610	18" diameter, by hand	↓	↓	8.50	1.882	Ea.	
	0700	Heavy or stoney soil						
	0710	Bare root seedlings, 3" to 5"	1 Clab	1 Common Building Laborer	470	.017	Ea.	
	0711	6" to 10"			255	.031	Ea.	
	0720	Potted, 2-1/4" diameter			101	.079	Ea.	
	0722	3" diameter	↓	↓	343	.023	Ea.	
	0730	Container, 1 gallon	2 Clab	2 Common Building Laborers	41.30	.387	Ea.	
	0735	5 gallon			14	1.143	Ea.	
	0750	Bagged and burlapped, 12" diameter ball, by hand	↓	↓	9.10	1.758	Ea.	

(from *Means Productivity Standards for Construction*)

Figure 6.10

attempted if it is based on a solid foundation of experience and considerable exposure to landscape industry methods and practices.

Equipment: There are four considerations for estimating the cost of equipment. They are:

- Choosing the proper type of equipment
- Judging the amount of time it will be used
- Applying the correct rental rate, including operator and fuel
- Including the cost to move the equipment on and off the job

The type of work to be done may suggest appropriate equipment. For example, large amounts of earthen materials to be moved in an easily accessible space may permit the largest equipment that is cost effective. Restricted access may require that materials be moved in a small tractor bucket or by hand with a wheelbarrow. Excavating and hauling may require front-end loaders and dump trucks or dump trailers; cutting and filling suggests bulldozers and/or scrapers and a roller compactor, and a water wagon. Productivity rates for various equipment options can be compared in Chapter 3, Figures 3.1 through 3.3.

Equipment costs may be classified in the following way:

1. Bare equipment (without operator or fuel) priced as rented per hour, day, week, or month. If operators and fuel (or any operating costs) are required, these may be priced out as separate labor and material items, respectively.

2. Bare equipment as above, but owned by the landscaper and charged to the job at an hourly depreciation rate figured by the owner for a fair return on the investment.

Weekly Payroll Estimate							
Labor Data			Hours per Week		Weekly Payroll		
Worker	Number	Rate	Estimated	Actual	Estimated	Actual	Variance
Foreman "A"	1	$19.25	40		$770.00		
Foreman "B"	1	17.25	20		345.00		
Workers "A"	2	15.50	40		620.00		
"B"	3	15.00	40		600.00		
"C"	1	13.00	25		325.00		
"D"	1	12.00	40		480.00		
Total Hours			205				
Total Wages					$3,140.00		
Payroll Wages*					$ 785.00		
TOTAL ESTIMATED PAYROLL					$3,925.00		

* For purposes of this example, 25% is added for payroll taxes. Actual percentages will vary from state to state and from company to company.

Figure 6.11

3. Operated equipment, complete including fuel, priced by the hour, day, week, or month and entered, in its entirety, as an equipment expense.

Quotations for equipment rental or lease costs can be obtained from local dealers and suppliers, or even from manufacturers. These costs can fluctuate and should be updated regularly.

Ownership costs must be determined within a company. There are many considerations beyond the up-front purchase price; these factors must be taken into account when figuring the cost of owning equipment. Interest rates and amortization schedules should be studied prior to the purchase. Insurance costs, storage fees, maintenance, taxes, and licenses, all added together, can become a significant percentage of the cost of owning equipment. Depreciation (a way of quantifying loss of value to the owner over time) is another important factor. All of these considerations should be reviewed prior to purchase in order to properly manage the ownership.

The operating costs of equipment, whether rented, leased, or owned, are available from the following sources (listed in order of reliability):

1. The company's own records.
2. Annual cost books containing equipment operating costs, such as *Means Building Construction Cost Data*.
3. Manufacturers' estimates.
4. Textbooks dealing with equipment operating costs.

These operating costs consist of fuel, lubrication, expendable parts replacement, minor maintenance, transportation, and mobilization costs. For estimating purposes, the equipment ownership and operating costs can be listed separately. In this way, the decision to rent, lease, or purchase can be decided project by project.

There are two commonly used methods for including equipment costs in a landscape estimate. The first is to include the cost of equipment as a part of the task for which it is used. This method is obvious for subcontract items where the machine work is subcontracted as a separate price. The advantage of this method is that costs are allocated to the division or task that actually incurs the expense. As a result, more accurate records can be kept for each construction component.

The second method for listing equipment costs is to keep all such costs separate and to include them as a part of Project Overhead. The advantage of this method is that all equipment costs are grouped together. The disadvantage is that for future estimating purposes, equipment costs will be known only by job and not by unit of construction. Under these circumstances, omissions could possibly occur.

Whichever method is used, the estimator must be consistent, and must be sure that all equipment costs are included, but not duplicated. The estimating method should be the same as that chosen for cost monitoring and accounting, so that the data will be available for future projects.

Subcontractors: Subcontractor quotations should be carefully examined to ensure the following:
- Are they complete as per the plans and specifications?
- Do they include sales tax?
- Do they involve any unusual scheduling requirements or constraints?

- Do they include a performance bond, or are they bondable?
- Do they include any unusual payment schedule?
- What is the experience of the subcontractor with the exact type of work involved?
- Is the price competitive or is it a "street" price?

Subcontractor quotations should be solicited and analyzed in the same way as material quotes. A primary concern is that the bid covers the work as per plans and specifications, and that all appropriate work alternates and allowances are included. Any exclusions should be clearly stated and explained. If the bid is received verbally, a form such as that in Figure 6.7 will help to assure that all items are included. Any unique scheduling or payment requirements must be noted and evaluated prior to submission of the prime bid. Such requirements could affect or restrict the normal progress of the project, and have an impact on the costs.

The estimator should note how long the subcontract bid will be honored. This time period usually varies from 30 to 90 days and is often included as a condition in complete bids. The general contractor may have to define the time limits of the prime bid based upon certain subcontractors. The estimator must also note any escalation clauses that may be included in subcontractor bids.

Reliability is another factor to be considered when soliciting and evaluating subcontractor bids. Reliability cannot be measured or priced until the project is actually under construction. Most landscape contractors tend to stay with the same subcontractors for just this reason. A certain unspoken communication exists in these established relationships and usually has a positive effect on the performance of the work. Such familiarity, however, can often erode the competitive nature of the bidding. To be competitive with the landscape bid, the estimator should always obtain comparison subcontract (and vendor) prices, whether these prices come from another subcontractor or are prepared by the estimator.

The estimator may question and verify the bonding capability and capacity of unfamiliar subcontractors. Taking such action may be necessary when bidding in a new location. Other than word-of-mouth, these inquiries may be the only way to confirm subcontractor reliability.

For major subcontract items it may be necessary to make up spreadsheets in order to list inclusions and omissions. This procedure ensures that there is an accounting for every item in the job. Time permitting, the estimator should do a takeoff and price these major subcontract items to compare with the sub-bids. If time does not permit a detailed takeoff, the estimator should at least budget the work. An assemblies estimate is ideal for this purpose.

Project Overhead: Some estimators list certain costs as project overhead. These are items required to perform the work, but not necessarily a direct part of specific landscape tasks. Project overhead includes items from project supervision to cleanup, from temporary utilities to permits. Some estimators may not agree that certain items (such as equipment and tools) should be included as Project Overhead, and might prefer to list such items in another division. Ultimately, it is not important *where* or *how* each item is incorporated into the estimate, but that *every item is included somewhere.*

Project overhead often includes time-related items including equipment rental, supervisory labor, and temporary utilities, etc. The cost for these items depends

upon the duration of the project. A preliminary schedule should therefore be developed *prior* to completion of the estimate so that time-related items can be properly counted.

Bonds: Bonds—bid bonds, performance bonds, etc.—may also be considered as project overhead. Bond requirements for a project are usually specified in the General Conditions portion of the specification. Costs for bonds are based on total project cost and are determined at the estimate summary stage. Listed below are a few common types:

Bid Bond: A form of bid security executed by the bidder or principal and by a surety (bonding company) to guarantee that the bidder will enter into a contract within a specified time and furnish any required Performance or Labor and Material Payment bonds.

Completion Bond: Also known as "Construction" or "Contract" bond. The guarantee by a surety that the construction contract will be completed and that it will be clear of all liens and encumbrances.

Labor and Material Payment Bond: The guarantee by a surety to the owner that the contractor will pay for all labor and materials used in the performance of the contract as per the construction documents. The claimants under the bond are those having direct contracts with the contractor or any subcontractor.

Performance Bond: (1) A guarantee that a contractor will perform a job according to the terms of the contracts. (2) A bond of the contractor in which a surety guarantees to the owner that the work will be performed in accordance with the contract documents. Except where prohibited by statute, the performance bond is frequently combined with the labor and material payment bond.

Surety Bond: A legal instrument under which one party agrees to be responsible for the debt, default, or failure to perform of another party.

Indirect Costs

The direct costs of a project must be itemized, tabulated, and totalled before the indirect costs can be applied to the estimate. It is indirect costs that have the most variation from contractor to contractor. The indirect costs are almost always defined as a percentage of direct costs and include:

- Sales tax (if required)
- Employment taxes
- Office or operating overhead (vs. project overhead)
- Profit
- Contingencies

Sales Tax: Sales tax varies from state to state and often from city to city within a state. Many states allow local jurisdictions, such as a county or city, to levy additional sales tax. Some localities also impose separate sales taxes on labor and equipment. Conversely, five states have no sales tax.

When bidding takes place in unfamiliar locations, the estimator should check with local agencies regarding the amount, and the method of payment of sales tax. Local authorities may require owners to withhold payments to out-of-state contractors until payment of all required sales tax has been verified. Sales tax is often taken for granted or even omitted. However, as can be seen in Figure 6.12, state sales tax can be as high as 7.00% of material costs. Indeed, this can represent a significant portion of the project's total cost. Conversely, some clients and/or their projects may be tax exempt, particularly those constructed

with public funds or for a non-profit organization. If this fact is unknown to the estimator, a large dollar amount of sales tax might be needlessly included in a bid.

Employment Taxes: As with sales taxes, the estimator must be familiar with local and federal regulations for amounts and payment of employment taxes. These may include, but are not limited to, Workers' Compensation, Federal and State Unemployment Insurance, and employer-paid Social Security tax and Medicare. National average rates for these taxes are shown in Figure 6.8 as percentages of labor costs.

Office or Operating Overhead: Office overhead, or the cost of doing business, is perhaps one of the main reasons why so many contractors are unable to realize a profit, or even to stay in business. If a contractor does not know the costs of operating the business, then, more than likely, these costs will not be recovered. Many companies survive, and even turn a profit, by simply adding a certain percentage for overhead to each job, without knowing how the percentage is derived or what is included. When annual volume changes signficantly, whether by increase or decrease, the previously used percentage for overhead may no longer be valid. Often when such a volume change occurs, the owner finds that the company is not doing as well as before and cannot determine the reasons. Chances are, overhead costs are not being fully recovered.

A list of typical types of operating costs for landscape contractors is found in Figure 6.13. Notice the columns of estimated annual costs. These estimates should be based upon records from prior years and should incorporate anticipated increases or decreases in costs for the coming year. At the end of a year, actual costs for each item should be determined, and variations between actual and estimated costs should be calculated and analyzed. This information can then be used, together with any other pertinent data, to predict the coming year's overhead figures.

State	Tax (%)	State	Tax (%)	State	Tax (%)	State	Tax (%)
Alabama	4	Illinois	6.25	Montana	0	Rhode Island	7
Alaska	0	Indiana	5	Nebraska	5	South Carolina	5
Arizona	5	Iowa	5	Nevada	6.5	South Dakota	4
Arkansas	4.625	Kansas	4.9	New Hampshire	0	Tennessee	6
California	7	Kentucky	6	New Jersey	6	Texas	6.25
Colorado	2.9	Louisiana	4	New Mexico	5	Utah	4.75
Connecticut	6	Maine	5.5	New York	4	Vermont	5
Delaware	0	Maryland	5	North Carolina	4	Virginia	4.5
District of Columbia	5.75	Massachusetts	5	North Dakota	5	Washington	6.5
Florida	6	Michigan	6	Ohio	5	West Virginia	6
Georgia	4	Minnesota	6.5	Oklahoma	4.5	Wisconsin	5
Hawaii	4	Mississippi	7	Oregon	0	Wyoming	4
Idaho	5	Missouri	4.225	Pennsylvania	6	Average	4.70 %

Figure 6.12

Means' Forms

**OVERHEAD
COST SHEET**

ITEM	PREVIOUS YEAR ACTUAL COSTS	CURRENT YEAR ESTIMATED COSTS	CURRENT YEAR ACTUAL COSTS	NEXT YEAR ESTIMATED COSTS
OFFICE PERSONNEL Salaries Payroll Taxes Benefits				
SECRETARIAL SERVICE ($ _____ per hr.)				
OFFICE COSTS Rent Utilities Telephone Supplies Postage				
INSURANCE Liability Vehicle				
LEGAL SERVICES				
ACCOUNTING				
ADVERTISING				
TRAVEL				
ENTERTAINING				
VEHICLES Gas Maintenance & Repairs Tax & License Depreciation				
EQUIPMENT Gas Maintenance & Repairs Tax & License Depreciation				
HAND TOOLS				
TOTAL COSTS				
TOTAL AVAILABLE WORK HOURS				
COST PER WORK HOUR				

Figure 6.13

Note the last category, "Cost per work hour." This figure should be based on the anticipated available work hours for a year (See Chapter 4 and Figure 4.1). The total annual overhead costs are divided by the total available work hours to determine the cost per hour that must be added to workers' wages in order to recover overhead costs. These overhead costs must be recovered (paid for) before any profit can be realized.

The estimator must also remember that if volume or manpower changes significantly, then the applicable costs for office overhead should be recalculated for current conditions. The same is true if there are changes in office staff. Remember that salaries are the major portion of office overhead costs.

Profit: Determining a fair and reasonable percentage to be included for profit is not an easy task. This responsibility is usually left to the owner or chief estimator. Experience is crucial in anticipating what profit the market will bear. The economic climate, competition, knowledge of the project, and familiarity with the landscape architect or owner all affect the way in which profit is determined.

Contingencies: Like profit, contingencies can be difficult to quantify. Especially appropriate in preliminary budgets, the addition of a contingency is meant to protect the contractor as well as give the owner a realistic estimate of project costs.

A contingency percentage should be based on the number of "unknowns" in a project. This percentage should be inversely proportional to the amount of planning detail that has been done for the project. If complete plans and specifications are supplied, and the estimate is thorough and precise, then there is little need for a contingency. Figure 6.14, from *Means Site Work & Landscape Cost Data*, lists suggested contingency percentages from 20% down to 3% based on the stage of planning and design development.

A method that is not recommended for including contingencies is "padding" or "rounding up" each individual item as it is priced. This can cause problems because the cost sheets will not show the actual costs separate from the "padding." At the summary, the estimator cannot determine exactly how much has been included as a contingency for the whole project. A much more accurate and controllable approach is the precise pricing of the estimate and the addition of one contingency amount at the bottom line. Using this method, the estimate prices become helpful historical records for the company.

The takeoff and pricing methods discussed in the preceding pages can be carried out neatly and effectively when the appropriate forms are used as guidelines. First, the quantity sheets are used for the material takeoff. Next, the data may be transferred to cost analysis or pricing sheets where items are priced and costs extended. Then, an estimate summary form, as shown in Figure 6.15, can be used to summarize the price totals for the general categories of a project. This process, transferring from one sheet to another, should be checked very carefully, as errors of transposition can easily occur. All major categories, such as trees or irrigation and their totals can be listed on this form, and subtotals figured. Appropriate markups for the indirect costs described above are then applied to the total dollar values. Generally, the sum of each column has different percentages added near the end of the estimate for the indirect costs. In summary:

Use Quantity Sheets and Complete in the Following Sequence:

1. Site Work Takeoff

01200 | Price & Payment Procedures

01250	Contract Modification Procedures	CREW	DAILY OUTPUT	LABOR-HOURS	UNIT	MAT.	LABOR	EQUIP.	TOTAL	TOTAL INCL O&P	
200	0010	**CONTINGENCIES** for estimate at conceptual stage				Project					20%	200
	0050	Schematic stage									15%	
	0100	Preliminary working drawing stage (Design Dev.)									10%	
	0150	Final working drawing stage				↓					3%	
300	0010	**CREWS** For building construction, see How To Use This Book										300
400	0010	**FACTORS** Cost adjustments										400
	0100	Add to construction costs for particular job requirements										
	1100	Equipment usage curtailment, add, minimum				Costs	1%	1%				
	1150	Maximum					3%	10%				
	1400	Material handling & storage limitation, add, minimum					1%	1%				
	1450	Maximum					6%	7%				
	2300	Temporary shoring and bracing, add, minimum					2%	5%				
	2350	Maximum					5%	12%				
	2400	Work inside prisons and high security areas, add, minimum						30%				
	2450	Maximum				↓		50%				
600	0010	**OVERTIME** For early completion of projects or where R01100-110										600
	0020	labor shortages exist, add to usual labor, up to				Costs		100%				

01255	Cost Indexes										
200	0010	**CONSTRUCTION COST INDEX** (Reference) over 930 zip code locations in										200
	0020	The U.S. and Canada, total bldg cost, min. (Clarksdale, MS)				%					66.20%	
	0050	Average									100%	
	0100	Maximum (New York, NY)				↓					134.60%	
500	0010	**LABOR INDEX** (Reference) For over 930 zip code locations in										500
	0020	the U.S. and Canada, minimum (Clarksdale, MS)				%		33.80%				
	0050	Average						100%				
	0100	Maximum (New York, NY)				↓		163.30%				
600	0011	**MATERIAL INDEX** For over 930 zip code locations in										600
	0020	the U.S. and Canada, minimum (Elizabethtown, KY)				%	92.10%					
	0040	Average					100%					
	0060	Maximum (Ketchikan, AK)				↓	143.90%					

01290	Payment Procedures										
800	0010	**TAXES** Sales tax, State, average R01100-090				%	4.70%					800
	0050	Maximum					7%					
	0200	Social Security, on first $80,400 of wages R01100-100						7.65%				
	0300	Unemployment, MA, combined Federal and State, minimum						2.10%				
	0350	Average						7%				
	0400	Maximum				↓		8%				

01300 | Administrative Requirements

01310	Project Management/Coordination	CREW	DAILY OUTPUT	LABOR-HOURS	UNIT	MAT.	LABOR	EQUIP.	TOTAL	TOTAL INCL O&P	
150	0010	**PERMITS** Rule of thumb, most cities, minimum				Job					.50%	150
	0100	Maximum				"					2%	

(from *Means Site Work & Landscape Cost Data 2002*)

Figure 6.14

Means Forms

**CONDENSED
ESTIMATE SUMMARY**

SHEET NO.

PROJECT

ESTIMATE NO.

LOCATION

TOTAL AREA/VOLUME

DATE

ARCHITECT

COST PER S.F./C.F.

NO. OF STORIES

PRICES BY:

EXTENSIONS BY:

CHECKED BY:

Figure 6.15

132

2. Hard Construction Takeoff

3. Planting Takeoff

4. Summary and Pricing of Each Category

When entering the extended totals, ignore the cents column and round all totals to the nearest dollar. In a column of totals, the cents will average out and be of no consequence. Each division is added and the results checked, preferably by someone other than the person doing the extensions.

The estimating process as a whole calls upon an accumulation of knowledge and experience. The first decision is to bid or not to bid. Once the facts have been carefully weighed and a decision made in favor of bidding, the estimating process is begun. Checklists, forms, and good working techniques aid in the process of information gathering and guard against oversights. The investigating and evaluation of a specific project and site conditions is one area in which effective communication between planners and contractors proves vital.

Chapter 7

Sample Takeoff and Estimate

Chapter Seven

Sample Takeoff and Estimate

The estimator, whether designer or contractor, foreman or manager, has one basic goal—to compute a relatively accurate cost for constructing a project. Why then do formal bid openings bring such a wide range of bids? It's because the skilled estimator does not merely compute the cost to construct a project; he or she computes the cost for that *particular company* to construct it. Estimators, even though they may use identical resources and the routines and methods outlined in earlier chapters, will still produce different true costs. Overhead, productivity, and purchasing power vary from company to company.

Estimating is a highly responsible job. Consideration must be given to the selection of suppliers and subcontractors; evaluations need to be made based on criteria such as reliability, price guarantees, and potential unexpected costs. When determining labor costs, it is more important to figure how much work is most likely to be accomplished in one day, rather than the amount that is possible under the best of circumstances. A company's labor costs are tied directly to the skill and productivity of its labor force. A good estimator knows his company's skills, costs, and capacity.

Not only does the estimator have to determine the costs for the project; he must also calculate the time required to complete the work. This determination is based on many factors: quantities derived from the estimate, time of year, availability of material, labor, and equipment resources.

The sample estimate in this chapter is based on an actual landscape project. A landscape plan (Figure 7.1) and the designer's specifications (referred to, but not shown) are the basis of the estimate. The plan defines the sample landscape project and represents the major features of the job. This plan is provided for illustrative purposes only. In actuality, such a project might require additional drawings with more plans and details. A full set of specifications would also be provided.

An initial scan of the plans produces a general impression. In actual practice, this overview should be verified and corrected by the site survey visit and the process of gathering information—perhaps with a Landscape Project Analysis form (See Chapter 4, Figures 4.2–4.6). Together, these procedures enable the estimator to see the full scope of the project, and provide guidelines for proper estimating method and sequence. A site visit and completed Landscape Project Analysis form may also reveal conditions not evident from the inspection of the plans alone. These conditions may have a bearing upon the cost of labor, equipment, and materials.

In this example, the owner will be awarding the contract, with advice from the landscape architect. The bidding will be selected competitively, and no bond will

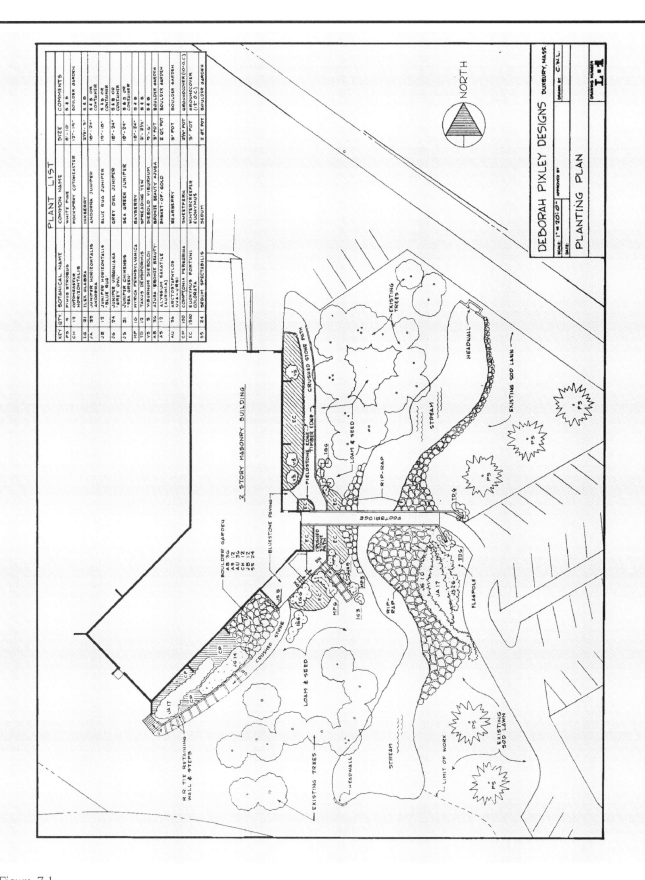

Figure 7.1

be required. In actual projects, plans and specs would have been provided by the landscape architect for the complete site development.

The example project is located 12 miles from the contractor's garage, and company employees are capable of performing most of the required work. The contractor has reliable and known subcontractors available to perform certain specialized sections of the work.

The takeoff process begins with a careful review of the scope of the project. This example is a five-acre site that is commercially zoned. The building on the site is owner-occupied. It is a two-story masonry building of good quality and serves as an office building and distribution center for a publishing company. All utilities are installed in the building. The site is located very near major highway access on good, paved roads. Soil tests and test pits identify a sandy soil. Fill and topsoil have been stockpiled on the site by the building excavating subcontractor.

The work area identified in the plans is only a part of the overall site and encompasses roughly 14,000 square feet, essentially all on the east side of the building. Special features and conditions include banks on both sides of a wet drainage ditch (stream) that will become a pond, an attractive focal point of the design. The steep sides of the stream banks are to be retained by stone rip rap. The planted area is to blend into existing natural wooded areas. Access to the site is by paved road to both paved parking areas. Access to the building from the front parking lot is by a concrete footbridge (by the building contractor) that spans the steep banks and the stream. This unique entrance will be used by both employees and visitors. Another entrance and parking lot for trucks and service are located further along the access drive. The area of work includes both sides of the pond banks and all building terraces and walkways.

The plans, specs, and Landscape Project Analysis form (based on the site visit) together form a "picture," or overall view of the work in the estimator's mind. An outline can now be made of the scope of the work. Such an outline could be set up on an Estimate Summary form to coincide with the organization of the project into basic "pricing categories." An example is shown in Figure 7.2.

This listing of the scope of the work can serve as a checklist of the major categories. The takeoff proceeds by breaking the categories down into various stages of detail. Note that a separate takeoff sheet is prepared for lists of site work, hard construction and planting. This is the process of defining the tasks and exactly what the work entails.

Area Measurements

Areas to be measured in landscape construction are often irregular and/or sloped. The estimator must perform various calculations in order to obtain the most accurate numbers.

There are three basic methods to determine area from a plan. The first is with a **planimeter**—a device which, when rolled along a designated perimeter, will measure area. The resulting measurement must then be converted to the scale of the drawing. **Trigonometry** can also be used to determine area. It is applied to the distances and bearings supplied by a survey. Sines and cosines are used to **calculate coordinates**, which are in turn used to calculate area. The planimeter may be used only if the drawing is to scale and the scale is known. The trigonometric method may be used on a drawing not to scale, but only if survey data is available. Both methods are accurate. The third method, calculating coordinates, is shown in Figure 7.3. This method is less accurate

CONDENSED ESTIMATE SUMMARY					

CONDENSED
ESTIMATE SUMMARY   SHEET NO.

PROJECT: Office Building				ESTIMATE NO. 02-1	
LOCATION:		TOTAL AREA / VOLUME		DATE: 2002	
ARCHITECT:		COST PER S.F. / C.F.		NO. OF STORIES	
PRICES BY: Means		EXTENSIONS BY: SHF		CHECKED BY: SHF	
DESCRIPTION	MATERIAL	LABOR	EQUIPMENT	SUBCONTRACT	TOTAL
Site Work					
Headwalls					
Rip Rap					
Grading					
Erosion Control					
Fountain/Aerator					
Flagpole					
Hard Construction					
Concrete					
Bluestone Patios					
Wood RR Ties					
- RR Tie Steps					
- RR Tie Retaining Wall					
- RR Tie Edging					
Fieldstone Edging					
Crushed Bluestone					
Plantings					
Trees, Shrubs, Groundcover					
Horticultural & Misc. Materials					
- Weed Barrier Filter Fabric					
- Tree Mulch Cover					
- Metal Edging					
Lawn					
- First Mowing					
Miscellaneous:					
Pruning & Cleanup					

Figure 7.2

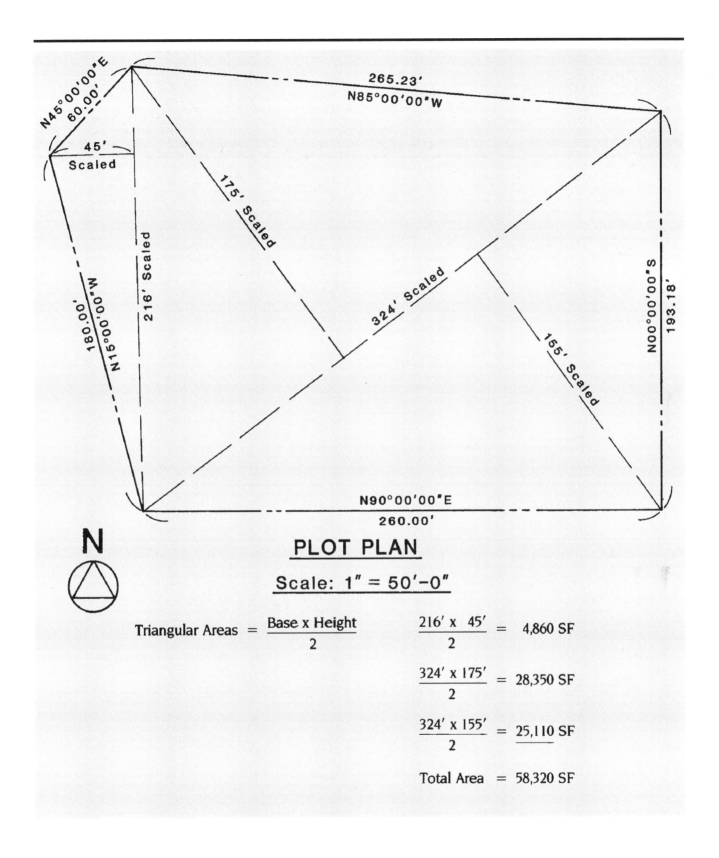

PLOT PLAN

Scale: 1" = 50'-0"

Triangular Areas = $\dfrac{\text{Base x Height}}{2}$

$\dfrac{216' \times 45'}{2}$ = 4,860 SF

$\dfrac{324' \times 175'}{2}$ = 28,350 SF

$\dfrac{324' \times 155'}{2}$ = 25,110 SF

Total Area = 58,320 SF

Figure 7.3

but can be used when a drawing is indicated to be in a certain scale. Check the drawing's accuracy with some measurement on the map such as a property line, that has already been noted. This method involves dividing the map area into triangles, squares, and rectangles and determining the area of each. Some dimensions must be scaled. This method can be performed quickly, and depending upon the scale of the site, it is accurate to within a few percent. Formulas for determining the area of geometric and irregular shapes are included in the Appendix.

The above methods are used to determine "map" or plan area—the superimposing of an uneven surface onto a horizontal plane. If the surface is sloped, the actual area will differ from the area as shown on the map. When the slope is known, the map area is converted using a conversion factor. This process is demonstrated in the Quantity Takeoff sheet for the sample project, Figure 7.6. A factor conversion chart is shown in Figure 7.4. If a contour map is available, slope can be determined by measuring the change in elevation versus the horizontal distance.

Certain graphic symbols are commonly used on landscape plans. Landscape plans may or may not include a key of symbols, and different designers may use different codes for the same items. It is important to review each set of plans individually and carefully. Refer to Chapter 5, Figure 5.2 for a chart of typical symbols.

In addition to measuring area, materials must also be identified and quantified along with the labor and equipment needed in each outlined category. The estimator can record these measurements on a quantity sheet for performing

Slope Area Conversion Chart		
Factors to Convert		
Horizontal Plan Dimensions to Actual, Inclined Dimensions		
Angle	Rise/Run	Factor
0°	Flat	1.000
4.8°	1/12	1.003
9.5°	1/6	1.014
14°	1/4	1.031
18.4°	1/3	1.054
26.6°	1/2	1.118
45°	1/1	1.414

Figure 7.4

extensions, or directly list the quantities on a pricing sheet. For purposes of this sample estimate, both methods are illustrated.

Most costs used in the sample estimate are from *Means Site Work & Landscape Cost Data*. In some cases, "local prices" are used where an estimator would be likely to solicit bids and/or labor costs from local suppliers and subcontractors. The methods shown in this sample estimate demonstrate how the estimator can use data such as that found in *Means Site Work & Landscape Cost Data* to verify the subcontractor bids or to develop budget costs.

Site Work

The site work portion of the estimate involves the rip rap slope, grading and spreading of topsoil, and the two headwalls of the pond. For purposes of this example, the headwalls and rip rap will be estimated as items that would normally be subcontracted; in other words, they will include the overhead and profit of the subcontractor. The landscape estimator would, in these cases, solicit bids from subcontractors for these certain portions of the work.

Construction around streams, ponds and just about any water area may require protection from siltation and bank side erosion according to state or federal mandate. For this project, the requirement is for a silt fence and the placement (and removal) of hay bales.

Rip Rap

The areas of placement of the rip rap slope for the project are shown in Figure 7.5. The actual map areas are measured from the plans using one of the methods described above. The dimensions and quantities can be entered on a quantity sheet as shown in Figure 7.6. From the site visit, the estimator has determined the average slope to be 1:2. The appropriate factor (from Figure 7.4) is applied to determine the *actual* area for installation of the rip rap. The estimator has determined that this portion of the work is to be subcontracted. Costs (including the installing contractor's overhead and profit) for rip rap are obtained from Figure 7.7 and entered on a cost analysis sheet (Figure 7.8).

This procedure represents one choice of method and sequence that can be used for all components of the estimate. No matter which procedure is used, the estimator should try to be consistent.

Grading

Various types of grading are required for this project. The estimator should consider: spreading and dressing topsoil for both planting beds and lawn areas, preparation for railroad tie edging and retaining walls, and preparation for patios and walks. Each of these different functions could be estimated individually, though the experienced estimator is likely to lump certain of the smaller items together. Measurements from the plan yield the following area quantities for basic grading work items:

Planting beds	3,353 S.F.
Lawn areas	5,650 S.F.
Patio, walk, and wall preparation	4,785 S.F.

Each of these areas will involve different types of work. Topsoil will be placed in the planting beds and most likely spread and dressed by hand. Topsoil for the lawn areas will be spread by machine and dressed by hand. Excavation and grading for the patio and walk areas will be completed by hand. For this example, the specifications require 6″ of topsoil for the planting bed and lawn areas.

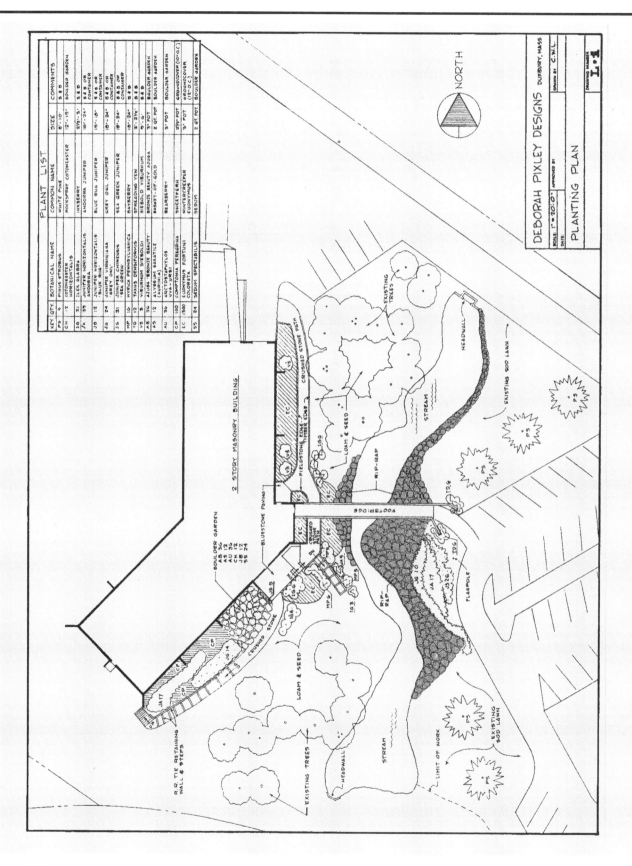

Figure 7.5

144

QUANTITY SHEET

PROJECT: Office Building ESTIMATE NO. 02-1

LOCATION: ARCHITECT: DATE: **2002**

TAKE OFF BY: SHF EXTENSIONS BY: SHF CHECKED BY: SHF

Description	NO.	L	W	Unit	AREA	Unit		Unit	VOLUME	Unit
Site Work										
Head Walls							2	E.A.		
Rip Rap		16'	11.5'		184	S.F.				
		29.5'	10.5'		310					
		15'	8'		120					
		13.5'	13'		176					
		24'	8'		192					
		90'	12'		1082					
					2062					
Slope Factor (x 1.118)					2305	S.F.	256	S.Y.		
Stream Side Erosion Control										
Silt Fence		188		L.F.						
Hay Bales, staked		188		L.F.						
Grading Plant Beds		88'	12'		1056	S.F.				
		24'	6'		144					
		19'	5'		95					
		16'	11'		176					
		16'	8'		128					
		44'	12'		528					
		52'	20'		1040					
		31'	6'		186					
					3353	S.F.	373	S.Y.		
Top Soil @ 6"									70	C.Y.
Lawns					5650	S.F.	628	S.Y.		
Top Soil @ 6"									119	C.Y.
Misc. Prep.					4785	S.F.	532	S.Y.		

Figure 7.6

		02370	Erosion & Sedimentation Control	CREW	DAILY OUTPUT	LABOR-HOURS	UNIT	2002 BARE COSTS MAT.	LABOR	EQUIP.	TOTAL	TOTAL INCL O&P	
300	0010		RIP-RAP Random, broken stone										300
	0100		Machine placed for slope protection	B-12G	62	.258	C.Y.	14.15	7.60	5.70	27.45	33.50	
	0110		3/8 to 1/4 C.Y. pieces, grouted	B-13	80	.700	S.Y.	35	17.80	9.05	61.85	76	
	0200		18" minimum thickness, not grouted	"	53	1.057	"	23.50	27	13.65	64.15	82.50	
	0300		Dumped, 50 lb. average	B-11A	800	.020	Ton	13.50	.55	1.03	15.08	16.80	
	0350		100 lb. average		700	.023		19.30	.62	1.18	21.10	23.50	
	0370		300 lb. average	▼	600	.027	▼	22.50	.73	1.37	24.60	27	
	0400		Gabions, galvanized steel mesh mats or boxes, stone filled, 6" deep	B-13	200	.280	S.Y.	12.65	7.15	3.62	23.42	29	
	0500		9" deep		163	.344		19.70	8.75	4.45	32.90	40	
	0600		12" deep		153	.366		22.50	9.30	4.74	36.54	44.50	
	0700		18" deep		102	.549		29	14	7.10	50.10	61.50	
	0800		36" deep	▼	60	.933	▼	49	24	12.10	85.10	104	
550	0010		EROSION CONTROL Jute mesh, 100 S.Y. per roll, 4' wide, stapled	B-80A	2,400	.010	S.Y.	.64	.23	.08	.95	1.15	550
	0060		Nylon, 3 dimensional geomatrix, 9 mil thick		700	.034		3.77	.80	.26	4.83	5.70	
	0062		12 mil thick		515	.047		5.10	1.09	.35	6.54	7.75	
	0064		18 mil thick	▼	460	.052		5.40	1.22	.40	7.02	8.30	
	0070		Paper biodegradable mesh	B-1	2,500	.010		.07	.23		.30	.44	
	0080		Paper mulch	B-64	20,000	.001		.05	.02	.01	.08	.10	
	0100		Plastic netting, stapled, 2" x 1" mesh, 20 mil	B-1	2,500	.010		.59	.23		.82	1.01	
	0120		Revegetation mat, webbed	2 Clab	1,000	.016	▼	4.71	.38		5.09	5.80	
	0160		Underdrain fabric, 18" x 100' roll	"	32	.500	Roll	19.65	11.75		31.40	40	
	0200		Polypropylene mesh, stapled, 6.5 oz./S.Y.	B-1	2,500	.010	S.Y.	1.22	.23		1.45	1.70	
	0300		Tobacco netting, or jute mesh #2, stapled	"	2,500	.010		.07	.23		.30	.44	
	0400		Soil sealant, liquid sprayed from truck	B-81	5,000	.005	▼	.40	.13	.11	.64	.75	
	1000		Silt fence, polypropylene, 3' high, ideal conditions	2 Clab	1,600	.010	L.F.	.29	.23		.52	.69	
	1100		Adverse conditions	"	950	.017	"	.29	.39		.68	.93	
	1130		Cellular confinement, poly, 3-dimen, 8' x 20' panels, 4" deep cell	B-6	1,600	.015	S.F.	1.58	.38	.11	2.07	2.45	
	1140		8" deep cells	"	1,200	.020	"	2.17	.51	.15	2.83	3.34	
	1200		Place and remove hay bales	A-2	3	8	Ton	51	190	52	293	405	
	1250		Hay bales, staked	"	2,500	.010	L.F.	2.04	.23	.06	2.33	2.66	
	1305		For less than 3 To 1 slope, add						15%				
	1310		For greater than 3 To 1 slope, add						25%				

		02390	Shore Protect/Mooring Structures										
150	0010		BULKHEADS Reinforced concrete, include footing and tie-backs										150
	0020		Up to 6' high, minimum	C-17C	28	2.964	L.F.	34.50	93	18.15	145.65	203	
	0060		Maximum		24.25	3.423		55	107	21	183	252	
	0100		12' high, minimum		20	4.150		89.50	130	25.50	245	330	
	0160		Maximum	▼	18.50	4.486	▼	104	141	27.50	272.50	365	
	0180		Precast bulkhead, complete, including										
	0190		vertical and battered piles, face panels, and cap										
	0195		Using 16' vertical piles				L.F.				225	260	
	0196		Using 20' vertical piles				"				240	275	
	0200		Steel sheeting, with 4' x 4' x 8" concrete deadmen, @ 10' O.C.										
	0210		12' high, shore driven	B-40	27	2.370	L.F.	56.50	72	81.50	210	268	
	0260		Barge driven	B-76	15	4.800	"	84.50	145	165	394.50	510	
	6000		Crushed stone placed behind bulkhead by clam bucket	B-12H	120	.133	C.Y.	14.55	3.93	5.85	24.33	28.50	
180	0010		BULKHEADS, RESIDENTIAL CANAL										180
	0020		Aluminum panel sheeting, incl. concrete cap and anchor										
	0030		Coarse compact sand, 4'-0" high, 2'-0" embedment	B-40	200	.320	L.F.	33	9.70	11	53.70	64	
	0040		3'-6" embedment		140	.457		39	13.85	15.70	68.55	82.50	
	0060		6'-0" embedment		90	.711		49.50	21.50	24.50	95.50	116	
	0120		6'-0" high, 2'-6" embedment		170	.376		43.50	11.40	12.95	67.85	80	

(from *Means Site Work & Landscape Cost Data 2002*)

Figure 7.7

COST ANALYSIS

PROJECT: Office Building	CLASSIFICATION:			ESTIMATE NO: 02-1		
LOCATION:	ARCHITECT:			DATE: 2002		
TAKE OFF BY: SHF	QUANTITIES BY: SHF	PRICES BY: Means	EXTENSIONS BY: BB	CHECKED BY:		

DESCRIPTION	SOURCE	QUANT.	UNIT	MATERIAL COST	MATERIAL TOTAL	LABOR COST	LABOR TOTAL	EQUIPMENT COST	EQUIPMENT TOTAL	SUBCONTRACT COST	SUBCONTRACT TOTAL	TOTAL COST	TOTAL TOTAL
Sitework													
Headwalls	G3030 310 2020	2	Ea.							2,475.00	4,950		
Rip Rap	02370 300 0200	256	S.Y.							82.50	21,120		
Grading													
Plant Beds	02920 340 3800	373	S.Y.			1.61	601						
Lawn	02920 340 5000	119	C.Y.			2.27	270	0.48	57				
Patio, Walk, Prep	02310 440 1150	532	S.Y.			0.83	442	0.08	43				
Place Topsoil	Crew B-10N	1	Day				343		264				
Erosion Control													
Silt Fence	02370 550 1000	188	L.F.	0.29	55	0.23	43						
Hay Bales	02370 550 1250	188	L.F.	2.04	384	0.23	43						
Fountain/Aerator	02815 225 0400	1	Ea.	2,950.00	2,950	118.00	118						
Flagpole	10355 400 0100	1	Ea.	605.00	605	217.00	217	91.00	91				
Flagpole Foundation	10355 400 7400	1	Ea.	415.00	415	91.00	91						
Total Site Work					$ 4,409		$ 2,168		$ 455		$ 26,070		$ 33,102

Figure 7.8

Figure 5.7, a conversion chart for materials, can be used to determine the amount of topsoil required. Sufficient quantities of topsoil have been stored on site so that costs required are for labor and equipment only. Quantities are derived in Figure 7.6, a quantity takeoff sheet, and costs are entered in Figure 7.8, a cost analysis sheet. Note that similar items, such as grading for plant beds and lawns, may be estimated in different ways. The grading for plant beds is priced by area (S.Y.) for a specific depth of topsoil, whereas grading for lawns is based on volume of material (C.Y.). Both methods are equally valid. The choice is often a matter of efficiency. Note that much of the work is done by hand in either case. See Figure 7.9 for the unit cost to spread conditioned topsoil by hand. (Note: The cost of topsoil material has been deleted on the estimate.) Equipment is required in order to place the topsoil for spreading and minor excavation. The cost of an appropriate crew and equipment (B-10N) is included (See Figure 7.10). Refer to Chapter 10 for a complete explanation of these crews and the use of *Means Site Work & Landscape Cost Data*.

	Area (S.F.)	C.Y./M.S.F.	Total C.Y.
Planting Beds	3,353	21	70.4
Lawns	5,650	21	118.6
6″ Topsoil required	9,003	21	189.0

Headwalls

The headwalls in this case are part of the landscape portion of the project. This work will be subcontracted. An assemblies cost (See Figure 7.11 from *Means Site Work & Landscape Cost Data*) is included in the estimate as a budget number until subcontractor bids are received. Note the assemblies cost includes all the system components, materials, equipment and labor. Such information is a handy check on a subcontractor's costs and specifications.

Hard Construction

A majority of the hard construction in this sample project is to be subcontracted. For those designated items—the bluestone patios and the railroad tie walls, steps, and edging—the costs include the subcontractors' overhead and profit. The project's owner has also added the installation of a flag pole and the installation of aeration—a fountain—in the pond as an enhancement of the company's headquarters building. These items will also be subcontracted.

It is sound estimating practice, even if a bid is solicited for a certain item, for the estimator to perform a takeoff and to price this same item. This approach allows the estimator to not only verify and crosscheck costs (against past jobs as well as bids for the current project), but also to schedule the work based on the derived quantities. Note that the productivity data in *Means Site Work & Landscape Cost Data* in Figure 7.9 is presented both as daily output (for a designated crew) and as labor-hours per unit of measurement. Productivity information in both formats can be used to determine duration times for scheduling. Figures 7.12 and 7.13 demonstrate the use of this data in calculating the time required for the bluestone patios. Figure 7.12 shows the references for crew, daily output and labor hours that are relevant. Figure 7.13 applies the labor-hour information to compute work days for this project.

As the quantities of work can be used to estimate the time required for certain items, so can the estimated time be used to determine the costs for other items. Such is the case for the fieldstone edging and crushed bluestone walks. See also the "plantings" estimate in Figure 7.17.

02900 | Planting

02920 | Lawns & Grasses

		CREW	DAILY OUTPUT	LABOR-HOURS	UNIT	MAT.	LABOR	EQUIP.	TOTAL	TOTAL INCL O&P
1350	300' haul	B-10B	15.40	.779	M.S.F.		22.50	53.50	76	93
1400	Alternate method, 75 HP dozer, 50' haul	B-10L	860	.014	C.Y.		.40	.34	.74	.98
1450	300' haul	"	114	.105			3.01	2.55	5.56	7.40
1500	200 HP dozer, 50' haul	B-10B	2,660	.005			.13	.31	.44	.54
1600	300' haul	"	570	.021			.60	1.44	2.04	2.51
1800	Rolling topsoil, hand push roller	1 Clab	3,200	.002	S.F.		.06		.06	.09
1850	Tractor drawn roller	B-66	10,666	.001	"		.02	.01	.03	.05
1900	Remove rocks & debris from grade, by hand	B-62	80	.300	M.S.F.		7.65	1.64	9.29	13.60
1920	With rock picker	B-10S	140	.086			2.45	1.97	4.42	5.90
2000	Root raking and loading, residential, no boulders	B-6	53.30	.450			11.50	3.35	14.85	21.50
2100	With boulders		32	.750			19.20	5.60	24.80	35.50
2200	Municipal, no boulders		200	.120			3.07	.89	3.96	5.70
2300	With boulders		120	.200			5.10	1.49	6.59	9.50
2400	Large commercial, no boulders	B-10B	400	.030			.86	2.06	2.92	3.57
2500	With boulders	"	240	.050			1.43	3.43	4.86	5.95
2600	Rough grade & scarify subsoil to receive topsoil, common earth									
2610	200 H.P. dozer with scarifier	B-11A	80	.200	M.S.F.		5.45	10.30	15.75	19.65
2620	180 H.P. grader with scarifier	B-11L	110	.145			3.98	3.92	7.90	10.40
2700	Clay and till, 200 H.P. dozer with scarifier	B-11A	50	.320			8.75	16.45	25.20	31.50
2710	180 H.P. grader with scarifier	B-11L	40	.400			10.95	10.80	21.75	28.50
3000	Scarify subsoil, residential, skid steer loader w/scarifiers, 50 HP	B-66	32	.250			7.45	4.87	12.32	16.60
3050	Municipal, skid steer loader w/scarifiers, 50 HP	"	120	.067			1.99	1.30	3.29	4.43
3100	Large commercial, 75 HP, dozer w/scarifier	B-10L	240	.050			1.43	1.21	2.64	3.51
3200	Grader with scarifier, 135 H.P.	B-11L	280	.057			1.56	1.54	3.10	4.09
3500	Screen topsoil from stockpile, vibrating screen, wet material (organic)	B-10P	200	.060	C.Y.		1.72	3.45	5.17	6.40
3550	Dry material	"	300	.040			1.14	2.30	3.44	4.27
3600	Mixing with conditioners, manure and peat	B-10R	550	.022			.62	.39	1.01	1.38
3650	Mobilization add for 2 days or less operation	B-34K	3	2.667	Job		66.50	235	301.50	360
3800	Spread conditioned topsoil, 6" deep, by hand	B-1	360	.067	S.Y.	2.48	1.61		4.09	5.25
3850	300 HP dozer	B-10M	27	.444	M.S.F.	268	12.70	38.50	319.20	355
3900	4" deep, by hand	B-1	470	.051	S.Y.	2.24	1.23		3.47	4.38
3920	300 H.P. dozer	B-10M	34	.353	M.S.F.	201	10.10	30.50	241.60	270
3940	180 H.P. grader	B-11L	37	.432	"	201	11.80	11.65	224.45	252
4000	Spread soil conditioners, alum. sulfate, 1#/S.Y., hand push spreader	A-1	17,500	.001	S.Y.	13.15	.01		13.16	14.50
4050	Tractor spreader	B-66	700	.011	M.S.F.	1,450	.34	.22	1,450.56	1,600
4100	Fertilizer, 0.2#/S.Y., push spreader	A-1	17,500	.001	S.Y.	.06	.01		.07	.09
4150	Tractor spreader	B-66	700	.011	M.S.F.	6.65	.34	.22	7.21	8.10
4200	Ground limestone, 1#/S.Y., push spreader	A-1	17,500	.001	S.Y.	.08	.01		.09	.11
4250	Tractor spreader	B-66	700	.011	M.S.F.	12.30	.34	.22	12.86	14.25
4300	Lusoil, 3#/S.Y., push spreader	A-1	17,500	.001	S.Y.	.42	.01		.43	.48
4350	Tractor spreader	B-66	700	.011	M.S.F.	46.50	.34	.22	47.06	52.50
4400	Manure, 18#/S.Y., push spreader	A-1	2,500	.003	S.Y.	2.49	.08	.02	2.59	2.89
4450	Tractor spreader	B-66	280	.029	M.S.F.	277	.85	.56	278.41	305
4500	Perlite, 1" deep, push spreader	A-1	17,500	.001	S.Y.	7.70	.01		7.71	8.45
4550	Tractor spreader	B-66	700	.011	M.S.F.	855	.34	.22	855.56	940
4600	Vermiculite, push spreader	A-1	17,500	.001	S.Y.	2.34	.01		2.35	2.59
4650	Tractor spreader	B-66	700	.011	M.S.F.	260	.34	.22	260.56	287
5000	Spread topsoil, skid steer loader and hand dress	B-62	270	.089	C.Y.	11.20	2.27	.48	13.95	16.35
5100	Articulated loader and hand dress	B-100	320	.037		11.20	1.07	1.56	13.83	15.65
5200	Articulated loader and 75HP dozer	B-10M	500	.024		11.20	.69	2.07	13.96	15.60
5300	Road grader and hand dress	B-11L	1,000	.016		11.20	.44	.43	12.07	13.45
6000	Tilling topsoil, 20 HP tractor, disk harrow, 2" deep	B-66	450	.018	M.S.F.		.53	.35	.88	1.18

(from *Means Site Work & Landscape Cost Data 2002*)

Figure 7.9

Crews

Crew No.	Bare Costs Hr.	Daily	Incl. Subs O & P Hr.	Daily	Cost Per Labor-Hour Bare Costs	Incl. O&P
Crew B-10K	Hr.	Daily	Hr.	Daily	Bare Costs	Incl. O&P
1 Equip. Oper. (med.)	$31.20	$249.60	$47.15	$377.20	$28.62	$43.60
.5 Laborer	23.45	93.80	36.50	146.00		
1 Centr. Water Pump, 6"		198.20		218.00		
1-20 Ft. Suction Hose, 6"		19.50		21.45		
2-50 Ft. Disch. Hoses, 6"		34.80		38.30	21.04	23.15
12 L.H., Daily Totals		$595.90		$800.95	$49.66	$66.75

Crew B-10L	Hr.	Daily	Hr.	Daily	Bare Costs	Incl. O&P
1 Equip. Oper. (med.)	$31.20	$249.60	$47.15	$377.20	$28.62	$43.60
.5 Laborer	23.45	93.80	36.50	146.00		
1 Dozer, 75 H.P.		291.20		320.30	24.27	26.69
12 L.H., Daily Totals		$634.60		$843.50	$52.89	$70.29

Crew B-10M	Hr.	Daily	Hr.	Daily	Bare Costs	Incl. O&P
1 Equip. Oper. (med.)	$31.20	$249.60	$47.15	$377.20	$28.62	$43.60
.5 Laborer	23.45	93.80	36.50	146.00		
1 Dozer, 300 H.P.		1034.00		1137.40	86.17	94.78
12 L.H., Daily Totals		$1377.40		$1660.60	$114.79	$138.38

Crew B-10N	Hr.	Daily	Hr.	Daily	Bare Costs	Incl. O&P
1 Equip. Oper. (med.)	$31.20	$249.60	$47.15	$377.20	$28.62	$43.60
.5 Laborer	23.45	93.80	36.50	146.00		
1 F.E. Loader, T.M., 1.5 C.Y		263.60		289.95	21.97	24.16
12 L.H., Daily Totals		$607.00		$813.15	$50.59	$67.76

Crew B-10O	Hr.	Daily	Hr.	Daily	Bare Costs	Incl. O&P
1 Equip. Oper. (med.)	$31.20	$249.60	$47.15	$377.20	$28.62	$43.60
.5 Laborer	23.45	93.80	36.50	146.00		
1 F.E. Loader, T.M., 2.25 C.Y.		498.40		548.25	41.53	45.69
12 L.H., Daily Totals		$841.80		$1071.45	$70.15	$89.29

Crew B-10P	Hr.	Daily	Hr.	Daily	Bare Costs	Incl. O&P
1 Equip. Oper. (med.)	$31.20	$249.60	$47.15	$377.20	$28.62	$43.60
.5 Laborer	23.45	93.80	36.50	146.00		
1 F.E. Loader, T.M., 2.5 C.Y.		690.60		759.65	57.55	63.31
12 L.H., Daily Totals		$1034.00		$1282.85	$86.17	$106.91

Crew B-10Q	Hr.	Daily	Hr.	Daily	Bare Costs	Incl. O&P
1 Equip. Oper. (med.)	$31.20	$249.60	$47.15	$377.20	$28.62	$43.60
.5 Laborer	23.45	93.80	36.50	146.00		
1 F.E. Loader, T.M., 5 C.Y.		971.20		1068.30	80.93	89.03
12 L.H., Daily Totals		$1314.60		$1591.50	$109.55	$132.63

Crew B-10R	Hr.	Daily	Hr.	Daily	Bare Costs	Incl. O&P
1 Equip. Oper. (med.)	$31.20	$249.60	$47.15	$377.20	$28.62	$43.60
.5 Laborer	23.45	93.80	36.50	146.00		
1 F.E. Loader, W.M., 1 C.Y.		214.40		235.85	17.87	19.65
12 L.H., Daily Totals		$557.80		$759.05	$46.49	$63.25

Crew B-10S	Hr.	Daily	Hr.	Daily	Bare Costs	Incl. O&P
1 Equip. Oper. (med.)	$31.20	$249.60	$47.15	$377.20	$28.62	$43.60
.5 Laborer	23.45	93.80	36.50	146.00		
1 F.E. Loader, W.M., 1.5 C.Y.		276.40		304.05	23.03	25.34
12 L.H., Daily Totals		$619.80		$827.25	$51.65	$68.94

Crew B-10U	Hr.	Daily	Hr.	Daily	Bare Costs	Incl. O&P
1 Equip. Oper. (med.)	$31.20	$249.60	$47.15	$377.20	$28.62	$43.60
.5 Laborer	23.45	93.80	36.50	146.00		
1 F.E. Loader, W.M., 5.5 C.Y.		777.60		855.35	64.80	71.28
12 L.H., Daily Totals		$1121.00		$1378.55	$93.42	$114.88

Crew B-10V	Hr.	Daily	Hr.	Daily	Bare Costs	Incl. O&P
1 Equip. Oper. (med.)	$31.20	$249.60	$47.15	$377.20	$28.62	$43.60
.5 Laborer	23.45	93.80	36.50	146.00		
1 Dozer, 700 H.P.		2924.00		3216.40	243.67	268.03
12 L.H., Daily Totals		$3267.40		$3739.60	$272.29	$311.63

Crew B-10W	Hr.	Daily	Hr.	Daily	Bare Costs	Incl. O&P
1 Equip. Oper. (med.)	$31.20	$249.60	$47.15	$377.20	$28.62	$43.60
.5 Laborer	23.45	93.80	36.50	146.00		
1 Dozer, 105 H.P.		432.60		475.85	36.05	39.66
12 L.H., Daily Totals		$776.00		$999.05	$64.67	$83.26

Crew B-10X	Hr.	Daily	Hr.	Daily	Bare Costs	Incl. O&P
1 Equip. Oper. (med.)	$31.20	$249.60	$47.15	$377.20	$28.62	$43.60
.5 Laborer	23.45	93.80	36.50	146.00		
1 Dozer, 410 H.P.		1374.00		1511.40	114.50	125.95
12 L.H., Daily Totals		$1717.40		$2034.60	$143.12	$169.55

Crew B-10Y	Hr.	Daily	Hr.	Daily	Bare Costs	Incl. O&P
1 Equip. Oper. (med.)	$31.20	$249.60	$47.15	$377.20	$28.62	$43.60
.5 Laborer	23.45	93.80	36.50	146.00		
1 Vibratory Drum Roller		303.40		333.75	25.28	27.81
12 L.H., Daily Totals		$646.80		$856.95	$53.90	$71.41

Crew B-11	Hr.	Daily	Hr.	Daily	Bare Costs	Incl. O&P
1 Equipment Oper. (med.)	$31.20	$249.60	$47.15	$377.20	$27.33	$41.83
1 Laborer	23.45	187.60	36.50	292.00		
16 L.H., Daily Totals		$437.20		$669.20	$27.33	$41.83

Crew B-11A	Hr.	Daily	Hr.	Daily	Bare Costs	Incl. O&P
1 Equipment Oper. (med.)	$31.20	$249.60	$47.15	$377.20	$27.33	$41.83
1 Laborer	23.45	187.60	36.50	292.00		
1 Dozer, 200 H.P.		823.40		905.75	51.46	56.61
16 L.H., Daily Totals		$1260.60		$1574.95	$78.79	$98.44

Crew B-11B	Hr.	Daily	Hr.	Daily	Bare Costs	Incl. O&P
1 Equipment Oper. (med.)	$31.20	$249.60	$47.15	$377.20	$27.33	$41.83
1 Laborer	23.45	187.60	36.50	292.00		
1 Dozer, 200 H.P.		823.40		905.75		
1 Air Powered Tamper		21.10		23.20		
1 Air Compr. 365 C.F.M.		163.00		179.30		
2-50 Ft. Air Hoses, 1.5" Dia.		9.40		10.35	63.56	69.91
16 L.H., Daily Totals		$1454.10		$1787.80	$90.89	$111.74

Crew B-11C	Hr.	Daily	Hr.	Daily	Bare Costs	Incl. O&P
1 Equipment Oper. (med.)	$31.20	$249.60	$47.15	$377.20	$27.33	$41.83
1 Laborer	23.45	187.60	36.50	292.00		
1 Backhoe Loader, 48 H.P.		178.60		196.45	11.16	12.28
16 L.H., Daily Totals		$615.80		$865.65	$38.49	$54.11

(from *Means Site Work & Landscape Cost Data 2002*)

Figure 7.10

G3030 Storm Sewer

The Headwall Systems are listed in concrete and two different stone wall materials for two different backfill slope conditions. The backfill slope directly affects the length of the wing walls. Walls are listed for three different culvert sizes 30″, 48″ and 60″ diameter. Excavation and backfill are included in the system components, and are figured from an elevation 2′ below the bottom of the pipe.

System Components	QUANTITY	UNIT	COST PER EACH		
			MAT.	INST.	TOTAL
SYSTEM G3030 310 2000					
HEADWALL C.I.P. CONCRETE FOR 30″ PIPE, 3′ LONG WING WALLS					
Excavation, hydraulic backhoe, 3/8 C.Y. bucket	2.500	C.Y.		151.20	151.20
Formwork, 2 uses	157.000	SFCA	241.40	1,230.49	1,471.89
Reinforcing in place including dowels	45.000	Lb.	20.25	57.60	77.85
Concrete, 3000 psi	2.600	C.Y.	197.60		197.60
Place concrete, spread footings, direct chute	2.600	C.Y.		89.49	89.49
Backfill, dozer	2.500	C.Y.		33.32	33.32
TOTAL			459.25	1,562.10	2,021.35

G3030 310	Headwalls	COST PER EACH		
		MAT.	INST.	TOTAL
2000	Headwall, 1-1/2 to 1 slope soil, C.I.P. conc, 30″pipe, 3′long wing walls	460	1,550	2,010
2020	Pipe size 36″, 3′-6″ long wing walls	575	1,900	2,475
2040	Pipe size 42″, 4′ long wing walls	695	2,200	2,895
2060	Pipe size 48″, 4′-6″ long wing walls	840	2,575	3,415
2080	Pipe size 54″, 5′-0″ long wing walls	995	2,975	3,970
2100	Pipe size 60″, 5′-6″ long wing walls	1,150	3,375	4,525
2120	Pipe size 72″, 6′-6″ long wing walls	1,550	4,350	5,900
2140	Pipe size 84″, 7′-6″ long wing walls	1,975	5,350	7,325
2500	$16/ton stone, pipe size 30″, 3′ long wing walls	71.50	570	641.50
2520	Pipe size 36″, 3′-6″ long wing walls	92	685	777
2540	Pipe size 42″, 4′ long wing walls	116	810	926
2560	Pipe size 48″, 4′-6″ long wing walls	143	955	1,098
2580	Pipe size 54″, 5′ long wing walls	172	1,100	1,272
2600	Pipe size 60″, 5′-6″ long wing walls	204	1,275	1,479
2620	Pipe size 72″, 6′-6″ long wing walls	282	1,700	1,982
2640	Pipe size 84″, 7′-6″ long wing walls	370	2,175	2,545
3000	$32/ton stone, pipe size 30″, 3′ long wing walls	143	570	713
3020	Pipe size 36″, 3′-6″ long wing walls	184	685	869
3040	Pipe size 42″, 4′ long wing walls	231	810	1,041
3060	Pipe size 48″, 4′-6″ long wing walls	285	955	1,240
3080	Pipe size 54″, 5′ long wing walls	345	1,100	1,445
3100	Pipe size 60″, 5′-6″ long wing walls	410	1,275	1,685
3120	Pipe size 72″, 6′-6″ long wing walls	565	1,700	2,265
3140	Pipe size 84″, 7′-6″ long wing walls	740	2,175	2,915
3500	$48/ton stone, pipe size 30″, 3′ long wing walls	215	570	785
3520	Pipe size 36″, 3′-6″ long wing walls	276	685	961

(from *Means Site Work & Landscape Cost Data 2002*)

Figure 7.11

02700 | Bases, Ballasts, Pavements & Appurtenances

02775 | Sidewalks

		CREW	DAILY OUTPUT	LABOR-HOURS	UNIT	2002 BARE COSTS MAT.	LABOR	EQUIP.	TOTAL	TOTAL INCL O&P	
275	0010 **SIDEWALKS, DRIVEWAYS, & PATIOS** No base										275
	0020 Asphaltic concrete, 2″ thick	B-37	720	.067	S.Y.	3.71	1.66	.16	5.53	6.80	
	0100 2-1/2″ thick	″	660	.073	″	4.70	1.81	.18	6.69	8.15	
	0110 Bedding for brick or stone, mortar, 1″ thick	D-1	300	.053	S.F.	.32	1.44		1.76	2.56	
	0120 2″ thick	″	200	.080		.80	2.16		2.96	4.19	
	0130 Sand, 2″ thick	B-18	8,000	.003		.13	.07	.01	.21	.27	
	0140 4″ thick	″	4,000	.006		.27	.14	.01	.42	.54	
	0300 Concrete, 3000 psi, CIP, 6 x 6 - W1.4 x W1.4 mesh,										
	0310 broomed finish, no base, 4″ thick	B-24	600	.040	S.F.	1.15	1.10		2.25	2.95	
	0350 5″ thick		545	.044		1.53	1.21		2.74	3.54	
	0400 6″ thick		510	.047		1.79	1.29		3.08	3.94	
	0440 For other finishes, see Div. 033-450										
	0450 For bank run gravel base, 4″ thick, add	B-18	2,500	.010	S.F.	.37	.23	.02	.62	.79	
	0520 8″ thick, add	″	1,600	.015		.74	.36	.03	1.13	1.42	
	0550 Exposed aggregate finish, add to above, minimum	B-24	1,875	.013		.07	.35		.42	.62	
	0600 Maximum		455	.053		.23	1.44		1.67	2.47	
	0700 Patterned surface, add to above min.		1,200	.020			.55		.55	.84	
	0710 Maximum		500	.048			1.31		1.31	2.01	

02778 | Steps

		CREW	DAILY OUTPUT	LABOR-HOURS	UNIT	2002 BARE COSTS MAT.	LABOR	EQUIP.	TOTAL	TOTAL INCL O&P	
280	0010 **STEPS** Incl. excav., borrow & concrete base, where applicable										280
	0100 Brick steps	B-24	35	.686	LF Riser	8.20	18.75		26.95	37.50	
	0200 Railroad ties	2 Clab	25	.640		2.75	15		17.75	26.50	
	0300 Bluestone treads, 12″ x 2″ or 12″ x 1-1/2″	B-24	30	.800		20	22		42	55.50	
	0500 Concrete, cast in place, see division 03310-240										
	0600 Precast concrete, see division 03480-800										

02780 | Unit Pavers

		CREW	DAILY OUTPUT	LABOR-HOURS	UNIT	2002 BARE COSTS MAT.	LABOR	EQUIP.	TOTAL	TOTAL INCL O&P	
800	0010 **STONE PAVERS**										800
	1100 Flagging, bluestone, irregular, 1″ thick,	D-1	81	.198	S.F.	4.20	5.35		9.55	12.80	
	1110 1-1/2″ thick		90	.178		4.96	4.80		9.76	12.80	
	1120 Pavers, 1/2″ thick		110	.145		7	3.93		10.93	13.70	
	1130 3/4″ thick		95	.168		8.90	4.55		13.45	16.80	
	1140 1″ thick		81	.198		9.55	5.35		14.90	18.70	
	1150 Snapped random rectangular, 1″ thick		92	.174		6.35	4.70		11.05	14.20	
	1200 1-1/2″ thick		85	.188		7.65	5.10		12.75	16.20	
	1250 2″ thick		83	.193		8.90	5.20		14.10	17.80	
	1300 Slate, natural cleft, irregular, 3/4″ thick		92	.174		4.51	4.70		9.21	12.15	
	1310 1″ thick		85	.188		5.25	5.10		10.35	13.60	

(from *Means Site Work & Landscape Cost Data 2002*)

Figure 7.12

The quantity takeoff and cost analysis sheet for the hard construction portion of the project are shown in Figures 7.14 and 7.15. In Chapter 10 detailed instructions on the use of all Means cost data are presented.

Plantings

The takeoff for plant materials is primarily a counting process. A plant list is often provided on the landscape plan or in the specifications. The quantities required may or may not be listed. In either case, the estimator should verify counts carefully to avoid omissions or duplication when determining quantities of plant material.

Plant and Landscape Material

In the sample estimate, the plant list and quantities have been provided by the designer. When the quantities are checked, these items can be transferred to a form that will allow for comparative pricing. Costs for plant material can vary greatly by region and season and should be obtained from local sources. An example of plant pricing is shown in Figure 7.16. Three vendors are used and, where possible, costs are compared. In addition the owner wishes to protect trees by creating designated mulched areas at tree bases. It will be necessary to install a metal edging and filter fabric weed barrier.

In this example, material and labor costs for plantings are estimated separately. To figure labor costs, the plant material is first divided into size categories so that appropriate costs can be applied to each size. Installation costs are dependent on root ball size and weight. An example of a labor estimate for plant material is shown in Figure 7.17. The labor costs in this example were derived by working back from crew cost and daily productivity figures (see Figure

Computing Work Days					
Item	Line #	Quantity	Unit	Labor-hours/Unit	Total Labor-hours
Gravel Base	02775-275-0450	453	SF	.010	4.53
Concrete Slab	02775-275-0310	453	SF	.040	18.12
Blue Stone Bedding	02775-275-0110	453	SF	.053	24.01
Flagging	02780-800-1250	453	SF	.193	87.43
Steps	02778-280-0300	25	LF	.800	20.00
			Total Labor-hours		154.09
			Total Labor-days (÷ 8)		19.26
			Total Days (2 workers)		10 days

Figure 7.13

QUANTITY SHEET

PROJECT: Office Building

LOCATION: ARCHITECT: DATE: 2002

TAKE OFF BY: SHF EXTENSIONS BY: SHF CHECKED BY: SHF

Description	NO.	L	W	D	AREA	Unit	RISERS	Unit	LENGTH	Unit	VOLUME	Unit
Hard Construction												
Bluestone		20'	8.5'		1 7 0	S.F.						
Flagging		16.5'	5'		8 3							
		12.5'	6.5'		8 1							
		irregular			2 5							
		9'	8'		7 2							
					4 3 1	S.F.						
5% waste					2 2	S.F.						
Total					4 5 3	S.F.						
Steps	5	5'					2 5	L.F.				
Concrete Slab				4"	4 5 3	S.F.						
Gravel Base				4"	4 5 3	S.F.						
Wood RR Ties												
Steps	14	4'					5 6	L.F.				
Edging		241'							2 4 1	L.F.		
Retaining Wall 2'		25'							2 5	L.F.		
	4'	60'							6 0	L.F.		
Fieldstone Edging		137'							1 3 7	L.F.		
Crushed Bluestone		227'	5'	3"	1 1 3 5	S.F.					11	C.Y.

Figure 7.14

154

COST ANALYSIS

PROJECT: Office Building   CLASSIFICATION: ESTIMATE NO: 02-1
LOCATION: ARCHITECT: As Shown   DATE: 2002
TAKE OFF BY: SHF   QUANTITIES BY: SHF   PRICES BY: RSM   EXTENSIONS BY: BB   CHECKED BY:

DESCRIPTION	SOURCE	QUANT.	UNIT	MATERIAL COST	MATERIAL TOTAL	LABOR COST	LABOR TOTAL	EQUIPMENT COST	EQUIPMENT TOTAL	SUBCONTRACT COST	SUBCONTRACT TOTAL	TOTAL COST	TOTAL TOTAL
Hard Construction													
Concrete													
4" Slab	02775 275 0310	453	S.F.							2.95	1,336		
4" Gravel Base	02775 275 0450	453	S.F.							0.79	358		
Bluestone													
Bedding	02775 275 0110	453	S.F.							2.56	1,160		
Flagging	800 1250	453	S.F.							17.80	8,063		
Steps	02778 280 0300	25	L.F.							55.50	1,388		
RR Tie													
Steps	02778 280 0200	56	L.F.							26.50	1,484		
Edging	02945 310 0600	241	L.F.							7.10	1,711		
Wood Tie Retaining Wall													
2' High	G2040 250 7000	25	L.F.							30.70	768		
4' High	G2040 250 7400	60	L.F.							69.50	4,170		
Fieldstone Edge	2 CLAB, 4 Hours	137	L.F.				188						
Crushed Bluestone, 3"													
Material	02775 275 1050	1135	S.F.	0.20	227								
Labor & Equipment	B-62 Crew	0.05	Day				307		65				
Total Hard Construction					$ 227		$ 495		$ 65		$ 20,438		$ 21,225

Figure 7.15

6.10) to obtain the planting cost. Costs for planting may also be easily obtained from *Means Site Work & Landscape Cost Data* in the "Planting" section of the landscaping unit price pages. Also useful is the appropriate crew and daily output data from the book, which can be used for scheduling purposes. See Chapter 10 of this book, "Using Means Site Work & Landscape Cost Data," for more information on the practical applications of crew and daily output data.

With simple calculations, the estimator can plan the duration of the planting activities based on the production rate of a particular crew. The durations for all activities should be calculated in the same manner in order to schedule the project and determine manpower allocation. Chapter 9 of this book, "Job Planning and Scheduling," provides a further explanation of scheduling methods.

Horticultural Material

Quantities of horticultural materials can be determined from several different sources. The specifications often include required quantities, such as "five pounds of ground limestone per hundred square feet." Quantities and costs for the sample project are shown in Figure 7.18, Cost Analysis Sheet for Planting, where they are listed by total area.

For plant beds and tree pits, excavation volumes must be measured and then offset by the root ball volumes in order to determine the required volume (quantity) of topsoil. This can be a tedious task requiring numerous repetitive calculations. The use of estimating aids such as the Surtee's Charts will help cut down the number of such calculations. An excerpt from the Surtee's Charts is shown in Figure 7.19. See the Appendix for a more extensive listing.

The measured area of the planting beds is also used to determine the volume of mulch needed. For the sample project, three inches of pine bark is specified for all planting beds. The chart in Figure 5.7 can be used to determine the quantity of mulch required. Costs can be determined by volume or by area (based on specific depth).

For Example:

Mulch depth	3 inches
Planting bed area	3,353 S.F.
Tree protection area	250 S.F.
Cubic yards per M.S.F. (at 1″ depth)	3.5 C.Y.
Total C.Y. required	38 C.Y.

For the sample project, the costs are from Figure 7.20, line 02910-500-0100. For the mulch requirements of individual tree pits, the surface area can be determined using the Surtee's Charts.

Lawns

In the sample estimate, costs for the seeded lawn have been determined by estimating the separate components: grading, spreading topsoil, horticultural material, and labor. The experienced landscape estimator will often develop a complete "assemblies" price based on the costs from past projects. This complete cost can be used as a comparison to assure that the unit price estimate is complete. For example, assemblies costs for lawns are shown in Figure 7.21, from *Means Site Work & Landscape Cost Data*. The most appropriate assembly for the project is line 1240. The complete assembly cost is $600 per thousand square feet. (See Chapter 10 for a complete discussion of the information presented in *Means Site Work & Landscape Cost Data*). This figure can be used as a cross-check for the costs as determined in the sample estimate.

QUANTITY SHEET

SHEET NO   1 of 7
ESTIMATE NO.: 02-1

PROJECT: Office Building
LOCATION: ARCHITECT: DATE: 2002
TAKE OFF BY: SHF EXTENSIONS BY: CHECKED BY: SHF

Description	NO.	DIMENSIONS		Vendor A	Unit	Vendor B	Unit	Vendor C	Unit	Total		Unit
Trees												
Pinus strobus	5	8'-10'	B&B	1 1 9				1 3 0		5 9 5		
Shrubs												
Cotoneaster horizontalis	12	12"-15"	Pot	1 3						1 5 6		
Ilex glabra	21	2-1/2'-3'	B&B	3 6						7 5 6		
Juniper												
Horizontalis andorra	39	18"-24"	B&B or Cont	1 8						7 0 2		
Horizontalis Blue Rug	12	15"-18"	B&B or Cont	1 3						1 5 6		
Virginia Grey Owl	24	18"-24"	B&B or Cont	1 8						4 3 2		
Chinensis Sea Green	31	18"-24"	B&B or Cont	2 0						6 2 0		
Myrica pennsylvanica	16	18"-24"	B&B or Cont	2 2						3 5 2		
Taxus densiformis	12	2'-2-1/2'	B&B	3 2						3 8 4		
Viburnum sieboldi	3	5'-6'	B&B	5 0						1 5 0		
Groundcover												
Ajuga "Bronze Beauty"	36	3" Pot		9 5		1 0 0		9 5		3 4 2 0		
Alyssum saxatile	12	2 Qt.	Pot	3 0 0		2 5 0		3 2 5		3 0		
Arctostaphylos uva-ursi	36	3" Pot		1 3 0				1 4 3		3 4 2 0		
Comptonia peregrina	100	2-1/2"	Pot					9 5		9 5		
Euonymus f. Colorata	1300	3" Pot		1		9 5		7 5		9 7 5		
Sedum spectabilis	24	2 Qt.	Pot			2 5 0				6 0		
Subtotal										5 5 3 1		
Delivery				8 5		2 0		2 5		1 3 5		
TOTAL										5 6 6 6 4 0		

Figure 7.16

Sample estimate costs:

	Material	Labor	Equip.
Grading		$ 270	$ 57
Place Topsoil (40% of total)		$ 137	$ 106
Seed, Fertilizer, Lime	$ 95		
Installation		$ 614	$ 179
	$ 95	$ 1021	$ 342
Total cost	$ 1,363		
Total area	5,650 S.F.		
Cost per M.S.F.	$ 241		

Note that the assemblies cost in Figure 7.21 includes $227.55 as a material cost for topsoil. This component is not required in the sample project. When the cost for topsoil is deducted, the assembly price is $372 per thousand square feet, which is within tolerable variances from the "actual" cost. Assemblies costs are useful not only for crosschecking purposes, but also for establishing budgets. However, for detailed estimating, the assemblies method may not allow for the variation needed to meet specific project requirements. For example, typically new lawn installations require the first time mowing by the installing contractor. The cost of this one-time mowing may be listed as a separate item.

Estimate Summary

At completion of site work, hard construction and planting takeoffs and summaries, all of the work has been identified, listed, and priced. All vendor quotes and subcontractor bids should be in hand (ideally, but not always realistically) and all costs should be determined "in house."

The costs for the major portions of the landscape work can now be transferred to an Estimate Summary form as shown in Figure 7.22. You may observe this appears much like the "overviews" summary (See Figure 7.2) that started the

Plant	Quantity	Unit Labor Cost	Total Cost	Crew	Daily Output	Time	
1 Groundcover	1472	$ .90	$1327	B-1	600	2.5	days
Potted Plants (approx. 1 gal.)	48	4.42	212	B-1	130	0.4	
Potted Plants (approx. 3 gal.)	122	6.53	796	B-1	80	1.5	
B & B Plants (approx. 18" ball)	15	17.69	265	B-1	30	0.5	
Trees	5	74.00	369	B-17	10	0.5	
		73.00*	292				
			$3,261			5.4	

* Equipment Cost

Figure 7.17

COST ANALYSIS

PROJECT: Office Building CLASSIFICATION:
LOCATION: ARCHITECT: ESTIMATE NO: 02-1
TAKE OFF BY: SHF QUANTITIES BY: SHF PRICES BY: Means DATE: 2002
EXTENSIONS BY: BB CHECKED BY: S.H.F.

DESCRIPTION	SOURCE/ DIMENSIONS	QUANT.	UNIT	MATERIAL COST	MATERIAL TOTAL	LABOR COST	LABOR TOTAL	EQUIPMENT COST	EQUIPMENT TOTAL	SUBCONTRACT COST	SUBCONTRACT TOTAL	TOTAL COST	TOTAL TOTAL
PLANTINGS													
Trees, Shrubs, Groundcover					5,666		2,969		292				
Metal Edge (Tree Protection)	02945 310 0051	94	L.F.	2.23	210	1.48	139						
Horticultural Materials													
Plant Beds													
Peat	4 C.Y. Bales	3	Ea.	5.25	16								
Fertilizer	50# 5-10-5	1	Ea.	10.15	10								
Bone Meal	25# Bag	1	Ea.	16.50	17								
Pine Bark Mulch	02910 500 0100	416	S.Y.	2.33	969	1.88	782						
Weed Barrier - Filter Fabric	02910 500 1050	43	S.Y.	0.74	32	0.19	8						
Lawn - 5650 S.F.													
Seed	25# Bag	1	Ea.	55.00	55								
Fertilizer	50# Bag	2	Ea.	12.50	25								
Lime	50# Bag	6	Ea.	2.55	15								
Installation	B-6 Crew	1	Day				614		179				
Initial Mowing	A-1 Crew	0.5	Day				94		30				
Total Plantings					$ 7,015		$ 4,606		$ 501				$ 12,122

Figure 7.18

159

Surtee's Tree Pits and Tree Balls
Cubic Feet Per Tree
For Estimating Excavation and Top Soil

Depths		1'	1¼'	1½'	1¾'	2'	2¼'	2½'	2¾'	3'	3¼'	3½'
Tree Pit	1'	.94	1.47	2.13	2.88	3.77	4.78	5.89	7.13	8.48	9.96	11.5
Ball		.68	1.07	1.54	2.10	2.73	3.42	4.30	5.20	6.19	7.38	8.4
Tree Pit	1¼'	1.16	1.85	2.65	3.60	4.71	5.93	7.37	8.90	10.6	12.4	14.4
Ball		.85	1.35	1.93	2.63	3.42	4.29	5.36	6.49	7.7	9.2	10.5
Tree Pit	1½'	1.40	2.22	3.08	4.32	5.65	7.16	8.83	10.7	12.7	15.0	17.3
Ball		1.02	1.62	2.32	3.15	4.10	5.19	6.39	7.8	9.2	10.9	12.7
Tree Pit	1¾'	1.65	2.58	3.70	5.04	6.60	8.20	10.3	12.5	14.8	17.4	20.2
Ball		1.20	1.88	3.72	3.68	4.78	6.03	7.5	9.1	10.7	12.7	14.7
Tree Pit	2'	1.87	2.95	4.26	5.76	7.54	9.55	11.8	14.3	17.0	19.9	23.0
Ball		1.38	2.15	3.10	4.20	5.49	6.92	8.5	10.4	12.3	14.5	16.8
Tree Pit	2¼'	2.10	3.32	4.78	6.48	8.48	10.7	13.2	16.0	19.1	22.4	26.0
Ball		1.55	2.43	3.48	4.73	6.19	7.5	9.6	11.7	13.8	16.4	18.9
Tree Pit	2½'	2.34	3.69	5.30	7.20	9.42	11.9	14.7	17.8	21.2	24.9	28.9
Ball		1.70	2.70	3.87	5.25	6.89	8.7	10.7	13.0	15.4	18.2	21.0
Tree Pit	2¾'	2.57	4.06	5.83	7.92	10.3	13.1	16.2	19.6	23.3	27.4	31.8
Ball		1.87	2.98	4.25	5.77	7.6	9.6	11.8	14.3	17.0	20.0	23.1
Tree Pit	3'	2.81	4.43	6.37	8.64	11.3	14.3	17.7	21.4	25.4	29.9	34.6
Ball		2.05	3.24	4.65	6.30	8.3	10.5	12.9	15.6	18.6	21.8	25.2
Tree Pit	3¼'	3.00	4.80	6.90	9.36	12.2	15.5	19.2	23.2	27.5	32.4	37.5
Ball		2.21	3.50	5.03	6.83	8.9	11.4	14.0	16.9	20.1	23.6	27.3
Tree Pit	3½'	3.28	5.17	7.41	10.1	13.2	16.7	20.7	25.0	29.6	34.9	40.4
Ball		2.39	3.77	5.42	7.4	9.6	12.2	15.0	18.2	21.7	25.4	29.4
Tree Pit	3¾'	3.50	5.53	7.96	10.8	14.2	17.9	22.2	26.7	31.7	37.1	43.3
Ball		2.56	4.04	3.80	7.9	10.3	13.1	16.1	19.5	23.2	27.2	31.5
Tree Pit	4'	3.74	5.90	8.50	11.5	15.1	19.1	23.7	28.5	33.8	39.9	46.2
Ball		2.73	4.31	6.19	8.4	11.0	14.0	17.2	20.8	24.8	29.0	33.6
Tree Pit	4¼'	3.97	6.28	9.01	12.3	16.0	20.3	25.1	30.3	36.0	42.3	49.1
Ball		2.90	4.58	6.58	8.9	11.8	14.8	18.3	22.1	26.3	30.8	35.7
Tree Pit	4½'	4.20	6.64	9.55	13.0	17.0	21.5	26.6	32.0	38.1	44.8	52.0
Ball		3.07	4.85	6.97	9.5	12.4	15.7	19.4	23.4	27.8	32.6	37.8
Tree Pit	4¾'	4.43	7.00	10.0	13.7	17.9	22.7	28.0	33.8	40.2	47.3	54.9
Ball		3.24	5.12	7.4	10.0	13.0	16.5	20.4	24.7	29.1	34.2	40.0
Tree Pit	5'	4.68	7.38	10.6	14.4	18.8	23.9	29.8	35.6	42.3	49.9	57.7
Ball		3.41	5.38	7.8	10.5	13.7	17.4	21.5	26.0	30.9	36.1	42.1
Tree Pit	5½'	5.14	8.12	11.7	15.8	20.7	26.3	32.4	39.2	46.7	54.8	63.5
Ball		3.76	5.93	8.5	11.6	15.1	19.1	23.7	28.6	34.0	40.0	46.3
Tree Pit	6'	5.41	8.86	12.7	17.3	22.6	28.7	35.4	42.8	50.9	57.8	69.3
Ball		4.10	6.46	9.3	12.6	16.5	20.9	25.9	31.2	37.1	43.6	50.5

Figure 7.19

		02890	Traffic Signs & Signals	CREW	DAILY OUTPUT	LABOR-HOURS	UNIT	2002 BARE COSTS				TOTAL INCL O&P	
								MAT.	LABOR	EQUIP.	TOTAL		
900	0200		Semi-actuated, detectors in side street only, add	L-9	.81	44.444	Total	2,525	1,225		3,750	4,725	900
	0300		Fully-actuated, detectors in all streets, add		.49	73.469		7,100	2,000		9,100	11,100	
	0400		For pedestrian pushbutton, add		.70	51.429		3,425	1,400		4,825	6,050	
	0500		Optically programmed signal only, add per head		1.64	21.951		2,625	600		3,225	3,875	
	0600		School flashing system, programmed	▼	.41	87.805	Signal	6,300	2,400		8,700	10,800	

02900 | Planting

		02905	Transplanting	CREW	DAILY OUTPUT	LABOR-HOURS	UNIT	2002 BARE COSTS				TOTAL INCL O&P	
								MAT.	LABOR	EQUIP.	TOTAL		
725	0010	**PLANTING**	Moving shrubs on site, 12" ball	B-62	28	.857	Ea.	22	4.67		26.67	38.50	725
	0100		24" ball	"	22	1.091		28	5.95		33.95	49.50	
	0300		Moving trees on site, 36" ball	B-6	3.75	6.400		164	47.50		211.50	305	
	0400		60" ball	"	1	24		615	179		794	1,150	
925	0010	**TREE REMOVAL**											925
	0100		Dig & lace, shrubs, broadleaf evergreen, 18"-24"	B-1	55	.436	Ea.		10.55		10.55	16.40	
	0200		2'-3'	"	35	.686			16.55		16.55	25.50	
	0300		3'-4'	B-6	30	.800			20.50	5.95	26.45	38	
	0400		4'-5'	"	20	1.200			30.50	8.95	39.45	57	
	1000		Deciduous, 12"-15"	B-1	110	.218			5.25		5.25	8.20	
	1100		18"-24"		65	.369			8.90		8.90	13.85	
	1200		2'-3'		55	.436			10.55		10.55	16.40	
	1300		3'-4'	B-6	50	.480			12.25	3.57	15.82	23	
	2000		Evergreeen, 18"-24"	B-1	55	.436			10.55		10.55	16.40	
	2100		2'-0" to 2'-6"		50	.480			11.60		11.60	18	
	2200		2'-6" to 3'-0"		35	.686			16.55		16.55	25.50	
	2300		3'-0" to 3'-6"		20	1.200			29		29	45	
	3000		Trees, deciduous, small, 2'-3'		55	.436			10.55		10.55	16.40	
	3100		3'-4'	B-6	50	.480			12.25	3.57	15.82	23	
	3200		4'-5'		35	.686			17.55	5.10	22.65	32.50	
	3300		5'-6'		30	.800			20.50	5.95	26.45	38	
	4000		Shade, 5'-6'		50	.480			12.25	3.57	15.82	23	
	4100		6'-8'		35	.686			17.55	5.10	22.65	32.50	
	4200		8'-10'		25	.960			24.50	7.15	31.65	46	
	4300		2" caliper		12	2			51	14.90	65.90	95	
	5000		Evergreen, 4'-5'		35	.686			17.55	5.10	22.65	32.50	
	5100		5'-6'		25	.960			24.50	7.15	31.65	46	
	5200		6'-7'		19	1.263			32.50	9.40	41.90	60	
	5300		7'-8'		15	1.600			41	11.90	52.90	76	
	5400		8'-10'	▼	11	2.182	▼		56	16.25	72.25	104	

		02910	Plant Preparation										
500	0010	**MULCH**											500
	0100		Aged barks, 3" deep, hand spread	1 Clab	100	.080	S.Y.	2.33	1.88		4.21	5.50	
	0150		Skid steer loader	B-63	13.50	2.963	M.S.F.	259	73	9.70	341.70	410	
	0200		Hay, 1" deep, hand spread	1 Clab	475	.017	S.Y.	.40	.39		.79	1.05	

(from *Means Site Work & Landscape Cost Data 2002*)

Figure 7.20

G2050 Landscaping

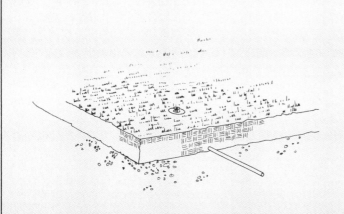

The Lawn Systems listed include different types of seeding, sodding and ground covers for flat and sloped areas. Costs are given per thousand square feet for different size jobs; residential, small commercial and large commercial. The size of the job relates to the type and productivity of the equipment being used. Components include furnishing and spreading screened loam, spreading fertilizer and limestone and mulching planted and seeded surfaces. Sloped surfaces include jute mesh or staking depending on the type of cover.

System Components	QUANTITY	UNIT	COST PER M.S.F.		
			MAT.	INST.	TOTAL
SYSTEM G2050 410 1000					
LAWN, FLAT AREA, SEEDED, TURF MIX, RESIDENTIAL					
Scarify subsoil, residential, skid steer loader	1.000	M.S.F.		16.60	16.60
Root raking, residential, no boulders	1.000	M.S.F.		21.39	21.39
Spread topsoil, skid steer loader	18.500	C.Y.	227.55	74.56	302.11
Spread ground limestone, push spreader	110.000	S.Y.	9.90	2.20	12.10
Spread fertilizer, push spreader	110.000	S.Y.	7.70	2.20	9.90
Till topsoil, 26" rototiller	110.000	S.Y.		39.60	39.60
Rake topsoil, screened loam	1.000	M.S.F.		19.45	19.45
Roll topsoil, push roller	18.500	C.Y.		1.67	1.67
Seeding, turf mix, push spreader	1.000	M.S.F.	6.90	36.50	43.40
Straw, mulch	110.000	S.Y.	36.30	67.10	103.40
TOTAL			288.35	281.27	569.62

G2050 410	Lawns & Ground Cover	COST PER M.S.F.		
		MAT.	INST.	TOTAL
1000	Lawn, flat area, seeded, turf mix, residential	288	282	570
1040	Small commercial	292	305	597
1080	Large commercial	300	260	560
1200	Shade mix, residential	292	282	574
1240	Small commercial	295	305	600
1280	Large commercial	310	260	570
1400	Utility mix, residential	294	282	576
1440	Small commercial	297	305	602
1480	Large commercial	330	260	590
2000	Sod, bluegrass, residential	530	655	1,185
2040	Small commercial	510	390	900
2080	Large commercial	485	315	800
2200	Bentgrass, residential	870	297	1,167
2240	Small commercial	810	385	1,195
2280	Large commercial	770	320	1,090
2400	Ground cover, english ivy, residential	1,050	735	1,785

(from *Means Site Work & Landscape Cost Data* 2002)

Figure 7.21

take-off process. In addition to the items listed in the pricing sheets, sales tax as required and certain other types of work may be specified. In this case, tree pruning (for all trees within the work area) and general site cleanup are required. The estimator must determine the extent of the work, as well as the appropriate crew and duration. For the sample project the equivalent of a B-85 crew (See Figure 7.23) is chosen for one day. Based on the site visit, the estimator feels that two laborers are required. One is subtracted from the daily crew cost in Figure 7.22.

For this example, overhead and profit are applied as in *Means Site Work & Landscape Cost Data*, and explained in Chapter 10. Ten percent is added to material and equipment costs for handling and ten percent is added to subcontract costs to cover supervision, management, and profit. However, 55.6% is added to the bare labor costs (shown in Figure 7.24) to cover employment taxes, insurance, office overhead, and profit.

The markups for each individual company will vary and should be calculated based on specific requirements and conditions. A discussion of types of costs is included in Chapter 6.

At this stage, the estimator has a final number ("Direct Costs Subtotal" in Figure 7.22) with which to work. Now is the time when sound judgment and experience are used to determine the bid price. Adjustments can be made (up and down) depending upon certain factors that may affect a final decision: the risk involved, competition from other bidders, thoroughness of the plans and specs, and above all, the years of experience—the qualification to make such a judgment. Some firms are so scientific in their calculations that every quoted price includes a lucky number.

A great deal of success in bidding can be attributed to the proper choice of jobs to bid. A landscape firm can go broke estimating every available job. The company must be able to recognize which jobs are too risky and when the competition is too keen, while not overlooking those which can be profitable. Again, knowledge of the marketplace and *experience* are the keys to successful bidding.

The primary purpose of this sample estimate (and this text) has not been to tell the reader how much an item will cost, but instead, how to develop a consistent and thorough approach to the estimating process. If such a pattern is developed, employing consistency, attention to detail, experience, and above all *common sense*, accurate estimates will follow.

If an estimate is thorough, organized, neat, and concise, the benefits go beyond winning contracts. The information and data that is developed will be useful throughout a project—for purchasing, change orders, cost accounting and control, and development of historical costs.

CONDENSED ESTIMATE SUMMARY

PROJECT: Office Building		ESTIMATE NO: 02-1
LOCATION:	TOTAL AREA/VOLUME	DATE: 2002
ARCHITECT:	COST PER S.F./C.F.	NO. OF STORIES
PRICES BY: RSM	EXTENSIONS BY: SHC	CHECKED BY:

DESCRIPTION	MATERIAL	LABOR	EQUIPMENT	SUBCONTRACT	TOTAL
Sitework	$ 4,409	$ 2,168	$ 455	$ 26,070	$ 33,102
Headwalls					
Rip Rap					
Grading					
Erosion Control					
Fountains/Aerator					
Flagpole					
Hard Construction	227	495	65	20,438	21,225
Concrete					
Bluestone Patios					
Wood RR Ties					
-RR Tie Steps					
-RR Tie Retaining Wall					
-RR Tie Edging					
Fieldstone Edging					
Crushed Bluestone					
Plantings	7,015	4,606	501		12,122
Trees, Shrubs, Groundcover					
Horticultural & Misc. Materials					
-Weed Barrier Filter Fabric					
-Tree Mulch Cover					
-Metal Edging					
Lawn					
-First Mowing					
Miscellaneous:		825	694		1,519
Pruning & Cleanup					
(B-85 Crew, 1 Day, minus 1 laborer)					
Sales Tax on Material (5%)	583				583
Direct Costs Subtotal	12,234	8,094	1,715	46,508	68,551
Overhead & Profit	1,223	4,500	172	4,651	10,546
10% M, 55.6% L, 10% E, 10% S					
TOTAL	$ 13,457	$ 12,594	$ 1,887	$ 51,159	$ 79,097

Figure 7.22

Crew No.	Bare Costs		Incl. Subs O & P		Cost Per Labor-Hour	
Crew B-76	Hr.	Daily	Hr.	Daily	Bare Costs	Incl. O&P
1 Dock Builder Foreman	$31.80	$254.40	$53.25	$426.00	$30.24	$48.98
5 Dock Builders	29.80	1192.00	49.90	1996.00		
2 Equip. Oper. (crane)	32.35	517.60	48.90	782.40		
1 Equip. Oper. Oiler	26.65	213.20	40.25	322.00		
1 Crawler Crane, 50 Ton		1027.00		1129.70		
1 Barge, 400 Ton		374.80		412.30		
1 Hammer, 15K Ft. Lbs.		320.60		352.65		
60 L.F. Leads, 15K Ft. Lbs.		456.00		501.60		
1 Air Compr., 600 C.F.M.		263.60		289.95		
2-50 Ft. Air Hoses, 3" Dia.		35.40		38.95	34.41	37.85
72 L.H., Daily Totals		$4654.60		$6251.55	$64.65	$86.83
Crew B-77	Hr.	Daily	Hr.	Daily	Bare Costs	Incl. O&P
1 Labor Foreman	$25.45	$203.60	$39.60	$316.80	$24.02	$37.23
3 Laborers	23.45	562.80	36.50	876.00		
1 Truck Driver (light)	24.30	194.40	37.05	296.40		
1 Crack Cleaner, 25 H.P.		64.40		70.85		
1 Crack Filler, Trailer Mtd.		138.20		152.00		
1 Flatbed Truck, 3 Ton		182.40		200.65	9.63	10.59
40 L.H., Daily Totals		$1345.80		$1912.70	$33.65	$47.82
Crew B-78	Hr.	Daily	Hr.	Daily	Bare Costs	Incl. O&P
1 Labor Foreman	$25.45	$203.60	$39.60	$316.80	$23.93	$37.11
4 Laborers	23.45	750.40	36.50	1168.00		
1 Truck Driver (light)	24.30	194.40	37.05	296.40		
1 Paint Striper, S.P.		177.40		195.15		
1 Flatbed Truck, 3 Ton		182.40		200.65		
1 Pickup Truck, 3/4 Ton		84.00		92.40	9.25	10.17
48 L.H., Daily Totals		$1592.20		$2269.40	$33.18	$47.28
Crew B-79	Hr.	Daily	Hr.	Daily	Bare Costs	Incl. O&P
1 Labor Foreman	$25.45	$203.60	$39.60	$316.80	$24.02	$37.23
3 Laborers	23.45	562.80	36.50	876.00		
1 Truck Driver (light)	24.30	194.40	37.05	296.40		
1 Thermo. Striper, T.M.		475.40		522.95		
1 Flatbed Truck, 3 Ton		182.40		200.65		
2 Pickup Truck, 3/4 Ton		168.00		184.80	20.65	22.71
40 L.H., Daily Totals		$1786.60		$2397.60	$44.67	$59.94
Crew B-80	Hr.	Daily	Hr.	Daily	Bare Costs	Incl. O&P
1 Labor Foreman	$25.45	$203.60	$39.60	$316.80	$25.75	$39.55
1 Laborer	23.45	187.60	36.50	292.00		
1 Truck Driver (light)	24.30	194.40	37.05	296.40		
1 Equip. Oper. (light)	29.80	238.40	45.05	360.40		
1 Flatbed Truck, 3 Ton		182.40		200.65		
1 Fence Post Auger, T.M.		377.80		415.60	17.51	19.26
32 L.H., Daily Totals		$1384.20		$1881.85	$43.26	$58.81
Crew B-80A	Hr.	Daily	Hr.	Daily	Bare Costs	Incl. O&P
3 Laborers	$23.45	$562.80	$36.50	$876.00	$23.45	$36.50
1 Flatbed Truck, 3 Ton		182.40		200.65	7.60	8.36
24 L.H., Daily Totals		$745.20		$1076.65	$31.05	$44.86
Crew B-80B	Hr.	Daily	Hr.	Daily	Bare Costs	Incl. O&P
3 Laborers	$23.45	$562.80	$36.50	$876.00	$25.04	$38.64
1 Equip. Oper. (light)	29.80	238.40	45.05	360.40		
1 Crane, Flatbed Mnt.		205.60		226.15	6.43	7.07
32 L.H., Daily Totals		$1006.80		$1462.55	$31.47	$45.71

Crew No.	Bare Costs		Incl. Subs O & P		Cost Per Labor-Hour	
Crew B-81	Hr.	Daily	Hr.	Daily	Bare Costs	Incl. O&P
1 Laborer	$23.45	$187.60	$36.50	$292.00	$26.55	$40.58
1 Equip. Oper. (med.)	31.20	249.60	47.15	377.20		
1 Truck Driver (heavy)	25.00	200.00	38.10	304.80		
1 Hydromulcher, T.M.		249.40		274.35		
1 Tractor Truck, 4x2		291.80		321.00	22.55	24.81
24 L.H., Daily Totals		$1178.40		$1569.35	$49.10	$65.39
Crew B-82	Hr.	Daily	Hr.	Daily	Bare Costs	Incl. O&P
1 Laborer	$23.45	$187.60	$36.50	$292.00	$26.63	$40.78
1 Equip. Oper. (light)	29.80	238.40	45.05	360.40		
1 Horiz. Borer, 6 H.P.		51.60		56.75	3.23	3.55
16 L.H., Daily Totals		$477.60		$709.15	$29.86	$44.33
Crew B-83	Hr.	Daily	Hr.	Daily	Bare Costs	Incl. O&P
1 Tugboat Captain	$31.20	$249.60	$47.15	$377.20	$27.33	$41.83
1 Tugboat Hand	23.45	187.60	36.50	292.00		
1 Tugboat, 250 H.P.		485.60		534.15	30.35	33.39
16 L.H., Daily Totals		$922.80		$1203.35	$57.68	$75.22
Crew B-84	Hr.	Daily	Hr.	Daily	Bare Costs	Incl. O&P
1 Equip. Oper. (med.)	$31.20	$249.60	$47.15	$377.20	$31.20	$47.15
1 Rotary Mower/Tractor		199.20		219.10	24.90	27.39
8 L.H., Daily Totals		$448.80		$596.30	$56.10	$74.54
Crew B-85	Hr.	Daily	Hr.	Daily	Bare Costs	Incl. O&P
3 Laborers	$23.45	$562.80	$36.50	$876.00	$25.31	$38.95
1 Equip. Oper. (med.)	31.20	249.60	47.15	377.20		
1 Truck Driver (heavy)	25.00	200.00	38.10	304.80		
1 Aerial Lift Truck, 80'		493.60		542.95		
1 Brush Chipper, 130 H.P.		182.60		200.85		
1 Pruning Saw, Rotary		17.90		19.70	17.35	19.09
40 L.H., Daily Totals		$1706.50		$2321.50	$42.66	$58.04
Crew B-86	Hr.	Daily	Hr.	Daily	Bare Costs	Incl. O&P
1 Equip. Oper. (med.)	$31.20	$249.60	$47.15	$377.20	$31.20	$47.15
1 Stump Chipper, S.P.		135.65		149.20	16.96	18.65
8 L.H., Daily Totals		$385.25		$526.40	$48.16	$65.80
Crew B-86A	Hr.	Daily	Hr.	Daily	Bare Costs	Incl. O&P
1 Equip. Oper. (medium)	$31.20	$249.60	$47.15	$377.20	$31.20	$47.15
1 Grader, 30,000 Lbs.		431.60		474.75	53.95	59.35
8 L.H., Daily Totals		$681.20		$851.95	$85.15	$106.50
Crew B-86B	Hr.	Daily	Hr.	Daily	Bare Costs	Incl. O&P
1 Equip. Oper. (medium)	$31.20	$249.60	$47.15	$377.20	$31.20	$47.15
1 Dozer, 200 H.P.		823.40		905.75	102.93	113.22
8 L.H., Daily Totals		$1073.00		$1282.95	$134.13	$160.37
Crew B-87	Hr.	Daily	Hr.	Daily	Bare Costs	Incl. O&P
1 Laborer	$23.45	$187.60	$36.50	$292.00	$29.65	$45.02
4 Equip. Oper. (med.)	31.20	998.40	47.15	1508.80		
2 Feller Bunchers, 50 H.P.		806.40		887.05		
1 Log Chipper, 22" Tree		1543.00		1697.30		
1 Dozer, 105 H.P.		291.20		320.30		
1 Chainsaw, Gas, 36" Long		39.60		43.55	67.01	73.71
40 L.H., Daily Totals		$3866.20		$4749.00	$96.66	$118.73

(from *Means Site Work & Landscape Cost Data 2002*)

Figure 7.23

Installing Contractor's Overhead & Profit

Below are the **average** installing contractor's percentage mark-ups applied to base labor rates to arrive at typical billing rates.

Column A: Labor rates are based on union wages averaged for 30 major U.S. cities. Base rates including fringe benefits are listed hourly and daily. These figures are the sum of the wage rate and employer-paid fringe benefits such as vacation pay, employer-paid health and welfare costs, pension costs, plus appropriate training and industry advancement funds costs.

Column B: Workers' Compensation rates are the national average of state rates established for each trade.

Column C: Column C lists average fixed overhead figures for all trades. Included are Federal and State Unemployment costs set at 7.0%; Social Security Taxes (FICA) set at 7.65%; Builder's Risk Insurance costs set at 0.34%; and Public Liability costs set at 1.55%. All the percentages except those for Social Security Taxes vary from state to state as well as from company to company.

Columns D and E: Percentages in Columns D and E are based on the presumption that the installing contractor has annual billing of $1,500,000 and up. Overhead percentages may increase with smaller annual billing. The overhead percentages for any given contractor may vary greatly and depend on a number of factors, such as the contractor's annual volume, engineering and logistical support costs, and staff requirements. The figures for overhead and profit will also vary depending on the type of job, the job location, and the prevailing economic conditions. All factors should be examined very carefully for each job.

Column F: Column F lists the total of Columns B, C, D, and E.

Column G: Column G is Column A (hourly base labor rate) multiplied by the percentage in Column F (O&P percentage).

Column H: Column H is the total of Column A (hourly base labor rate) plus Column G (Total O&P).

Column I: Column I is Column H multiplied by eight hours.

Abbr.	Trade	A Base Rate Incl. Fringes Hourly	A Daily	B Workers' Comp. Ins.	C Average Fixed Overhead	D Overhead	E Profit	F Total Overhead & Profit %	F Amount	H Rate with O & P Hourly	I Daily
Skwk	Skilled Workers Average (35 trades)	$30.95	$247.60	16.8%	16.5%	13.0%	10%	56.3%	$17.40	$48.35	$386.80
	Helpers Average (5 trades)	22.75	182.00	18.5		11.0		56.0	12.75	35.50	284.00
	Foreman Average, Inside ($.50 over trade)	31.45	251.60	16.8		13.0		56.3	17.70	49.15	393.20
	Foreman Average, Outside ($2.00 over trade)	32.95	263.60	16.8		13.0		56.3	18.55	51.50	412.00
Clab	Common Building Laborers	23.45	187.60	18.1		11.0		55.6	13.05	36.50	292.00
Asbe	Asbestos/Insulation Workers/Pipe Coverers	33.45	267.60	16.2		16.0		58.7	19.65	53.10	424.80
Boil	Boilermakers	36.25	290.00	14.7		16.0		57.2	20.75	57.00	456.00
Bric	Bricklayers	30.50	244.00	16.0		11.0		53.5	16.30	46.80	374.40
Brhe	Bricklayer Helpers	23.50	188.00	16.0		11.0		53.5	12.55	36.05	288.40
Carp	Carpenters	30.00	240.00	18.1		11.0		55.6	16.70	46.70	373.60
Cefi	Cement Finishers	28.70	229.60	10.6		11.0		48.1	13.80	42.50	340.00
Elec	Electricians	35.45	283.60	6.7		16.0		49.2	17.45	52.90	423.20
Elev	Elevator Constructors	37.10	296.80	7.7		16.0		50.2	18.60	55.70	445.60
Eqhv	Equipment Operators, Crane or Shovel	32.35	258.80	10.6		14.0		51.1	16.55	48.90	391.20
Eqmd	Equipment Operators, Medium Equipment	31.20	249.60	10.6		14.0		51.1	15.95	47.15	377.20
Eqlt	Equipment Operators, Light Equipment	29.80	238.40	10.6		14.0		51.1	15.25	45.05	360.40
Eqol	Equipment Operators, Oilers	26.65	213.20	10.6		14.0		51.1	13.60	40.25	322.00
Eqmm	Equipment Operators, Master Mechanics	32.80	262.40	10.6		14.0		51.1	16.75	49.55	396.40
Glaz	Glaziers	30.00	240.00	13.8		11.0		51.3	15.40	45.40	363.20
Lath	Lathers	28.75	230.00	11.1		11.0		48.6	13.95	42.70	341.60
Marb	Marble Setters	30.10	240.80	16.0		11.0		53.5	16.10	46.20	369.60
Mill	Millwrights	31.75	254.00	10.6		11.0		48.1	15.25	47.00	376.00
Mstz	Mosaic & Terrazzo Workers	29.25	234.00	9.8		11.0		47.3	13.85	43.10	344.80
Pord	Painters, Ordinary	27.15	217.20	13.8		11.0		51.3	13.95	41.10	328.80
Psst	Painters, Structural Steel	27.90	223.20	48.4		11.0		85.9	23.95	51.85	414.80
Pape	Paper Hangers	27.10	216.80	13.8		11.0		51.3	13.90	41.00	328.00
Pile	Pile Drivers	29.80	238.40	24.9		16.0		67.4	20.10	49.90	399.20
Plas	Plasterers	28.10	224.80	15.8		11.0		53.3	15.00	43.10	344.80
Plah	Plasterer Helpers	23.70	189.60	15.8		11.0		53.3	12.65	36.35	290.80
Plum	Plumbers	35.95	287.60	8.3		16.0		50.8	18.25	54.20	433.60
Rodm	Rodmen (Reinforcing)	34.25	274.00	28.3		14.0		68.8	23.55	57.80	462.40
Rofc	Roofers, Composition	26.60	212.80	32.6		11.0		70.1	18.65	45.25	362.00
Rots	Roofers, Tile & Slate	26.75	214.00	32.6		11.0		70.1	18.75	45.50	364.00
Rohe	Roofers, Helpers (Composition)	19.80	158.40	32.6		11.0		70.1	13.90	33.70	269.60
Shee	Sheet Metal Workers	35.10	280.80	11.7		16.0		54.2	19.00	54.10	432.80
Spri	Sprinkler Installers	36.20	289.60	8.7		16.0		51.2	18.55	54.75	438.00
Stpi	Steamfitters or Pipefitters	36.20	289.60	8.3		16.0		50.8	18.40	54.60	436.80
Ston	Stone Masons	30.65	245.20	16.0		11.0		53.5	16.40	47.05	376.40
Sswk	Structural Steel Workers	34.25	274.00	39.8		14.0		80.3	27.50	61.75	494.00
Tilf	Tile Layers	29.15	233.20	9.8		11.0		47.3	13.80	42.95	343.60
Tilh	Tile Layers Helpers	23.35	186.80	9.8		11.0		47.3	11.05	34.40	275.20
Trlt	Truck Drivers, Light	24.30	194.40	14.9		11.0		52.4	12.75	37.05	296.40
Trhv	Truck Drivers, Heavy	25.00	200.00	14.9		11.0		52.4	13.10	38.10	304.80
Sswl	Welders, Structural Steel	34.25	274.00	39.8		14.0		80.3	27.50	61.75	494.00
Wrck	*Wrecking	23.45	187.60	41.2		11.0		78.7	18.45	41.90	335.20

*Not included in averages

(from *Means Site Work & Landscape Cost Data 2002*)

Figure 7.24

Chapter 8

Bidding for Jobs

Chapter Eight
Bidding for Jobs

Obtaining a contract to perform a landscape project is the goal of all the estimating and pricing discussed in previous chapters. Your estimate and pricing becomes a proposal, that is a **bid**, for a contract to perform specific work. That bid will be an offer to complete a job for a stated sum of money. This bid amount is the result of carefully figured costs for materials, equipment, and labor, and includes the necessary markups for overhead and profit. Under some circumstances, that offer may be a legal binder to perform.

Bidding is a systematic process aimed at gaining a desirable work contract. It is also a strategy, and like all good strategies, should incorporate both advance preparations and final stage flexibility.

Bidding is also hard work. Putting a bid together is a job, simplified by proper organization. Routine and systematic procedures can be valuable organizational tools, because they make bidding easier and help guard against costly errors.

The importance of proper bidding methods and skills is demonstrated by the interest this topic generates within the industry. Trade associations run bidding workshops as a part of their educational and training programs. The key to successful bidding and competition is obtaining precise cost information for all direct costs. Good productivity data is also essential for producing competitive landscape project bids. The best source of such data is detailed records from previous jobs. Collecting accurate productivity data is a joint effort of management and landscape foremen, and should be based on work over a substantial period of time for greater accuracy. Be sure to keep labor cost records and daily time sheets as illustrated in Chapter 6 and file them carefully.

The bidding procedure can be viewed from several different perspectives. The client's goal is to obtain the best work for the lowest price. A client puts together a bid package with these aims in mind. The bidders' qualifications as well as prices are carefully analyzed by the client who wants quality work, a conscientious performance, and follow-up corrections, if necessary. Typical qualifications of bidders are discussed in Chapter 1.

From the bidder's point of view, the goal is not only winning the contract, but also the profitable and timely completion of the project. The exact percentage or amount of the profit may be one of the "estimated" items in a bid package. Many experienced contractors do not use a predetermined markup for overhead and profit for every job, but determine such costs on a job-by-job basis. After all, many variables may influence the costs applicable to any particular project. The size of the job and its desirability are obvious factors. Other points to consider are:

- Economic circumstances
- Number and quality of competitors
- Need for work

The contractor must take into account competition from other bidders. Strong competition puts pressure on the bidder to lower his profit percentage. Other factors that limit profit include the possibility of increased overhead, and self-imposed limitations, such as those required for a company growth plan. In other words, the need for work may outweigh the "need" for large profits (on a short term basis).

With the large number of small owner/foreman businesses in the landscape industry, there is a particularly large pitfall open for struggling contractors entering the competitive bidding scene. Caution must be taken against inadvertently "buying a contract," that is to say, working at no profit—or possibly at a loss. Too much optimism may be costly. Caution is advised against bids that are based on imagined maximum labor production and lowest possible material costs. Even large established firms must carefully scrutinize their bids to be sure they are based on sound estimating practice, guaranteed price quotes, and firm bids from known subcontractors. Advantages shift back and forth among bidders, and there will be highly desirable work prospects at certain times. The profit on a job should be large enough to permit the growth of company assets. Too low, and the company does not prosper; too high, and the company will not win contracts.

The bidder wants to bid as low as possible and hopefully close to the next lowest bid. A large gap between his bid and the next lowest bid shows that the bidder has failed to see the advantages he had over his competitors. The bidder needs to procure the contract with a low bid *and* make a profit.

Activities and requirements for successful bidding include:
- Accurate quantity takeoff
- Accurate pricing (good source of cost data)
- Dependable subcontractors
- Careful planning for realistic time scheduling
- Anticipation of the methods used to perform the work

While many landscape decisions are inevitably made in the field, as much project planning as possible should be outlined before bidding. By highlighting options and strategies, unanticipated problems can be minimized. Bidding is a time to sort and analyze information and determine answers.

Bidding Strategies

A strategy is a detailed plan for reaching your goal or achieving an advantage. The strategies of bidding are well charted by Paul J. Cook in his book *Bidding for Contractors*, published by R.S. Means Company, Inc. The need for work is always the major determining factor that influences bidding for a contract. But other factors, such as desirability, should also be critically analyzed. Cook lists and explains 14 different conditions that may influence bidding decisions:

1. Size (cost of the project in dollars)
2. Location of project (travel distance)
3. Relationship with client
4. Type of, and familiarity with, construction
5. Probable level of competition
6. Labor market
7. Subcontractor market
8. Quality of drawings and specifications
9. Quality of supervision
10. Special risks

11. Completion time and penalty
12. Estimating and bidding time
13. Need for work
14. Other special advantages or disadvantages

If all conditions are primarily positive, the project should be highly desirable and the bidding competitive. If most of these conditions are negative, the project should be less desirable and the bidding conservative.

The Bid Package

The American Society of Landscape Architects (ASLA) *Handbook of Professional Practice* suggests that the formality of the bid procedure and documents should correspond with the size of the job. Simple jobs should be simply documented. Large, highly detailed, costly jobs should be appropriately detailed and documented. Generally, good specifications are brief while remaining complete and adequate so as not to discourage the competing contractors and/or increase the bid. The ASLA recommends, as a minimum, simple and concise drawings, specifications offering a clear understanding of the work to be done, the amount and schedule of payments, and the completion date.

Simple bid packages may consist of the client's requirements written on a standard proposal form. An example of how a simple, minimum bid proposal should be presented is shown in Figure 8.1. The project requirements should be clearly and completely presented as an integral part of the proposal.

Landscape projects that are professionally managed or performed for the government—whether federal, state, county, or city—often have **prepared bid packages**. The bid package has two main parts, one for the client and one for the bidder. The client's responsibility is to provide:
- Drawings and plans, including graphic details.
- Written information and specifications as part of the drawings.

When this information is extensive (as is typical in the case of government projects), the specifications may be called the "Project Manual" and may consist of the following segments:
- Advertisement for bids, or Invitation to bid
- Bid and contract requirements
  - Instructions to bidders
  - Bid forms
  - Bond forms
  - Experience qualification forms
  - Contract forms (agreement)
- Standard clauses
  - Labor laws
  - Miscellaneous laws, rules, regulations
  - Taxes, permits, licenses, inspections
- General and special conditions
- Technical specifications pertaining to the various trades and subtrades (often organized by Index Divisions)
- Requirements for acceptance of the completed work by the owner and release by the contractor

Means® Forms

PROPOSAL

FROM:
_____
_____
_____

TO: _____
_____
_____

PROPOSAL NO.	_____
DATE	_____
PROJECT	_____
LOCATION	_____
	_____
CONSTRUCTION TO BEGIN	_____
COMPLETION DATE	_____

Gentlemen:

The undersigned proposes to furnish all materials and necessary equipment and perform all labor necessary to complete the following work:

_____
_____
_____
_____
_____
_____
_____
_____
_____
_____
_____
_____
_____
_____
_____

All of the above work to be completed in a substantial and workmanlike manner

☐ for the sum of _____ dollars ($_____)

☐ to be paid for at actual cost of Labor, Materials and Equipment plus _____ percent (____%)

Payments to be made as follows:_____

_____The entire amount of the contract to be paid within_____ after completion.

Any alteration or deviation from the plans and specifications will be executed only upon written orders for same and will be added to or deducted from the sum quoted in this contract. All additional agreements must be in writing.

The Contractor agrees to carry Workmen's Compensation and Public Liability Insurance and to pay all taxes on material and labor furnished under this contract as required by Federal laws and the laws of the State in which this work is performed.

Respectfully submitted,

Contractor _____

By_____

ACCEPTANCE

You are hereby authorized to furnish all material, equipment and labor required to complete the work described in the above proposal, for which the undersigned agrees to pay the amount stated in said proposal and according to the terms thereof.

Date _____ 20 ____

_____

_____

Figure 8.1

The author and R. S. Means suggest the use of standard forms, contract documents and specifications for landscape professionals. Many organizations provide good, fill-in-the-blank-type forms, or forms that may be customized on your computer. These organizations include the Associated General Contractors of America, American Society of Landscape Architects and the American Nursery and Landscape Association. Contact information on these organizations may be found in the Appendix.

Examples and excerpts of bid documents that might be used by a city, "Invitation to Bid" and "Instructions to Bidders" are shown in Figures 8.2 and 8.3. A sample "Proposal/Bid Form" is featured in Figure 8.4.

In the "Invitation to Bid" basic information about the project is presented. The "Instructions to Bidders" provides information and requirements important to the contract. The "Proposal/Bid Form" is an example of a bid form that would be completed by the contractor.

Documents such as these have important legal, insurance and/or surety consequences. Consultation with an attorney and insurance and/or surety consultant is encouraged when completing or modifying any documents of these types.

Unit Price proposals are typically divided into separate, task-related categories or systems which can be used by the client for comparative purposes. The "units" in a Unit Price proposal are typically those items estimated as assemblies. For example, excavating 100 cubic yards of common earth to be priced on a C.Y. basis. This type of bid is also appropriate if the project parameters have not been completely detailed. The bidder can provide costs based on "estimated" quantities. Total costs can then vary based on actual installed quantities.

Overhead and profit are usually included in the costs for each item in this type of unit pricing. The total bid amount is the same as a lump sum bid for the same job, but in this case, the project is broken down. Unit Price bids are legitimate methods and should provide reliable estimates. Unfortunately, the Unit Price method is sometimes used by the client or designer as a basis for canceling or manipulating individual costly items; in such cases, serious doubt can be cast upon the integrity of the proposed design solution if items are detailed solely on the basis of cost. The character of a particular material or item may be integral to the unity or beauty of a project. When such an item is changed or deleted, the entire project may lose its intended value.

Lump Sum Bids provide one price for all the materials and labor required according to the plans and specs. In many cases, the bidder may wish to list some unit prices in his Lump Sum Bid, especially if work areas are subject to individual interpretation or if certain items are excluded from the bid. For example, an area that is difficult to estimate for seeding could be safely bid by stating that the bid price is based on "not more than 15,000 square yards of grass seeding."

Putting Together a Bid

Bidding a large project means getting to know the person(s) connected with the project as well as the site. The matter of qualifications statement is discussed in Chapter 1. The development of the lowest possible costs is explained in Chapters 5 and 6.

Putting together a bid is a step typically shared by management or the owner in conference with the estimator and foreman. The cost estimate is the first item to be checked. Verifying the estimate requires another review of the drawings and specs. This is the time to search for oversights and contradictions in the cost

information and for potential problems in the drawings and specs. Make a thorough analysis of the work proposed. If any problems are discovered, contract requirements and obligations will have to be clarified.

An ideal bid is made up entirely of detailed, accurate, estimated costs and firm, reliable, subcontractor quotes. An actual bid may be something less than ideal and may contain costs representing budgets, "guesstimates," and allowances. These types of costs should be kept to a minimum. Unfortunately, bidding schedules do not always allow enough time to complete proper estimates. When putting a bid together for a job, the estimator may be forced by time constraints to use cost information that is not as accurate and dependable as a detailed estimate would be. Until the last moment, however, every effort should be made to confirm costs and receive commitments for both subcontract and material prices.

The basic requirements of the bidder are to respond to and complete the bid documents and requests, and to provide an offer to perform specific work, often within a stated time frame, in return for a specified price. The contractor's bid consists of all known costs, compiled and analyzed as carefully as possible. Included in this figure is a crucial amount for overhead and profit, and the bid bond, if one is required. The bid bond cost is calculated last because it is always based on the total amount of the bid. For example, a 0.6% bid bond on a $100,000 contract would cost $600.

Formal Bid Openings

When a bid package indicates a formal bid time and procedure, the instructions must be followed closely. Formal bid openings usually begin at the exact minute of the opening deadline. As a rule, a bid arriving after the opening ritual will not be accepted. At formal, public bid openings, it is a good idea to record all the bids submitted for the project. A review of competitors' bidding patterns can guide you on future projects.

The Bid Award

Only one bidder will be awarded the sought-after contract, and congratulations are in order for the company that is chosen. Acceptance of a bid is the maximum vote of confidence in a bidder's work. Knowledge gained from the experience is the only reward of the unsuccessful bidder. In such a case, one should put this hindsight to work on the next bid. The lessons on the current market, competition, profit margins, and bidding procedures cannot be completely learned from books.

CITY OF NORTHUMBERLAND
OFFICE OF PARKS AND RECREATION
540 North Seward Street
NORTHUMBERLAND, MA

NOTICE TO CONTRACTORS

INVITATION FOR PROPOSALS/BIDS for Case 132: Street Tree Planting on Atlantic Avenue, Chestnut Street, Main Street, Summer Street, East and West Elm Street and additional locations along other public ways.

The City of Northumberland, acting through the Office of Parks and Recreation, 540 North Seward Street, Northumberland, MA, hereby invites sealed bids for the project described above. All bids must be submitted before 12 noon on Monday, April 8, 2002, at which time the bids/proposals will be opened and read aloud.

Bids shall be submitted on a form available from the Office of Parks and Recreation, hereinafter referred to as the Awarding Authority. All bids shall be clearly identified as a bid for "Case 132 Tree Planting" marked on the envelope. All bids must be signed by the bidder.

SCOPE OF WORK includes: Furnishing all labor, materials, and equipment necessary for Cutting and Removing Pavement, Tree Pit Excavation, Furnishing and Planting Trees, Maintaining and Guaranteeing Trees.

SPECIFICATIONS AND PLANS will be available Friday, March 15, 2002 at the Parks and Recreation Office to all interested parties who present a $50.00 certified check, payable to the City of Northumberland for each set. Specifications must be returned in good condition within thirty (30) days of the bid opening in order for the bidder to receive return of the check.

BID DEPOSITS in the amount of 5% of the bid, payable to the City of Northumberland shall be submitted in the form of bid bond, certified check, treasurer's check, or cashier's check. A bid bond must be of a surety company qualified to do business under the laws of the Commonwealth of Massachusetts and made payable to the City of Northumberland.

Figure 8.2

CITY OF NORTHUMBERLAND
OFFICE OF PARKS AND RECREATION

Instructions to Bidders

1. GENERAL

All Proposals submitted hereto shall be received by the Office of Parks and Recreation, 540 North Seward Street, Northumberland, MA before 12 noon, Monday, April 8, 2002. Proposals not received by that time and date will not be considered.

All Proposals must be submitted on a City of Northumberland Proposal/Bid Form available from the Office of Parks and Recreation.

The City of Northumberland Office of Parks and Recreation, hereinafter referred to as the Awarding Authority, will solicit all Proposals. The Comissioner of Parks and Recreation will record receipt of all Proposals and evaluate Proposals against a cost estimate prepared and maintained by the Office. The lowest responsible and eligible Proposal that is within 10% of the Office's cost estimate will be awarded the project, subject to successful execution of contracts.

All submitted Proposals shall be complete. Any omission of any item in a Proposal received shall be considered accidental, and it is understood that in submitting a Proposal, the contractor is committing to the entire project as described and enumerated in the Scope of Work.

2. SITE INSPECTION

Contractors are required to inspect the tree planting sites. Any contractor who submits a proposal but has not conducted an inspection of the sites will be rejected as unresponsive and ineligible to submit a Proposal on the project.

3. PROPOSAL QUALIFICATIONS

All contractors shall abide by the Terms and Conditions of Contractor Rules and Regulations of the City of Northumberland. Said terms and conditions are incorporated in the Proposal/Bid Form and are binding on all contractors submitting bids. In particular, any contractor working under two projects financed by the Awarding Authority at the time of the Bid Opening will not be considered a "responsible" bidder, unless at least one of the two is 90% complete. This provision may be waived by the Commissioner of Parks and Recreation only by prior approval, and only in these instances where a contractor can prove that he/she is capable of performing under more than two concurrent contracts.

4. SUBCONTRACTORS

All Proposals will include a list of the names, addresses, telephone numbers and applicable state license numbers of any subcontractors who will be working for the contractor on this project. Proposals will indicate what portions of the Scope of Work are to be conducted by subcontractors.

Contractors may not change subcontractors without the written approval of the Comissioner of Parks and Recreation.

5. CONTRACT AWARD

The Awarding Authority will evaluate all Proposals received and recommend any eligible contractor with the lowest responsible Proposal.

Figure 8.3

6. MINORITY/WOMEN BUSINESS ENTERPRISES

The Awarding Authority encourages minority and women business enterprises certified by the State Office of Minority Business Assistance to compete for contracts. If a contractor or any subcontractor used in connection with a project is SOMBA certified, evidence of the same should be provided on the Proposal Form.

7. CHANGE ORDERS; MODIFICATION OF SCOPE OF WORK

No change to the specifications set forth in SCOPE OF WORK document shall be allowed without an approved Change Order signed by the Comissioner of Parks and Recreation and for which financial approval has been granted by same.

8. METHOD OF PAYMENT; CONTRACTOR BILLING PROCEDURES

The Contractor shall be eligible to submit invoices for payment to the Awarding Authority at intervals equal to twenty-five percent (25%) of the total contract cost, including labor and material. Upon approval of work completed, as determined by the Comissioner of Parks and Recreation who will inspect performance and progress at reasonable and customary hours, the Awarding Authority will process contractor invoices. Checks will be issued by the City of Northumberland Treasurer. The Awarding Authority reserves the right to adjust the amount of payment issued where inspection results so justify. In all cases, ten percent (10%) of each invoice amount shall be withheld as performance surety and released only when all contractual obligations have been met by the contractor, including closeout documentation required by the Awarding Authority.

9. PROJECT SCHEDULE

The Contractor selected for this project must be prepared to begin work no later than May 10, 2002. The work is to be completed within ninety days (90 days) of the start of work. Extensions may be granted for cause. Contractors must indicate in their Proposals the date on which they can start and finish this job.

Figure 8.3 *(cont.)*

PROPOSAL/BID FORM
Office of Parks and Recreation
Northumberland, MA

Date: _____   Case: # 132

SUBMIT SEALED PROPOSALS MARKED "BID: Case 132, Tree Planting", TO:
City of Northumberland
Office of Parks and Recreation
540 North Seward Street
Northumberland, MA

FROM: _____
Contractor

_____
Street and Mailing Address

_____
Town   Zip Code

_____
Telephone #

CONTRACTOR'S PROPOSAL/BID STATEMENT

1. The CONTRACTOR having inspected the SITES of Case 132, TREE PLANTING and having read the PROPOSAL/BID SPECIFICATION AND SCOPE OF WORK dated March 15, 2002 and related Drawings or other items furnished by the OFFICE OF PARKS AND RECREATION pertaining to the PROJECT, hereby offers to provide all labor, materials and equipment necessary to complete the PROJECT as set forth in the PROPOSAL/BID SPECIFICATION AND SCOPE OF WORK for a total CONTRACT PRICE OF: $ _____ , also shown as

_____ (Dollars)
(Contract Price must be written in full)

SIGNED:

_____
Contractor   Date

Proposals are due by 12 noon April 8, 2002
ALL SUBCONTRACTORS MUST BE LISTED ON LAST PAGE

2. The CONTRACTOR commits to providing all services as would constitute a complete PROJECT as described in the PROPOSAL/BID SPECIFICATION AND SCOPE OF WORK. Any omission of items from the PROPOSAL/BID is by error of the CONTRACTOR, who agrees to abide by the SCOPE OF WORK AND THE SIGNED CONTRACT PRICE in full, upon acceptance of contract award.

3. The CONTRACTOR understands that the Awarding Authority reserves the right to reject any and all PROPOSAL/BIDS.

Figure 8.4

4. The CONTRACTOR agrees to commence work on the PROJECT within twenty (20) days of the date of issuance of a NOTICE TO PROCEED, and understands that either failure to commence work within said twenty days, or to complete all work set forth in the SCOPE OF WORK within ninety (90) days of commencement, shall be cause for termination of all AGREEMENTS, contracts and other binding documents unless waiver of the same has been previously authorized in writing by the Awarding Authority.

5. The CONTRACTOR agrees to ABIDE by all terms and conditions of Contractor Participation set by the Awarding Authority, and in submitting this PROPOSAL/BID indicates his/her understanding of and assent to said terms and conditions.

6. The CONTRACTOR is currently carrying the required Workers' Compensation Insurance, liability insurance at the minimum amounts of $300,000, property damage, $500,000, personal injury, and holds a valid Massachusetts Construction Supervisor's License. Evidence of the same shall be required as a condition of PROPOSAL/BID award.

7. CONTRACT COST BREAKDOWN
         (REFER TO PROPOSAL/BID SPECIFICATION AND SCOPE OF WORK)

Item #1
    Contractor Labor Cost $ _____

    Subcontractor Labor Cost $ _____

    Materials Cost $ _____

                              Total $ _____

Item #2
    Contractor Labor Cost $ _____

    Subcontractor Labor Cost $ _____

    Materials Cost $ _____

                              Total $ _____

Item #3
    Contractor Labor Cost $ _____

    Subcontractor Labor Cost $ _____

    Materials Cost $_____

                              Total $ _____

Item #4
    Contractor Labor Cost $ _____

    Subcontractor Labor Cost $ _____

    Materials Cost $ _____

                              Total $ _____

Figure 8.4 *(cont.)*

Item #5
    Contractor Labor Cost $ _____

    Subcontractor Labor Cost $ _____

    Materials Cost $ _____

                       Total $ _____

Item #6
    Contractor Labor Cost $ _____

    Subcontractor Labor Cost $ _____

    Materials Cost $ _____

                       Total $ _____

         All Inclusive   TOTAL $ _____

ALL SUBCONTRACTORS MUST BE LISTED

Trade	Company Name	Address	Telephone #	License #

PLEASE INDICATE THE DATES YOU CAN START AND COMPLETE THIS PROJECT:

STARTING DATE: _____

ENDING DATE: _____

Figure 8.4 (cont.)

Chapter 9
Job Planning and Scheduling

Chapter Nine
Job Planning and Scheduling

Work scheduling, purchasing and allocation of assets are your new priorities after winning a desirable contract. Management now takes over the planning and scheduling of labor, materials and equipment—items all considered by the experienced estimator throughout the estimating and bidding process.

Proper job planning—of both time and costs—is an essential ingredient for job profit. Without logical schedules and cost planning, decisions made on the job could result in an interruption of progress and work flow. Down time and confusion may be the costly effects.

The Planning Team

The best schedule makes the most efficient use of these four major factors in the landscape industry—manpower, materials, machinery, and money. Keep in mind that none of these is available on immediate notice. Work scheduling often becomes a combination of juggling and precise planning. Experienced contractors try to rely on sound planning efforts to reduce the juggling act. Planning consists of designing a series of activities to occur in such a way as to bring about the most efficient and effective performance of a job. These goals are accomplished by arranging the activities in a logical order and assigning each a starting time, a duration time, and a completion time.

Most contracting companies develop a routine of some sort for planning. The management team now has the responsibility for planning and scheduling the project, and should use all the information from the estimator. The quantity takeoff prepared by the estimator becomes an information resource for management to use when putting together a plan and schedule for the job.

The objectives of job planning include foreseeing any problems and establishing the following:
- Critical paths
- The *logical* sequence of events.
- The *best* work sequence.
- The impact of deviations ("What happens if...?").
- Material requirements and delivery schedules.
- Ability to meet the completion date.

The Job Schedule

Scheduling involves drawing up an outline or a simple bar chart to describe the general sequence of construction. Where and when will the work begin? In the sample project (Chapter 7), the major components of the work will start with the stone rip rap and the placing of paving materials on the site. Activity begins at the stream level, progressing upward from there to the top of the bank. The work ends with the lawn seeding and a final cleanup and removal of debris.

Lists are made of the tasks required to complete each activity. Many companies make up their own checklist forms in order to avoid oversights. For some jobs "planting" may be too general a description and might need to be more specifically broken down into: "tree planting," "staking," "wrapping," and "mulching." Then on to "shrub planting" as a separate activity. For each of these activities, a crew makeup and an appropriate amount of time must be designated. Figure 9.1, a simple calendar, is an example of how preliminary job planning might begin. Here a combination of "critical path" and "best work sequence" shows work that must be completed before other work can start and also other tasks that may take place at the same time. The possibilities of concurrent activities may eliminate down time.

Plan, Coordinate, Target

When the basic time frames have been established, the crews are planned on the basis of the skills required as well as the number of workers needed to perform the work within the required time frame. The planner must coordinate all work with the delivery times obtained from suppliers. Targets of specific work goals should be established and may be timed to a certain day. For example: May 10 – bluestone patios complete.

Time Schedules

In order to arrive at a schedule for the project, the planner must determine the amount of time required to do the complete job. Part of this process is determining what work must be completed before other tasks can begin or proceed, and how many tasks can be done at the same time.

Activities will be directed on site and records kept by the well-informed supervisor or foreman. The scheduling and management of the job should be based on the labor hours determined in the estimate for each phase of the work. "In place" labor records from actual jobs will be used for future estimating purposes. Other important scheduling factors include:

- The owner's requirements for job start and completion dates.
- Material delivery dates (purchase orders should be processed with confirmation of guaranteed prices and delivery dates).
- Work by subcontractors (contracts must be let with firm agreements on the scope of work and the required job duration or date of completion).

Established landscape firms have learned the value of creating and using a chart and calendar to schedule large projects. These individual project calendars should be checked against a master calendar listing the company's other scheduled work. Figure 9.2 shows how such a calendar might be set up. This particular example might be used to schedule crews. Note that there are no more than two jobs scheduled on any day. This may reflect the available work force (supervisory and labor) for a particular company.

The methods of scheduling may be simple or sophisticated, depending on the requirements of the job and the preferences of the planner. Whatever method is used, experienced managers rely on three basic scheduling principles:

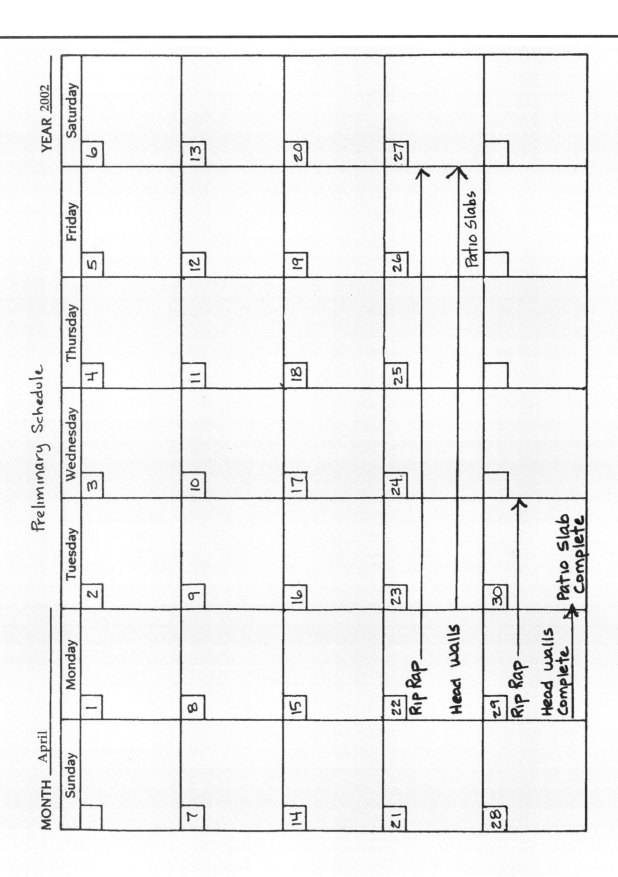

Preliminary Schedule

MONTH April

YEAR 2002

Sunday	Monday	Tuesday	Wednesday	Thursday	Friday	Saturday
	1	2	3	4	5	6
7	8	9	10	11	12	13
14	15	16	17	18	19	20
21	22 Rip Rap	23	24	25	26	27
28	29 Rip Rap	30				

Head walls

Head walls Complete

Patio Slab Complete

Patio Slabs

Figure 9.1a

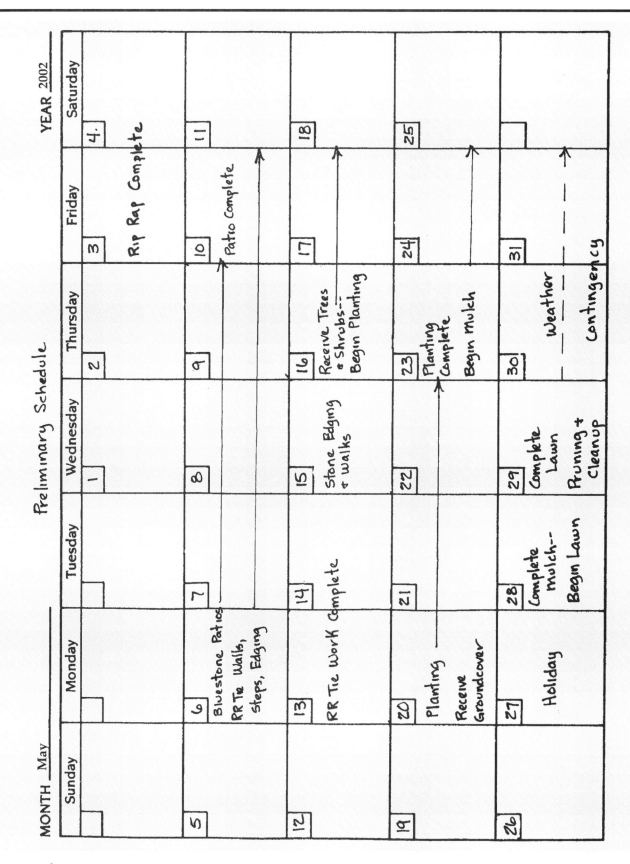

Preliminary Schedule

Figure 9.1b

186

Master Project Calendar

MONTH **May**   YEAR **2002**

Sunday	Monday	Tuesday	Wednesday	Thursday	Friday	Saturday
			1	2	3 Med. Co. Quincy	4
5	6 Griffin Newton	7 Griffin Newton	8 Marks Hingham	9 Griffin Newton / Marks Hingham	10 Johnson Braintree	11
12	13 Johnson Braintree / Kojak Cambridge	14 Johnson Braintree / Kojak Cambridge	15 Costs Co. Kingston / Johnson Braintree	16 Costs Co. Kingston	17 Costs Co. Kingston	18
19	20 Costs Co. Kingston	21 Costs Co. Kingston	22 Costs Co. Kingston	23 Costs Co. Kingston	24 Costs Co. Kingston	25
26	27 Holiday	28 Costs Co Kingston	29 Costs Co. Kingston	30 Costs Co. Kingston (complete) / Larson Newton	31 Larson Newton	

Figure 9.2

- Interconnected activities
- Restraints
- Sequence of installation and duration times

An **interconnected activity** is one which may run at the same time as another activity. Examples are tree planting and patio installation; these two different aspects of the job may occur on the same day or days if there are no conflicts and sufficient labor is available.

Restraints should be analyzed and appropriate plans made to deal with them. On a construction site the work of other trades and their need for access can be a significant restraint on landscape work. There are various types of restraints, fitting into several categories. A simple example is an activity that cannot be started before another is finished, such as a crushed stone drip edge to be in place before the lawn sod installation. The following questions reflect some important considerations regarding restraints:

- Is site access a factor?
- Will material arrive on schedule?
- What facilities and utilities are required and available?
- Will subcontractors perform as required?
- What risks are present?

Some risk factors may occur only at certain phases of a project, while others, such as security of goods and materials, may exist for the duration. To make a schedule, management needs to know which activities must be completed before another can begin, and which activities can be run concurrently.

Sequence of Installation and Duration Time

Sequence of installation and duration time for activities must be plotted on calendars and charts so that specific dates can be assigned. When charting workdays, it is important to allow for a certain amount of lost time. Cold, heat, and rain are all factors that must be taken into consideration.

Determine and list the durations according to actual time sequence as determined by the restraints. For example, when using a bar chart, the durations of listed activities are drawn on a time-scaled chart. Each activity is reviewed with respect to the previously defined restraints. The following questions are posed:

- Which, if any, activity must begin prior to this one?
- Which activity must run at the same time?
- Which activity must proceed after this one?

If the crew, equipment, and materials cannot all be effectively utilized during the scheduled time frame, then the schedule must be adjusted. Figure 9.3 is a bar chart that lists the various work activities for the sample project in Chapter 7. The activities are listed in the order they are scheduled with appropriate durations.

This chart lists the number of working days which can be determined using the methods described in Chapter 7. The bar chart is a refinement of the calendar, and lists the activities individually. The working days should also be shown on a calendar (Figure 9.1) with target dates. Adjustments for Saturdays, Sundays, holidays, and weather days should be taken into account when target dates are set up.

Job scheduling should be done by the manager and verified by the job foreman. Experienced managers provide foremen with written job activities and do not

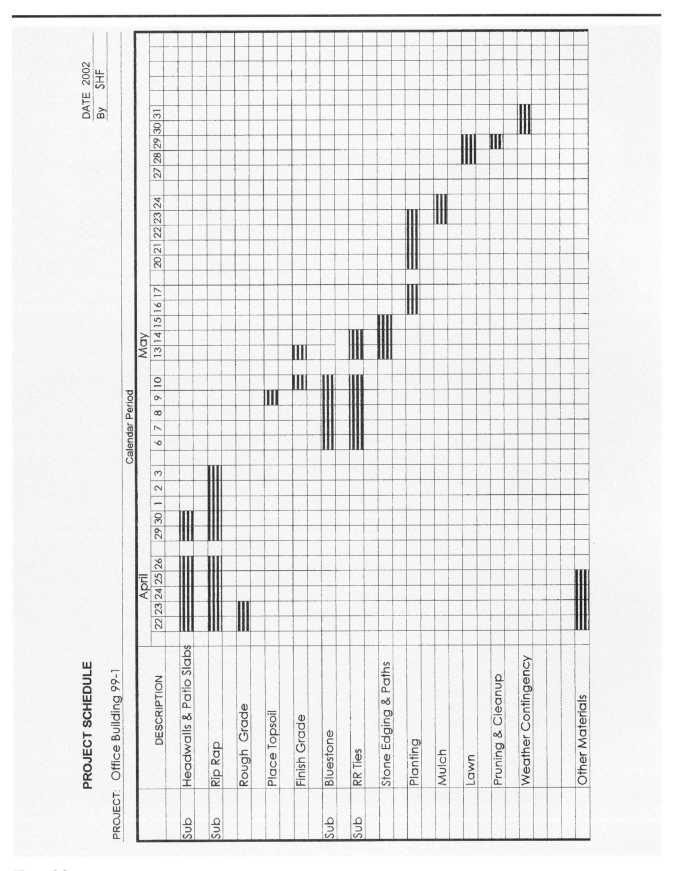

Figure 9.3

depend on memory for all of the details and required sequences. Management responsibilities regarding scheduling are handled in the following sequence:

1. Visualizing the installation process
2. Interpreting the project requirements
3. Preliminary scheduling
4. Making preparations
5. Scheduling
6. Determining the methods of construction
7. Allocating equipment and workers
8. Planning implementation
9. Arranging mobilization
10. Determining and arranging the cash flow

In scheduling, it is important to be aware of the effects of adjacent work carried out by the other trades involved in the project. For example, the installation of fence by others may involve excavation that could result in damage to nearby plantings. The responsibility should be established for "cleaning up" or repairing and replacing damage to the landscaper's work. If conflicts arise regarding materials or other factors, the conditions of the contract generally describe the procedures that should be used to resolve these questions.

While it is important to establish a schedule at the start, there is room for adjustment in the course of the project. In case of crisis, a well-developed schedule can give a broad overview of the options for adjusting work activities and salvaging work time. Throughout the project, all four of the critical resources of manpower, materials, machinery and money must be individually controlled. As the project progresses, records should be kept of time spent and materials used. Adjustments should be made, if necessary, to improve efficiency.

Project Budget

Planning is essential on jobs where payments depend upon specific completion dates. When the contractor's payment schedule relies upon certain timely activities, a chart listing and "timing" those activities may help control costly restraints, oversights, and delayed payments. Planning is especially critical when financial penalties may be imposed on the contractor for failure to perform by the established contract deadlines. Figure 9.4 is a projected payment chart from *Means Scheduling Manual* by F. William Horsley. This chart can be used to determine cash flow requirements for a particular project. Expanded, this method can be used to help predict requirements for a season or year.

Money is a primary consideration in job planning and activity scheduling. An important part of scheduling may be submitting invoices for completed work or for delivered materials. Scheduling may be tied to the payment agreement. If anticipated or required, the cost of borrowing money must also be considered —in estimating as well as planning. Contract agreements usually control payment requisitions. Typical contract requirements are: 1) specific dates (deadlines) for requisitions, 2) work periods that may be invoiced, 3) required inventories and acceptance of work and materials in place.

Schedule Review

Job planning is only effective if it has the agreement of all who are involved in the work or who are in a position to influence the progress of the work. When the schedule or job plan is finally drawn up on paper, it is vital that it be thoroughly checked over by the concerned parties for any potential problems or limitations.

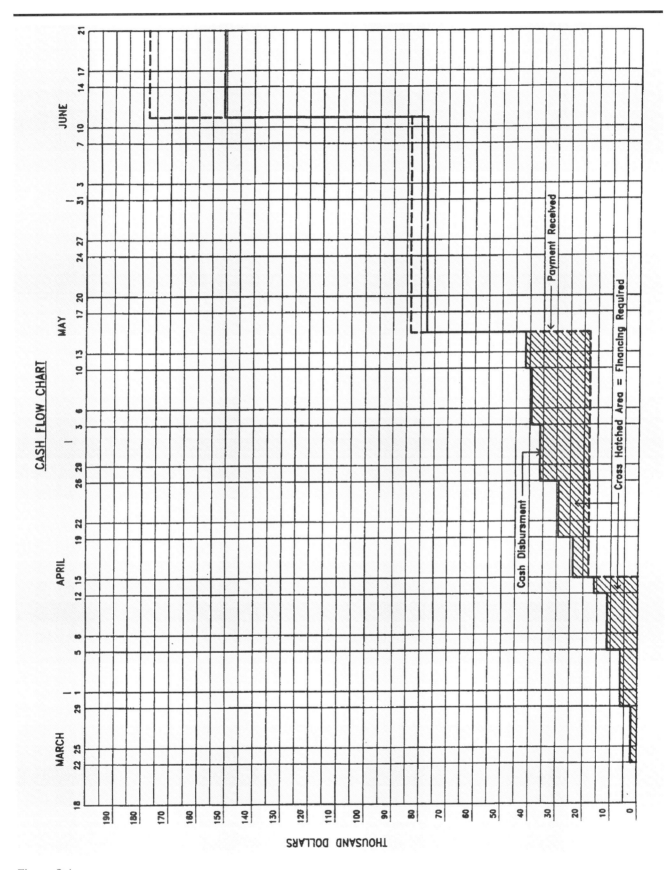

Figure 9.4

A problem involving any of the four major factors (**manpower**, **materials**, **machinery**, or **money**) has the potential to adversely affect the work schedule and consequently, the successful completion of the project. A careful review should identify any such problems or restrictions at an early stage and should help to achieve a proper rate of production. If there are unavoidable constraints, the schedule must be adapted.

Work Completion

Success in job planning requires not only an initial review, but also an ongoing process of checking off completed work. Communication regarding current and future activities between management and other personnel is a vital component. Construction sites are always in a state of change, and potential problems, which may arise at any time, must be recognized and resolved quickly. Adjusting schedules should not mean merely extending the time duration. Better solutions may involve allocating more resources or using manpower, machinery, materials, or money more productively.

Like many other activities discussed in this book, planning builds upon prior experience and information gathering. Records of past job performance are important as productivity data for your company. They may alert you, for example, to equipment advantages or impediments. Review old schedules with notations of actual versus anticipated production. These are the truest and most accurate measures of work capacity.

How To Use Means Site Work & Landscape Cost Data

Chapter Ten

How to Use Means Site Work & Landscape Cost Data

The principles of landscape estimating—from an overview of the entire process to a detailed discussion of techniques for surveying the site, recording information, pricing, bidding, and scheduling—have been discussed in previous chapters. The sample takeoff and estimate in Chapter 7 demonstrates these methods in practice. The prices used in the sample estimate are from *Means Site Work & Landscape Cost Data*. This chapter describes the components and uses of this annual cost source, along with the methods by which these costs are obtained and organized.

Using Cost Data

Users of *Means Site Work & Landscape Cost Data* are chiefly interested in obtaining quick, reasonable, average prices for site work and landscape estimates. This data is especially useful for unfamiliar items. This is the primary purpose of the annual book—to eliminate guesswork when pricing unknowns. Many people use the cost data, whether for bids or verification of quotations or budgets, without being fully aware of how the prices are obtained and derived. Without this knowledge, this resource is not being used to fullest advantage. In addition to the basic cost data, the book also contains a wealth of information to aid the estimator, the contractor, the designer, and the owner to better plan and manage landscape projects. Productivity data is provided in order to assist with scheduling, and national union labor rates are analyzed. Tables and charts for location and time adjustments are also included to help the estimator tailor the prices to a specific location. The costs in *Means Site Work & Landscape Cost Data* consist of thousands of unit price line items and systems, or assembly, prices. In addition to providing a complete, all-inclusive price, the assemblies can also be used as checklists to assure that all required items are included in a particular segment of the project.

Data Format

The first section of *Means Site Work & Landscape Cost Data* lists unit prices. The data is organized according to the 16 divisions of the MasterFormat as created by the Construction Specifications Institute, Inc. This index was developed with cooperation from representatives of all parties concerned with the building

construction industry and has been accepted by the American Institute of Architects (AIA) and the Associated General Contractors of America, Inc. (AGC), as well as most manufacturers of building materials. In *Means Site Work & Landscape Cost Data*, relevant parts of other divisions are included along with Division 2 – Site Work. The following is a list of all the MasterFormat divisions.

Construction Specifications Institute, Inc., MasterFormat Divisions

Division 1 – General Requirements

Division 2 – Site Construction

Division 3 – Concrete

Division 4 – Masonry

Division 5 – Metals

Division 6 – Wood & Plastics

Division 7 – Thermal & Moisture Protection

Division 8 – Doors & Windows

Division 9 – Finishes

Division 10 – Specialties

Division 11 – Equipment

Division 12 – Furnishings

Division 13 – Special Construction

Division 14 – Conveying Systems

Division 15 – Mechanical

Division 16 – Electrical

The second section of *Means Site Work & Landscape Cost Data*, **Assemblies**, contains thousands of costs for landscape and other site work systems. Components of the systems are fully detailed and accompanied by illustrations.

The third section, **Reference**, is a collection of technical tables and reference information. It also provides estimating procedures for some types of work and explanations of cost development which support and supplement the unit price and assemblies cost data.

The prices presented in *Means Site Work & Landscape Cost Data* are national averages. Material and equipment costs are developed through annual contact with manufacturers, dealers, distributors, and contractors throughout the United States. Means' staff of engineers is constantly updating prices and keeping abreast of changes and fluctuations within the industry. Labor rates are the national average of each trade as determined from union agreements from thirty major U.S. cities. Labor costs for each item are derived from productivity data which reflects actual working conditions and normal work performance. Following is a list of factors and assumptions on which the Means costs are based:

Quality

The costs are based on methods, materials, and workmanship in accordance with U.S. government standards and represent good, sound construction practice.

Overtime

The costs, as presented, include no allowance for overtime. If overtime or premium time is anticipated, labor costs must be factored accordingly. See

Figure 10.1 for suggested relationship of work days per week, hours per day and production efficiency as estimated over 1 to 4 weeks.

Productivity

The daily output figures are based on an eight-hour workday, during daylight hours. The chart in Figure 10.1 shows that as the number of hours worked per day (over eight) increases, and as the days per week (over five) increase, production efficiency decreases.

Size of Project

Costs in *Means Site Work & Landscape Cost Data* are based on commercial and industrial buildings which cost $500,000 and up for the total projects, including the landscape portion. Large residential projects are also included. The total value of each job influences material costs and productivity. All of the prices in the example in Chapter 7 are based on high volume materials and production costs. You should adjust your prices according to local circumstances and the particular job.

Local Factors

Weather conditions, season of the year, local labor restrictions, work near wetlands, and unusual zoning requirements can all have a significant impact on site work costs. The availability of a skilled labor force, sufficient materials, and even adequate energy and utilities will also affect costs. These factors vary in impact and are not necessarily dependent upon location. They must be reviewed for each project in every area.

In presenting prices in *Means Site Work & Landscape Cost Data*, certain rounding rules are employed to make the numbers easy to use without significantly affecting accuracy. The rules are used consistently and are as follows:

Prices		Rounded
From	To	to nearest
$ 0.01	$ 5.00	$ 0.01
5.01	20.00	0.05
20.01	100.00	1.00
100.01	1,000.00	5.00
1,000.01	10,000.00	25.00
10,000.01	50,000.00	100.00
50,000.01	up	500.00

Unit Price Section

The unit price section of *Means Site Work & Landscape Cost Data* contains a great deal of information in addition to unit costs for landscape and site work construction components. Figure 10.2 is a typical page from *Means Site Work & Landscape Cost Data*, showing a partial listing of planting costs for trees, shrubs, and ground cover. Note that prices are included for several sizes, with separate listings for bare root, potted, and bagged and burlapped plants. In addition, a suggested crew of workers is indicated for the job. The crews are the basis of the installed costs and labor-hour units. Productivity and cost data are broken down and itemized in this way to provide for the most detailed pricing possible. This price breakdown also allows for the opportunity to adjust for local variations on individual cost elements.

Within each individual line item, there is a description of the construction component, information regarding typical crews designated to perform the work, and productivity shown in labor-hours. Costs are presented as "bare," or unburdened, as well as with markups for overhead and profit. Figure 10.3 is a graphic representation of how to read a Unit Price page from *Means Site Work & Landscape Cost Data.*

Line Numbers

Every construction item in the Means unit price cost data books has a unique line number. This line number acts as an address so that each item can be quickly located and/or referenced. The numbering system is based on the classification by division. In Figure 10.3, note the bold number in reverse type, 03300. This number represents the **major subdivision**, in this case, "Cast-In-Place Concrete" of Division 3 – Concrete. All 16 divisions are organized in this manner. Within each subdivision, the data is broken down into **major classifications**. These major classifications are **listed alphabetically** and are designated by bold type for both numbers and descriptions. Each item, or line, is further defined by an individual number. As shown in Figure 10.3, the full line number for each item consists of: a major subdivision number, a major classification number, and an item line number. Each full line number describes a unique construction element. For example, in Figure 10.3, the line number for Concrete in place, footings, strip, 18″ x 9″, plain is 03310-240-3900.

Days per Week	Hours per Day	Production Efficiency					Payroll Cost Factors	
		1 Week	2 Weeks	3 Weeks	4 Weeks	Average 4 Weeks	@ 1-1/2 times	@ 2 times
	8	100%	100%	100%	100%	100%	100%	100%
	9	100	100	95	90	96.25	105.6	111.1
5	10	100	95	90	85	91.25	110.0	120.0
	11	95	90	75	65	81.25	113.6	127.3
	12	90	85	70	60	76.25	116.7	133.3
	8	100	100	95	90	96.25	108.3	116.7
	9	100	95	90	85	92.50	113.0	125.9
6	10	95	90	85	80	87.50	116.7	133.3
	11	95	85	70	65	78.75	119.7	139.4
	12	90	80	65	60	73.75	122.2	144.4
	8	100	95	85	75	88.75	114.3	128.6
	9	95	90	80	70	83.75	118.3	136.5
7	10	90	85	75	65	78.75	121.4	142.9
	11	85	80	65	60	72.50	124.0	148.1
	12	85	75	60	55	68.75	126.2	152.4

Figure 10.1

02912	General Planting	CREW	DAILY OUTPUT	LABOR-HOURS	UNIT	2002 BARE COSTS				TOTAL INCL O&P
						MAT.	LABOR	EQUIP.	TOTAL	
350	0010	**PLANTING** Trees, shrubs and ground cover										350
0100	Light soil									
0110	Bare root seedlings, 3" to 5"	1 Clab	960	.008	Ea.		.20		.20	.30
0120	6" to 10"		520	.015			.36		.36	.56
0130	11" to 16"		370	.022			.51		.51	.79
0140	17" to 24"		210	.038			.89		.89	1.39
0200	Potted, 2-1/4" diameter		840	.010			.22		.22	.35
0210	3" diameter		700	.011			.27		.27	.42
0220	4" diameter	▼	620	.013			.30		.30	.47
0300	Container, 1 gallon	2 Clab	84	.190			4.47		4.47	6.95
0310	2 gallon		52	.308			7.20		7.20	11.25
0320	3 gallon		40	.400			9.40		9.40	14.60
0330	5 gallon		29	.552			12.95		12.95	20
0400	Bagged and burlapped, 12" diameter ball, by hand	▼	19	.842			19.75		19.75	30.50
0410	Backhoe/loader, 48 H.P.	B-6	40	.600			15.35	4.46	19.81	28.50
0415	15" diameter, by hand	2 Clab	16	1			23.50		23.50	36.50
0416	Backhoe/loader, 48 H.P.	B-6	30	.800			20.50	5.95	26.45	38
0420	18" diameter by hand	2 Clab	12	1.333			31.50		31.50	48.50
0430	Backhoe/loader, 48 H.P.	B-6	27	.889			22.50	6.60	29.10	42.50
0440	24" diameter by hand	2 Clab	9	1.778			41.50		41.50	65
0450	Backhoe/loader 48 H.P.	B-6	21	1.143			29	8.50	37.50	54.50
0470	36" diameter, backhoe/loader, 48 H.P.	"	17	1.412	▼		36	10.50	46.50	67
0550	Medium soil									
0560	Bare root seedlings, 3" to 5"	1 Clab	672	.012	Ea.		.28		.28	.43
0561	6" to 10"		364	.022			.52		.52	.80
0562	11" to 16"	▼	260	.031	▼		.72		.72	1.12
0563	17" to 24"	1 Clab	145	.055	Ea.		1.29		1.29	2.01
0570	Potted, 2-1/4" diameter		590	.014			.32		.32	.49
0572	3" diameter		490	.016			.38		.38	.60
0574	4" diameter	▼	435	.018			.43		.43	.67
0590	Container, 1 gallon	2 Clab	59	.271			6.35		6.35	9.90
0592	2 gallon		36	.444			10.40		10.40	16.20
0594	3 gallon		28	.571			13.40		13.40	21
0595	5 gallon		20	.800			18.75		18.75	29
0600	Bagged and burlapped, 12" diameter ball, by hand	▼	13	1.231			29		29	45
0605	Backhoe/loader, 48 H.P.	B-6	28	.857			22	6.40	28.40	40.50
0607	15" diameter, by hand	2 Clab	11.20	1.429			33.50		33.50	52
0608	Backhoe/loader, 48 H.P.	B-6	21	1.143			29	8.50	37.50	54.50
0610	18" diameter, by hand	2 Clab	8.50	1.882			44		44	68.50
0615	Backhoe/loader, 48 H.P.	B-6	19	1.263			32.50	9.40	41.90	60
0620	24" diameter, by hand	2 Clab	6.30	2.540			59.50		59.50	92.50
0625	Backhoe/loader, 48 H.P.	B-6	14.70	1.633			42	12.15	54.15	77.50
0630	36" diameter, backhoe/loader, 48 H.P.	"	12	2	▼		51	14.90	65.90	95
0700	Heavy or stoney soil									
0710	Bare root seedlings, 3" to 5"	1 Clab	470	.017	Ea.		.40		.40	.62
0711	6" to 10"		255	.031			.74		.74	1.15
0712	11" to 16"		182	.044			1.03		1.03	1.60
0713	17" to 24"		101	.079			1.86		1.86	2.89
0720	Potted, 2-1/4" diameter		101	.079			1.86		1.86	2.89
0722	3" diameter		343	.023			.55		.55	.85
0724	4" diameter	▼	305	.026			.62		.62	.96
0730	Container, 1 gallon	2 Clab	41.30	.387			9.10		9.10	14.15
0732	2 gallon		25.20	.635			14.90		14.90	23
0734	3 gallon		19.60	.816			19.15		19.15	30

(from *Means Site Work & Landscape Cost Data 2002*)

Figure 10.2

How to Use the Unit Price Pages

The following is a detailed explanation of a sample entry in the Unit Price Section. Next to each bold number below is the item being described with appropriate component of the sample entry following in parenthesis. Some prices are listed as bare costs, others as costs that include overhead and profit of the installing contractor. In most cases, if the work is to be subcontracted, the general contractor will need to add an additional markup (R.S. Means suggests using 10%) to the figures in the column "Total Incl. O&P."

Division Number/Title (03300/Cast-In-Place Concrete)

Use the Unit Price Section Table of Contents to locate specific items. The sections are classified according to the CSI MasterFormat (1995 Edition).

Line Numbers (03310 240 3900)

Each unit price line item has been assigned a unique 12-digit code based on the CSI MasterFormat classification.

- Level One - CSI-MasterFormat Division
- Level Two - CSI

03300
03310-240-3900

- Means 12-digit Line Number
- Level Four - Means
- Level Three - CSI

Description (Concrete-In-Place, etc.)

Each line item is described in detail. Sub-items and additional sizes are indented beneath the appropriate line items. The first line or two after the main item (in boldface) may contain descriptive information that pertains to all line items beneath this boldface listing.

Items which include the symbol **CN** are updated in the Key Material Price Section of *The Change Notice* quarterly publication.

Reference Number Information

| R03310 -010 | You'll see reference numbers shown in bold rectangles at the beginning of some sections. These refer to related items in the |

Reference Section, visually identified by a vertical gray bar on the edge of pages.

The relation may be: (1) an estimating procedure that should be read before estimating, (2) an alternate pricing method, or (3) technical information.

The "R" designates the Reference Section. The numbers refer to the MasterFormat classification system.

It is strongly recommended that you review all reference numbers that appear within the section in which you are working.

Note: Not all reference numbers appear in all Means publications.

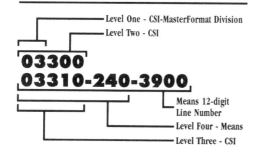

03300 | Cast-In-Place Concrete

03310	Structural Concrete		CREW	DAILY OUTPUT	LABOR-HOURS	UNIT	MAT.	LABOR	EQUIP.	TOTAL	TOTAL INCL O&P	
240	0010	CONCRETE IN PLACE Including forms... reinforcing										240
	0050	steel, including finishing unless otherwise indicated	R03310 -010									
	3800	Footings, spread under 1 C.Y.	C-14C	38.07	2.942	C.Y.	100	84.50	.94	185.44	244	
	3850	Over 5 C.Y.		81.04	1.382		92	40	.44	132.44	164	
	3900	Footings, strip, 18" x 9", plain		41.04	2.729		91	78.50	.87	170.37	225	
	3950	36" x 12", reinforced		61.55	1.820		92.50	52.50	.58	145.58	185	
	4000	Foundation mat, under 10 C.Y.		38.67	2.896		124	83.50	.93	208.43	268	
	4050	Over 20 C.Y.		56	2.086		110	57	.64	167.64	209	
	4200	Grade walls, 8" thick, 8' high	C-14D	45	2.64		126	130	15.65	271.65	360	
	4250	14' high		27.26	7.337		149	219	26.50	394.50	540	
	4260	12" thick, 8' high		64.32	3.109		111	93	11.15	215.15	279	
	4270	14' high		40.01	4.999		119	149	17.95	285.95	385	

Figure 10.3

Crew (C-14C)

The "Crew" column designates the typical trade or crew used to install the item. If an installation can be accomplished by one trade and requires no power equipment, that trade and the number of workers are listed (for example, "2 Carpenters"). If an installation requires a composite crew, a crew code designation is listed (for example, "C-14C"). You'll find full details on all composite crews in the Crew Listings.

* For a complete list of all trades utilized in this book and their abbreviations, see the inside back cover.

Crews

Crew No.	Bare Costs		Incl. Subs O & P		Cost Per Labor-Hour	
Crew C-14C	Hr.	Daily	Hr.	Daily	Bare Costs	Incl. O&P
1 Carpenter Foreman (out)	$32.00	$256.00	$49.80	$398.40	$28.79	$45.29
6 Carpenters	30.00	1440.00	46.70	2241.60		
2 Rodmen (reinf.)	34.25	548.00	57.80	924.80		
4 Laborers	23.45	750.40	36.50	1168.00		
1 Cement Finisher	28.70	229.60	42.50	340.00		
1 Gas Engine Vibrator		35.60		39.15	.32	.35
112 L.H., Daily Totals		$3259.60		$5111.95	$29.11	$45.64

Productivity: Daily Output (41.04)/Labor-Hours (2.729)

The "Daily Output" represents the typical number of units the designated crew will install in a normal 8-hour day. To find out the number of days the given crew would require to complete the installation, divide your quantity by the daily output. For example:

Quantity	÷	Daily Output	=	Duration
100 C.Y.	÷	41.04/ Crew Day	=	2.44 Crew Days

The "Labor-Hours" figure represents the number of labor-hours required to install one unit of work. To find out the number of labor-hours required for your particular task, multiply the quantity of the item times the number of labor-hours shown. For example:

Quantity	x	Productivity Rate	=	Duration
100 C.Y.	x	2.724 Labor-Hours/ C.Y.	=	272.4 Labor-Hours

Unit (C.Y.)

The abbreviated designation indicates the unit of measure upon which the price, production, and crew are based (C.Y. = Cubic Yard). For a complete listing of abbreviations refer to the Abbreviations Listing in the Reference Section of this book.

Bare Costs:

Mat. (Bare Material Cost) (91)

The unit material cost is the "bare" material cost with no overhead and profit included. *Costs shown reflect national average material prices for January of the current year and include delivery to the job site. No sales taxes are included.*

Labor (78.50)

The unit labor cost is derived by multiplying bare labor-hour costs for Crew C-14C by labor-hour units. The bare labor-hour cost is found in the Crew Section under C-14C. (If a trade is listed, the hourly labor cost—the wage rate—is found on the inside back cover.)

Labor-Hour Cost Crew C-14C	x	Labor-Hour Units	=	Labor
$28.79	x	2.729	=	$78.50

Equip. (Equipment) (.87)

Equipment costs for each crew are listed in the description of each crew. Tools or equipment whose value justifies purchase or ownership by a contractor are considered overhead as shown on the inside back cover. The unit equipment cost is derived by multiplying the bare equipment hourly cost by the labor-hour units.

Equipment Cost Crew C-14C	x	Labor-Hour Units	=	Equip.
.32	x	2.729	=	.87

Total (170.37)

The total of the bare costs is the arithmetic total of the three previous columns: mat., labor, and equip.

Material	+	Labor	+	Equip.	=	Total
$91	+	$78.50	+	$.87	=	$170.37

Total Costs Including O&P

This figure is the sum of the bare material cost plus 10% for profit; the bare labor cost plus total overhead and profit (per the inside back cover or, if a crew is listed, from the crew listings); and the bare equipment cost plus 10% for profit.

Material is Bare Material Cost + 10% = 91 + 9.10	=	$100.10
Labor for Crew C-14C = Labor-Hour Cost (45.29) x Labor-Hour Units (2.729)	=	$123.60
Equip. is Bare Equip. Cost + 10% = .87 + .09	=	$ .96
Total (Rounded)	=	$225

Figure 10.3 (*cont.*)

Line Description

Each line has a text description of the item for which costs are listed. The description may be self-contained and all-inclusive. Other lines are indented and rely on the text above for a complete description. All indented items are delineations (by size, color, material, etc.) or breakdowns of previously described items. An extensive index is provided in the back of *Means Site Work & Landscape Cost Data* to aid in locating particular items.

Crew

For each construction element (each line item), a minimum typical crew is designated as appropriate to perform the work. The crew may include one or more trades, foremen, craftsmen and helpers, and any equipment required for proper installation of the described item. If an individual trade installs the item using only hand tools, the smallest efficient number of tradesmen will be indicated; 1 Clab (common laborer), 1 Skwk (skilled worker), 1 Ston (stone mason), etc. A complete list of abbreviations for trades is shown in Figure 10.4. If more than one trade is required to install the item and/or if powered equipment is needed, a crew number will be designated (B-18, B-36, etc.). A complete listing of crews is presented after the reference section of *Means Site Work & Landscape Cost Data* (See Figure 10.5 for an example Crew page). On these pages, each crew is broken down into the following components:

1. Number and size of workers designated.
2. Number, size, and type of any equipment required.
3. Hourly labor costs listed two ways: "bare"—base rate including fringe benefits; and billing rate—including the installing contractor's overhead and profit. (See Figure 10.4 from the inside back cover of *Means Site Work & Landscape Cost Data* for union labor rate information).
4. Daily equipment costs, based on the weekly equipment rental cost divided by five, plus the hourly operating cost, times eight hours. This cost is listed two ways: as a bare cost and with a 10% markup to cover handling and management costs.
5. Labor and equipment are further broken down into: cost per labor-hour for labor, and cost per labor-hour for equipment.
6. The total daily labor-hours for the crew.
7. The total bare costs per day for the crew, including equipment.
8. The total daily cost of the crew including the installing contractor's overhead and profit.

The total daily cost of the required crew is used to calculate the unit installation cost for each item (for both bare costs and cost including overhead and profit).

The crew designation does not mean that this is the only crew that can perform the work. Crew size and content have been developed and chosen based on practical experience and feedback from contractors. These designations represent a labor and equipment makeup commonly found in the industry. The most appropriate crew for a given task is best determined based on particular project requirements. Unit costs may vary if crew sizes or content are significantly changed.

Figure 10.6 is a page from Division 01596 of *Means Site Work & Landscape Cost Data*. This type of page lists the equipment costs used in the presentation and calculation of the crew costs and unit price data. Rental costs are shown as daily, weekly, and monthly rates. The Hourly Operating Cost represents the cost

R01100-070 Contractor's Overhead & Profit

Below are the **average** installing contractor's percentage mark-ups applied to base labor rates to arrive at typical billing rates.

Column A: Labor rates are based on union wages averaged for 30 major U.S. cities. Base rates including fringe benefits are listed hourly and daily. These figures are the sum of the wage rate and employer-paid fringe benefits such as vacation pay, employer-paid health and welfare costs, pension costs, plus appropriate training and industry advancement funds costs.

Column B: Workers' Compensation rates are the national average of state rates established for each trade.

Column C: Column C lists average fixed overhead figures for all trades. Included are Federal and State Unemployment costs set at 7.0%; Social Security Taxes (FICA) set at 7.65%; Builder's Risk Insurance costs set at 0.34%; and Public Liability costs set at 1.55%. All the percentages except those for Social Security Taxes vary from state to state as well as from company to company.

Columns D and E: Percentages in Columns D and E are based on the presumption that the installing contractor has annual billing of $1,500,000 and up. Overhead percentages may increase with smaller annual billing. The overhead percentages for any given contractor may vary greatly and depend on a number of factors, such as the contractor's annual volume, engineering and logistical support costs, and staff requirements. The figures for overhead and profit will also vary depending on the type of job, the job location, and the prevailing economic conditions. All factors should be examined very carefully for each job.

Column F: Column F lists the total of Columns B, C, D, and E.

Column G: Column G is Column A (hourly base labor rate) multiplied by the percentage in Column F (O&P percentage).

Column H: Column H is the total of Column A (hourly base labor rate) plus Column G (Total O&P).

Column I: Column I is Column H multiplied by eight hours.

		A		B	C	D	E	F	G	H	I
		Base Rate Incl. Fringes		Workers' Comp. Ins.	Average Fixed Overhead	Overhead	Profit	Total Overhead & Profit		Rate with O & P	
Abbr.	Trade	Hourly	Daily					%	Amount	Hourly	Daily
Skwk	Skilled Workers Average (35 trades)	$30.95	$247.60	16.8%	16.5%	13.0%	10.0%	56.3%	$17.40	$48.35	$386.80
	Helpers Average (5 trades)	22.75	182.00	18.5		11.0		56.0	$12.75	35.50	284.00
	Foreman Average, Inside ($0.50 over trade)	31.45	251.60	16.8		13.0		56.3	17.70	49.15	393.20
	Foreman Average, Outside ($2.00 over trade)	32.95	263.60	16.8		13.0		56.3	18.55	51.50	412.00
Clab	Common Building Laborers	23.45	187.60	18.1		11.0		55.6	13.05	36.50	292.00
Asbe	Asbestos/Insulation Workers/Pipe Coverers	33.45	267.60	16.2		16.0		58.7	19.65	53.10	424.80
Boil	Boilermakers	36.25	290.00	14.7		16.0		57.2	20.75	57.00	456.00
Bric	Bricklayers	30.50	244.00	16.0		11.0		53.5	16.30	46.80	374.40
Brhe	Bricklayer Helpers	23.50	188.00	16.0		11.0		53.5	12.55	36.05	288.40
Carp	Carpenters	30.00	240.00	18.1		11.0		55.6	16.70	46.70	373.60
Cefi	Cement Finishers	28.70	229.60	10.6		11.0		48.1	13.80	42.50	340.00
Elec	Electricians	35.45	283.60	6.7		16.0		49.2	17.45	52.90	423.20
Elev	Elevator Constructors	37.10	296.80	7.7		16.0		50.2	18.60	55.70	445.60
Eqhv	Equipment Operators, Crane or Shovel	32.35	258.80	10.6		14.0		51.1	16.55	48.90	391.20
Eqmd	Equipment Operators, Medium Equipment	31.20	249.60	10.6		14.0		51.1	15.95	47.15	377.20
Eqlt	Equipment Operators, Light Equipment	29.80	238.40	10.6		14.0		51.1	15.25	45.05	360.40
Eqol	Equipment Operators, Oilers	26.65	213.20	10.6		14.0		51.1	13.60	40.25	322.00
Eqmm	Equipment Operators, Master Mechanics	32.80	262.40	10.6		14.0		51.1	16.75	49.55	396.40
Glaz	Glaziers	30.00	240.00	13.8		11.0		51.3	15.40	45.40	363.20
Lath	Lathers	28.75	230.00	11.1		11.0		48.6	13.95	42.70	341.60
Marb	Marble Setters	30.10	240.80	16.0		11.0		53.5	16.10	46.20	369.60
Mill	Millwrights	31.75	254.00	10.6		11.0		48.1	15.25	47.00	376.00
Mstz	Mosaic and Terrazzo Workers	29.25	234.00	9.8		11.0		47.3	13.85	43.10	344.80
Pord	Painters, Ordinary	27.15	217.20	13.8		11.0		51.3	13.95	41.10	328.80
Psst	Painters, Structural Steel	27.90	223.20	48.4		11.0		85.9	23.95	51.85	414.80
Pape	Paper Hangers	27.10	216.80	13.8		11.0		51.3	13.90	41.00	328.00
Pile	Pile Drivers	29.80	238.40	24.9		16.0		67.4	20.10	49.90	399.20
Plas	Plasterers	28.10	224.80	15.8		11.0		53.3	15.00	43.10	344.80
Plah	Plasterer Helpers	23.70	189.60	15.8		11.0		53.3	12.65	36.35	290.80
Plum	Plumbers	35.95	287.60	8.3		16.0		50.8	18.25	54.20	433.60
Rodm	Rodmen (Reinforcing)	34.25	274.00	28.3		14.0		68.8	23.55	57.80	462.40
Rofc	Roofers, Composition	26.60	212.80	32.6		11.0		70.1	18.65	45.25	362.00
Rots	Roofers, Tile and Slate	26.75	214.00	32.6		11.0		70.1	18.75	45.50	364.00
Rohe	Roofer Helpers (Composition)	19.80	158.40	32.6		11.0		70.1	13.90	33.70	269.60
Shee	Sheet Metal Workers	35.10	280.80	11.7		16.0		54.2	19.00	54.10	432.80
Spri	Sprinkler Installers	36.20	289.60	8.7		16.0		51.2	18.55	54.75	438.00
Stpi	Steamfitters or Pipefitters	36.20	289.60	8.3		16.0		50.8	18.40	54.60	436.80
Ston	Stone Masons	30.65	245.20	16.0		11.0		53.5	16.40	47.05	376.40
Sswk	Structural Steel Workers	34.25	274.00	39.8		14.0		80.3	27.50	61.75	494.00
Tilf	Tile Layers	29.15	233.20	9.8		11.0		47.3	13.80	42.95	343.60
Tilh	Tile Layer Helpers	23.35	186.80	9.8		11.0		47.3	11.05	34.40	275.20
Trlt	Truck Drivers, Light	24.30	194.40	14.9		11.0		52.4	12.75	37.05	296.40
Trhv	Truck Drivers, Heavy	25.00	200.00	14.9		11.0		52.4	13.10	38.10	304.80
Sswl	Welders, Structural Steel	34.25	274.00	39.8		14.0		80.3	27.50	61.75	494.00
Wrck	*Wrecking	23.45	187.60	41.2	▼	11.0	▼	78.7	18.45	41.90	335.20

*Not included in Averages.

(from *Means Site Work & Landscape Cost Data* 2002)

Figure 10.4

Crews

Crew No.	Bare Costs		Incl. Subs O & P		Cost Per Labor-Hour	
Crew B-10K	**Hr.**	**Daily**	**Hr.**	**Daily**	**Bare Costs**	**Incl. O&P**
1 Equip. Oper. (med.)	$31.20	$249.60	$47.15	$377.20	$28.62	$43.60
.5 Laborer	23.45	93.80	36.50	146.00		
1 Centr. Water Pump, 6"		198.20		218.00		
1-20 Ft. Suction Hose, 6"		19.50		21.45		
2-50 Ft. Disch. Hoses, 6"		34.80		38.30	21.04	23.15
12 L.H., Daily Totals		$595.90		$800.95	$49.66	$66.75
Crew B-10L	**Hr.**	**Daily**	**Hr.**	**Daily**	**Bare Costs**	**Incl. O&P**
1 Equip. Oper. (med.)	$31.20	$249.60	$47.15	$377.20	$28.62	$43.60
.5 Laborer	23.45	93.80	36.50	146.00		
1 Dozer, 75 H.P.		291.20		320.30	24.27	26.69
12 L.H., Daily Totals		$634.60		$843.50	$52.89	$70.29
Crew B-10M	**Hr.**	**Daily**	**Hr.**	**Daily**	**Bare Costs**	**Incl. O&P**
1 Equip. Oper. (med.)	$31.20	$249.60	$47.15	$377.20	$28.62	$43.60
.5 Laborer	23.45	93.80	36.50	146.00		
1 Dozer, 300 H.P.		1034.00		1137.40	86.17	94.78
12 L.H., Daily Totals		$1377.40		$1660.60	$114.79	$138.38
Crew B-10N	**Hr.**	**Daily**	**Hr.**	**Daily**	**Bare Costs**	**Incl. O&P**
1 Equip. Oper. (med.)	$31.20	$249.60	$47.15	$377.20	$28.62	$43.60
.5 Laborer	23.45	93.80	36.50	146.00		
1 F.E. Loader, T.M., 1.5 C.Y		263.60		289.95	21.97	24.16
12 L.H., Daily Totals		$607.00		$813.15	$50.59	$67.76
Crew B-10O	**Hr.**	**Daily**	**Hr.**	**Daily**	**Bare Costs**	**Incl. O&P**
1 Equip. Oper. (med.)	$31.20	$249.60	$47.15	$377.20	$28.62	$43.60
.5 Laborer	23.45	93.80	36.50	146.00		
1 F.E. Loader, T.M., 2.25 C.Y.		498.40		548.25	41.53	45.69
12 L.H., Daily Totals		$841.80		$1071.45	$70.15	$89.29
Crew B-10P	**Hr.**	**Daily**	**Hr.**	**Daily**	**Bare Costs**	**Incl. O&P**
1 Equip. Oper. (med.)	$31.20	$249.60	$47.15	$377.20	$28.62	$43.60
.5 Laborer	23.45	93.80	36.50	146.00		
1 F.E. Loader, T.M., 2.5 C.Y.		690.60		759.65	57.55	63.31
12 L.H., Daily Totals		$1034.00		$1282.85	$86.17	$106.91
Crew B-10Q	**Hr.**	**Daily**	**Hr.**	**Daily**	**Bare Costs**	**Incl. O&P**
1 Equip. Oper. (med.)	$31.20	$249.60	$47.15	$377.20	$28.62	$43.60
.5 Laborer	23.45	93.80	36.50	146.00		
1 F.E. Loader, T.M., 5 C.Y.		971.20		1068.30	80.93	89.03
12 L.H., Daily Totals		$1314.60		$1591.50	$109.55	$132.63
Crew B-10R	**Hr.**	**Daily**	**Hr.**	**Daily**	**Bare Costs**	**Incl. O&P**
1 Equip. Oper. (med.)	$31.20	$249.60	$47.15	$377.20	$28.62	$43.60
.5 Laborer	23.45	93.80	36.50	146.00		
1 F.E. Loader, W.M., 1 C.Y.		214.40		235.85	17.87	19.65
12 L.H., Daily Totals		$557.80		$759.05	$46.49	$63.25
Crew B-10S	**Hr.**	**Daily**	**Hr.**	**Daily**	**Bare Costs**	**Incl. O&P**
1 Equip. Oper. (med.)	$31.20	$249.60	$47.15	$377.20	$28.62	$43.60
.5 Laborer	23.45	93.80	36.50	146.00		
1 F.E. Loader, W.M., 1.5 C.Y.		276.40		304.05	23.03	25.34
12 L.H., Daily Totals		$619.80		$827.25	$51.65	$68.94

Crew No.	Bare Costs		Incl. Subs O & P		Cost Per Labor-Hour	
Crew B-10U	**Hr.**	**Daily**	**Hr.**	**Daily**	**Bare Costs**	**Incl. O&P**
1 Equip. Oper. (med.)	$31.20	$249.60	$47.15	$377.20	$28.62	$43.60
.5 Laborer	23.45	93.80	36.50	146.00		
1 F.E. Loader, W.M., 5.5 C.Y.		777.60		855.35	64.80	71.28
12 L.H., Daily Totals		$1121.00		$1378.55	$93.42	$114.88
Crew B-10V	**Hr.**	**Daily**	**Hr.**	**Daily**	**Bare Costs**	**Incl. O&P**
1 Equip. Oper. (med.)	$31.20	$249.60	$47.15	$377.20	$28.62	$43.60
.5 Laborer	23.45	93.80	36.50	146.00		
1 Dozer, 700 H.P.		2924.00		3216.40	243.67	268.03
12 L.H., Daily Totals		$3267.40		$3739.60	$272.29	$311.63
Crew B-10W	**Hr.**	**Daily**	**Hr.**	**Daily**	**Bare Costs**	**Incl. O&P**
1 Equip. Oper. (med.)	$31.20	$249.60	$47.15	$377.20	$28.62	$43.60
.5 Laborer	23.45	93.80	36.50	146.00		
1 Dozer, 105 H.P.		432.60		475.85	36.05	39.66
12 L.H., Daily Totals		$776.00		$999.05	$64.67	$83.26
Crew B-10X	**Hr.**	**Daily**	**Hr.**	**Daily**	**Bare Costs**	**Incl. O&P**
1 Equip. Oper. (med.)	$31.20	$249.60	$47.15	$377.20	$28.62	$43.60
.5 Laborer	23.45	93.80	36.50	146.00		
1 Dozer, 410 H.P.		1374.00		1511.40	114.50	125.95
12 L.H., Daily Totals		$1717.40		$2034.60	$143.12	$169.55
Crew B-10Y	**Hr.**	**Daily**	**Hr.**	**Daily**	**Bare Costs**	**Incl. O&P**
1 Equip. Oper. (med.)	$31.20	$249.60	$47.15	$377.20	$28.62	$43.60
.5 Laborer	23.45	93.80	36.50	146.00		
1 Vibratory Drum Roller		303.40		333.75	25.28	27.81
12 L.H., Daily Totals		$646.80		$856.95	$53.90	$71.41
Crew B-11	**Hr.**	**Daily**	**Hr.**	**Daily**	**Bare Costs**	**Incl. O&P**
1 Equipment Oper. (med.)	$31.20	$249.60	$47.15	$377.20	$27.33	$41.83
1 Laborer	23.45	187.60	36.50	292.00		
16 L.H., Daily Totals		$437.20		$669.20	$27.33	$41.83
Crew B-11A	**Hr.**	**Daily**	**Hr.**	**Daily**	**Bare Costs**	**Incl. O&P**
1 Equipment Oper. (med.)	$31.20	$249.60	$47.15	$377.20	$27.33	$41.83
1 Laborer	23.45	187.60	36.50	292.00		
1 Dozer, 200 H.P.		823.40		905.75	51.46	56.61
16 L.H., Daily Totals		$1260.60		$1574.95	$78.79	$98.44
Crew B-11B	**Hr.**	**Daily**	**Hr.**	**Daily**	**Bare Costs**	**Incl. O&P**
1 Equipment Oper. (med.)	$31.20	$249.60	$47.15	$377.20	$27.33	$41.83
1 Laborer	23.45	187.60	36.50	292.00		
1 Dozer, 200 H.P.		823.40		905.75		
1 Air Powered Tamper		21.10		23.20		
1 Air Compr. 365 C.F.M.		163.00		179.30		
2-50 Ft. Air Hoses, 1.5" Dia.		9.40		10.35	63.56	69.91
16 L.H., Daily Totals		$1454.10		$1787.80	$90.89	$111.74
Crew B-11C	**Hr.**	**Daily**	**Hr.**	**Daily**	**Bare Costs**	**Incl. O&P**
1 Equipment Oper. (med.)	$31.20	$249.60	$47.15	$377.20	$27.33	$41.83
1 Laborer	23.45	187.60	36.50	292.00		
1 Backhoe Loader, 48 H.P.		178.60		196.45	11.16	12.28
16 L.H., Daily Totals		$615.80		$865.65	$38.49	$54.11

from *Means Site Work & Landscape Cost Data 2002*)

Figure 10.5

01590 | Equipment Rental

				UNIT	HOURLY OPER. COST	RENT PER DAY	RENT PER WEEK	RENT PER MONTH	CREW EQUIPMENT COST/DAY	
200	2900	Rake, spring tooth, with tractor	R01590 -100	Ea.	1.14	190	571	1,725	123.30	200
	3000	Roller, tandem, gas, 3 to 5 ton			5.15	127	380	1,150	117.20	
	3050	Diesel, 8 to 12 ton	R02315 -400		4.30	223	670	2,000	168.40	
	3100	Towed type, vibratory, gas 12.5 H.P., 2 ton			2.70	255	765	2,300	174.60	
	3150	Sheepsfoot, double 60" x 60"	R02315 -450		.85	110	330	990	72.80	
	3200	Pneumatic tire diesel roller, 12 ton			6.10	315	945	2,825	237.80	
	3250	21 to 25 ton			10.25	590	1,775	5,325	437	
	3300	Sheepsfoot roller, self-propelled, 4 wheel, 130 H.P.			29.80	875	2,630	7,900	764.40	
	3320	300 H.P.			41.55	975	2,930	8,800	918.40	
	3350	Vibratory steel drum & pneumatic tire, diesel, 18,000 lb.			11.30	355	1,065	3,200	303.40	
	3400	29,000 lb.			18.95	470	1,415	4,250	434.60	
	3410	Rotary mower, brush, 60", with tractor			7.15	237	710	2,125	199.20	
	3450	Scrapers, towed type, 9 to 12 C.Y. capacity			3.37	161	482	1,450	123.35	
	3500	12 to 17 C.Y. capacity			3.58	214	643	1,925	157.25	
	3550	Scrapers, self-propelled, 4 x 4 drive, 2 engine, 14 C.Y. capacity			69.40	1,450	4,320	13,000	1,419	
	3600	2 engine, 24 C.Y. capacity			101.35	2,275	6,815	20,400	2,174	
	3650	Self-loading, 11 C.Y. capacity			31.35	825	2,470	7,400	744.80	
	3700	22 C.Y. capacity			61.35	1,475	4,410	13,200	1,373	
	3710	Screening plant 110 hp. w / 5' x 10'screen			15.85	370	1,115	3,350	349.80	
	3720	5' x 16' screen	▼		17.20	475	1,420	4,250	421.60	
	3850	Shovels, see Cranes division 01590-600								
	3860	Shovel/backhoe bucket, 1/2 C.Y.		Ea.	.85	53.50	160	480	38.80	
	3870	3/4 C.Y.			.85	61.50	185	555	43.80	
	3880	1 C.Y.			.90	71.50	215	645	50.20	
	3890	1-1/2 C.Y.			1	170	510	1,525	110	
	3910	3 C.Y.			1.15	305	920	2,750	193.20	
	3950	Stump chipper, 18" deep, 30 H.P.			3.08	185	555	1,675	135.65	
	4110	Tractor, crawler, with bulldozer, torque converter, diesel 75 H.P.			12.15	325	970	2,900	291.20	
	4150	105 H.P.			17.20	490	1,475	4,425	432.60	
	4200	140 H.P.			19.80	510	1,530	4,600	464.40	
	4260	200 H.P.			29.80	975	2,925	8,775	823.40	
	4310	300 H.P.			39.20	1,200	3,600	10,800	1,034	
	4360	410 H.P.			53.65	1,575	4,725	14,200	1,374	
	4380	700 H.P.			109.65	3,400	10,235	30,700	2,924	
	4400	Loader, crawler, torque conv., diesel, 1-1/2 C.Y., 80 H.P.			9.70	310	930	2,800	263.60	
	4450	1-1/2 to 1-3/4 C.Y., 95 H.P.			11.70	380	1,145	3,425	322.60	
	4510	1-3/4 to 2-1/4 C.Y., 130 H.P.			16.05	615	1,850	5,550	498.40	
	4530	2-1/2 to 3-1/4 C.Y., 190 H.P.			23.20	840	2,525	7,575	690.60	
	4560	3-1/2 to 5 C.Y., 275 H.P.			31.15	1,200	3,610	10,800	971.20	
	4610	Tractor loader, wheel, torque conv., 4 x 4, 1 to 1-1/4 C.Y., 65 H.P.			10.05	223	670	2,000	214.40	
	4620	1-1/2 to 1-3/4 C.Y., 80 H.P.			11.05	315	940	2,825	276.40	
	4650	1-3/4 to 2 C.Y., 100 H.P.			11.55	335	1,000	3,000	292.40	
	4710	2-1/2 to 3-1/2 C.Y., 130 H.P.			14.55	425	1,270	3,800	370.40	
	4730	3 to 4-1/2 C.Y., 170 H.P.			18.10	565	1,700	5,100	484.80	
	4760	5-1/4 to 5-3/4 C.Y., 270 H.P.			32.95	855	2,570	7,700	777.60	
	4810	7 to 8 C.Y., 375 H.P.			50.20	1,100	3,305	9,925	1,063	
	4870	12-1/2 C.Y., 690 H.P.			93.50	2,350	7,015	21,000	2,151	
	4880	Wheeled, skid steer, 10 C.F., 30 H.P. gas			5.85	140	420	1,250	130.80	
	4890	1 C.Y., 78 H.P., diesel	▼		7.60	223	670	2,000	194.80	
	4891	Attachments for all skid steer loaders								
	4892	Auger		Ea.	.46	77.50	232	695	50.10	
	4893	Backhoe			.64	107	320	960	69.10	
	4894	Broom			.66	110	331	995	71.50	
	4895	Forks	▼		.21	34.50	104	310	22.50	

(from *Means Site Work & Landscape Cost Data 2002*)

Figure 10.6

of fuel, lubrication, and routine maintenance. Equipment costs used in the crews are calculated as follows:

Line number	01590-200-3950
Equipment	Stump chipper, 18″ deep, 30 H.P.
Rent per week	$555
Hourly operating cost	$3.08

$$\frac{\text{Weekly rental}}{\text{5 days per week}} + (\text{Hourly Oper. Cost} \times 8 \text{ hrs/day} = \text{Crew's Equipment Cost}$$

$$\frac{\$555}{5} + (\$3.08 \times 8) = \$135.64$$

Units

The unit column (See Figure 10.3) defines the component, such as ton or M.S.F., for which the costs have been calculated. It is this "unit" on which Unit Price Estimating is based. The units, as used, represent standard estimating and quantity takeoff procedures. However, the estimator should always check to be sure that the units taken off are the same as those priced. A list of standard abbreviations is included at the back of *Means Site Work & Landscape Cost Data.*

Bare Costs

There are four columns listed under "Bare Costs" (bare costs are listed for all unit prices except Division 01590, Equipment). Bare costs are presented as: "Material," "Labor," "Equipment," and "Total," and represent the actual cost of construction items to the contractor. In other words, bare costs are those which *do not* include the overhead and profit of the installing contractor.

Material costs are based on the national average, contractor purchase price delivered to the job site. Delivered costs are assumed to be within a 20-mile radius of metropolitan areas. No sales tax is included in the material price because of variations from state to state.

The prices are based on quantities that would normally be purchased for landscape projects costing $5,000 to $10,000 and up. Material costs represent wholesale prices. Prices for small quantities must be adjusted accordingly. If more current costs for materials are available for the appropriate location, it is recommended that adjustments be made to the unit costs to reflect any cost difference.

Labor costs are calculated by multiplying the "Bare Labor Cost" per labor-hour times the number of labor-hours, from the "Labor-Hours" column. The "Bare" labor rate is determined by adding the base rate plus fringe benefits. The base rate is the actual hourly wage of a worker used in figuring payroll. It is from this figure that employee deductions are taken (federal withholding, Social Security, Medicare, state withholding). Fringe benefits include all employer-paid benefits, above and beyond the payroll amount (employer-paid health, vacation pay, pension, profit sharing). The "Bare Labor Cost" is, therefore, the actual amount that the contractor must pay directly for construction workers. Figure 10.4 shows labor rates for the 35 construction trades plus skilled worker, helper, and foreman averages. These rates are the averages of union wage agreements effective January 1 of the current year from 30 major cities in the United States. The "Bare Labor Cost" for each trade, as used in *Means Site Work & Landscape Cost*

Data, is shown in column "A" as the base rate including fringes. Refer to the "Crew" column to determine what rate is used to calculate the "Bare Labor Cost" for a particular line item.

Equipment costs are calculated by multiplying the "Bare Equipment Cost" per labor-hour, from the appropriate "Crew" listing, times the labor-hours in the "Labor-Hours" column. The calculation of the equipment portion of installation costs is outlined earlier in this chapter.

The **Total Bare Costs** are the arithmetical sum of the "Bare Material Cost," "Bare Labor Cost," and "Bare Equipment Cost" columns. The "Total Bare Cost" of any particular line item is the amount that a contractor will directly pay for that item. This is, in effect, the contractor's wholesale price.

Total Including Overhead and Profit

The prices in the "Total Including Overhead and Profit" column might also be called the "billing rate." These prices are, on the average, what the installing contractor would charge for the particular item of work.

The installing contractor could be either the general contractor or a subcontractor. If these costs are used for an item to be installed by a subcontractor, the general contractor should include an additional percentage (usually 10 to 20%) to cover the expenses of supervision and management.

The costs in the "Total Including Overhead and Profit" column are the arithmetical sum of the following three calculations:

1. Bare material cost plus 10%
2. Labor cost, including overhead and profit, per labor-hour times the number of labor-hours.
3. Equipment cost (bare cost plus 10%) per labor-hour times the number of labor-hours.

In order to increase the crew cost to include overhead and profit, labor and equipment costs are treated separately. Ten percent is added to the bare equipment cost for handling, management, etc. Labor costs are increased by percentages for overhead and profit, depending upon trade, as shown in Figure 10.4. The resulting rates are listed in the right hand columns of the same figure. The following items are included in the increase for overhead and profit, also shown in Figure 10.4:

Workers' Compensation and Employer's Liability: Workers' Compensation and Employer's Liability Insurance rates vary from state to state and are tied into the construction trade safety records in that particular state. Rates also vary by trade according to the hazard involved. (See Figure 10.7 from *Means Site Work & Landscape Cost Data*.) The proper authorities will most likely keep the contractor well informed of the rates and obligations.

State and Federal Unemployment Insurance: The employer's tax rate is adjusted by a merit-rating system according to the number of former employees applying for benefits. Contractors who find it possible to offer a maximum of steady employment can enjoy a reduction in the unemployment tax rate.

Employer-Paid Social Security (FICA): The tax rate is assigned annually by the federal government. It is a percentage of an employee's salary up to a maximum annual contribution.

Builder's Risk and Public Liability: These insurance rates vary according to the trades involved and the state in which the work is done.

R01100-060   Workers' Compensation Insurance Rates by Trade

The table below tabulates the national averages for Workers' Compensation insurance rates by trade and type of building. The average "Insurance Rate" is multiplied by the "% of Building Cost" for each trade. This produces

the "Workers' Compensation Cost" by % of total labor cost, to be added for each trade by building type to determine the weighted average Workers' Compensation rate for the building types analyzed.

Trade	Insurance Rate (% Labor Cost) Range		Average	% of Building Cost Office Bldgs.	Schools & Apts.	Mfg.	Workers' Compensation Office Bldgs.	Schools & Apts.	Mfg.
Excavation, Grading, etc.	3.8 % to	24.7%	10.5%	4.8%	4.9%	4.5%	.50%	.51%	.47%
Piles & Foundations	5.9 to	62.5	24.8	7.1	5.2	8.7	1.76	1.29	2.16
Concrete	5.9 to	36.8	16.9	5.0	14.8	3.7	.85	2.50	.63
Masonry	5.3 to	31.1	15.9	6.9	7.5	1.9	1.10	1.19	.30
Structural Steel	5.9 to	112.0	39.5	10.7	3.9	17.6	4.23	1.54	6.95
Miscellaneous & Ornamental Metals	4.9 to	25.3	12.8	2.8	4.0	3.6	.36	.51	.46
Carpentry & Millwork	5.9 to	43.6	18.0	3.7	4.0	0.5	.67	.72	.09
Metal or Composition Siding	5.9 to	32.2	16.5	2.3	0.3	4.3	.38	.05	.71
Roofing	5.9 to	85.9	32.3	2.3	2.6	3.1	.74	.84	1.00
Doors & Hardware	4.1 to	25.5	10.9	0.9	1.4	0.4	.10	.15	.04
Sash & Glazing	5.7 to	38.8	13.7	3.5	4.0	1.0	.48	.55	.14
Lath & Plaster	5.2 to	53.5	15.7	3.3	6.9	0.8	.52	1.08	.13
Tile, Marble & Floors	3.7 to	22.6	9.8	2.6	3.0	0.5	.25	.29	.05
Acoustical Ceilings	3.5 to	26.7	11.0	2.4	0.2	0.3	.26	.02	.03
Painting	5.9 to	27.6	13.7	1.5	1.6	1.6	.21	.22	.22
Interior Partitions	5.9 to	43.6	18.0	3.9	4.3	4.4	.70	.77	.79
Miscellaneous Items	1.1 to	128.0	17.6	5.2	3.7	9.7	.91	.65	1.70
Elevators	2.1 to	17.0	7.7	2.1	1.1	2.2	.16	.08	.17
Sprinklers	2.5 to	19.5	8.7	0.5	—	2.0	.04	—	.17
Plumbing	3.0 to	16.9	8.2	4.9	7.2	5.2	.40	.59	.43
Heat., Vent., Air Conditioning	3.3 to	32.5	11.6	13.5	11.0	12.9	1.57	1.28	1.50
Electrical	2.4 to	10.5	6.7	10.1	8.4	11.1	.68	.56	.74
Total	2.0 % to	132.9%	—	100.0%	100.0%	100.0%	16.87%	15.39%	18.88%
			Overall Weighted Average	17.05%					

Workers' Compensation Insurance Rates by States

The table below lists the weighted average Workers' Compensation base rate for each state with a factor comparing this with the national average of 16.8%.

State	Weighted Average	Factor	State	Weighted Average	Factor	State	Weighted Average	Factor
Alabama	31.9%	190	Kentucky	19.7%	117	North Dakota	14.8%	88
Alaska	11.0	65	Louisiana	27.2	162	Ohio	19.1	114
Arizona	11.0	65	Maine	21.7	129	Oklahoma	21.8	130
Arkansas	14.2	85	Maryland	11.8	70	Oregon	13.6	81
California	18.5	110	Massachusetts	20.4	121	Pennsylvania	22.8	136
Colorado	26.4	157	Michigan	18.5	110	Rhode Island	20.9	124
Connecticut	20.0	119	Minnesota	27.7	165	South Carolina	13.7	82
Delaware	11.5	68	Mississippi	20.4	121	South Dakota	14.5	86
District of Columbia	21.9	130	Missouri	17.6	105	Tennessee	15.8	94
Florida	27.8	165	Montana	17.6	105	Texas	15.8	94
Georgia	24.8	148	Nebraska	15.7	93	Utah	12.9	77
Hawaii	16.7	99	Nevada	17.3	103	Vermont	16.4	98
Idaho	10.7	64	New Hampshire	24.9	148	Virginia	10.9	65
Illinois	23.2	138	New Jersey	9.0	54	Washington	9.2	55
Indiana	7.2	43	New Mexico	16.7	99	West Virginia	13.0	77
Iowa	13.4	80	New York	15.3	91	Wisconsin	13.0	77
Kansas	10.1	60	North Carolina	13.0	77	Wyoming	6.5	39
			Weighted Average for U.S. is	17.0% of payroll = 100%				

Rates in the following table are the base or manual costs per $100 of payroll for Workers' Compensation in each state. Rates are usually applied to straight time wages only and not to premium time wages and bonuses.

The weighted average skilled worker rate for 35 trades is 16.8%. For bidding purposes, apply the full value of Workers' Compensation directly to total

labor costs, or if labor is 38%, materials 42% and overhead and profit 20% of total cost, carry 38/80 x 16.8% = 8.0% of cost (before overhead and profit) into overhead. Rates vary not only from state to state but also with the experience rating of the contractor.

Rates are the most current available at the time of publication.

(from *Means Site Work & Landscape Cost Data 2002*)

Figure 10.7

Overhead: The column listed as "Overhead" provides percentages to be added for office or operating overhead. This is the cost of doing business. The percentages are presented as national averages by trade as shown in Figure 10.4. (Note that the operating overhead costs are applied to *labor only* in *Means Site Work & Landscape Cost Data*.)

Profit: The percentage is the fee added by the contractor to offer both a return on investment and an allowance to cover the risk involved in the type of construction being bid as well as a consideration for future growth of the company. The profit percentage may vary from 4% on large, straightforward projects, to as much as 25% on smaller, high-risk jobs. Profit percentages are directly affected by economic conditions, the expected number of bidders, and the estimated risk involved in the project. For estimating purposes, *Means Site Work & Landscape Cost Data* assumes 10% as a reasonable average profit factor (as applied to labor costs).

Assemblies Cost Tables

Means' assemblies data are divided into 7 "UNIFORMAT II" divisions, which organize the components of construction into logical groupings. The assemblies approach was devised to provide a quick and easy method for estimating even when only preliminary design data is available. The groupings, or assemblies, are presented in such a way that the estimator can easily vary components within the system as well as substitute one system for another. This arrangement is extremely useful when adapting to budget, design, or other considerations. Figure 10.8 shows how the data is presented in the Assemblies pages, and Figure 10.9, taken from *Means Site Work & Landscape Cost Data*, is an example system for headwalls.

Each assembly is illustrated and accompanied by a detailed description. The book lists the components and sizes of each assembly, usually in the order of construction. Alternates for the most commonly variable components are also listed. Further, each individual component can be found in the Unit Price Section, if a required alternate is not listed in Assemblies.

Quantity

A unit of measure is established for each assembly. For example, lawn assemblies are measured by the square foot area to be seeded or planted; retaining walls are measured by the linear foot; tree pits are measured as "each." Within each assembly, the components are measured by industry standard, using the same units as in the Unit Price section.

Material

The cost of each component in the Material column is the "Bare Material Cost," plus 10% handling, for the unit and quantity as defined in the "Quantity" column.

Installation

Installation costs as listed in the Assemblies pages contain both labor and equipment costs. The labor rate includes the "Bare Labor Cost" plus the installing contractor's overhead and profit. These rates are shown in Figure 10.4. The equipment rate is the "Bare Equipment Cost" plus 10%.

How to Use the Assemblies Cost Tables

The following is a detailed explanation of a sample Assemblies Cost Table. Most Assembly Tables are separated into three parts:
1) an illustration of the system to be estimated; 2) the components and related costs of a typical system; and 3) the costs for similar systems with dimensional and/or size variations. For costs of the components that comprise these systems or "assemblies," refer to the Unit Price Section. Next to each bold number below is the item being described with the appropriate component of the sample entry following in parenthesis. In most cases, if the work is to be subcontracted, the general contractor will need to add an additional markup (R.S. Means suggests using 10%) to the "Total" figures.

System/Line Numbers (G2040 210)

Each Assemblies Cost Line has been assigned a unique identification number based on the UNIFORMAT II classification system.

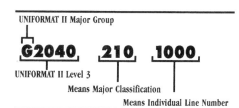

UNIFORMAT II Major Group

G2040 , **210** , **1000** ,

UNIFORMAT II Level 3

Means Major Classification

Means Individual Line Number

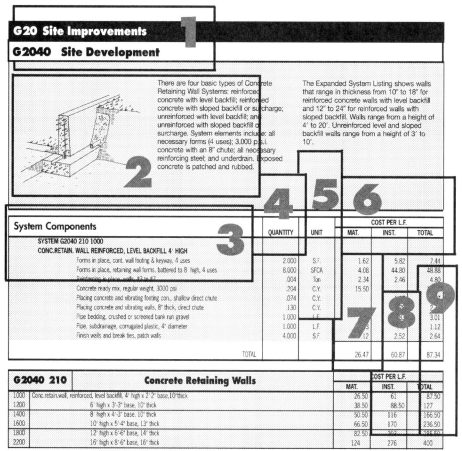

G20 Site Improvements
G2040 Site Development

There are four basic types of Concrete Retaining Wall Systems: reinforced concrete with level backfill; reinforced concrete with sloped backfill or surcharge; unreinforced with level backfill; and unreinforced with sloped backfill or surcharge. System elements include: all necessary forms (4 uses); 3,000 p.s.i. concrete with an 8" chute; all necessary reinforcing steel; and underdrain. Exposed concrete is patched and rubbed.

The Expanded System Listing shows walls that range in thickness from 10" to 18" for reinforced concrete walls with level backfill and 12" to 24" for reinforced walls with sloped backfill. Walls range from a height of 4' to 20'. Unreinforced level and sloped backfill walls range from a height of 3' to 10'.

System Components	QUANTITY	UNIT	COST PER L.F. MAT.	COST PER L.F. INST.	COST PER L.F. TOTAL
SYSTEM G2040 210 1000					
CONC.RETAIN. WALL REINFORCED, LEVEL BACKFILL 4' HIGH					
Forms in place, cont. wall footing & keyway, 4 uses	2.000	S.F.	1.62	5.82	7.44
Forms in place, retaining wall forms, battered to 8' high, 4 uses	8.000	SFCA	4.08	44.80	48.88
Reinforcing in place, walls, #3 to #7	.004	Ton	2.34	2.46	4.80
Concrete ready mix, regular weight, 3000 psi	.204	C.Y.	15.50		
Placing concrete and vibrating footing con., shallow direct chute	.074	C.Y.			
Placing concrete and vibrating walls, 8" thick, direct chute	.130	C.Y.			
Pipe bedding, crushed or screened bank run gravel	1.000	L.F.			3.01
Pipe, subdrainage, corrugated plastic, 4" diameter	1.000	L.F.			1.12
Finish walls and break ties, patch walls	4.000	S.F.	.12	2.52	2.64
TOTAL			26.47	60.87	87.34

G2040 210	Concrete Retaining Walls	COST PER L.F. MAT.	COST PER L.F. INST.	COST PER L.F. TOTAL
1000	Conc.retain.wall, reinforced, level backfill, 4' high x 2'-2" base,10"thick	26.50	61	87.50
1200	6' high x 3'-3" base, 10" thick	38.50	88.50	127
1400	8' high x 4'-3" base, 10" thick	50.50	116	166.50
1600	10' high x 5'-4" base, 13" thick	66.50	170	236.50
1800	12' high x 6'-6" base, 14" thick	82.50	202	285.50
2200	16' high x 8'-6" base, 16" thick	124	276	400

(from *Means Site Work & Landscape Cost Data 2002*)

Figure 10.8

Illustration

At the top of most assembly tables is an illustration, a brief description, and the design criteria used to develop the cost.

System Components

The components of a typical system are listed separately to show what has been included in the development of the total system price. The table below contains prices for other similar systems with dimensional and/or size variations.

Quantity

This is the number of line item units required for one system unit. For example, we assume that it will take 2 S.F. of footing forms per L.F. of wall.

Unit of Measure for Each Item

The abbreviated designation indicates the unit of measure, as defined by industry standards, upon which the price of the component is based. For example, reinforcing is priced per ton and concrete is priced per C.Y.

Unit of Measure for Each System (Cost per L.F.)

Costs shown in the three right hand columns have been adjusted by the component quantity and unit of measure for the entire system. In this example, "Cost per L.F." is the unit of measure for this system or "assembly."

Materials (26.47)

This column contains the Materials Cost of each component. These cost figures are bare costs plus 10% for profit.

Installation (60.87)

Installation includes labor and equipment plus the installing contractor's overhead and profit. Equipment costs are the bare rental costs plus 10% for profit. The labor overhead and profit is defined on the inside back cover of this book.

Total (87.34)

The figure in this column is the sum of the material and installation costs.

Material Cost	+	Installation Cost	=	Total
$26.47	+	$60.87	=	$87.34

Figure 10.8 (cont.)

G30 Site Mechanical Utilities

G3030 Storm Sewer

The Headwall Systems are listed in concrete and two different stone wall materials for two different backfill slope conditions. The backfill slope directly affects the length of the wing walls. Walls are listed for three different culvert sizes 30″, 48″ and 60″ diameter. Excavation and backfill are included in the system components, and are figured from an elevation 2′ below the bottom of the pipe.

System Components	QUANTITY	UNIT	COST PER EACH MAT.	COST PER EACH INST.	COST PER EACH TOTAL
SYSTEM G3030 310 2000					
HEADWALL C.I.P. CONCRETE FOR 30″ PIPE, 3′ LONG WING WALLS					
Excavation, hydraulic backhoe, 3/8 C.Y. bucket	2.500	C.Y.		151.20	151.20
Formwork, 2 uses	157.000	SFCA	241.40	1,230.49	1,471.89
Reinforcing in place including dowels	45.000	Lb.	20.25	57.60	77.85
Concrete, 3000 psi	2.600	C.Y.	197.60		197.60
Place concrete, spread footings, direct chute	2.600	C.Y.		89.49	89.49
Backfill, dozer	2.500	C.Y.		33.32	33.32
TOTAL			459.25	1,562.10	2,021.35

G3030 310	Headwalls	COST PER EACH MAT.	COST PER EACH INST.	COST PER EACH TOTAL
2000	Headwall, 1-1/2 to 1 slope soil, C.I.P. conc, 30″pipe, 3′long wing walls	460	1,550	2,010
2020	Pipe size 36″, 3′-6″ long wing walls	575	1,900	2,475
2040	Pipe size 42″, 4′ long wing walls	695	2,200	2,895
2060	Pipe size 48″, 4′-6″ long wing walls	840	2,575	3,415
2080	Pipe size 54″, 5′-0″ long wing walls	995	2,975	3,970
2100	Pipe size 60″, 5′-6″ long wing walls	1,150	3,375	4,525
2120	Pipe size 72″, 6′-6″ long wing walls	1,550	4,350	5,900
2140	Pipe size 84″, 7′-6″ long wing walls	1,975	5,350	7,325
2500	$16/ton stone, pipe size 30″, 3′ long wing walls	71.50	570	641.50
2520	Pipe size 36″, 3′-6″ long wing walls	92	685	777
2540	Pipe size 42″, 4′ long wing walls	116	810	926
2560	Pipe size 48″, 4′-6″ long wing walls	143	955	1,098
2580	Pipe size 54″, 5′ long wing walls	172	1,100	1,272
2600	Pipe size 60″, 5′-6″ long wing walls	204	1,275	1,479
2620	Pipe size 72″, 6′-6″ long wing walls	282	1,700	1,982
2640	Pipe size 84″, 7′-6″ long wing walls	370	2,175	2,545
3000	$32/ton stone, pipe size 30″, 3′ long wing walls	143	570	713
3020	Pipe size 36″, 3′-6″ long wing walls	184	685	869
3040	Pipe size 42″, 4′ long wing walls	231	810	1,041
3060	Pipe size 48″, 4′-6″ long wing walls	285	955	1,240
3080	Pipe size 54″, 5′ long wing walls	345	1,100	1,445
3100	Pipe size 60″, 5′-6″ long wing walls	410	1,275	1,685
3120	Pipe size 72″, 6′-6″ long wing walls	565	1,700	2,265
3140	Pipe size 84″, 7′-6″ long wing walls	740	2,175	2,915
3500	$48/ton stone, pipe size 30″, 3′ long wing walls	215	570	785
3520	Pipe size 36″, 3′-6″ long wing walls	276	685	961

(from *Means Site Work & Landscape Cost Data 2002*)

Figure 10.9

Reference Numbers

Throughout the Unit Price and Assemblies sections there are reference numbers within bold boxes. These numbers serve as footnotes, referring the reader to illustrations, charts, and estimating reference tables in the "Reference Numbers" section. Also, many reference numbers explain how unit cost prices are developed. Figure 10.10 shows an example reference number (for grass seeding) as it appears on a Unit Price page.

Figure 10.11 shows the corresponding page from the Reference section. Suggestions, hints and design criteria for many types of site work systems are included to aid the designer/estimator in making appropriate choices.

City Cost Indexes

The unit prices in *Means Site Work & Landscape Cost Data* are national averages. When they are to be applied to a particular location, these prices must be adjusted to local conditions. R.S. Means Company, Inc. has developed the City Cost Indexes for just that purpose. *Means Site Work & Landscape Cost Data* contains average construction cost indexes for over 300 major U.S. and Canadian cities, based on a 30 major city average of 100. Please note that for each city there is a weighted average based on total project costs. This average is based on the relative contribution of each division to the construction process as a whole. Figure 10.12 is a sample page from the City Cost Index.

In addition to adjusting the figures in *Means Site Work & Landscape Cost Data* for particular locations, the City Cost Index can also be used to adjust costs from one city to another.

For example, the price of a certain landscape job is known for City A. In order to budget the costs for the same type of project in City B, the following calculation can be made:

$$\frac{\text{City B Index}}{\text{City A Index}} \times \text{City A Cost} = \text{City B Cost}$$

Historical Cost Indexes

While City Cost Indexes provide a means to adjust prices for location, the Historical Cost Indexes (also included in *Means Site Work & Landscape Cost Data* and shown in Figure 10.13) provide a means to adjust for time. Using the same principle as above, a time-adjustment factor can be calculated:

$$\frac{\text{Index for Year X}}{\text{Index for Year Y}} \times \text{Time-Adjustment Factor}$$

This time-adjustment factor can be used to determine the budget costs for a particular type of project in Year X, based on costs for a similar building type known from Year Y. Used together, the two indexes allow for cost adjustments from one city during a given year, to another city in another year (the present or otherwise).

For example, a project constructed in San Francisco in 1974 originally cost $50,000. How much will a similar project cost in Phoenix in 2002? Adjustment factors are developed as shown above using data from Figures 10.12 (City Cost Index) and 10.13 (Historical Cost Index):

$$\frac{\text{Phoenix Index}}{\text{San Francisco Index}} = \frac{89.4}{124.4} = 0.72$$

$$\frac{\text{2002 Index}}{\text{1974 Index}} = \frac{126.1}{41.4} = 3.05$$

		02920	Lawns & Grasses	CREW	DAILY OUTPUT	LABOR-HOURS	UNIT	MAT.	LABOR	EQUIP.	TOTAL	TOTAL INCL O&P	
340	6250		6″ deep	A-1	750	.011	S.Y.		.25	.08	.33	.48	340
510	0010		SEEDING Athletic field mix, 8#/M.S.F., push spreader R02920-500	1 Clab	8	1	M.S.F.	16.60	23.50		40.10	55	510
	0100		Tractor spreader	B-66	52	.154		16.60	4.58	3	24.18	28.50	
	0200		Hydro or air seeding, with mulch & fertil.	B-81	80	.300		18.25	7.95	6.75	32.95	39.50	
	0400		Birdsfoot trefoil, .45#/M.S.F., push spreader	1 Clab	8	1		6.85	23.50		30.35	44	
	0500		Tractor spreader	B-66	52	.154		6.85	4.58	3	14.43	17.80	
	0600		Hydro or air seeding, with mulch & fertil.	B-81	80	.300		13.20	7.95	6.75	27.90	34	
	0800		Bluegrass, 4#/M.S.F., common, push spreader	1 Clab	8	1		14.40	23.50		37.90	52.50	
	0900		Tractor spreader	B-66	52	.154		14.40	4.58	3	21.98	26	
	1000		Hydro or air seeding, with mulch & fertil.	B-81	80	.300		24	7.95	6.75	38.70	45.50	
	1100		Baron, push spreader	1 Clab	8	1		19.05	23.50		42.55	57.50	
	1200		Tractor spreader	B-66	52	.154		19.05	4.58	3	26.63	31.50	
	1300		Hydro or air seeding, with mulch & fertil.	B-81	80	.300		26	7.95	6.75	40.70	48.50	
	1500		Clover, 0.67#/M.S.F., white, push spreader	1 Clab	8	1		1.25	23.50		24.75	38	
	1600		Tractor spreader	B-66	52	.154		1.25	4.58	3	8.83	11.65	
	1700		Hydro or air seeding, with mulch and fertil.	B-81	80	.300		6.90	7.95	6.75	21.60	27	
	1800		Ladino, push spreader	1 Clab	8	1		4.94	23.50		28.44	42	
	1900		Tractor spreader	B-66	52	.154		4.94	4.58	3	12.52	15.70	
	2000		Hydro or air seeding, with mulch and fertil.	B-81	80	.300		21.50	7.95	6.75	36.20	43.50	
	2200		Fescue 5.5#/M.S.F., tall, push spreader	1 Clab	8	1		9.80	23.50		33.30	47.50	
	2300		Tractor spreader	B-66	52	.154		9.80	4.58	3	17.38	21	
	2400		Hydro or air seeding, with mulch and fertilizer	B-81	80	.300		32.50	7.95	6.75	47.20	55	
	2500		Chewing, push spreader	1 Clab	8	1		9.80	23.50		33.30	47.50	
	2600		Tractor spreader	B-66	52	.154		9.80	4.58	3	17.38	21	
	2700		Hydro or air seeding, with mulch and fertil.	B-81	80	.300		32.50	7.95	6.75	47.20	55	
	2800		Creeping, push spreader	1 Clab	8	1		7.55	23.50		31.05	45	
	2810		Tractor spreader	B-66	26	.308		7.55	9.15	6	22.70	29	
	2820		Hydro or air seeding, with mulch and fertilizer	B-81	80	.300		25	7.95	6.75	39.70	47	
	2900		Crown vetch, 4#/M.S.F., push spreader	1 Clab	8	1		36	23.50		59.50	76	
	3000		Tractor spreader	B-66	52	.154		36	4.58	3	43.58	50	
	3100		Hydro or air seeding, with mulch and fertilizer	B-81	80	.300		49.50	7.95	6.75	64.20	74	
	3300		Rye, 10#/M.S.F., annual, push spreader	1 Clab	8	1		4.78	23.50		28.28	42	
	3400		Tractor spreader	B-66	52	.154		4.78	4.58	3	12.36	15.50	
	3500		Hydro or air seeding, with mulch and fertilizer	B-81	80	.300		10.50	7.95	6.75	25.20	31	
	3600		Fine textured, push spreader	1 Clab	8	1		7	23.50		30.50	44	
	3700		Tractor spreader	B-66	52	.154		7	4.58	3	14.58	17.95	
	3800		Hydro or air seeding, with mulch and fertilizer	B-81	80	.300		15.40	7.95	6.75	30.10	36.50	
	4000		Shade mix, 6#/M.S.F., push spreader	1 Clab	8	1		9.40	23.50		32.90	47	
	4100		Tractor spreader	B-66	52	.154		9.40	4.58	3	16.98	20.50	
	4200		Hydro or air seeding, with mulch and fertilizer	B-81	80	.300		20.50	7.95	6.75	35.20	42.50	
	4400		Slope mix, 6#/M.S.F., push spreader	1 Clab	8	1		9.40	23.50		32.90	47	
	4500		Tractor spreader	B-66	52	.154		9.40	4.58	3	16.98	20.50	
	4600		Hydro or air seeding, with mulch and fertilizer	B-81	80	.300		23.50	7.95	6.75	38.20	45.50	
	4800		Turf mix, 4#/M.S.F., push spreader	1 Clab	8	1		6.30	23.50		29.80	43.50	
	4900		Tractor spreader	B-66	52	.154		6.30	4.58	3	13.88	17.15	
	5000		Hydro or air seeding, with mulch and fertilizer	B-81	80	.300		15.70	7.95	6.75	30.40	37	
	5200		Utility mix, 7#/M.S.F., push spreader	1 Clab	8	1		11	23.50		34.50	48.50	
	5300		Tractor spreader	B-66	52	.154		11	4.58	3	18.58	22.50	
	5400		Hydro or air seeidng, with mulch and fertilizer	B-81	80	.300		41	7.95	6.75	55.70	65	
	5600		Wildflower, .10#/M.S.F., push spreader	1 Clab	8	1		3.85	23.50		27.35	40.50	
	5700		Tractor spreader	B-66	52	.154		3.85	4.58	3	11.43	14.50	

(from *Means Site Work & Landscape Cost Data 2002*)

Figure 10.10

R02920-500 Seeding

The type of grass is determined by light, shade and moisture content of soil plus intended use. Fertilizer should be disked 4″ before seeding. For steep slopes disk five tons of mulch and lay two tons of hay or straw on surface per acre after seeding. Surface mulch can be staked, lightly disked or tar emulsion sprayed. Material for mulch can be wood chips, peat moss, partially rotted hay or straw, wood fibers and sprayed emulsions. Hemp seed blankets with fertilizer are also available. For spring seeding, watering is necessary. Late fall seeding may have to be reseeded in the spring. Hydraulic seeding, power mulching, and aerial seeding can be used on large areas.

R02920-510 Plant Spacing Chart

This chart may be used when plants are to be placed equidistant from each other, staggering their position in each row.

Plant Spacing (Inches)	Row Spacing (Inches)	Plants Per (CSF)	Plant Spacing (Feet)	Row Spacing (Feet)	Plants Per (MSF)
			4	3.46	72
6	5.20	462	5	4.33	46
8	6.93	260	6	5.20	32
10	8.66	166	8	6.93	18
12	10.39	115	10	8.66	12
15	12.99	74	12	10.39	8
18	15.59	51.32	15	12.99	5.13
21	18.19	37.70	20	17.32	2.89
24	20.78	28.87	25	21.65	1.85
30	25.98	18.48	30	25.98	1.28
36	31.18	12.83	40	34.64	0.72

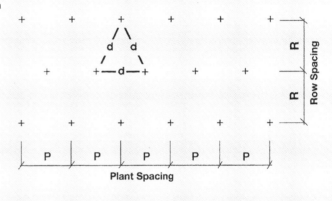

(from *Means Site Work & Landscape Cost Data 2002*)

Figure 10.11

City Cost Indexes

DIVISION		UNITED STATES 30 CITY AVERAGE			ALABAMA BIRMINGHAM			HUNTSVILLE			MOBILE			MONTGOMERY			TUSCALOOSA		
		MAT.	INST.	TOTAL	MAT.	INST.	TOTAL	MAT.	INST.	TOTAL	MAT.	INST.	TOTAL	MAT.	INST.	TOTAL	MAT.	INST.	TOTAL
01590	EQUIPMENT RENTAL	.0	100.0	100.0	.0	101.6	101.6	.0	101.5	101.5	.0	98.0	98.0	.0	98.0	98.0	.0	101.5	101.5
02	SITE CONSTRUCTION	100.0	100.0	100.0	87.3	93.8	92.2	85.3	92.9	91.1	96.4	86.7	89.0	96.9	87.2	89.6	85.8	92.6	91.0
03100	CONCRETE FORMS & ACCESSORIES	100.0	100.0	100.0	91.5	76.7	78.6	93.3	55.6	60.5	93.3	58.7	63.3	91.7	53.1	58.2	93.2	43.7	50.2
03200	CONCRETE REINFORCEMENT	100.0	100.0	100.0	92.9	85.5	88.6	92.9	85.9	88.8	95.9	63.2	76.8	95.9	84.5	89.2	92.9	84.8	88.2
03300	CAST-IN-PLACE CONCRETE	100.0	100.0	100.0	93.8	66.8	82.9	88.7	63.5	78.5	93.7	61.6	80.7	95.3	55.5	79.3	92.4	53.0	76.5
03	CONCRETE	100.0	100.0	100.0	89.2	76.1	82.7	86.8	65.8	76.3	89.7	62.2	76.0	90.4	61.7	76.1	88.6	56.8	72.8
04	MASONRY	100.0	100.0	100.0	85.6	72.8	77.8	85.5	57.7	68.5	86.1	58.2	69.1	86.6	40.4	58.4	85.8	42.9	59.6
05	METALS	100.0	100.0	100.0	98.5	95.6	97.5	98.2	94.4	96.8	96.8	85.6	92.7	96.8	93.5	95.6	97.2	94.0	96.1
06	WOOD & PLASTICS	100.0	100.0	100.0	92.1	76.9	84.3	91.3	53.9	72.1	91.3	58.8	74.6	89.5	53.9	71.2	91.3	42.8	66.4
07	THERMAL & MOISTURE PROTECTION	100.0	100.0	100.0	96.1	80.2	88.6	95.8	72.3	84.7	95.8	73.5	85.3	95.5	66.5	81.8	95.8	65.2	81.3
08	DOORS & WINDOWS	100.0	100.0	100.0	96.4	78.5	92.1	96.4	60.0	87.6	96.4	59.2	87.4	96.4	61.1	87.9	96.4	60.2	87.7
09200	PLASTER & GYPSUM BOARD	100.0	100.0	100.0	110.1	76.7	88.5	106.9	53.0	72.1	106.9	58.1	75.3	106.9	53.0	72.1	106.9	41.5	64.7
095,098	CEILINGS & ACOUSTICAL TREATMENT	100.0	100.0	100.0	95.7	76.7	82.9	95.7	53.0	67.0	95.7	58.1	70.4	95.7	53.0	67.0	95.7	41.5	59.3
09600	FLOORING	100.0	100.0	100.0	101.2	58.0	90.6	101.2	50.2	88.6	109.8	62.9	98.2	109.8	32.5	90.7	101.2	47.7	88.0
097,099	WALL FINISHES, PAINTS & COATINGS	100.0	100.0	100.0	92.6	54.7	70.4	92.6	53.7	69.8	92.6	62.1	74.7	92.6	61.0	74.1	92.6	52.5	69.1
09	FINISHES	100.0	100.0	100.0	98.4	70.6	83.9	97.8	53.2	74.6	101.8	59.4	79.7	101.9	48.9	74.3	97.8	43.9	69.7
10 - 14	TOTAL DIV. 10000 - 14000	100.0	100.0	100.0	100.0	81.5	96.1	100.0	74.9	94.8	100.0	71.1	94.0	100.0	72.6	94.3	100.0	69.7	93.7
15	MECHANICAL	100.0	100.0	100.0	99.9	69.8	86.5	99.9	52.0	78.6	99.9	65.2	84.5	99.9	46.9	76.3	99.9	41.2	73.8
16	ELECTRICAL	100.0	100.0	100.0	96.3	64.8	74.4	96.7	72.5	79.8	96.7	59.5	70.8	96.3	72.2	79.6	96.7	64.8	74.5
01 - 16	WEIGHTED AVERAGE	100.0	100.0	100.0	96.2	75.8	86.4	95.8	67.2	82.0	96.7	66.5	82.1	96.8	62.7	80.3	95.9	59.7	78.4

DIVISION		ALASKA ANCHORAGE			FAIRBANKS			JUNEAU			ARIZONA FLAGSTAFF			MESA/TEMPE			PHOENIX		
		MAT.	INST.	TOTAL	MAT.	INST.	TOTAL	MAT.	INST.	TOTAL	MAT.	INST.	TOTAL	MAT.	INST.	TOTAL	MAT.	INST.	TOTAL
01590	EQUIPMENT RENTAL	.0	118.9	118.9	.0	118.9	118.9	.0	118.9	118.9	.0	93.5	93.5	.0	94.0	94.0	.0	94.6	94.6
02	SITE CONSTRUCTION	135.4	135.4	135.4	119.2	135.4	131.5	131.2	135.4	134.4	86.4	99.4	96.3	83.1	99.0	95.2	83.5	99.8	95.9
03100	CONCRETE FORMS & ACCESSORIES	131.1	115.5	117.6	132.7	122.4	123.7	132.5	115.5	117.8	106.0	71.2	75.8	103.0	70.6	74.9	104.3	76.7	80.4
03200	CONCRETE REINFORCEMENT	141.5	102.7	118.9	118.9	102.7	109.5	105.2	102.7	103.7	103.7	78.6	89.1	103.9	71.2	84.7	102.1	79.2	88.7
03300	CAST-IN-PLACE CONCRETE	189.8	117.6	160.7	158.3	118.2	142.1	190.6	117.6	161.2	97.3	84.7	92.2	99.2	76.6	90.1	99.3	84.7	93.4
03	CONCRETE	153.7	113.1	133.5	130.0	116.3	123.2	149.8	113.1	131.6	122.5	77.0	99.9	100.1	72.6	86.4	99.7	79.6	89.7
04	MASONRY	195.4	122.8	151.0	182.4	122.8	146.0	184.6	122.8	146.9	101.4	63.1	78.0	109.3	57.6	77.7	96.2	72.6	81.8
05	METALS	130.0	98.4	118.4	130.0	98.8	118.6	130.3	98.4	118.6	98.0	70.9	88.1	98.3	68.9	87.6	99.6	73.5	90.1
06	WOOD & PLASTICS	118.0	113.5	115.7	118.3	122.3	120.3	118.0	113.5	115.7	107.0	70.7	88.3	101.0	77.5	89.0	102.2	77.7	89.6
07	THERMAL & MOISTURE PROTECTION	199.7	115.4	159.7	195.7	118.9	159.3	196.4	115.4	158.0	111.2	73.5	93.4	108.6	68.5	89.6	108.5	75.9	93.1
08	DOORS & WINDOWS	128.0	105.9	122.7	125.1	111.0	121.7	125.1	105.9	120.5	101.1	72.2	94.1	98.0	70.5	91.4	99.2	75.9	93.6
09200	PLASTER & GYPSUM BOARD	129.7	113.9	119.4	129.7	122.9	125.3	129.7	113.9	119.4	90.9	69.9	77.3	91.5	76.8	82.0	92.0	76.9	82.3
095,098	CEILINGS & ACOUSTICAL TREATMENT	129.4	113.9	118.9	129.4	122.9	125.0	129.4	113.9	118.9	102.9	69.9	80.7	105.6	76.8	86.2	105.6	76.9	86.3
09600	FLOORING	127.3	126.3	127.1	127.5	126.3	127.2	127.3	126.3	127.1	98.9	58.7	89.0	102.1	73.2	95.0	102.4	76.4	96.0
097,099	WALL FINISHES, PAINTS & COATINGS	116.2	107.8	111.3	116.2	117.9	117.2	116.2	107.8	111.3	98.7	55.7	73.5	109.9	59.9	80.6	109.9	69.0	85.9
09	FINISHES	140.2	116.9	128.1	138.0	123.2	130.3	138.7	116.9	127.4	97.1	66.6	81.2	98.5	70.0	83.6	98.7	75.6	86.7
10 - 14	TOTAL DIV. 10000 - 14000	100.0	114.1	102.9	100.0	115.2	103.2	100.0	114.1	102.9	100.0	82.1	96.3	100.0	77.5	95.3	100.0	83.2	96.5
15	MECHANICAL	108.2	108.0	108.1	108.2	117.3	112.2	108.2	108.0	108.1	100.2	83.1	92.6	100.1	73.0	88.0	100.1	83.2	92.6
16	ELECTRICAL	161.7	110.8	126.3	164.6	110.8	127.2	164.6	110.8	127.2	100.4	55.8	69.4	98.1	37.7	56.1	107.2	66.9	79.2
01 - 16	WEIGHTED AVERAGE	134.1	113.7	124.3	129.5	117.2	123.6	132.6	113.7	123.5	102.5	73.4	88.4	99.6	67.2	83.9	99.8	78.2	89.4

DIVISION		ARIZONA PRESCOTT			TUCSON			ARKANSAS FORT SMITH			JONESBORO			LITTLE ROCK			PINE BLUFF		
		MAT.	INST.	TOTAL	MAT.	INST.	TOTAL	MAT.	INST.	TOTAL	MAT.	INST.	TOTAL	MAT.	INST.	TOTAL	MAT.	INST.	TOTAL
01590	EQUIPMENT RENTAL	.0	93.5	93.5	.0	94.0	94.0	.0	85.1	85.1	.0	106.6	106.6	.0	85.1	85.1	.0	85.1	85.1
02	SITE CONSTRUCTION	73.6	99.0	92.9	80.3	99.6	94.9	77.9	83.7	82.3	101.8	98.8	99.5	77.7	83.7	82.3	79.9	83.7	82.8
03100	CONCRETE FORMS & ACCESSORIES	100.9	65.3	70.0	103.7	76.2	79.8	101.5	47.4	54.6	85.7	54.4	58.5	95.6	52.0	57.8	77.5	51.9	55.3
03200	CONCRETE REINFORCEMENT	103.7	75.2	87.1	101.0	78.6	87.9	95.6	73.7	82.8	91.5	52.8	68.9	95.8	69.7	80.6	95.8	69.7	80.6
03300	CAST-IN-PLACE CONCRETE	97.2	71.9	87.0	99.3	84.5	93.3	91.2	68.8	82.2	86.9	62.8	77.2	91.2	68.8	82.2	83.7	68.8	77.7
03	CONCRETE	107.0	69.3	88.2	99.5	79.2	89.4	87.8	60.7	74.3	84.4	58.7	71.6	87.5	61.9	74.8	85.1	61.9	73.5
04	MASONRY	101.9	68.7	81.6	96.7	63.0	76.1	96.8	58.5	73.4	90.8	53.8	68.2	95.0	58.5	72.7	114.4	58.5	80.2
05	METALS	98.1	68.2	87.2	98.9	71.6	88.9	96.7	72.8	87.9	90.9	80.6	87.2	96.3	71.5	87.2	95.4	71.4	86.6
06	WOOD & PLASTICS	102.2	64.2	82.7	102.7	77.7	89.9	104.8	46.4	74.8	89.1	55.8	72.0	101.5	52.5	76.3	81.5	52.5	66.6
07	THERMAL & MOISTURE PROTECTION	109.4	69.8	90.7	109.2	70.1	90.7	99.2	53.2	77.4	109.1	57.5	84.7	98.1	53.8	77.1	97.8	53.8	76.9
08	DOORS & WINDOWS	101.1	64.6	92.3	96.6	75.9	91.1	96.6	49.4	85.2	98.1	53.3	87.3	96.6	52.6	86.0	92.0	52.6	82.5
09200	PLASTER & GYPSUM BOARD	88.9	63.1	72.3	92.3	76.9	82.4	96.0	45.7	63.5	102.1	55.0	71.6	96.0	51.9	67.5	89.3	51.9	65.1
095,098	CEILINGS & ACOUSTICAL TREATMENT	102.9	63.1	76.2	107.0	76.9	86.8	101.9	45.7	64.1	102.5	55.0	70.5	101.9	51.9	68.3	97.6	51.9	66.9
09600	FLOORING	97.2	58.5	87.7	101.5	58.7	91.0	118.1	74.4	107.3	79.1	51.6	72.3	119.4	74.4	108.3	106.8	74.4	98.8
097,099	WALL FINISHES, PAINTS & COATINGS	98.7	55.7	73.5	107.4	55.7	77.2	95.8	65.3	78.0	84.7	58.7	69.5	95.8	50.0	69.0	95.8	50.0	69.0

(from *Means Site Work & Landscape Cost Data* 2002)

Figure 10.12

The table below lists both the Means Historical Cost Index based on Jan. 1, 1993 = 100 as well as the computed value of an index based on Jan. 1, 2002 costs. Since the Jan. 1, 2002 figure is estimated, space is left to write in the actual index figures as they become available through either the quarterly "Means Construction Cost Indexes" or as printed in the "Engineering News-Record." To compute the actual index based on Jan. 1, 2002 = 100, divide the Historical Cost Index for a particular year by the actual Jan. 1, 2002 Construction Cost Index. Space has been left to advance the index figures as the year progresses.

Year	Historical Cost Index Jan. 1, 1993 = 100 Est.	Historical Cost Index Jan. 1, 1993 = 100 Actual	Current Index Based on Jan. 1, 2002 = 100 Est.	Current Index Based on Jan. 1, 2002 = 100 Actual
Oct 2002				
July 2002				
April 2002				
Jan 2002	126.1		100.0	100.0
July 2001		125.1	99.2	
2000		120.9	95.9	
1999		117.6	93.3	
1998		115.1	91.3	
1997		112.8	89.5	
1996		110.2	87.4	
1995		107.6	85.3	
1994		104.4	82.8	
1993		101.7	80.7	
1992		99.4	78.9	
1991		96.8	76.8	
1990		94.3	74.8	
1989		92.1	73.1	
1988		89.9	71.3	

Year	Historical Cost Index Jan. 1, 1993 = 100 Actual	Current Index Based on Jan. 1, 2002 = 100 Est.	Current Index Based on Jan. 1, 2002 = 100 Actual
July 1987	87.7	69.5	
1986	84.2	66.8	
1985	82.6	65.5	
1984	82.0	65.0	
1983	80.2	63.6	
1982	76.1	60.4	
1981	70.0	55.5	
1980	62.9	49.9	
1979	57.8	45.8	
1978	53.5	42.4	
1977	49.5	39.3	
1976	46.9	37.2	
1975	44.8	35.5	
1974	41.4	32.8	
1973	37.7	29.9	
1972	34.8	27.6	
1971	32.1	25.5	
1970	28.7	22.8	

Year	Historical Cost Index Jan. 1, 1993 = 100 Actual	Current Index Based on Jan. 1, 2002 = 100 Est.	Current Index Based on Jan. 1, 2002 = 100 Actual
July 1969	26.9	21.3	
1968	24.9	19.7	
1967	23.5	18.6	
1966	22.7	18.0	
1965	21.7	17.2	
1964	21.2	16.8	
1963	20.7	16.4	
1962	20.2	16.0	
1961	19.8	15.7	
1960	19.7	15.6	
1959	19.3	15.3	
1958	18.8	14.9	
1957	18.4	14.6	
1956	17.6	14.0	
1955	16.6	13.2	
1954	16.0	12.7	
1953	15.8	12.5	
1952	15.4	12.2	

Adjustments to Costs

The Historical Cost Index can be used to convert National Average building costs at a particular time to the approximate building costs for some other time.

Example:

Estimate and compare construction costs for different years in the same city.

To estimate the National Average construction cost of a building in 1970, knowing that it cost $900,000 in 2002:

INDEX in 1970 = 28.7

INDEX in 2002 = 126.1

Note: The City Cost Indexes for Canada can be used to convert U.S. National averages to local costs in Canadian dollars.

Time Adjustment using the Historical Cost Indexes:

$$\frac{\text{Index for Year A}}{\text{Index for Year B}} \times \text{Cost in Year B} = \text{Cost in Year A}$$

$$\frac{\text{INDEX 1970}}{\text{INDEX 2002}} \times \text{Cost 2002} = \text{Cost 1970}$$

$$\frac{28.7}{126.1} \times \$900,000 = .228 \times \$900,000 = \$205,200$$

The construction cost of the building in 1970 is $205,200.

(from *Means Site Work & Landscape Cost Data 2002*)

Figure 10.13

Original cost × location adjustment × time adjustment = Proposed new cost.

$50,000 × 0.72 × 3.05 = $109,800

Understanding how *Means Site Work & Landscape Cost Data* prices are obtained and organized makes this annual cost book a more valuable tool for the landscape estimator.

Estimating Maintenance Costs

Chapter Eleven

Estimating Maintenance Costs

Maintenance is a large segment of the landscape industry—in both number of dollars and amount of work. The scope of work that any one business may encompass could include campus or corporate facilities, sports stadiums, and even highways. There are also hundreds of thousands of small businesses focusing on lawn care services for the residential and small commercial customer. Many firms have risen to multi-millions in billings by offering highly specialized technical services. *Service* is the key word in landscape maintenance.

The methods used to procure contracts and plan maintenance proposals are similar to those proposed in Chapter 1 for design and new construction. Potential clients need to review a landscape firm's qualifications, licenses and references. The landscape contractor proposing to perform the work will need to define the scope of the job based on the client's needs and the requirements of the site. The maintenance professional who wins the job must then follow up with effective planning and expert performance. Like other businesses, landscape maintenance firms must not only continue to seek new clients, but keep their existing accounts.

Assessing your firm's capabilities and goals allows you to define and pursue the size and type of jobs that will be most rewarding to your company. Large volume commercial, public and facility accounts may have fairly extensive bid requirements similar to those described in Chapter 4, "How to Estimate." Not all maintenance contracts in your location are going to be both manageable and profitable. Employee expertise and cost-effective equipment are important factors in determining exactly which jobs will be most profitable for your firm. Here again, the *Information*, *Capability* and *Capacity* of the maintenance company is the knowledge base relied on in making decisions to bid or perform contracts.

The scope of work performed by maintenance companies varies from basic lawn care to full service exterior maintenance carried out year-round in all weather conditions. The variety and extent of these services provides both the challenges and advantages in maintenance contracting. Although some companies offer a range of services that include maintenance with design/build, the industry increasingly acknowledges the separate and distinct nature of new construction versus ongoing maintenance.

Other chapters of this book have focused on the special characteristics of each and every landscape project. While it is true that each site is unique, the maintenance business deals in repetition, as similar services are performed

over and over at the same site. Consequently, heavy emphasis is placed on achieving—and being able to reliably predict— good productivity. Cost effective equipment and skilled operators are the key to profitability. The biggest expense in the maintenance business is typically labor, and when equipment breaks down, the loss is compounded by personnel down time.

Division of Maintenance Tasks

Maintain, Repair, Replace, and *Enhance* are functions of a maintenance company. Figures 11.1 through 11.4 show examples of these job divisions and their reliance on labor, equipment and materials with excerpts from *Means Site Work & Landscape Cost Data.* In Figure 11.1 the site maintenance task descriptions (except fertilizing) show that approximately 90% of all costs are for the crew performing the work. Repair work is also typically labor-intensive. The walkway repair estimate on line number 02985-700-5910 demonstrates this point—labor accounts for $3.41 of the total $7.77 bare costs per square yard. Keep in mind that these references are based on an assumption of a full day's work by specific equipment and crew. Your own historical records of previous jobs are the most accurate predictors of your company's productivity.

Landscape Materials

Material costs, to a large extent, are a reflection of a company's buying power. Timeliness, storage, and transportation are other factors. A discussion of materials common to the landscape industry is found in Chapter 2, "Materials and Methods," with further details in the Appendix.

The landscape materials in Chapter 2 are familiar to the maintenance contractor, whose job is to maintain, repair, replace and sometimes enhance the original installation. Individual site conditions, including the size of the property, will influence the cost per square foot of doing the work. Cost variables include the site conditions, contractor's selection of the most cost-effective equipment, and the cost of materials, which may decrease when purchased in substantial quantity. As shown in Figure 11.1, lawn aeration, for example, may have a bare cost ranging from $0.36 to $2.61 per 1000 square feet depending on site conditions and equipment.

Replacing and enhancing materials, such as mulch and plantings—activities that are performed seasonally—give companies an opportunity for increased revenues. The market for the sales of perishable seasonal ornamentals may be competitive. Volume costs for trees, shrubs and groundcover may be found in Figure 11.2 from the unit cost section of *Means Site Work & Landscape Cost Data.* Anticipated productivity for a day of planting trees, shrubs and groundcover of various sizes at sites with different soil types is shown in Figure 11.3.

Note: *The work and materials shown in these and other examples and illustrations in this chapter are priced for large volume work, and prices do not consider the travel time, and loading and unloading between clients in one work day. Chapter 10 includes discussion of crews and other elements included in* Means Site Work & Landscape Cost Data.

Vehicles and Equipment

The type, variety and quantity of vehicles and equipment that a landscape firm should own are management budget decisions based on the operating budget and planned scope of work to be performed. Capital investments in vehicles and equipment and the needed planning for these purchases are discussed in Chapter 3, "Equipment."

Purchasing the "best" equipment is a challenge. When deciding what type of equipment to purchase, experienced users and mechanics are often the best

02985	Site Maintenance	CREW	DAILY OUTPUT	LABOR-HOURS	UNIT	2002 BARE COSTS				TOTAL INCL O&P
						MAT.	LABOR	EQUIP.	TOTAL	
700	0010	**SITE MAINTENANCE**									700
0800	Flower bed maintenance									
0810	Cultivate bed-no mulch	1 Clab	14	.571	M.S.F.		13.40		13.40	21
0830	Fall clean-up of flower bed, including pick-up mulch for re-use		1	8			188		188	292
0840	Fertilize flower bed, dry granular 3 lb./c.s.f.		85	.094		9.25	2.21		11.46	13.65
1130	Police, hand pickup	↓	30	.267			6.25		6.25	9.75
1140	Vacuum (outside)	A-1	48	.167			3.91	1.26	5.17	7.50
1200	Spring prepare	1 Clab	2	4	↓		94		94	146
1300	Weed mulched bed	1 Clab	20	.400	M.S.F.		9.40		9.40	14.60
1310	Unmulched bed	↓	8	1	↓		23.50		23.50	36.50
3000	Lawn maintenance									
3010	Aerate lawn, 18" cultivating width, walk behind	A-1	95	.084	M.S.F.		1.97	.64	2.61	3.77
3040	48" cultivating width	B-66	750	.011			.32	.21	.53	.71
3060	72" cultivating width	"	1,100	.007	↓		.22	.14	.36	.49
3100	Edge lawn, by hand at walks	1 Clab	16	.500	C.L.F.		11.75		11.75	18.25
3150	At planting beds	"	7	1.143			27		27	41.50
3200	Using gas powered edger at walks	A-1	88	.091			2.13	.69	2.82	4.08
3250	At planting beds		24	.333	↓		7.80	2.53	10.33	14.95
3260	Vacuum, 30" gas, outdoors with hose	↓	96	.083	M.L.F.		1.95	.63	2.58	3.73
3400	Weed lawn, by hand	1 Clab	3	2.667	M.S.F.		62.50		62.50	97.50
4510	Power rake	A-1	45	.178	"		4.17	1.35	5.52	8
4700	Seeding lawn, see Division 02920-510									
4750	Sodding, see Division 02920-600									
5900	Road & walk maintenance									
5910	Asphaltic concrete paving, cold patch, 2" thick	B-37	350	.137	S.Y.	4.03	3.41	.33	7.77	10.05
5913	3" thick	"	260	.185	"	5.75	4.59	.45	10.79	13.95
5915	De-icing roads and walks									
5920	Calcium Chloride in truckload lots see Division 02340-160									
6000	Ice melting comp., 90% Calc. Chlor., effec. to -30°F									
6010	50-80 lb. poly bags, med. applic. 19 lbs./M.S.F., by hand	1 Clab	60	.133	M.S.F.	14.85	3.13		17.98	21
6050	With hand operated rotary spreader		110	.073		14.85	1.71		16.56	19
6100	Rock salt, med. applic. on road & walkway, by hand		60	.133		3.72	3.13		6.85	8.95
6110	With hand operated rotary spreader		110	.073		3.72	1.71		5.43	6.75
6130	Hosing, sidewalks & other paved areas	↓	30	.267	↓		6.25		6.25	9.75
6260	Sidewalk, brick pavers, steam cleaning	A-1	950	.008	S.F.	.05	.20	.06	.31	.44
6400	Sweep walk by hand	1 Clab	15	.533	M.S.F.		12.50		12.50	19.45
6410	Power vacuum	A-1	100	.080			1.88	.61	2.49	3.59
6420	Drives & parking areas with power vacuum	1 Clab	120	.067	↓		1.56		1.56	2.43
6600	Shrub maintenance									
6640	Shrub bed fertilize dry granular 3 lbs./M.S.F.	1 Clab	85	.094	M.S.F.	.88	2.21		3.09	4.41
6800	Weed, by handhoe		8	1			23.50		23.50	36.50
6810	Spray out		32	.250			5.85		5.85	9.15
6820	Spray after mulch	↓	48	.167	↓		3.91		3.91	6.10
7100	Tree maintenance									
7200	Fertilize, tablets, slow release, 30 gram/tree	1 Clab	100	.080	Ea.	.31	1.88		2.19	3.26
7420	Pest control, spray		24	.333		14.40	7.80		22.20	28
7430	Systemic	↓	48	.167	↓	13.40	3.91		17.31	21

(from *Means Site Work & Landscape Cost Data 2002*)

Figure 11.1

02930 | Exterior Plants

		CREW	DAILY OUTPUT	LABOR-HOURS	UNIT	2002 BARE COSTS MAT.	LABOR	EQUIP.	TOTAL	TOTAL INCL O&P	
915											**915**
9330	3-1/2" to 4" Cal.				Ea.	193			193	212	
9335	4" to 4-1/2" Cal.					285			285	315	
9340	4-1/2" to 5" Cal.					455			455	505	
9345	5" to 5-1/2" Cal.					500			500	550	
9350	Bare root, 10' to 12'					62.50			62.50	69	
9355	12' to 14'				↓	80			80	88	
9400	Tilia tomentosa, (Silver Linden), Z4, B&B										
9410	6' to 8'				Ea.	74.50			74.50	81.50	
9420	8' to 10'					89			89	98	
9430	10' to 12'					109			109	120	
9440	2" to 2-1/2" Cal.					116			116	127	
9450	2-1/2" to 3" Cal.				↓	143			143	157	
9500	Ulmus americana, (American Elm), Z3, B&B										
9510	6' to 8'				Ea.	31			31	34	
9600	Zeklova serrata, (Japanese Keaki Tree), Z4, B&B										
9610	1-1/2" to 2" Cal.				Ea.	86			86	94.50	
9620	2" to 2-1/2" Cal.					130			130	143	
9630	2-1/2" to 3" Cal.				↓	159			159	175	
920	**TREES, CONIFERS** zone 2-7										**920**
0010											
1000	Abies balsamea nana, (Dwarf Balsam Fir), Z3, cont										
1001	1 gal				Ea.	6.60			6.60	7.25	
1002	15" to 18"					65			65	71.50	
1003	18" to 24"				↓	86.50			86.50	95	
1050	Abies concolor, (White Fir), Z4, B&B										
1051	2' to 3'				Ea.	33.50			33.50	37	
1052	3' to 4'					47			47	51.50	
1053	4' to 5'					55			55	60	
1054	5' to 6'					67.50			67.50	74	
1055	6' to 8'				↓	141			141	155	
1100	Abies concolor violacea, Z4, cont/BB										
1101	5' to 6'				Ea.	132			132	145	
1102	6' to 7'				"	162			162	178	
1150	Abies fraseri, (Fraser Balsam Fir), Z5, B&B										
1151	5' to 6'				Ea.	67.50			67.50	74	
1152	6' to 7'				"	74.50			74.50	81.50	
1200	Abies iasiocarpa arizonica, (Cork Fir), Z5, cont/BB										
1201	2' to 3'				Ea.	53.50			53.50	59	
1202	3' to 4'					90			90	99	
1203	4' to 5'					153			153	168	
1204	5' to 6'					137			137	151	
1205	6' to 7'					190			190	209	
1206	8' to 10'					229			229	252	
1207	10' to 12'				↓	320			320	350	
1250	Abies iasiocarpa compacta, (Dwarf Alpine Fir), Z5, cont/BB										
1251	18" to 24"				Ea.	44			44	48	
1252	2' to 3'					84			84	92	
1253	3' to 4'					173			173	191	
1254	4' to 5'					256			256	281	
1255	5' to 6'				↓	310			310	340	
1300	Abies koreana, (Korean Fir), Z5, B&B										

(from *Means Site Work & Landscape Cost Data 2002*)

Figure 11.2

02900 | Planting

02912	General Planting	CREW	DAILY OUTPUT	LABOR-HOURS	UNIT	MAT.	LABOR	EQUIP.	TOTAL	TOTAL INCL O&P	
							2002 BARE COSTS				
350	0010	**PLANTING** Trees, shrubs and ground cover										350
	0100	Light soil										
	0110	Bare root seedlings, 3" to 5"	1 Clab	960	.008	Ea.		.20		.20	.30	
	0120	6" to 10"		520	.015			.36		.36	.56	
	0130	11" to 16"		370	.022			.51		.51	.79	
	0140	17" to 24"		210	.038			.89		.89	1.39	
	0200	Potted, 2-1/4" diameter		840	.010			.22		.22	.35	
	0210	3" diameter		700	.011			.27		.27	.42	
	0220	4" diameter	▼	620	.013			.30		.30	.47	
	0300	Container, 1 gallon	2 Clab	84	.190			4.47		4.47	6.95	
	0310	2 gallon		52	.308			7.20		7.20	11.25	
	0320	3 gallon		40	.400			9.40		9.40	14.60	
	0330	5 gallon		29	.552			12.95		12.95	20	
	0400	Bagged and burlapped, 12" diameter ball, by hand	▼	19	.842			19.75		19.75	30.50	
	0410	Backhoe/loader, 48 H.P.	B-6	40	.600			15.35	4.46	19.81	28.50	
	0415	15" diameter, by hand	2 Clab	16	1			23.50		23.50	36.50	
	0416	Backhoe/loader, 48 H.P.	B-6	30	.800			20.50	5.95	26.45	38	
	0420	18" diameter by hand	2 Clab	12	1.333			31.50		31.50	48.50	
	0430	Backhoe/loader, 48 H.P.	B-6	27	.889			22.50	6.60	29.10	42.50	
	0440	24" diameter by hand	2 Clab	9	1.778			41.50		41.50	65	
	0450	Backhoe/loader 48 H.P.	B-6	21	1.143			29	8.50	37.50	54.50	
	0470	36" diameter, backhoe/loader, 48 H.P.	"	17	1.412	▼		36	10.50	46.50	67	
	0550	Medium soil										
	0560	Bare root seedlings, 3" to 5"	1 Clab	672	.012	Ea.		.28		.28	.43	
	0561	6" to 10"		364	.022			.52		.52	.80	
	0562	11" to 16"	▼	260	.031	▼		.72		.72	1.12	
	0563	17" to 24"	1 Clab	145	.055	Ea.		1.29		1.29	2.01	
	0570	Potted, 2-1/4" diameter		590	.014			.32		.32	.49	
	0572	3" diameter		490	.016			.38		.38	.60	
	0574	4" diameter	▼	435	.018			.43		.43	.67	
	0590	Container, 1 gallon	2 Clab	59	.271			6.35		6.35	9.90	
	0592	2 gallon		36	.444			10.40		10.40	16.20	
	0594	3 gallon		28	.571			13.40		13.40	21	
	0595	5 gallon		20	.800			18.75		18.75	29	
	0600	Bagged and burlapped, 12" diameter ball, by hand	▼	13	1.231			29		29	45	
	0605	Backhoe/loader, 48 H.P.	B-6	28	.857			22	6.40	28.40	40.50	
	0607	15" diameter, by hand	2 Clab	11.20	1.429			33.50		33.50	52	
	0608	Backhoe/loader, 48 H.P.	B-6	21	1.143			29	8.50	37.50	54.50	
	0610	18" diameter, by hand	2 Clab	8.50	1.882			44		44	68.50	
	0615	Backhoe/loader, 48 H.P.	B-6	19	1.263			32.50	9.40	41.90	60	
	0620	24" diameter, by hand	2 Clab	6.30	2.540			59.50		59.50	92.50	
	0625	Backhoe/loader, 48 H.P.	B-6	14.70	1.633			42	12.15	54.15	77.50	
	0630	36" diameter, backhoe/loader, 48 H.P.	"	12	2	▼		51	14.90	65.90	95	
	0700	Heavy or stoney soil										
	0710	Bare root seedlings, 3" to 5"	1 Clab	470	.017	Ea.		.40		.40	.62	
	0711	6" to 10"		255	.031			.74		.74	1.15	
	0712	11" to 16"		182	.044			1.03		1.03	1.60	
	0713	17" to 24"		101	.079			1.86		1.86	2.89	
	0720	Potted, 2-1/4" diameter		101	.079			1.86		1.86	2.89	
	0722	3" diameter		343	.023			.55		.55	.85	

(from *Means Site Work & Landscape Cost Data 2002*)

Figure 11.3

sources for advice. In-house expertise in operation and maintenance should be called upon in the equipment purchase process. It is some companies' business practice to count on in-house servicing and work their equipment until it falls apart. The lost productivity of such equipment can detract significantly from any savings that are achieved by putting off new equipment purchases. Some examples of relative productivity of various-size machines are shown in Chapter 3, "Equipment." Keeping detailed records of the service of a piece of equipment is not only important to maintaining long equipment life and regular availability, but may also be helpful in the event a decision is made to sell used equipment. Economic models may be used to forecast the present and future values of cash earmarked for capital investment, as illustrated in Chapter 3.

Work Crews or Teams

The composition of a crew (the number of people and their task responsibilities and necessary tools and equipment) is a management decision. Trade journals routinely feature real-life scenarios and opinions on the efficiency and effectiveness of teams. Each business will learn by applying productivity information from their own historical time and work records. (See examples of mowing, tree pruning and shrub pruning productivity in Figure 11.4. Generic information on suggested crew make-up is available in cost books, such as *Means Site Work & Landscape Cost Data*, but no information is as reliable as your own time and productivity records from similar work over a period of time.

Site Inspection

Profitable maintenance operations require a thorough knowledge of every account site. Site inspection is covered in Figure 4.2, the landscape project analysis form found in Chapter 4, "How to Estimate." Topography and access on a site often determine the methods and equipment that can be used for that site. Figure 11.5 is a simple form that can be used to perform a maintenance survey when assembling a maintenance proposal. Later in this chapter there is an example of the kind of data that would be recorded about a site, based on the site inspection or analysis.

Scheduling and Travel Time

A landscape maintenance company's work calendar schedule is quite different from that of the landscape contractor who performs only new design and construction. The example in Chapter 9, "Job Planning and Scheduling," is a master project calendar for a landscape contractor. It suggests two job sites running concurrently. In contrast, a maintenance crew may easily work at more than two sites in one day, and many more in a weekly work schedule.

Effective management of multiple sites and the transfer of crew and equipment between those locations is a number one priority task. The most efficient use of labor and equipment is vital to your company's existence and advancement. Not only the time spent performing the work, but also travel between accounts is a cost that must be captured in billings to clients. Travel time is one aspect of scheduling—an art successful managers learn to practice. Scheduling a logical sequence of work and team of workers, and restricting performance to contract requirements are required functions of crew leaders. Large firms may outfit certain vehicles for a particular team and type of work.

The purchase of materials also goes on the manager's planning schedule. Having materials available when they are needed is vital to good productivity. Proper planning helps to ensure that materials are there when needed, and also purchased at a reasonable cost. Other important scheduling concerns include

02935 | Plant Maintenance

		CREW	DAILY OUTPUT	LABOR-HOURS	UNIT	2002 BARE COSTS				TOTAL INCL O&P	
						MAT.	LABOR	EQUIP.	TOTAL		
300	0180	Water soluable, hydro spread, 1.5 # /MSF	B-64	600	.027	M.S.F.	2	.64	.45	3.09	3.68	**300**
	0190	Add for weed control				↓	.29			.29	.32	
600	0010	**MOWING**										**600**
	1650	Mowing brush, tractor with rotary mower										
	1660	Light density	B-84	22	.364	M.S.F.		11.35	9.05	20.40	27	
	1670	Medium density		13	.615			19.20	15.30	34.50	46	
	1680	Heavy density	↓	9	.889			27.50	22	49.50	66.50	
	4000	Lawn mowing, improved areas, 16" hand push	1 Clab	48	.167			3.91		3.91	6.10	
	4050	Power mower, 18" - 22"		65	.123			2.89		2.89	4.49	
	4100	22" - 30"	↓	110	.073			1.71		1.71	2.65	
	4150	30" - 32"	A-1	140	.057			1.34	.43	1.77	2.57	
	4160	Riding mower, 36" - 44"	B-66	300	.027			.79	.52	1.31	1.77	
	4170	48" - 58"	"	480	.017	↓		.50	.32	.82	1.11	
	4175	Mowing with tractor & attachments										
	4180	3 gang reel, 7'	B-66	930	.009	M.S.F.		.26	.17	.43	.57	
	4190	5 gang reel, 12'		1,200	.007			.20	.13	.33	.44	
	4200	Cutter or sickle-bar, 5', rough terrain		210	.038			1.14	.74	1.88	2.54	
	4210	Cutter or sickle-bar, 5', smooth terrain		340	.024	↓		.70	.46	1.16	1.56	
	4220	Drainage channel, 5' sickle bar	↓	5	1.600	Mile		47.50	31	78.50	107	
	4250	Lawnmower, rotary type, sharpen (all sizes)	1 Clab	10	.800	Ea.		18.75		18.75	29	
	4260	Repair or replace part	"	7	1.143	"		27		27	41.50	
	5000	Edge trimming with weed whacker	A-1	5,760	.001	L.F.		.03	.01	.04	.06	
700	0010	**TREE PRUNING**										**700**
	0020	1-1/2" caliper	1 Clab	84	.095	Ea.		2.23		2.23	3.48	
	0030	2" caliper		70	.114			2.68		2.68	4.17	
	0040	2-1/2" caliper		50	.160			3.75		3.75	5.85	
	0050	3" caliper	↓	30	.267			6.25		6.25	9.75	
	0060	4" caliper, by hand	2 Clab	21	.762			17.85		17.85	28	
	0070	Aerial lift equipment	B-85	38	1.053			26.50	18.25	44.75	61	
	0100	6" caliper, by hand	2 Clab	12	1.333			31.50		31.50	48.50	
	0110	Aerial lift equipment	B-85	20	2			50.50	34.50	85	116	
	0200	9" caliper, by hand	2 Clab	7.50	2.133			50		50	78	
	0210	Aerial lift equipment	B-85	12.50	3.200			81	55.50	136.50	186	
	0300	12" caliper, by hand	2 Clab	6.50	2.462			57.50		57.50	90	
	0310	Aerial lift equipment	B-85	10.80	3.704			93.50	64.50	158	215	
	0400	18" caliper by hand	2 Clab	5.60	2.857			67		67	104	
	0410	Aerial lift equipment	B-85	9.30	4.301			109	74.50	183.50	250	
	0500	24" caliper, by hand	2 Clab	4.60	3.478			81.50		81.50	127	
	0510	Aerial lift equipment	B-85	7.70	5.195			131	90	221	300	
	0600	30" caliper, by hand	2 Clab	3.70	4.324			101		101	158	
	0610	Aerial lift equipment	B-85	6.20	6.452			163	112	275	375	
	0700	36" caliper, by hand	2 Clab	2.70	5.926			139		139	216	
	0710	Aerial lift equipment	B-85	4.50	8.889			225	154	379	515	
	0800	48" caliper, by hand	2 Clab	1.70	9.412			221		221	345	
	0810	Aerial lift equipment	B-85	2.80	14.286	↓		360	248	608	830	
710	0010	**SHRUB PRUNING**										**710**
	6700	Prune, shrub bed	1 Clab	7	1.143	M.S.F.		27		27	41.50	
	6710	Shrub under 3' height		190	.042	Ea.		.99		.99	1.54	
	6720	4' height		90	.089			2.08		2.08	3.24	
	6730	Over 6'		50	.160			3.75		3.75	5.85	
	7350	Prune trees from ground	↓	20	.400	↓		9.40		9.40	14.60	

(from *Means Site Work & Landscape Cost Data* 2002)

Figure 11.4

Landscape Maintenance Analysis Short Form

Date _____

Travel Time From _____ To _____

Travel Minutes _____ Travel Miles _____

Project _____ Location _____

Owner _____ Project Manager _____

Building Type _____ Building Size _____

Quality: Economy: ☐ Average: ☐ Custom: ☐ Luxury: ☐
Outdoor surface parking: S.F. _____ No. of parking spaces req.: S.F. _____

Lawn area: S.F. _____

Landscape planting area: S.F. _____

Other area: S.F. _____

Zoning: Residential ☐ Commercial ☐ Industrial ☐ None ☐ Other ☐
Zoning Requirements _____

General Inspection	Spring	Summer	Fall	Winter
Overall appearance				
Maintainability				
Repairs/replacements				
Code compliance				
Roads, Walks, and Parking Lots				
Surface Conditions				
Curbing				
Drainage and Erosion Controls				
Surface drainage				
Manholes, catch basins				
Retention, detention				
Drains				
Lawns				
Level				
Moderate slope				
Steep slope				
Plant beds				
Flower beds				
Other plantings				
Trees				
Waste disposal				

Figure 11.5

the seasonal deadlines related to plant growth cycles and winter snow and ice control.

Scheduling includes identifying the day of service, the tasks to be performed, the estimated hours for each task, and the type of equipment and materials required. For that purpose, managers prepare daily service tickets (forms) listing crew members, equipment, and materials as well as the required tasks to be accomplished, and the projected duration. The ticket also serves as a report from the crew leader who enters actual figures alongside the estimates. Further information on the variety of issues and constraints important in scheduling may be found in Chapter 9, "Job Planning and Scheduling."

Facilities Personnel as Landscape Managers

The facilities manager or maintenance manager oversees his/her annual budget for general and preventive maintenance. He or she may elect to contract an outside firm to provide service at any one of various levels. Much decision-making focuses on the desirability (or cost effectiveness) of using in-house staff versus outside contractors. Maintenance cost formulas are developed to address the cost of materials, labor, and equipment. Whether the work is performed by in-house staff or outside contractors, there are indirect costs (such as benefits, procurement and service) that must be applied to staff, materials, and equipment. In addition, the contractor adds a profit percentage to materials, labor, and equipment usage.

What advantages does a facility gain by subcontracting grounds work? The cost difference between in-house and subcontracted work in some cases may be negligible, since the subcontractors' cost of materials, labor, and equipment may be lower. Subcontractors can also be more efficient than in-house staff, since they specialize only in this type of work. Another advantage of subcontracting landscape maintenance work is that grounds care equipment requires storage space. Materials such as fuel and chemicals also need to be stored, and there may be associated regulatory requirements. Additional factors include the time and cost both to train personnel and to purchase special materials. Insurance and liability are other costs to consider. Workers' Compensation rates, for example, vary according to job classifications.

Facilities personnel who opt to outsource landscape work need to conduct a site survey to qualify the jobs that must be done. Figure 11.6, A Survey for a Maintenance Proposal, is a handy tool for this purpose. On large campuses and noncontiguous areas, a survey is needed for each designated area. The measurements and counting in a landscape survey are the base of information for the diagnosis and prescriptions for landscape care and maintenance. Decisions may then be made on needed services and the frequency and sequence of those services. Figure 11.6 details the steps and categories to be considered in the review and provides space to fill in the needed information. The purpose of the survey form is to arrive at a quantity takeoff as detailed in Chapter 5, "How to Take Off Quantities." The next step after the takeoff is calculating and applying labor-hours, equipment use, supervisory time, and materials to arrive at direct costs for the performance of the segments of the job.

Commercial, institutional, and other facility groundskeeping budgets may include various "levels" of landscape maintenance for different sites, depending on factors such as visibility, pedestrian traffic, vehicle traffic, and other special needs and circumstances. Owners require the most cost-effective landscape maintenance plan that meets their desired standards. Facilities managers compare their in-house staff costs with those of outside maintenance contractors.

Survey For Maintenance Proposal

Date _____

Summary Description of Area: Residential ☐   Commercial ☐   Industrial ☐   Other ☐

_____

_____

Building Type _____

QUALITY: Economy: ☐   Average: ☐   Custom: ☐   Luxury: ☐

LAWN AREA(S)   Measure in linear feet and convert to square feet

Describe AREA	L x W	S.F.	LEVEL	MODERATE GRADE	STEEP GRADE

MULCHED BED AREA(S)   Measure in linear feet and convert to square feet. Describe type of edge and plant materials.

Describe AREA	L x W	S.F.	LEVEL	MODERATE GRADE	STEEP GRADE

OTHER GROUND AREAS   Uncultivated, unpaved, "natural" areas, other

Describe AREA	L x W	S.F.	LEVEL	MODERATE GRADE	STEEP GRADE

Figure 11.6

Special Considerations/Obstacles for lawn and plants areas: _____

_____

_____

IRRIGATION SYSTEM Describe: _____

Control Box _____   # Zones: _____   Heads/Emitters/other _____

Special Considerations/Obstacles for Irrigation Areas: _____

_____

_____

PAVED AREAS for SWEEPING, ICE/SNOW CONTROL

SIDEWALKS Measure in linear feet and convert to square feet

Describe AREA	L × W	S.F.	LEVEL	MODERATE GRADE	STEEP GRADE

STEPS Count number in each sequence

Describe AREA	L × W	S.F	LEVEL	MODERATE GRADE	STEEP GRADE

PATIOS and TERRACES Measure in linear feet and convert to square feet

Describe AREA	L × W	S.F.	LEVEL	MODERATE GRADE	STEEP GRADE

Figure 11.6 *(cont.)*

Special Considerations/Obstacles for sidewalks, steps, patios: _____

_____

_____

DRIVEWAYS Measure in linear feet and convert to square feet

Describe AREA	L × W	S.F.	LEVEL	MODERATE GRADE	STEEP GRADE

PARKING AREAS Measure in linear feet and convert to square feet

Describe AREA	L × W	S.F	LEVEL	MODERATE GRADE	STEEP GRADE

CURBS Measure in linear feet and convert to square feet

Describe AREA	L × W	S.F.	LEVEL	MODERATE GRADE	STEEP GRADE

Special Considerations/Obstacles for Paved Areas: _____

_____

_____

Figure 11.6 (*cont.*)

The cost of labor and equipment as calculated using in-house resources versus subcontracted is estimated in Figure 11.7 from *Means Facilities Maintenance and Repair Cost Data*. Another chart from the same book, Figure 11.8, estimates the cost of travel time using in-house staff compared to contractor's personnel traveling to and from the job site.

The Landscape Contractor's Ongoing Performance Analysis

Existing contracts should be reviewed on a regular basis to ensure the costs and productivity are in keeping with standards established by the firm. Material expenditures should also be reviewed to make sure they are required purchases. Productivity and the quality of labor performance must be evaluated and recorded. Variations between budget and actual costs to date should be analyzed. Periodic reviews are also the time to ensure that travel time and all costs associated with trucks and operations are included in the price of servicing an account. (Pricing the true cost of owning and operating equipment is discussed in Chapter 3, "Equipment.")

Developing a Maintenance Proposal: An Example

Before a cost estimate is created, the decision is made "to bid or not to bid" for the contract. Assuming the property falls within the firm's accessible geographical area and the property is in reasonable condition, the estimating will get under way. Commercial clients seeking maintenance proposals typically contract for one-, two- and three-year terms. The two-and three-year terms are common for large-scope developments, such as campuses. The following example is based on the small commercial project described in Chapter 7.

Site Analysis

The first step is the site visit and analysis. This involves inspecting the site and interviewing the client to learn his or her specific requirements, access and/or noise limitations, and any other pertinent information.

> *This property consists of five acres with a commercial building and distribution center occupied by the owner. There are parking lots on both the east and west side of the building. Good quality landscape and lawn exist on the east side only. The west parking lot is for loading and has natural wooded edges all along the perimeter. The property is located 12 miles from the lawn care company's garage and within the service area of other accounts. At this commercial building, weekend appearance is not a primary concern. The terrain of the site (its slopes, obstructions, and tree line) is noted. A stream runs through the property, and its steep banks are held by stone rip rap. The remainder of the terrain is relatively flat except for some rip rap slopes and mulched planting beds. The terrain—its slopes, tree line, irrigation, and obstructions—will determine the type of mowers to be used and also the largest effective piece(s) of equipment. Good quality mowing is required with no scalping or turn divots. (Note: The operating noise at an occupied site can be a factor in the selection of equipment.)*

For a larger facility, such as an office park or shopping mall, the "Landscape Project Analysis Form," Figure 4.2 in Chapter 4, may be needed to record details pertinent to the site. The conditions will have a bearing on the cost of labor, equipment, and materials. Maintenance companies are very familiar with the capacities of their equipment and apply that information to their decisions to bid jobs. For example, if a 32" walk-behind mower covers 140 M.S.F. in an 8-hour work day, a formula would indicate one M.S.F production in 0.057 hours in similar conditions.

Crew No.	Bare Costs		In-House Costs		Incl. Subs O&P		Cost Per Labor-Hour		
Crew A-16	Hr.	Daily	Hr.	Daily	Hr.	Daily	Bare Costs	In House	Incl. O&P
1 Maintenance Laborer	$17.60	$140.80	$21.65	$173.20	$21.65	$173.20	$17.60	$21.65	$27.10
1 Lawn Mower, large		86.00		86.00		94.60	10.75	10.75	11.83
8 M.H., Daily Totals		$226.80		$259.20		$267.80	$28.35	$32.40	$38.93
Crew A-17	Hr.	Daily	Hr.	Daily	Hr.	Daily	Bare Costs	In House	Incl. O&P
1 Maintenance Laborer	$17.60	$140.80	$21.65	$173.20	$21.65	$173.20	$17.60	$21.65	$27.10
1 Light Truck, 1.5 Ton		155.60		155.60		171.15	19.45	19.45	21.40
8 M.H., Daily Totals		$296.40		$328.80		$344.35	$37.05	$41.10	$48.50
Crew A-18	Hr.	Daily	Hr.	Daily	Hr.	Daily	Bare Costs	In House	Incl. O&P
1 Maintenance Laborer	$17.60	$140.80	$21.65	$173.20	$21.65	$173.20	$17.60	$21.65	$27.10
1 Farm Tractor w/ Attachment		179.00		179.00		196.90	22.38	22.38	24.61
8 M.H., Daily Totals		$319.80		$352.20		$370.10	$39.98	$44.03	$51.71
Crew B-1	Hr.	Daily	Hr.	Daily	Hr.	Daily	Bare Costs	In House	Incl. O&P
1 Labor Foreman (outside)	$25.45	$203.60	$34.25	$274.00	$34.25	$274.00	$24.12	$32.45	$39.95
2 Laborers	23.45	375.20	31.55	504.80	31.55	504.80			
24 M.H., Daily Totals		$578.80		$778.80		$778.80	$24.12	$32.45	$39.95
Crew B-18	Hr.	Daily	Hr.	Daily	Hr.	Daily	Bare Costs	In House	Incl. O&P
1 Labor Foreman (outside)	$25.45	$203.60	$34.25	$274.00	$34.25	$274.00	$24.12	$32.45	$39.95
2 Laborers	23.45	375.20	31.55	504.80	31.55	504.80			
1 Vibrating Compactor		55.60		55.60		61.15	2.32	2.32	2.55
24 M.H., Daily Totals		$634.40		$834.40		$839.95	$26.44	$34.77	$42.50
Crew B-21	Hr.	Daily	Hr.	Daily	Hr.	Daily	Bare Costs	In House	Incl. O&P
1 Labor Foreman (out)	$25.45	$203.60	$34.25	$ 274.00	$34.25	$ 274.00	$27.44	$36.46	$44.98
1 Skilled Worker	30.95	247.60	41.25	330.00	41.25	330.00			
1 Laborer	23.45	187.60	31.55	252.40	31.55	252.40			
.5 Equip. Oper. (crane)	32.35	129.40	41.10	164.40	41.10	164.40			
.5 S.P. Crane, 5 Ton		157.70		157.70		173.45	5.63	5.63	6.20
28 M.H., Daily Totals		$925.90		$1178.50		$1194.25	$33.07	$42.09	$51.18
Crew B-25B	Hr.	Daily	Hr.	Daily	Hr.	Daily	Bare Costs	In House	Incl. O&P
1 Labor Foreman	$25.45	$ 203.60	$34.25	$ 274.00	$34.25	$ 274.00	$26.20	$34.48	$42.62
7 Laborers	23.45	1313.20	31.55	1766.80	31.55	1766.80			
4 Equip. Oper. (medium)	31.20	998.40	39.65	1268.80	39.65	1268.80			
1 Asphalt Paver, 130 H.P.		1290.00		1290.00		1419.00			
2 Rollers, Steel Wheel		336.80		336.80		370.50			
1 Roller, Pneumatic Wheel		237.80		237.80		261.60	19.42	19.42	21.37
96 M.H., Daily Totals		$4379.80		$5174.20		$5360.70	$45.62	$53.90	$63.99
Crew B-35	Hr.	Daily	Hr.	Daily	Hr.	Daily	Bare Costs	In House	Incl. O&P
1 Laborer Foreman (out)	$25.45	$ 203.60	$34.25	$ 274.00	$34.25	$ 274.00	$29.13	$37.81	$46.86
1 Skilled Worker	30.95	247.60	41.25	330.00	41.25	330.00			
1 Welder (plumber)	35.95	287.60	44.85	358.80	44.85	358.80			
1 Laborer	23.45	187.60	31.55	252.40	31.55	252.40			
1 Equip. Oper. (crane)	32.35	258.80	41.10	328.80	41.10	328.80			
1 Equip. Oper. Oiler	26.65	213.20	33.85	270.80	33.85	270.80			
1 Electric Welding Mach.		79.95		79.95		87.95			
1 Hyd. Excavator, .75 C.Y.		457.00		457.00		502.70	11.19	11.19	12.31
48 M.H., Daily Totals		$1935.35		$2351.75		$2405.45	$40.32	$49.00	$59.17
Crew B-37	Hr.	Daily	Hr.	Daily	Hr.	Daily	Bare Costs	In House	Incl. O&P
1 Labor Foreman (outside)	$25.45	$ 203.60	$34.25	$ 274.00	$34.25	$ 274.00	$24.84	$33.06	$40.77
4 Laborers	23.45	750.40	31.55	1009.60	31.55	1009.60			
1 Equip. Oper. (light)	29.80	238.40	37.90	303.20	37.90	303.20			
1 Tandem Roller, 5 Ton		117.20		117.20		128.90	2.44	2.44	2.69
48 M.H., Daily Totals		$1309.60		$1704.00		$1715.70	$27.28	$35.50	$43.46

(from *Means Facilities Maintenance & Repair Cost Data 2002*)

Figure 11.7

The following table is used to estimate the cost of in-house staff or contractor's personnel to travel to and from the job site. The amount incurred must be added to the in-house total labor cost or contractor's billing application to calculate the total cost with travel.

In-House Staff–Travel Times versus Costs

Travel Time versus Costs	Crew Abbr.	Skwk	Clab	Clam	Asbe	Bric	Carp	Elec	Pord	Plum	Rofc	Shee	Stpi
	Rate with Mark-ups	$41.25	$31.55	$21.65	$44.40	$40.40	$40.40	$43.65	$35.40	$44.85	$39.65	$45.00	$45.20
Round Trip Travel Time (hours)	Crew size												
0.50	1	20.63	15.78	10.83	22.20	20.20	20.20	21.83	17.70	22.43	19.83	22.50	22.60
	2	41.25	31.55	21.65	44.40	40.40	40.40	43.65	35.40	44.85	39.65	45.00	45.20
	3	61.88	47.33	32.48	66.60	60.60	60.60	65.48	53.10	67.28	59.48	67.50	67.80
0.75	1	30.94	23.66	16.24	33.30	30.30	30.30	32.74	26.55	33.64	29.74	33.75	33.90
	2	61.88	47.33	32.48	66.60	60.60	60.60	65.48	53.10	67.28	59.48	67.50	67.80
	3	92.81	70.99	48.71	99.90	90.90	90.90	98.21	79.65	100.91	89.21	101.25	101.70
1.00	1	41.25	31.55	21.65	44.40	40.40	40.40	43.65	35.40	44.85	39.65	45.00	45.20
	2	82.50	63.10	43.30	88.80	80.80	80.80	87.30	70.80	89.70	79.30	90.00	90.40
	3	123.75	94.65	64.95	133.20	121.20	121.20	130.95	106.20	134.55	118.95	135.00	135.60
1.50	1	61.88	47.33	32.48	66.60	60.60	60.60	65.48	53.10	67.28	59.48	67.50	67.80
	2	123.75	94.65	64.95	133.20	121.20	121.20	130.95	106.20	134.55	118.95	135.00	135.60
	3	185.63	141.98	97.43	199.80	181.80	181.80	196.43	159.30	201.83	178.43	202.50	203.40
2.00	1	82.50	63.10	43.30	88.80	80.80	80.80	87.30	70.80	89.70	79.30	90.00	90.40
	2	165.00	126.20	86.60	177.60	161.60	161.60	174.60	141.60	179.40	158.60	180.00	180.80
	3	247.50	189.30	129.90	266.40	242.40	242.40	261.90	212.40	269.10	237.90	270.00	271.20

Installing Contractors–Travel Times versus Costs

Travel Time versus Costs	Crew Abbr.	Skwk	Clab	Clam	Asbe	Bric	Carp	Elec	Pord	Plum	Rofc	Shee	Stpi
	Rate with O & P	$50.85	$38.85	$27.10	$54.75	$49.85	$49.70	$54.65	$43.80	$56.00	$47.90	$55.90	$56.40
Round Trip Travel Time (hours)	Crew size												
0.50	1	25.43	19.43	13.55	27.38	24.93	24.85	27.33	21.90	28.00	23.95	27.95	28.20
	2	50.85	38.85	27.10	54.75	49.85	49.70	54.65	43.80	56.00	47.90	55.90	56.40
	3	76.28	58.28	40.65	82.13	74.78	74.55	81.98	65.70	84.00	71.85	83.85	84.60
0.75	1	38.14	29.14	20.33	41.06	37.39	37.28	40.99	32.85	42.00	35.93	41.93	42.30
	2	76.28	58.28	40.65	82.13	74.78	74.55	81.98	65.70	84.00	71.85	83.85	84.60
	3	114.41	87.41	60.98	123.19	112.16	111.83	122.96	98.55	126.00	107.78	125.78	126.90
1.00	1	50.85	38.85	27.10	54.75	49.85	49.70	54.65	43.80	56.00	47.90	55.90	56.40
	2	101.70	77.70	54.20	109.50	99.70	99.40	109.30	87.60	112.00	95.80	111.80	112.80
	3	152.55	116.55	81.30	164.25	149.55	149.10	163.95	131.40	168.00	143.70	167.70	169.20
1.50	1	76.28	58.28	40.65	82.13	74.78	74.55	81.98	65.70	84.00	71.85	83.85	84.60
	2	152.55	116.55	81.30	164.25	149.55	149.10	163.95	131.40	168.00	143.70	167.70	169.20
	3	228.83	174.83	121.95	246.38	224.33	223.65	245.93	197.10	252.00	215.55	251.55	253.80
2.00	1	101.70	77.70	54.20	109.50	99.70	99.40	109.30	87.60	112.00	95.80	111.80	112.80
	2	203.40	155.40	108.40	219.00	199.40	198.80	218.60	175.20	224.00	191.60	223.60	225.60
	3	305.10	233.10	162.60	328.50	299.10	298.20	327.90	262.80	336.00	287.40	335.40	338.40

(from *Means Facilities Maintenance & Repair Cost Data 2002*)

Figure 11.8

Quantity and Scope of Work

First outline the scope of work:

For the sample project, services included are: Weekly mowing of all lawn areas, mulching grass clippings, and removing excess clippings. Trim carefully at edges. Blow off walks, patios, road edges and groundcover area of beds and rip rap. Every four weeks, power edge the hard edges. The time span of the work begins in late March and runs through November. This information is necessary to determine the number of labor hours required to perform each contract with the available equipment.

Mowing: Measure the amount of turf area and mulched planting bed area. Select the most efficient and effective size and type of equipment depending on the access, configuration, and topography of the designated mowing areas. The efficiency of a mower increases dramatically with the cut width. Mulching mowers may minimize cleanup. Creative managers may have solutions such as turf growth regulators and changing troublesome areas to groundcover or other non-lawn surfaces. The typical unit of measure for turf lawns is square feet, with areas divided according to the type of mowing equipment that may be used.

Edging: This task is a part of every mowing. Both the soft edges (to be trimmed) and the hard edges (to be edged) are measured. Edging (machine and chemical) is needed at both hard surfaces and soft surfaces. The size and type of string trimmers and mechanical edgers must be taken into account. The typical unit of measure is linear feet, with areas designated as to the type of edging needed.

Pruning: The typical unit of measurement is area of shrub beds and size and type of shrubs. The pruning at this site will be hand work, at the appropriate time of year. The junipers are intended to be natural and require control only at paths. Shade trees and pines are to be pruned at dormant times as needed.

Fertilizing and Weed Control: Testing for pH and nutrient levels is required in order to choose appropriate materials and applications and to determine the schedule and number of applications. The typical measurement is square feet of surface area. Special consideration is given for restrictions regarding application near standing water and wetlands. Weekly maintenance also includes treating weeds in mulched areas with selective herbicide and hand weeding in groundcover beds as needed.

Choosing Crew and Equipment

The experienced estimator visualizes the work and determines the time required using his/her company's crew and equipment. In addition, the cost of each crew member, the cost of owning and operating each truck and unit of equipment, and the cost of materials must be computed. (See Chapter 3 for more information on equipment costs.)

For this example, a two-person crew will handle the weekly servicing of the account. Due to the noncontiguous and irregular areas of lawn, a 32" walk-behind power mower will be used. A power edger will be used to tidy the edges. Along the base of the wood retainers, a turf growth regulator may be applied to reduce wear at the edging. The blowing off of walkways and patios will be accomplished with a backpack blower chosen to provide as quiet as possible operation. At the paved surface edges, a power edger will be used monthly.

Using this equipment, the weekly mowing of 10 M.S.F. of turf will take an average of 0.57 hours for one laborer to complete (02935-600-4150). Power edge 2000 L.F. around

obstacles (02985-700-3250), and blow off 4800 S.F. of walkways and patios (02985-700-6410) can be expected to take 0.67 and 0.38 hours respectively. Treat weeds in the mulched areas and the plant beds (02985-700-1300). Every month the 1600 L.F. of parking lot edges will be power edged (02985-700-3200).

The pruning will take place seasonally and, on the basis of 3400 S.F. of plant beds, is estimated to require 3.89 labor hours. The time estimate is low because the plant material is intended to remain natural. Tree care may be set up so the ornamental trees could be pruned over the winter season as needed. Assuming this is a high profile account, it will be serviced on a weekly basis from late April to late November.

In the climate of eastern Massachusetts, a spring cleanup of the site will be a special consideration. Beds would be flat spade-edged, and a power edger used where possible. A fresh edge will be created around the mulched tree area. All lawn areas will be power-raked or aerated. Hand-raking of all the groundcover and planting beds will also be required. A new application of mulch will be applied as required. Pruning will be performed to remove winter damage. Estimate of the total labor hours for spring cleanup is 8 labor-hours.

All direct and indirect costs are taken into account in estimating. Chapter 4, "How to Estimate," lists in detail the various types of indirect costs, and also provides a methodology to save time and deliver accurate numbers when doing a quantity takeoff. Figure 6.13 from Chapter 6, "The Skill of Pricing," is a useful form for calculating typical overhead costs. Details on the recovery of overhead costs may be found in both Chapters 4 and 6.

In summary, the development of a cost estimate for the servicing of a maintenance account is a step-by-step process. All of the steps taken to produce a true cost are very similar to those detailed in Chapter 7, "The Sample Takeoff and Estimate." For all bidding, a detailed and systematic list of all labor-hours, equipment and materials is essential in order to produce an accurate list of quantities and a record of true costs. Chapter 6 provides an example of a materials quantity takeoff form, as well as other standard forms that are useful in recording and listing costs. When all direct job costs are listed, your maintenance proposal is completed by the addition of your company's rate for overhead and profit. This is a percentage rate unique to your company. Chapter 8, "Bidding for Jobs," includes further suggestions on putting together a "proposal package."

A *Final* Word

All successful business management is a blend of good common sense and practical experience. In the landscape industry, managers and workers often find themselves holding the best jobs on earth. Their work is never completed! From decorative planting and on through the snow-plowing season, their efforts give immediate results and instant client satisfaction. Such is the secret of success in the landscape business.

Appendix

ESTIMATING

SITE WORK

HARD CONSTRUCTION

PLANTING & WEATHER

PROFESSIONAL REFERENCES

ABBREVIATIONS

Conversion Factors

To change cubic feet to gallons:
Multiply the number of cubic feet by 7.48.
For approximate results, multiply by 7½.

To change gallons to cubic feet:
Multiply the number of gallons by 0.1337.

To change cubic inches to gallons:
Divide the number of cubic inches by 231,
or multiply by 0.004329.

To change cubic feet to bushels:
Divide the number of cubic feet by 1.244.
For approximate results, multiply the
number of cubic feet by ⅘.

To change cubic inches to bushels:
Divide the number of cubic inches by 2150.42
or multiply the number of cubic inches by
0.000465.

To change bushels to cubic feet:
Multiply the number of bushels by 1.244. For
approximate results, multiply the number by ⅝.

**To change temperature in degrees
Centigrade to degrees Fahrenheit:**
Multiply Centigrade temperature
by ⁹⁄₅ and add 32°.
Example: 30° C. = 30 x ⁹⁄₅ + 32 = 86° F.

**To change temperature in degrees
Fahrenheit to degrees Centigrade:**
Subtract 32 from Fahrenheit reading
and multiply by ⁵⁄₉.
Example: 86° F. = 86-32 = 54 x ⁵⁄₉ = 30° C.

To change cubic yards to cubic feet:
Multiply cubic yards by 27.

To change cubic feet to cubic yards:
Divide cubic feet by 27.

To change hectares to acres:
Multiply hectares by 2.471.

(from *Landscape Designer & Estimator's Guide, Third Edition,* American Nursery & Landscape Association, Washington, DC)

Metric Conversion Factors

Description: This table is primarily for converting customary U.S. units in the left hand column to SI metric units in the right hand column. In addition, conversion factors for some commonly encountered Canadian and non-SI metric units are included.

	If You Know	Multiply By		To Find
Length	Inches	x	25.4[a]	= Millimeters
	Feet	x	0.3048[a]	= Meters
	Yards	x	0.9144[a]	= Meters
	Miles (statute)	x	1.609	= Kilometers
Area	Square inches	x	645.2	= Square millimeters
	Square feet	x	0.0929	= Square meters
	Square yards	x	0.8361	= Square meters
Volume (Capacity)	Cubic inches	x	16,387	= Cubic millimeters
	Cubic feet	x	0.02832	= Cubic meters
	Cubic yards	x	0.7646	= Cubic meters
	Gallons (U.S. liquids)[b]	x	0.003785	= Cubic meters[c]
	Gallons (Canadian liquid)[b]	x	0.004546	= Cubic meters[c]
	Ounces (U.S. liquid)[b]	x	29.57	= Milliliters[c,d]
	Quarts (U.S. liquid)[b]	x	0.9464	= Liters[c,d]
	Gallons (U.S. liquid)[b]	x	3.785	= Liters[c,d]
Force	Kilograms force[d]	x	9.807	= Newtons
	Pounds force	x	4.448	= Newtons
	Pounds force	x	0.4536	= Kilograms force[d]
	Kips	x	4448	= Newtons
	Kips	x	453.6	= Kilograms force[d]
Pressure, Stress, Strength (Force per unit area)	Kilograms force per square centimeter[d]	x	0.09807	= Megapascals
	Pounds force per square inch (psi)	x	0.006895	= Megapascals
	Kips per square inch	x	6.895	= Megapascals
	Pounds force per square inch (psi)	x	0.07031	= Kilograms force per square centimeter[d]
	Pounds force per square foot	x	47.88	= Pascals
	Pounds force per square foot	x	4.882	= Kilograms force per square meter[d]
Bending Moment Or Torque	Inch-pounds force	x	0.01152	= Meter-kilograms force[d]
	Inch-pounds force	x	0.1130	= Newton-meters
	Foot-pounds force	x	0.1383	= Meter-kilograms force[d]
	Foot-pounds force	x	1.356	= Newton-meters
	Meter-kilograms force[d]	x	9.807	= Newton-meters
Mass	Ounces (avoirdupois)	x	28.35	= Grams
	Pounds (avoirdupois)	x	0.4536	= Kilograms
	Tons (metric)	x	1000[a]	= Kilograms
	Tons, short (2000 pounds)	x	907.2	= Kiloprams
	Tons, short (2000 pounds)	x	0.9072	= Megagrams[e]
Mass per Unit Volume	Pounds mass per cubic foot	x	16.02	= Kilograms per cubic meter
	Pounds mass per cubic yard	x	0.5933	= Kilograms per cubic meter
	Pounds mass per gallon (U.S. liquid)[b]	x	119.8	= Kilograms per cubic meter
	Pounds mass per gallon (Canadian liquid)[b]	x	99.78	= Kilograms per cubic meter
Temperature	Degrees Fahrenheit	(F-32)/1.8		= Degrees Celsius
	Degrees Fahrenheit	(F+459.67)/1.8		= Degrees Kelvin
	Degrees Celsius	C+273.15		= Degrees Kelvin

[a]The factor given is exact
[b]One U.S. gallon = 0.8327 Canadian gallon
[c]1 liter = 1000 milliliters = 1000 cubic centimeters
   1 cubic decimeter = 0.001 cubic meter
[d]Metric but not SI unit
[e]Called "tonne" in England and "metric ton" in other metric countries

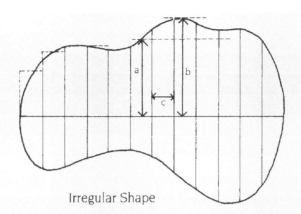

Irregular Shape

For each segment:

$$\text{Area} = \frac{(a + b)c}{2}$$

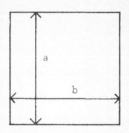

Square Area = ab

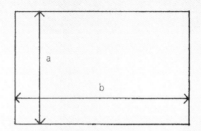

Rectangle Area = ab

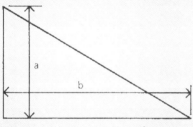

$$\text{Triangle Area} = \frac{ab}{2}$$

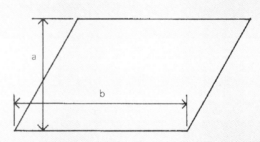

Parallelogram Area = ab

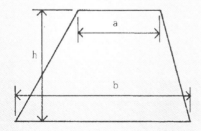

$$\text{Trapezoid Area} = \frac{(a + b)h}{2}$$

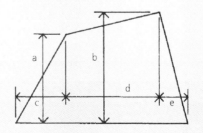

$$\text{Trapezium Area} = \frac{bd + ad + be + ac}{2}$$

Area Calculations

Conversion of Inches to Decimal Parts per Foot												
	0	1″	2″	3″	4″	5″	6″	7″	8″	9″	10″	11″
0	0	.08	.17	.25	.33	.42	.50	.58	.67	.75	.83	.92
1/8″	.01	.09	.18	.26	.34	.43	.51	.59	.68	.76	.84	.93
1/4″	.02	.10	.19	.27	.35	.44	.52	.60	.69	.77	.85	.94
3/8″	.03	.11	.20	.28	.36	.45	.53	.61	.70	.78	.86	.95
1/2″	.04	.12	.21	.29	.37	.46	.54	.62	.71	.79	.87	.96
5/8″	.05	.14	.22	30	39	.47	.55	.64	.72	.80	.89	.97
3/4″	.06	.15	.23	.31	.40	.48	.56	.65	.73	.81	.90	.98
7/8″	.07	.16	.24	.32	.41	.49	.57	.66	.74	.82	.91	.99

Design Weight for Various Materials

Type		Description	Weight Per C.F.	Type		Description	Weight Per C.F.
Bituminous	Coal	Anthracite	97	Masonry	Ashlar	Granite	168
		Bituminous	84			Limestone, crystalline	168
		Peat, turf, dry	47			Limestone, oolitic	135
		Coke	75			Marble	173
	Petroleum	Unrefined	54			Sandstone	144
		Refined	50		Rubble, in mortar	Granite	153
		Gasoline	42			Limestone, crystalline	147
	Pitch		69			Limestone, oolitic	138
	Tar	Bituminous	75			Marble	156
Concrete	Plain	Stone aggregate	144			Sandstone	137
		Slag aggregate	132		Brick	Pressed	140
		Expanded slag aggregate	100			Common	120
		Haydite (burned clay agg.)	90			Soft	100
		Vermiculite/perlite, load bearing	70-105		Cement	Portland, loose	90
		Vermiculite & perlite, non load bear	25-50			Portland set	183
	Rein-forced	Stone aggregate	150		Lime	Gypsum, loose	53-64
		Slag aggregate	138		Mortar	Set	103
		Lightweight aggregates	30-106	Metals	Aluminum Brass	Cast, hammered	165
Earth	Clay	Dry	63			Cast, rolled	534
		Damp, plastic	110		Bronze Copper	7.9 to 14% Sn	509
		and gravel, dry	100			Cast, rolled	556
	Dry	Loose	76		Iron	Cast, pig	450
		Packed	95			Wrought	485
	Moist	Loose	78		Lead Monel		710
		Packed	96				556
	Mud	Flowing	108		Steel	Rolled	490
		Packed	115		Tin Zinc	Cast, hammered	459
	Riprap	Limestone	80-85			Cast rolled	440
		Sandstone	90	Timber	Cedar	White or red	22
		Shale	105		Fir	Douglas	32
	Sand & gravel	Dry, loose	90-105			Eastern	25
		Dry, packed	100-120		Maple	Hard	43
		Wet	118-120			White	33
Gases	Air	0°C., 760 mm.	.0807		Oak	Red or Black	41
	Gas	Natural	.0385			White	46
Liquids	Alcohol	100%	49		Pine	White	26
	Water	4°C., maximum density	62.5			Yellow, long leaf	44
		Ice	56			Yellow, short leaf	38
		Snow, fresh fallen	8		Redwood	California	26
		Sea water	64		Spruce	White or Black	27

Computation
Volume of Excavated Material

(Depth in inches and feet)	(Cubic yards per square surface foot)
2"	.006
4"	.012
6"	.019
8"	.025
10"	.031
1'	.037
2'	.074
3'	.111
4'	.148
5'	.185
6'	.222
7'	.259
8'	.296
9'	.333
10'	.370

(No swellage factor applied)

Example: Excavation required: 20' x 30' x 4' = 600 times .148 = 88.8 Cu. Yds.

(from *Landscape Designer & Estimator's Guide*, Third Edition, American Nursery & Landscape Association, Washington, DC)

SITE CONSTRUCTION

Maximum Grades and Slopes
for Various Use Areas

Use	Ratio Horizontal to Vertical	Percentage
Entrance walk	10:1	10%
Driveway	6.7:1	15%
Ramps	5:1	20%
Grass Bank	3:1	33.3%
Planted Bank	2:1	50.0%
Steps	1.5:1	66.6%

Minimum Grades for Surface Drainage

Use	Ratio Horizontal to Vertical	Percentage
Patio	1" in 10 feet	(.8% slope)
Open Lawn - Well Drained	1" in 8 feet	(1% slope)
Open Lawn - Heavy Soil	1" in 4 feet	(2% slope)
Around Building Foundation And Areas Requiring Good Drainage	1" in 2 feet	(5% slope)

(from *Landscape Designer & Estimator's Guide, Third Edition*, American Nursery & Landscape Association Washington, DC)

Parking Lot Specifications
Layout Data Based on 9' x 19' Parking Stall Size

φ	P	A	C	W	N	G	D	L	P'	W'
Angle of Stall	Parking Depth	Aisle Width	Curb Length	Width Overall	Net Car Area	Gross Car Area	Distance Last Car	Lost Area	Parking Depth	Width Overall
90°	19'	24'	9'	62'	171 S.F.	171 S.F.	9'	0	19'	62'
60°	21'	18'	10.4'	60'	171 S.F.	217 S.F.	7.8'	205 S.F.	18.8'	55.5'
45°	19.8'	13'	12.8'	52.7'	171 S.F.	252 S.F.	6.4'	286 S.F.	16.6'	46.2'

Note: Square foot per car areas do not include the area of the travel lane.

90° Stall Angle: The main reason for use of this stall angle is to achieve the highest car capacity. This may be sound reasoning for employee lots with all day parking, but in most (in & out) lots there is difficulty in entering the stalls and no traffic lane direction. This may outweigh the advantage of high capacity.

60° Stall Angle: This layout is used most often due to the ease of entering and backing out, also the traffic aisle may be smaller.

45° Stall Angle: Requires a small change of direction from the traffic aisle to the stall, so the aisle may be reduced in width.

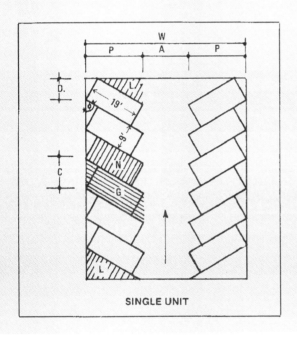

SINGLE UNIT

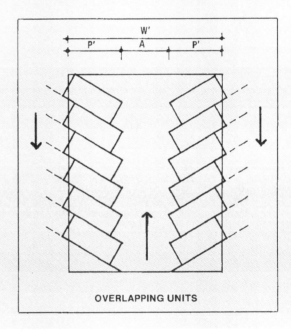

OVERLAPPING UNITS

SITE CONSTRUCTION

EARTHWORK EQUIPMENT

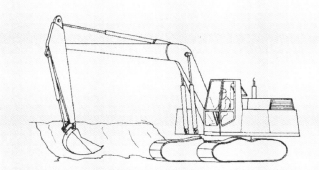

Excavator-Track Mounted

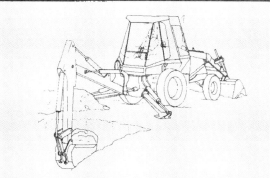

Rubber-Tired Backhoe

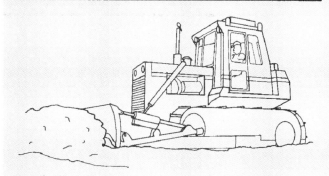

Straight Blade Bulldozer

Rubber-Tired Front End Loader

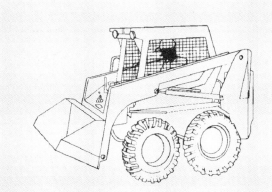

Skid Steer Loader

Dump Truck

EARTHWORK EQUIPMENT

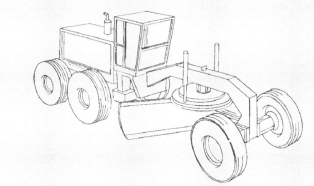

Grader

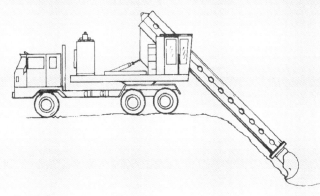

Gradall

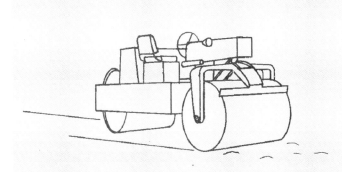

Roller

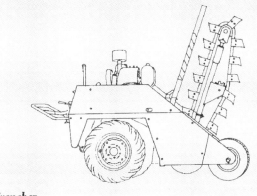

Trencher

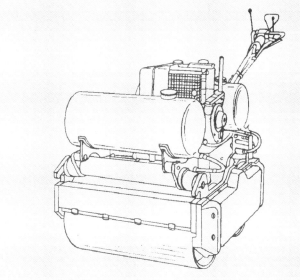

Compactor Roller

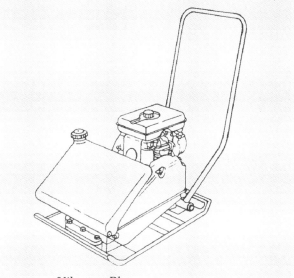

Compactor - Vibratory Plate

CONCRETE EQUIPMENT

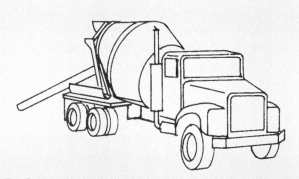

Ready Mix Truck

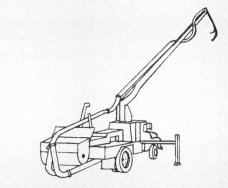

Concrete Pump

Concrete Bucket

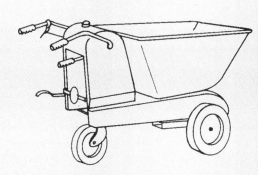

Concrete Cart

Concrete Mixer

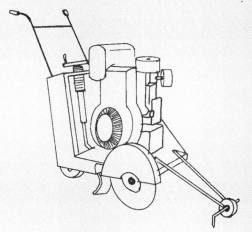

Concrete Saw

CONCRETE EQUIPMENT

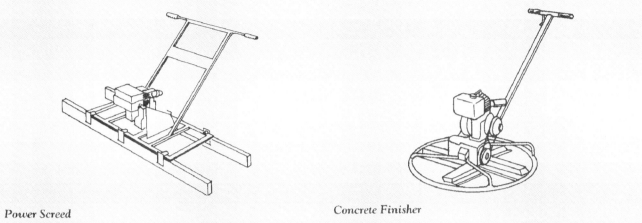

Power Screed   *Concrete Finisher*

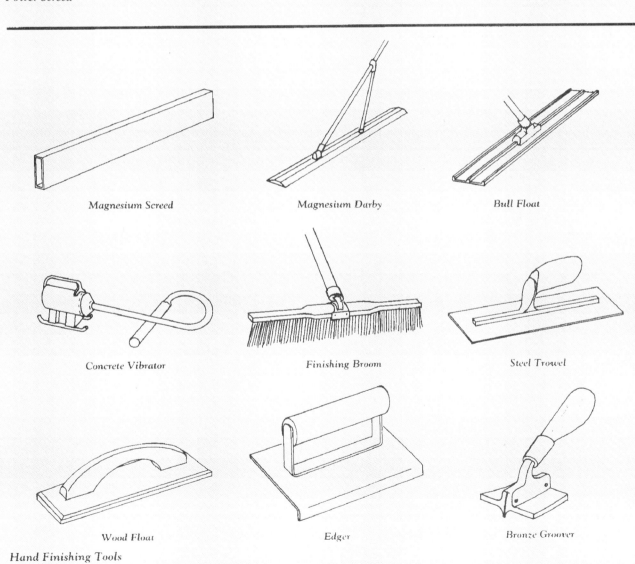

Magnesium Screed   *Magnesium Darby*   *Bull Float*

Concrete Vibrator   *Finishing Broom*   *Steel Trowel*

Wood Float   *Edger*   *Bronze Groover*

Hand Finishing Tools

DEWATERING

Excavation dewatering is the process of removing surface and ground water which may interfere with the excavation and construction of a structure. Methods used for removal of surface water are ditching, or gravity flow, and pumping.

The use of ditches to remove surface water by gravity flow may be economical where the angle of repose of the earth is steep and the amount of required excavation of the site is minimal. Where surface water is a common feature in the geographic location, the dewatering ditch may be planned as part of the final landscaping or topographical design of the site.

The removal of surface water by pumping is the alternative to the ditching method. Depending on the condition and the amount of the water to be removed, diaphragm or centrifugal pumps may be used. Where the water contains large amounts of solids, the diaphragm type is recommended. The more efficient centrifugal pumps should be used in cases which require removal of large volumes of surface water. Regardless of the type of pump selected, it should be located as close to the water as possible to minimize lift. Ideally, it should rest in a sump at a low point of the excavation. The inlet to the pump should be fitted with a trash screen to protect the pump and be set in a mesh enclosure to prevent clogging. Placing the inlet in a wooden box may keep it from settling in mud and sludge.

Water may be removed prior to excavation by lowering the water table around the site with the installation of well points or deep wells and pumping. A well point is a section of perforated pipe that is jetted vertically into place below the ground water level and then connected by riser pipes to a horizontal header at the ground surface. Well points and their accompanying risers are spaced along the header at intervals ranging from 2-1/2′ to 10′ on center. A pump is then connected to the header pipe, and the ground water is drawn from the water table, which, in time, is lowered to the depth of the well points (usually a maximum of 15′). Deeper well points are installed by locating headers at successively lower levels and operating the pump at the lowest of these levels. The flow of ground water into the well points depends on the porosity of the soil surrounding them. Where the soil is comprised of clay or consists of material which restricts its porosity, sand fill may be placed around the well points to facilitate the flow of water into them. The deep well system is a more complex and costly operation than the well point system because of the depth of installation involved and the drilling and lining of the shafts. Deep wells can be driven to depths of 50′ and deeper and are spaced at wider intervals than well points.

Because all types of dewatering operations may require continuous pumping, a standby pump and extra operating equipment should be readily available to cope with breakdowns. To save on overtime wages for uninterrupted pumping operations that last for a week or longer, the assignment of four men rotating six-hour shifts computes to a total of only eight hours overtime wages per man per week.

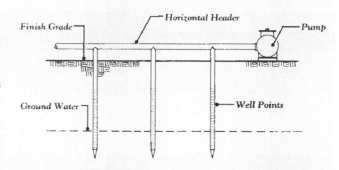

Man-hours

Description	m/hr	Unit
Excavate Drainage Trench, 2′ Wide		
2′ Deep	.178	cu yd
3′ Deep	.160	cu yd
Sump Pits, By Hand		
Light Soil	1.130	cu yd
Heavy Soil	2.290	cu yd
Pumping 8 Hours, Diaphragm or		
Centrifugal Pump		
Attended 2 hours per Day	3.000	day
Attended 8 hours per Day	12.000	day
Pumping 24 Hours, Attended 24 Hours, 4 Men		
at 6 Hour Shifts, 1 Week Minimum	25.140	day
Relay Corrugated Metal Pipe, Including		
Excavation, 3′ Deep		
12″ Diameter	.209	lf
18″ Diameter	.240	lf
Sump Hole Construction, Including Excavation,		
with 12″ Gravel Collar		
Corrugated Pipe		
12″ Diamter	.343	lf
18″ Diameter	.480	lf
Wood Lining, Up to 4′ x 4′	.080	sfca
Well-point System, Single Stage, Install and		
Remove, per Length of Header		
Minimum	.750	lf
Maximum	2.000	lf
Wells, 10′ to 20′ Deep with Steel Casing		
2′ Diameter		
Minimum	.145	vlf
Average	.245	vlf
Maximum	.490	vlf

OPEN SITE DRAINAGE SYSTEMS

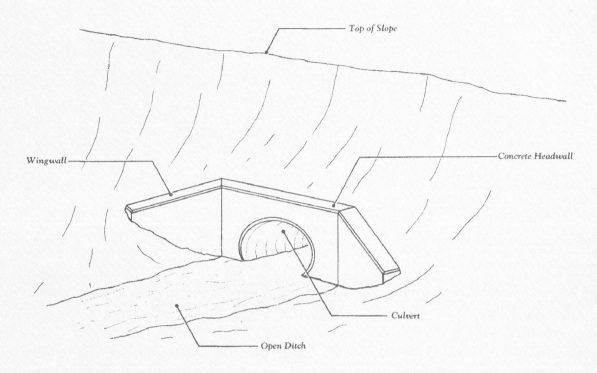

The flow of storm water runoff on the surfaces of slopes and the embankments of swales and ditches must be controlled to prevent erosion and the undermining of site structures and pavements. Where the vegetative cover is insufficient to control surface erosion, transverse water diversion ditches should be placed at the top of the slope. Where the end of the intercepting ditch becomes too steep or must follow the slope, a paved spillway section may be installed to conduct the flow. Paving may be required where the flow in a ditch or swale exceeds the runoff limits for bare earth or turf grass. The paving materials commonly used for these installations include stone rubble, asphalt, and concrete. Concrete drop structures, which are similar in construction to catch basins, may also be installed at critical locations along the ditch to reduce the volume of the flow and to allow some of the runoff to be carried by pipe to safe remote discharge locations.

Culverts may also be employed to conduct storm water runoff, especially under roads, highways, and railroad beds. Small culverts of only a few feet in diameter may be constructed from sections of reinforced concrete pipe, corrugated metal, or plastic. Large culverts require more complex installations which may be constructed from reinforced concrete pipe of up to 8′ in diameter, precast box culverts of up to 12′ in height, corrugated steel or aluminum arches of up to 6′ in radius, or multi-plate steel arches. Poured-in-place concrete bridges may even be required for extremely large-scale culvert installations. Regardless of the size of the culvert, the structure, wherever possible, should be placed at right angles to the roadway or rail bed to minimize the length of the structure and to reduce its cost.

Care should be exercised in planning and constructing the entrances and exits of culverts so that appropriately designed and installed headwalls will protect and retain the surrounding fill. For small culverts which are correctly aligned on slight slopes, a simple straight headwall constructed perpendicular to the flow serves as adequate protection. For larger culverts and moderate to steep slopes, wing walls must be placed alongside the straight headwall to prevent erosion of the sloped fill and undermining of the culvert itself. In situations where the flow changes abruptly at a culvert, the wing walls must be skewed in a direction to coincide with the natural stream. In addition to the headwall, a paved apron may also be required where high intake or exit flow velocities can cause further erosion or undermining.

The materials used for the construction of culverts, headwalls and culvert piping vary according to the size of the structure and the conditions of its placement. Large field constructed headwalls are normally constructed from poured-in-place concrete or from building stones set in mortar. Precast culvert boxes may be ordered with custom end walls at an additional cost. Some types of small culvert piping can be ordered with special sections with flared ends which can function as headwalls. Concrete culvert pipe may be ordered with a vitreous lining which greatly improves the pipe's hydraulic characteristics. Corrugated metal pipe also achieves greater hydraulic efficiency with the addition of a specially ordered paved invert.

OPEN SITE DRAINAGE SYSTEMS (CONT.)

Man-hours

Description	m/hr	Unit
Paving, Asphalt, Ditches	.185	sq yd
Concrete, Ditches	.360	sq yd
Filter Stone Rubble	.258	cu yd
Paving, Ashpalt, Aprons	.320	sq yd
Concrete, Aprons	.620	sq yd
Drop Structure	8.000	Ea.
Culverts, Reinforced Concrete, 12″ Diameter	.162	lf
24″ Diameter	.183	lf
48″ Diameter	.280	lf
72″ Diameter	.431	lf
96″ Diameter	.560	lf
Flared Ends, 12″ Diameter	1.080	Ea.
24″ Diameter	1.750	Ea.
Corrugated Metal, 12″ Diameter	.114	lf
24″ Diameter	.175	lf
48″ Diameter	.560	lf
72″ Diameter	1.240	lf
Reinforced Plastic, 12″ Diameter	.280	lf
Precast Box Culvert, 6′ x 3′	.343	lf
8′ x 8′	.480	lf
12′ x 8′	.716	lf
Aluminum Arch Culvert, 17″ x 11″	.150	lf
35″ x 24″	.300	lf
57″ x 38″	.800	lf
Multi-plate Arch, Steel	.014	lb

Corrugated Metal Culvert

Man-hours (cont.)

Description	m/hr	Unit
Headwall, Concrete, 30″ Diameter Pipe,		
3′ Wing Walls	28.750	Ea.
4′-3″ Wing Walls	33.500	Ea.
60″ Diameter Pipe, 5′-6″ Wing Walls	63.250	Ea.
8′-0″ Wing Walls	76.650	Ea.
Stone, 30″ Diameter Pipe, 3′ Wing Walls	12.650	Ea.
4′-3″ Wing Walls	14.800	Ea.
60″ Diameter Pipe, 5′-6″ Wing Walls	30.200	Ea.
8′-0″ Wing Walls	37.200	Ea.

		Reinforcing Bars		
			Nominal Dimensions - Round Sections	
Bar Size Designation	Weight Pounds Per Foot	Diameter Inches	Cross-Sectional Area-Sq. Inches	Perimeter Inches
#3	.376	.375	.11	1.178
#4	.668	.500	.20	1.571
#5	1.043	.625	.31	1.963
#6	1.502	.750	.44	2.356
#7	2.044	.875	.60	2.749
#8	2.670	1.000	.79	3.142
#9	3.400	1.128	1.00	3.544
#10	4.303	1.270	1.27	3.990
#11	5.313	1.410	1.56	4.430
#14	7.650	1.693	2.25	5.320
#18	13.600	2.257	4.00	7.090

	Common Stock Styles of Welded Wire Fabric						
	New Designation	Old Designation	Steel Area Per Foot				Approximate Weight Per 100 Sq. Ft.
			Longitudinal		Transverse		
	Spacing - Cross Sectional Area (IN.)-(Sq. IN. 100)	Spacing Wire Gauge (IN.)-(AS & W)	IN.	CM	IN.	CM	LB	KG
Rolls	6 x 6-W1.4 x W1.4	6 x 6-10 x 10	0.028	0.071	0.028	0.071	21	9.53
	6 x 6-W2.0 x W2.0	6 x 6-8 x 8 (1)	0.040	0.102	0.040	0.102	29	13.15
	6 x 6-W2.9 x W2.9	6 x 6-6 x 6	0.058	0.147	0.053	0.147	42	19.05
	6 x 6-W4.0 x W4.0	6 x 6-4 x 4	0.080	0.203	0.080	0.203	58	26.31
	4 x 4-W1.4 x W1.4	4 x 4-10 x 10	0.042	0.107	0.042	0.107	31	14.06
	4 x 4-W2.0 x W2.0	4 x 4-8 x 8 (1)	0.060	0.152	0.060	0.152	43	19.50
	4 x 4-W2.9 x W2.9	4 x 4-6 x 6	0.087	0.221	0.087	0.221	62	28.12
	4 x 4-W4.0 x W4.0	4 x 4-4 x 4	0.120	0.305	0.120	0.305	85	38.56
Sheets	6 x 6-W2.9 x W2.9	6 x 6-6 x 6	0.058	0.147	0.058	0.147	42	19.05
	6 x 6-W4.0 x W4.0	6 x 6-4 x 4	0.080	0.203	0.080	0.203	58	26.31
	6 x 6-W5.5 x W5.5	6 x 6-2 x 2 (2)	0.110	0.279	0.110	0.279	80	36.29
	6 x 6-W4.0 x W4.0	4 x 4-4 x 4	0.120	0.305	0.120	0.305	85	38.56

NOTES
1. Exact W-number size for 8 gauge is W2.1
2. Exact W-number size for 2 gauge is W5.4

HARD CONSTRUCTION

Brick Quantities for Use in Paving			
Estimating Mortarless Paving Units			
Paver Face Dimensions (actual inches)		Paver Face Area (in sq. in.)	Paver Units (per sq. ft.)
w x l			
4	8	32.0	4.5
3¾	8	30.0	4.8
3⅝	7⅝	27.6	5.2
3⅞	8¼	32.0	4.5
3⅞	7¾	30.0	4.8
3¾	7½	28.2	5.1
3¾	7¾	29.1	5.0
3⅝	11⅝	42.1	3.4
3⅝	8	29.0	5.0
3⅝	11¾	42.6	3.4
3⁹⁄₁₆	8	28.5	5.1
3½	7¾	27.1	5.3
3½	7½	26.3	5.5
3⅜	7½	25.3	5.7
4	4	16.0	9.0
6	6	36.0	4.0
7⅝	7⅝	58.1	2.5
7¾	7¾	60.1	2.4
8	8	64.0	2.3
8	16	128.0	1.1
12	12	144.0	1.0
16	16	256.0	0.6
6	6 Hexagon	31.2	4.6
8	8 Hexagon	55.4	2.6
12	12 Hexagon	124.7	1.2

NOTE: The above table does not include waste.
Allow at least 5% for waste and breakage.

(courtesy Brick Industry Association)

Brick Quantities For Use In Paving

Brick Paver Units*

Face Dimensions (actual size in inches)		Thickness
w x	l	
4	8	The unit thickness of brick pavers varies. The most popular thicknesses are 2¼ in. and 1⅝ in. The range of thickness is generally from ¾ in. to 2½ in.
3¾	8	
3¾	7½	
3⅝	7⅝	
3½	7½	
6	6	
8	8	
6	6 Hexagon	
8	8 Hexagon	

*Table 1 is based on BIA survey conducted in 1973. According to the survey approximately 38 sizes are manufactured.

Brick Paving Units and Mortar Quantities

Brick Paver Units	Paver Units per sq. ft.	Cubic Feet of Mortar Joints per 1000 Units	
w x l x t		⅜-in. Joint	½-in. Joint
3⅝ x 8 x 2¼[a]	4.3	5.86	—
3⅝ x 7⅝ x 2¼	4.5	5.68	—
3¾ x 8 x 2¼	4.0	—	8.0
3⅝ x 7⅝ x 1¼	4.5	3.15	—
3¾ x 8 x 1⅛	4.0	—	4.0

[a]Running bond pattern only

NOTE: No waste was included for brick and mortar in above quantities. Allow 5% for brick and 25% for mortar.

Mortar Bed and Soft Cushion Base of Sand and Portland Cement

Material	Cubic per 100 sq. ft.	Weight of Material lb. per cu. ft.
½-in. cushion of: cement-sand (1:6)	4.17	
portland cement		15.67
sand		80.00
½-in. Type N mortar bed (1:1:6)	4.17	
portland cement		15.67
hydrated lime		6.67
sand		80.00

(courtesy Brick Industry Association)

ASPHALT PAVEMENT

Asphalt pavements transfer and distribute traffic loads to the subgrade. The pavement is made up of two layers of material, the wearing course and the base course. The wearing course consists of two layers: the thin surface course and the thicker binder course that bonds the surface course to the heavy base layer underneath. The base consists of one layer that varies in thickness, type of material, and design, according to the bearing value of the subgrade material. If the subgrade material has a low-bearing value, either the thickness or the flexural strength of the base must be increased to spread the load over a larger area.

Increasing the flexural strength of the base course can be accomplished in two ways, one of which is to mix asphalt with the base material. The addition of the asphalt doubles the load distributing ability of a conventional granular base. A second method of increasing flexural strength is to add a layer of geotextile stabilization fabric between the base and the subgrade. This fabric not only adds tensile strength to the base, but also prevents the subgrade material from pumping up and contaminating the base during load cycles.

The thicknesses of the various courses within the pavement vary with each layer, according to the intended use of the pavement and, as noted earlier for the base course, the bearing value of the subgrade. For example, pavement may contain a 1″ surface course, a 2″-3″ binder course, and a 5″ or more base course. Standard commercial parking lot pavement may consist of 2-1/2″ of wearing surface and 8″ of granular base, while a highway may require a full-depth pavement with 5-1/2″ of asphalt base and 4″ of wearing surface. Granular base courses usually range from 6″ to 18″ in thickness. The cost of the asphalt mix for a pavement depends on the quality of the aggregate used in the various layers. Generally, the surface mixes contain smaller, higher-grade aggregates and, therefore, cost more than the heavier base mixes.

The installation of pavement material involves several steps and requires highly specialized equipment. Asphalt mix is delivered by truck to the hopper on the front end of the paver and is carried back to the spreading screws by bar feeders. The screws deposit a continuous flow of mix in front of the screed unit, which controls the thickness of the course being spread by the machine. The width of the mat may be increased with extensions added to the screed unit. Automatic sensors, which follow a previously set string line or a ski that rides on an adjacent grade, guide the screed unit to maintain the correct grade of the paved surface. After the pavement has been spread, steel-wheeled or pneumatic-tired rollers compact the asphalt in three separate rollings: the first, to achieve the desired density; the second, to seal the surface; and the third, to remove compactor roller marks and to smooth the wearing surface.

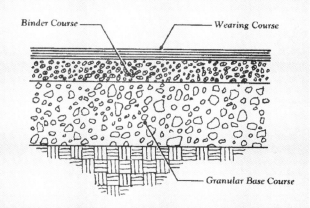

Asphalt Pavement

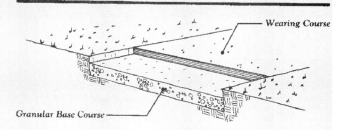

Bituminous Sidewalk

MAN-HOURS

Description	m/hr	Unit
Subgrade, Grade and Roll		
Small Area	.024	sq yd
Large Area	.011	sq yd
Base Course		
Bank Run Gravel, Spread Compact		
6″ Deep	.004	sq yd
18″ Deep	.013	sq yd
Crushed Stone, Spread Compact		
6″ Deep	.016	sq yd
18″ Deep	.029	sq yd
Asphalt Concrete Base		
4″ Thick	.053	sq yd
8″ Thick	.089	sq yd
Stabilization Fabric, Polypropylene, 6 oz./sq yd	.002	sq yd
Asphalt Pavement, Wearing Course		
1-1/2″ Thick	.026	sq yd
3″ Thick	.052	sq yd

PAVEMENT RECYCLING

The process of recycling used asphalt pavement provides a means of reclaiming and rejuvenating old pavement materials so that they can be respread. Generally, all of the methods of recycling involve the tearing up or breaking of the old material, pulverizing it into uniform consistency at a treatment plant or with on-site machines, combining it with new materials, and reinstalling the paving mixture.

The reclaiming part of the recycling process includes the loosening and removing of all or part of the worn-out asphalt pavement. The method used for removal of the existing paved surface depends on the thickness of the pavement to be recycled and the nature of the underlying base. If the base is concrete and the entire layer of pavement above it is to be removed, a ripper or scarifier, which has been mounted on a dozer, loader, or motor grader, can be used. If the base is composed of gravel, the total pavement can be removed with a pavement breaker. Another method, which can be implemented with any type of base material, is to sawcut the pavement into manageable sized strips that can be removed with a backhoe or gradall. Regardless of the method used in tearing up or breaking the old pavement, the loosened, variously sized pieces must be loaded for stockpiling and eventual pulverization.

The pulverization of the old asphalt pavement material can be accomplished on the site with three types of machines designed for this procedure: the stabilizer, the cold planer, or the miller. The actual pulverizing of the old material is performed by a rotating drum with inlaid carbide cutting teeth, called the "cutter," within the planer unit. If the planer is track-mounted, material with depths of just above 0″ to a maximum of 5″ to 12″ can be processed; for wheel-mounted machines, the maximum falls between 3″ and 7″ in depth. The width of the cutter varies.

After the material has been pulverized, several methods of handling it can be employed, depending on how it is to be used when respread. The recycled pavement may be blended with the base as it is being pulverized to upgrade the strength of the base; it may be left behind in a windrow; or it may be deposited into a truck with an elevating loader. The pulverized material may also be deposited into a traveling hammermill or portable crushing plant and processed into a uniformly graded mixture that is suitable for respreading.

Two operations may be implemented for rejuvenating the pulverized old pavement: cold-mix recycling and hot-mix recycling. Cold-mix recycling involves the combining-in-place of asphalt emulsions or cutbacks with the reclaimed pavement materials at the installation site. If, as often happens, the reclaimed pavement has been respread over the roadway after pulverization, asphaltic emulsion is sprayed on the material from a distribution tanker and then blade-mixed with motor graders. In another cold-mix method, the emulsion is added during the mixing with a stabilizer connected to the tanker. Some planers are also equipped with blending and asphalt emulsion spray bars, and therefore perform three tasks—pulverization, addition of emulsion, and mixing—and function as self-contained, mobile recycling plants.

The hot-mix recycling process is carried out at an asphalt recycling facility, rather than at the removal and/or installation site. In the hot-mix recycling operation, stockpiled recycled pavement must be crushed and screened before being mixed with new aggregate and asphalt. The proportion of old to new material depends on the new mix design and type of plant in which the recycling operation is taking place. In a batch plant, the new mix usually consists of 30% old material and 70% new; in a continuous mix plant, the new mix is usually composed of 70% old material and 30% new. The reason for the superior efficiency of continuous mix plants is that both the recycled material and the new aggregate are directly heated. In the batch plant operation, the recycled pavement is heated only mixing it with superheated new aggregate. Additional savings in both operations can be realized by utilizing recycled aggregate materials in addition to the recycled pavement.

Man-hours

Description	m/hr	Unit
Asphalt Pavement Demolition		
Hydraulic Hammer	.035	sq yd
Ripping Pavement, Load and Sweep	.007	sq yd
Crush and Screen, Traveling Hammermill		
3″ Deep	.004	sq yd
6″ Deep	.007	sq yd
12″ Deep	.012	sq yd
Pulverizing, Crushing, and Blending into Base		
4″ Pavement		
Over 15,000 sq yd	.027	sq yd
5,000 to 15,000 sq yd	.029	sq yd
8″ Pavement		
Over 15,000 sq yd	.029	sq yd
5,000 to 15,000 sq yd	.032	sq yd
Remove, Rejuvenate and Spread, Mixer-Paver	.026	sq yd
Profiling, Load and Sweep		
1″ Deep	.002	sq yd
3″ Deep	.006	sq yd
6″ Deep	.011	sq yd
12″ Deep	.019	sq yd

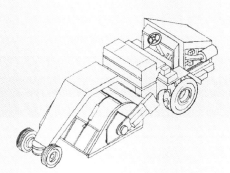

Pulverizer

CURBS

Curbs are set along the sides of roadways to protect the unpaved roadside and to provide erosion-free means of drainage for the road surface. Commonly used curb materials include cast-in-place concrete, precast concrete, bituminous concrete, asphalt, and stone (usually granite). The methods of curb installation vary with the type of curbing material.

Cast-in-place concrete curbs can be formed and cast or placed monolithically with a form-and-place machine. In the latter method, the concrete is placed into a large retaining bin on the machine, formed into the shape of the curb, and then placed as the machine moves along at a set pace. Bituminous concrete curbing can be formed and placed in the same way. In both the cast-in-place and monolithic methods, gutters can be placed as an integral part of the curb.

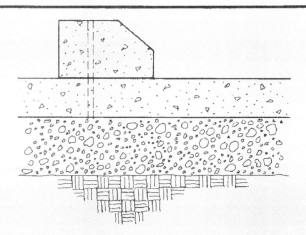

Precast Concrete Parking Bumper

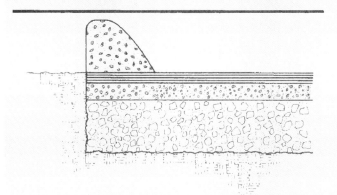

Bituminous Curb

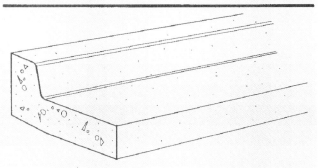

Cast-in-Place Concrete Curb and Gutter

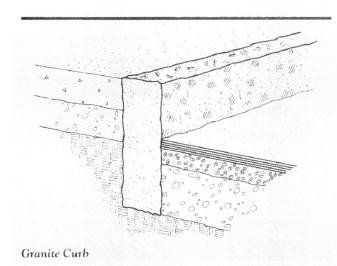

Granite Curb

Man-hours

Description	m/hr	Unit
Curbs, Bituminous, Plain, 8″ Wide, 6″ High, 50 lf/ton	.032	lf
8″ Wide, 8″ High, 44 lf/ton	.036	lf
Bituminous Berm, 12″ Wide, 3″ to 6″ High, 35 lf/ton, before Pavement	.046	lf
12″ Wide, 1-1/2″ to 4″ High, 60 lf/ton, Laid with Pavement	.030	lf
Concrete, 6″ x 18″, Cast-in-place, Straight	.096	lf
6″ x 18″ Radius	.107	lf
Precast, 6″ x 18″, Straight	.160	lf
6″ x 18″ Radius	.172	lf
Granite, Split Face, Straight, 5″ x 16″	.112	lf
6″ x 18″	.124	lf
Radius Curbing, 6″ x 18″, Over 10′ Radius	.215	lf
Corners, 2′ Radius	.700	Ea.
Edging, 4-1/2″ x 12″, straight	.187	lf
Curb inlets, (guttermouth) straight	1.366	Ea.
Monolithic concrete curb and gutter, cast in place with 6′ high curb and 6″ thick gutter		
24″ wide, .055 cy per lf	.128	lf
30″ wide, .066 cy per lf	.141	lf

BULKHEAD RETAINING WALLS

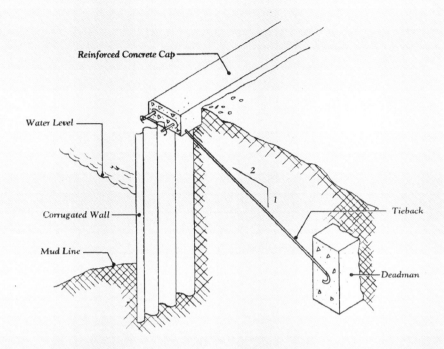

Reinforced Concrete Cap

Water Level

Corrugated Wall

Mud Line

Tieback

Deadman

2

1

Bulkhead retaining walls are usually used for canal bank and shoreline protection. Sheet piling is installed with a continuous cap that is anchored at regular intervals with tiebacks connected to a deadman buried in the retained bank. Three types of sheet piling are used for these walls: asbestos-cement, aluminum, and steel. The choice of anchor material to be used depends on a number of variables, including the amount of force to be withstood by the wall, its height, and climate considerations. Aluminum and steel sheet piling can be installed with either a pile driving hammer or jetting; asbestos-cement can be erected only with jetting.

Asbestos-cement sheeting, because it does not have the strength of aluminum or steel sheeting, is restricted in its use to sheltered waterways with tidal variations of less than 2'. It is available in panels measuring 3'-6" in width and 3' to 10' in length. The maximum allowable exposed face is 5' in height or less, with a maximum embedment of 6'-6". It resists corrosion, but it cannot be used in climates that experience a regular freeze-thaw cycle. After the piling is installed and anchored with tie rods at spacings of 10', a reinforced concrete cap is formed and placed to maintain wall alignment. Asbestos-cement sheeting can also be used as a knee wall to protect the toe of a larger bulkhead where severe tidal and erosion forces must be resisted.

Aluminum sheet piling, because it is stronger than asbestos-cement piling, can be used in waterways and bays where wave action is considerable. Also, this sheeting is not restricted by climate or corrosive environments. It is available in panels measuring 5' in width and 13' in length which can be installed with a maximum exposed face of 8'. Longer aluminum sheet piling is available in interlocking Z and U shaped sections which can be used in conjunction with walers when the exposed face must be 12' or more in

height. After the piling is installed and secured, a concrete cap, similar to the cap used for asbestos-cement walls, or an aluminum cap, is installed to maintain alignment and to anchor one end of the tieback.

Steel sheet piling possesses the greatest strength of the three types. With appropriate use of walers, steel sheeting can be used to heights of 30' and can withstand severe tidal and wave forces. Galvanized or aluminum coatings can be applied to provide corrosion protection when needed. The sheeting profile is only 3" deep, as compared with 9" to 16" for Z shaped steel sheeting. The thickness ranges from 5 to 12 gauge to suit the specific application. Successive panels interlock to simplify alignment during driving. Steel sheeting is superior to other types when difficult driving conditions are encountered.

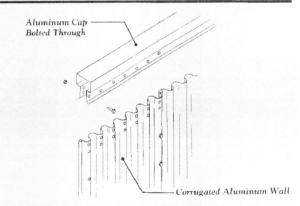

Aluminum Cap
Bolted Through

Corrugated Aluminum Wall

Aluminum Bulkhead Retaining Wall - Aluminum Cap

BULKHEAD RETAINING WALLS (cont.)

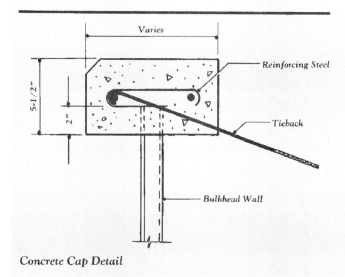

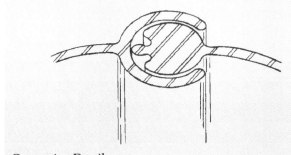

Concrete Cap Detail

Connection Detail

Man-hours

Description	m/hr	Unit
Asbestos-Cement Sheeting, by Jetting, Including Cap and Anchors, Coarse Compact Sand,		
2'-6" Embedment	.267	lf
5'-6" Embedment	.533	lf
Loose Silty Sand		
2'-6" Embedment	.200	lf
5'-6" Embedment	.400	lf
Aluminum Panel Sheeting, Vibratory Hammer Driven, Including Cap and Anchors, Coarse Compact Sand,		
2'-0" Embedment	.320	lf
5'-6" Embedment	.674	lf
Loose Silty Sand,		
3'-0" Embedment	.312	lf
5'-6" Embedment	.492	lf
Steel Sheet Piling, Exposed Face		
Shore Driven	.067	sf
Barge Driven	.116	sf

CONCRETE RETAINING WALLS

Concrete retaining walls are freestanding structures used to retain earth. They take up much less space than bin- or crib-type wall structures and can be used in situations where very high retaining walls are needed. When soil conditions are normal and the backfill is level, the forces of earth pressure on the wall vary with the height. However, normal earth pressure forces can be increased several times by special conditions such as water, sloped backfill, and building, highway, or railroad bed surcharges. Concrete retaining walls must be built to resist the tendency for sliding and overturning which these forces generate.

There are two basic types of concrete retaining walls: gravity and cantilever. A gravity wall resists sliding and overturning by its mass alone. The cross-sectional shape is usually trapezoidal—narrowest at the top and widest at the base where the forces of the retained earth are greatest. Since the width at the base is greater than 50% of the wall's height, the volume of concrete and related cost become prohibitive if the wall rises above 10'.

A cantilever wall consists of two segments: a vertical wall stem and a horizontal base slab. The wall stem acts as a cantilever fixed at the base. Vertical reinforcing bars resist bending in the stem, and horizontal bars resist bending in the base. Cantilever wall thickness may be constant for structures of less than 10' in height. Higher walls may require a section that increases in width toward the base by means of a 1:12 slope on the inside face. This slope may also be included on the outside face for aesthetic effect. The wall stem is usually keyed into the base, and the base may be keyed into the underlying, undisturbed earth to resist sliding.

Because retaining walls are not usually designed to withstand hydraulic pressure, provisions must be made to remove any groundwater that might collect behind the structure. This condition can be prevented by placing a blanket of drainage stone backfill behind the wall and placing weep holes at about 10' intervals at the bottom of the wall. To remove the water entirely, perforated pipe, surrounded by drainage stone, can be installed along the inside face at the base of the wall prior to backfilling.

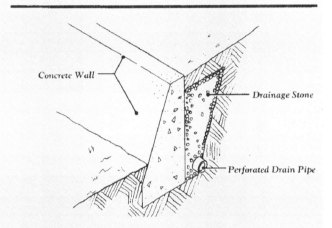

Gravity Retaining Wall

Man-hours

Description	m/hr	Unit
Concrete Retaining Wall		
Footing Formwork	.066	sfca
Wall Formwork, Under 8' High	.049	sfca
Under 16' High	.079	sfca
Wall Formwork, Battered to 16' High	.150	sfca
Footing Reinforcing Bars	15.240	ton
Wall Reinforcing Bars	10.670	ton
Footing Concrete, Direct Chute	.400	cu yd
Pumped	.640	cu yd
Crane and Bucket	.711	cu yd
Wall Concrete, Direct Chute	.480	cu yd
Pumped	.674	cu yd
Crane and Bucket	.711	cu yd
Perforated, Clay, 4" Diameter	.060	lf
6" Diameter	.076	lf
8" Diameter	.083	lf
Bituminous, 4" Diameter	.032	lf
6" Diameter	.035	lf
Porous Concrete, 4" Diameter	.072	lf
6" Diameter	.076	lf
8" Diameter	.090	lf
Drainage Stone, 3/4" Diameter	.092	cu yd
Backfill, Dozer	.010	cu yd
Compaction, Vibrating Plate, 12" Lifts	.044	cu yd

Cantilever Retaining Wall

GABION RETAINING WALLS

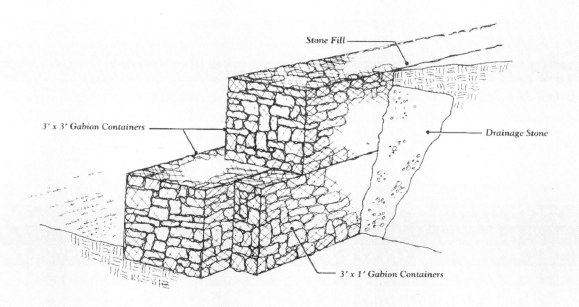

Stone Fill

3' x 3' Gabion Containers

Drainage Stone

3' x 1' Gabion Containers

Gabion retaining walls are designed and built to hold back earth with their weight and mass. Although they have the greatest mass of retaining wall types, they are among the least expensive to erect. The basic components of the walls include individual gabion containers, wire or plastic, and the 4″ to 8″ stone with which the containers are filled. The containers are 3′ in width and range from 1′ to 3′ in height and 6′ to 12′ in length.

The process of installing the walls involves several steps. Empty containers are arranged, one course at a time and one or more deep, and then filled. During the installation and filling process, care must be taken not to damage the galvanized or plastic coating on the wire mesh. The stone on the exposed face of the wall may be set by hand with the balance of each of the containers filled by machine. Voids within the container average about 35% of its total volume.

Special construction techniques may add to the life and effectiveness of gabion walls. Either face of the wall may be stepped, for example, and added stability may be realized by tilting the wall into the retained earth at a 1:6 slope. In clay soils, additional gabions, spaced from 13′ to 30′ on center, should run traverse to the wall line, from the outside face to beyond the slip plane of the retained bank. If drainage is a problem, especially in instances where the retained earth supports a highway or railroad bed, a blanket of drainage stone should be placed behind the wall. This drainage system helps in preventing fines from washing through and undermining the wall's backfill.

Man-hours

Description	m/hr	Unit
Gabion with stone fill		
3′ x 6′ x 1′	.280	Ea.
3′ x 6′ x 3′	1.020	Ea.
3′ x 9′ x 1′	.431	Ea.
3′ x 9′ x 3′	1.510	Ea.
3′ x 12′ x 1′	.560	Ea.
3′ x 12′ x 3′	2.240	Ea.
Drainage stone, 3/4″ diameter	.092	cu yd
Backfill Dozer	.010	cu yd
Compaction, roller, 12″ lifts	.014	cu yd

MASONRY RETAINING WALLS

Masonry retaining walls may be constructed of block, brick or stone.

Brick or block walls are usually placed on a concrete footing that acts as a leveling pad and distributes imposed loads to the subsoil. Both the wall and the footing may be reinforced. Voids in the masonry are usually filled with mortar or grout, and the wall capped with a suitable material. Solid masonry walls should include porous backfill against the back of the wall and weep holes or drainage piping to eliminate hydrostatic head.

Stone retaining walls may be constructed dry or mortar set with or without a suitable concrete footing. All masonry retaining walls should be placed a sufficient depth below grade to eliminate the danger of frost heave. Mortar set walls should include an adequate drainage system.

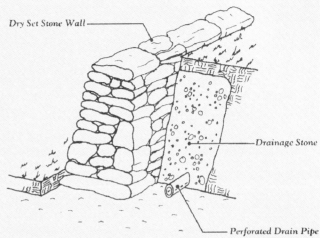

Stone Retaining Wall

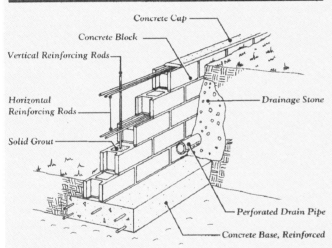

Masonry Retaining Wall

Man-hours

Description	m/hr	Unit
Masonry Retaining Wall, 8" Thick, 4' High		
Continous Wall Footing	.140	lf
Concrete Block Wall Including Reinforcing and Grouting	.610	lf
Fill in Trench Crushed Bank Run	.010	lf
Perforated Asbestos Cement Drain, 4" Diameter	.062	lf
Masonry Retaining Wall, 10" Thick, 6' High		
Continuous Wall Footing	.218	lf
Concrete Block Wall Including Reinforcing and Grouting	.957	lf
Fill in Trench Crushed Bank Run	.015	lf
Perforated Asbestos Cement Drain, 4" Diameter	.062	lf
Masonry Retaining Wall, 12" Thick, 8' High		
Continuous Wall Footing	.278	lf
Concrete Block Wall Including Reinforcing and Grouting	1.548	lf
Fill in Trench Crushed Bank Run	.020	lf
Perforated Asbestos Cement Drain, 4" Diameter	.062	lf
Stone Retaining Wall, 3' Above Grade, Dry Set	2.742	lf
Mortar Set	2.400	lf
6' Above Grade, Dry Set	4.114	lf
Mortar Set	3.600	lf

Note: Units are per lf of wall.

HARD CONSTRUCTION

WOOD RETAINING WALLS

Wood retaining walls are usually constructed of redwood, cedar, pressure-treated lumber, or creosoted lumber.

The three systems normally used to construct these walls are wood post, post-and-board, and wood tie.

Wood post walls consist of posts placed side by side and anchored a suitable distance below the subgrade in order to resist overturning.

Post-and-board walls are erected of spaced, anchored posts, horizontal wood sheathing, and a wood cap.

Wood tie walls are constructed of railroad or landscape ties. These are anchored by steel rods driven thru holes in the ties.

Wood retaining walls are normally used for their pleasing aesthetic effect and are not suitable for high cuts or heavy surcharges.

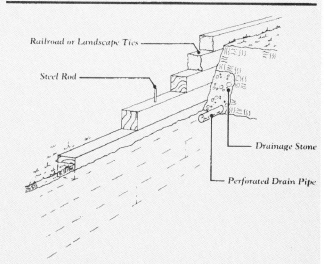

Wood Tie Retaining Wall

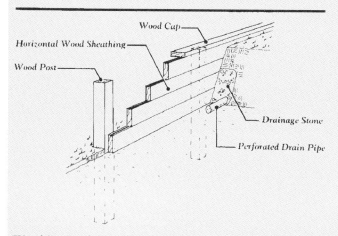

Wood Post and Board Retaining Wall

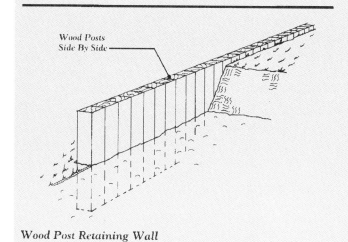

Wood Post Retaining Wall

Man-hours

Description	m/hr	Unit
Wood Post and Board Retaining Wall		
4' High		
Redwood Posts, Plank and Cap	.664	lf
Porous Backfill	.010	lf
Perforated Pipe	.062	lf
6' High		
Redwood Posts, Plank and Cap	.742	lf
Porous Backfill	.015	lf
Perforated Pipe	.062	lf
8' High		
Redwood Posts, Plank and Cap	1.307	lf
Porous Backfill	.020	lf
Perforated Pipe	.062	lf
Wood Post Retaining Wall		
2' High Redwood Posts	.358	lf
Porous Fill	.005	lf
Perforated Pipe	.062	lf
4' High Redwood Posts	1.074	lf
Porous Fill	.010	lf
Perforated Pipe	.062	lf
6' High Redwood Posts	2.505	lf
Porous Fill	.015	lf
Perforated Pipe	.062	lf
Wood Tie Retaining Wall		
4' High Redwood Ties	.689	lf
Porous Fill	.010	lf
Perforated Pipe	.062	lf
6' High Redwood Ties	1.034	lf
Porous Fill	.015	lf
Perforated Pipe	.062	lf

FENCING

Fences are usually composed of a series of vertical posts set into the earth and spanned with rails, panels, or stretched metal fencing fabric. They are installed for many reasons, including privacy, safety, security, weather protection, cosmetics, and mandate of local codes. Fence posts may be installed and secured by direct driving or by setting them in concrete or compacted fill in predug post holes. The most commonly used fencing materials are wood (usually cedar or redwood), galvanized steel, aluminum, and plastic-coated steel.

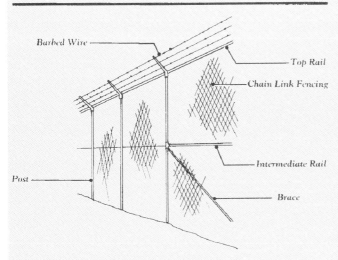

Chain Link Fence, Industrial

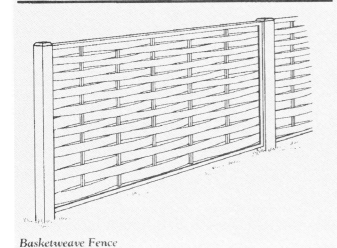

Basketweave Fence

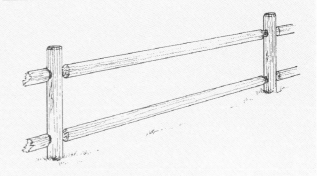

Stockade Fence

Open Rail Rustic Fence

Man-hours

Description	m/hr	Unit
Fence, Chain Link, Industrial Plus 3 Strands		
Barbed Wire, 2" Line Post @ 10' on Center		
1-5/8" Top Rail, 6' High	.096	lf
Corners, Add	.600	Ea.
Braces, Add	.300	Ea.
Gate, Add	.686	Ea.
Residential, 11 Gauge Wire, 1-5/8" Line		
Post @ 10' on Center 1-3/8"		
Top Rail, 3' High	.048	lf
4' High	.060	lf
Gate, Add	.400	Ea.
Tennis Courts, 11 Gauge Wire, 1-3/4"		
Mesh, 2-1/2" Line Posts, 1-5/8" Top Rail,		
10' High	.155	lf
12' High	.185	lf
Corner Posts, 3" Diameter, Add	.800	Ea.
Fence, Security, 12' High	.960	lf
16' High	1.200	lf
Fence, Wood, Cedar Picket, 2 Rail, 3' High	.150	lf
Gate, 3'-6", Add	.533	Ea.
Cedar Picket, 3 Rail, 4' High	.160	lf
Gate, 3'-6", Add	.585	Ea.
Open Rail Rustic, 2 Rail, 3' High	.150	lf
Stockade, 6' High	.150	lf
Board, Shadow Box, 1" x 6" Treated Pine,		
6' High	.150	lf

HARD CONSTRUCTION

Calculations For Lawn and Soil Maintenance

Pounds Per 1000 S.F. Nomograph

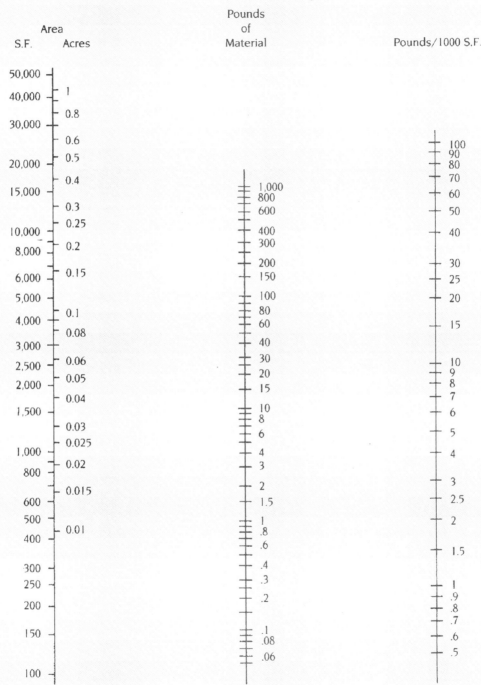

Use by placing a straight edge to known or given points on any 2 scales and reading the unknown on the remaining scale. Example: How many pounds of material will be needed to treat an 8000 S.F. lawn at 5 lbs/1000 S.F.?

Answer: 40 lbs.

Prepared By: Harold Davidson, Department of Horticulture, Michigan State University

(from *Landscape Designer & Estimator's Guide*, Third Edition, American Nursery & Landscape Association, Washington, DC)

PLANTING
& WEATHER

Conversion Chart for Loam, Baled Peat, and Mulch			
Loam Requirements		Mulch Requirements (Bulk Peat, Crushed Stone, Shredded Bark, Wood Chips)	
Depth per 10,000 S.F.	Cubic yards required	Depth per 1,000 S.F.	Cubic yards required
2 inches	70	1 inch	3-1/2
4　〃	140	2 inches	7
6　〃	210	3　〃	10-1/2
		4　〃	14
Per 1,000 S.F.		Per 100 S.F.	
2 inches	7	1 inch	1/3
4　〃	14	2 inches	2/3
6　〃	21	3　〃	1
		4　〃	1-1/3

Baled (or Compressed) Peat	
Per 100 S.F.	Bales Required
1 inch	one 4 cubic foot bale
2 inches	two 4 cubic foot bales
3　〃	two 6 cubic foot bales
4　〃	one 4 cubic foot bales and two 6 cubic foot bales

Note: Opened and spread, peat from bales will be about 2-1/2 times the volume of the unopened bale.

				Surtee's Landscape Service Charts					
				Ball Sizes — Weight, Etc.					
Diam.	Depth	Area S.F.	Cubic Feet	Weight Lbs.	Diam.	Depth	Area S.F.	Cubic Feet	Weight Lbs.
8″	6″	0.35	0.15	13	26″	20″	′′	5.37	457
8″	8″	′′	0.21	18	26″	21″	′′	5.64	480
10″	6″	0.54	0.24	21	27″	12″	3.98	3.49	297
10″	8″	′′	0.32	28	27″	15″	′′	4.36	370
10″	10″	′′	0.39	34	27″	18″	′′	5.23	444
12″	6″	0.78	0.34	29	27″	20″	′′	5.81	491
12″	9″	′′	0.52	45	27″	22″	′′	6.39	532
12″	12″	′′	0.68	58	27″	24″	′′	6.97	588
14″	6″	1.08	0.47	40	28″	14″	4.28	4.36	370
14″	8″	′′	0.63	53	28″	16″	′′	4.99	424
14″	10″	′′	0.78	66	28″	18″	′′	5.62	477
14″	12″	′′	0.94	80	28″	20″	′′	6.24	530
14″	14″	′′	1.10	94	28″	22″	′′	6.87	583
15″	8″	1.23	0.72	62	28″	24″	′′	7.49	637
15″	10″	′′	0.90	76	30″	15″	4.91	5.37	456
15″	12″	′′	1.07	91	30″	18″	′′	6.44	547
15″	14″	′′	1.26	107	30″	21″	′′	7.51	638
15″	15″	′′	1.35	115	30″	24″	′′	8.58	729
16″	10″	1.40	1.13	96	30″	27″	′′	9.65	820
16″	12″	′′	1.21	103	33″	15″	5.94	6.50	552
16″	14″	′′	1.42	120	33″	18″	′′	7.80	663
16″	15″	′′	1.52	129	33″	21″	′′	9.10	773
18″	12″	1.77	1.54	131	33″	24″	′′	10.40	884
18″	14″	′′	1.81	155	33″	27″	′′	11.69	994
18″	16″	′′	2.05	175	36″	18″	7.07	9.27	788
20″	12″	2.18	1.91	163	36″	21″	′′	10.83	920
20″	14″	′′	2.24	191	36″	24″	′′	12.37	1052
20″	15″	′′	2.39	203	36″	27″	′′	13.91	1183
20″	16″	′′	2.54	216	36″	30″	′′	15.46	1314
20″	18″	′′	2.87	244	39″	18″	8.30	10.77	916
21″	12″	2.40	2.10	178	39″	21″	′′	12.69	1079
21″	15″	′′	2.63	224	39″	24″	′′	14.52	1129
21″	18″	′′	3.15	268	39″	27″	′′	16.35	1270
21″	20″	′′	3.50	298	39″	30″	′′	18.15	1411
22″	12″	2.64	2.31	196	39″	33″	′′	19.97	1550
22″	15″	′′	2.89	246	40″	18″	8.73	11.46	974
22″	16″	′′	3.08	262	40″	21″	′′	13.38	1137
22″	18″	′′	3.46	294	40″	24″	′′	15.29	1300
22″	21″	′′	4.04	343	40″	27″	′′	17.19	1461
24″	12″	3.14	2.74	233	40″	30″	′′	19.10	1623
24″	15″	′′	3.44	292	40″	33″	′′	21.00	1785
24″	16″	′′	3.65	310	40″	36″	′′	22.92	1948
24″	18″	′′	4.13	351	42″	18″	9.62	12.63	1074
24″	21″	′′	4.80	408	42″	21″	′′	14.74	1253
26″	12″	3.69	3.23	275	42″	24″	′′	16.85	1432
26″	14″	′′	3.77	320	42″	27″	′′	18.95	1610
26″	15″	′′	4.03	343	42″	30″	′′	21.05	1789
26″	16″	′′	4.30	365	42″	33″	′′	23.15	1970
26″	18″	′′	4.83	411	42″	36″	′′	25.25	2146

PLANTING & WEATHER

273

					Surtee's Landscape Service Charts				
					Ball Sizes — Weight, Etc.				
Diam.	Depth	Area S.F.	Cubic Feet	Weight Lbs.	Diam.	Depth	Area S.F.	Cubic Feet	Weight Lbs.
45″	18″	11.05	14.51	1234	60″	33″	19.64	47.26	4017
45″	21″	″	16.93	1439	60″	36″	″	51.56	4383
45″	24″	″	19.35	1644	60″	39″	″	55.86	4748
45″	27″	″	21.77	1849	60″	42″	″	60.15	5113
45″	30″	″	24.18	2054	66″	21″	23.75	36.38	3092
45″	33″	″	26.59	2260	66″	24″	″	41.56	3533
45″	36″	″	29.00	2465	66″	27″	″	46.75	3974
48″	21″	12.57	19.24	16.35	66″	30″	″	51.96	4417
48″	24″	″	22.00	1870	66″	33″	″	57.15	4858
48″	27″	″	24.75	2104	66″	36″	″	62.34	5299
48″	30″	″	27.50	2337	66″	39″	″	67.54	5741
48″	33″	″	30.25	2571	66″	42″	″	72.74	6183
48″	36″	″	33.00	2804	72″	24″	28.28	49.49	4207
48″	39″	″	35.75	3038	72″	27″	″	55.67	4732
50″	21″	13.64	20.89	1776	72″	30″	″	61.85	5257
50″	24″	″	23.87	2029	72″	33″	″	68.04	5784
50″	27″	″	26.86	2283	72″	36″	″	74.23	6310
50″	30″	″	29.84	2536	72″	39″	″	80.42	6836
50″	33″	″	32.82	2790	72″	42″	″	86.62	7363
50″	36″	″	35.80	3043	78″	24″	33.18	58.06	4935
50″	39″	″	38.79	3296	78″	27″	″	65.32	5552
50″	42″	″	41.78	3550	78″	30″	″	72.58	6170
51″	21″	14.18	21.72	1846	78″	33″	″	79.84	6786
51″	24″	″	24.82	2110	78″	36″	″	87.11	7404
51″	27″	″	27.92	2373	78″	39″	″	94.36	8021
51″	30″	″	31.02	2637	78″	42″	″	101.61	8637
51″	33″	″	34.12	2900	78″	45″	″	108.86	9253
51″	36″	″	37.22	3163	78″	48″	″	116.11	9870
51″	39″	″	40.33	3428	84″	24″	38.49	67.36	5725
51″	42″	″	43.43	3692	84″	27″	″	75.78	6441
54″	21″	15.91	24.36	2071	84″	30″	″	84.20	7157
54″	24″	″	27.84	2367	84″	33″	″	92.62	7873
54″	27″	″	31.32	2663	84″	36″	″	101.04	8588
54″	30″	″	34.80	2959	84″	39″	″	109.46	9304
54″	33″	″	38.28	3255	84″	42″	″	117.88	10020
54″	36″	″	41.76	3559	84″	45″	″	126.30	10736
54″	39″	″	45.24	3846	84″	48″	″	134.72	11451
54″	42″	″	48.73	4142	90″	24″	44.18	77.32	6572
57″	21″	17.71	27.11	2305	90″	27″	″	86.98	7393
57″	24″	″	31.00	2635	90″	30″	″	96.64	8214
57″	27″	″	34.88	2965	90″	33″	″	106.30	9036
57″	30″	″	38.76	3294	90″	36″	″	115.96	9857
57″	33″	″	42.63	3623	90″	39″	″	125.63	10679
57″	36″	″	46.50	3952	90″	42″	″	135.30	11500
57″	39″	″	50.37	4281	90″	45″	″	144.97	12323
57″	42″	″	54.24	4610	90″	48″	″	154.63	13144
60″	21″	19.64	30.07	2556	96″	30″	50.27	109.96	9347
60″	24″	″	34.37	2921	96″	33″	″	120.96	10282
60″	27″	″	38.67	3286	96″	36″	″	131.96	11217
60″	30″	″	42.96	3652	96″	39″	″	142.96	12152

		Surtee's Landscape Service Charts							
		Ball Sizes — Weight, Etc.							
Diam.	Depth	Area S.F.	Cubic Feet	Weight Lbs.	Diam.	Depth	Area S.F.	Cubic Feet	Weight Lbs.
96″	42″	50.27	153.96	13087	138″	39″	103.87	295.38	25107
96″	45″	″	164.96	14022	138″	42″	″	318.11	27039
96″	48″	″	175.96	14957	138″	45″	″	340.83	28971
102″	30″	56.75	124.14	10552	138″	48″	″	363.55	30902
102″	33″	″	136.55	11607	138″	54″	″	409.08	34764
102″	36″	″	148.96	12662	138″	60″	″	454.43	38627
102″	39″	″	161.37	13717	144″	36″	113.09	269.86	25233
102″	42″	″	173.78	14771	144″	39″	″	321.60	27336
102″	45″	″	186.20	15827	144″	42″	″	346.34	29439
102″	48″	″	198.62	16883	144″	45″	″	371.08	31542
108″	30″	63.62	139.17	11830	144″	48″	″	395.82	33645
108″	33″	″	153.09	13013	144″	54″	″	445.30	37850
108″	36″	″	167.01	14196	144″	60″	″	494.77	42055
108″	39″	″	180.93	15379	150″	36″	122.72	322.14	27382
108″	42″	″	194.85	16562	150″	39″	″	348.99	29664
108″	45″	″	208.76	17745	150″	42″	″	375.84	31946
108″	48″	″	222.67	18927	150″	45″	″	402.69	34228
114″	30″	70.88	155.05	13179	150″	48″	″	429.53	36510
114″	33″	″	170.56	14498	150″	54″	″	480.22	41074
114″	36″	″	186.07	15816	150″	60″	″	536.90	45637
114″	39″	″	201.58	17135	156″	36″	132.73	348.42	29616
114″	42″	″	217.08	18452	156″	39″	″	377.45	32083
114″	45″	″	232.58	19770	156″	42″	″	406.48	34551
114″	48″	″	248,08	21087	156″	45″	″	435.51	37019
120″	30″	78.54	171.81	14603	156″	48″	″	464.54	39487
120″	33″	″	188.98	16063	156″	54″	″	522.61	44423
120″	36″	″	206.16	17524	156″	60″	″	580.69	49359
120″	39″	″	223.34	18984	162″	36″	143.14	375.74	31938
120″	42″	″	240.52	20444	162″	39″	″	407.06	34600
120″	45″	″	257.70	21905	162″	42″	″	438.38	37262
120″	48″	″	274.89	23366	162″	45″	″	469.69	39924
126″	30″	86.59	189.42	16101	162″	48″	″	501.00	42586
126″	33″	″	208.36	17711	162″	54″	″	563.62	47908
126″	36″	″	227.30	19321	162″	60″	″	626.24	53230
126″	39″	″	246.24	20931	168″	36″	153.94	404.09	34348
126″	42″	″	265.18	22541	168″	39″	″	437.77	37212
126″	45″	″	284.12	24150	168″	42″	″	471.45	40072
126″	48″	″	303.06	25760	168″	45″	″	505.13	42934
126″	54″	″	340.94	28980	168″	48″	″	538.80	45796
126″	60″	″	378.83	32200	168″	54″	″	606.14	51521
132″	36″	95.03	249.46	21204	168″	60″	″	673.48	57246
132″	39″	″	270.24	22970	180″	36″	176.71	463.86	39428
132″	42″	″	291.03	24736	180″	39″	″	502.52	42714
132″	45″	″	311.81	26503	180″	42″	″	541.17	46000
132″	48″	″	332.60	28270	180″	45″	″	579.83	49286
132″	54″	″	374.16	31805	180″	48″	″	618.48	52572
132″	60″	″	415.76	35340	180″	54″	″	695.80	59143
138″	36″	103.87	272.65	23175	180″	60″	″	773.11	65714

PLANTING & WEATHER

Surtee's Tree Pits and Tree Balls
Cubic Feet Per Tree
For Estimating Excavation and Top Soil

Diameters / Depths		1'	1¼'	1½'	1¾'	2'	2¼'	2½'	2¾'	3'	3¼'	3½'
Tree Pit	1'	.94	1.47	2.13	2.88	3.77	4.78	5.89	7.13	8.48	9.96	11.5
Ball		.68	1.07	1.54	2.10	2.73	3.42	4.30	5.20	6.19	7.38	8.4
Tree Pit	1¼'	1.16	1.85	2.65	3.60	4.71	5.93	7.37	8.90	10.6	12.4	14.4
Ball		.85	1.35	1.93	2.63	3.42	4.29	5.36	6.49	7.7	9.2	10.5
Tree Pit	1½'	1.40	2.22	3.08	4.32	5.65	7.16	8.83	10.7	12.7	15.0	17.3
Ball		1.02	1.62	2.32	3.15	4.10	5.19	6.39	7.8	9.2	10.9	12.7
Tree Pit	1¾'	1.65	2.58	3.70	5.04	6.60	8.20	10.3	12.5	14.8	17.4	20.2
Ball		1.20	1.88	3.72	3.68	4.78	6.03	7.5	9.1	10.7	12.7	14.7
Tree Pit	2'	1.87	2.95	4.26	5.76	7.54	9.55	11.8	14.3	17.0	19.9	23.0
Ball		1.38	2.15	3.10	4.20	5.49	6.92	8.5	10.4	12.3	14.5	16.8
Tree Pit	2¼'	2.10	3.32	4.78	6.48	8.48	10.7	13.2	16.0	19.1	22.4	26.0
Ball		1.55	2.43	3.48	4.73	6.19	7.5	9.6	11.7	13.8	16.4	18.9
Tree Pit	2½'	2.34	3.69	5.30	7.20	9.42	11.9	14.7	17.8	21.2	24.9	28.9
Ball		1.70	2.70	3.87	5.25	6.89	8.7	10.7	13.0	15.4	18.2	21.0
Tree Pit	2¾'	2.57	4.06	5.83	7.92	10.3	13.1	16.2	19.6	23.3	27.4	31.8
Ball		1.87	2.98	4.25	5.77	7.6	9.6	11.8	14.3	17.0	20.0	23.1
Tree Pit	3'	2.81	4.43	6.37	8.64	11.3	14.3	17.7	21.4	25.4	29.9	34.6
Ball		2.05	3.24	4.65	6.30	8.3	10.5	12.9	15.6	18.6	21.8	25.2
Tree Pit	3¼'	3.00	4.80	6.90	9.36	12.2	15.5	19.2	23.2	27.5	32.4	37.5
Ball		2.21	3.50	5.03	6.83	8.9	11.4	14.0	16.9	20.1	23.6	27.3
Tree Pit	3½'	3.28	5.17	7.41	10.1	13.2	16.7	20.7	25.0	29.6	34.9	40.4
Ball		2.39	3.77	5.42	7.4	9.6	12.2	15.0	18.2	21.7	25.4	29.4
Tree Pit	3¾'	3.50	5.53	7.96	10.8	14.2	17.9	22.2	26.7	31.7	37.1	43.3
Ball		2.56	4.04	3.80	7.9	10.3	13.1	16.1	19.5	23.2	27.2	31.5
Tree Pit	4'	3.74	5.90	8.50	11.5	15.1	19.1	23.7	28.5	33.8	39.9	46.2
Ball		2.73	4.31	6.19	8.4	11.0	14.0	17.2	20.8	24.8	29.0	33.6
Tree Pit	4¼'	3.97	6.28	9.01	12.3	16.0	20.3	25.1	30.3	36.0	42.3	49.1
Ball		2.90	4.58	6.58	8.9	11.8	14.8	18.3	22.1	26.3	30.8	35.7
Tree Pit	4½'	4.20	6.64	9.55	13.0	17.0	21.5	26.6	32.0	38.1	44.8	52.0
Ball		3.07	4.85	6.97	9.5	12.4	15.7	19.4	23.4	27.8	32.6	37.8
Tree Pit	4¾'	4.43	7.00	10.0	13.7	17.9	22.7	28.0	33.8	40.2	47.3	54.9
Ball		3.24	5.12	7.4	10.0	13.0	16.5	20.4	24.7	29.1	34.2	40.0
Tree Pit	5'	4.68	7.38	10.6	14.4	18.8	23.9	29.8	35.6	42.3	49.9	57.7
Ball		3.41	5.38	7.8	10.5	13.7	17.4	21.5	26.0	30.9	36.1	42.1
Tree Pit	5½'	5.14	8.12	11.7	15.8	20.7	26.3	32.4	39.2	46.7	54.8	63.5
Ball		3.76	5.93	8.5	11.6	15.1	19.1	23.7	28.6	34.0	40.0	46.3
Tree Pit	6'	5.41	8.86	12.7	17.3	22.6	28.7	35.4	42.8	50.9	57.8	69.3
Ball		4.10	6.46	9.3	12.6	16.5	20.9	25.9	31.2	37.1	43.6	50.5

Surtee's Tree Pits and Tree Balls
Cubic Feet Per Tree
For Estimating Excavation and Top Soil

Diameters / Depths		3¾'	4'	4¼'	4½'	4¾'	5'	5½'	6'	6½'	7'	7½'
Tree Pit	1'	13.3	15.1	17.0	19.1	21.2	23.6	28.5	33.9	39.8	46.2	53.0
Ball		9.7	11.0	12.4	13.9	15.5	17.4	20.8	24.7	29.0	33.7	38.7
Tree Pit	1¼'	16.6	18.8	21.3	23.8	26.5	29.5	35.6	42.4	49.8	57.7	66.3
Ball		12.2	13.8	15.5	17.4	19.4	21.7	26.0	30.9	36.3	42.1	48.3
Tree Pit	1½'	19.9	22.6	25.5	28.6	31.9	35.4	42.8	50.9	59.7	69.3	79.5
Ball		14.5	16.5	18.6	20.9	23.2	25.8	31.2	37.1	43.6	50.5	58.0
Tree Pit	1¾'	23.2	26.4	29.7	33.4	37.2	41.2	49.9	59.4	69.7	80.8	92.8
Ball		16.9	19.1	21.7	24.4	27.1	30.1	36.4	43.4	50.8	58.9	67.7
Tree Pit	2'	26.5	30.2	34.0	38.2	42.0	47.1	57.0	67.9	79.6	92.4	106.3
Ball		19.2	21.9	24.8	27.8	31.0	34.4	41.6	49.5	58.1	67.4	77.3
Tree Pit	2¼'	29.8	33.9	38.3	43.0	47.8	53.0	64.1	76.4	89.6	103.9	119.3
Ball		21.6	24.6	27.9	31.3	34.9	39.7	46.8	55.7	65.3	75.8	87.0
Tree Pit	2½'	33.1	37.7	42.5	47.7	53.1	59.0	71.3	84.9	99.6	115.5	132.6
Ball		24.1	27.3	31.0	34.7	38.8	43.0	52.0	61.9	72.6	84.2	96.7
Tree Pit	2¾'	36.5	41.5	46.8	52.5	58.5	64.8	78.4	93.3	109.5	127.0	145.8
Ball		26.4	30.0	34.1	38.1	42.6	47.3	57.2	68.0	79.9	92.6	106.3
Tree Pit	3'	39.8	45.3	51.0	57.3	63.8	70.6	85.5	101.8	119.5	138.5	159.0
Ball		28.8	32.8	37.0	41.5	46.5	51.6	62.3	74.2	87.1	101.0	116.0
Tree Pit	3¼'	43.1	49.0	55.3	62.0	69.1	76.5	92.6	110.3	129.4	150.1	172.3
Ball		31.4	35.7	40.1	45.0	50.4	55.9	67.5	80.4	94.4	109.5	125.6
Tree Pit	3½'	46.4	52.8	59.6	66.8	74.3	82.5	99.7	118.7	139.4	161.7	185.6
Ball		33.9	38.5	43.2	48.5	54.4	60.2	72.7	86.6	101.6	112.9	135.3
Tree Pit	3¾'	49.7	56.6	63.8	71.6	79.7	88.4	106.8	127.3	149.3	173.8	198.8
Ball		36.4	41.2	46.3	52.2	58.1	64.4	77.5	92.3	108.7	126.3	145.0
Tree Pit	4'	53.0	60.3	68.1	76.3	85.0	94.2	113.0	135.7	159.3	184.8	212.1
Ball		38.9	44.0	49.4	55.7	62.0	68.7	82.8	98.5	116.1	134.7	154.6
Tree Pit	4¼'	56.3	64.1	72.3	81.1	90.3	100.1	121.0	144.2	169.2	196.3	225.3
Ball		41.4	46.8	52.5	59.2	65.9	73.0	88.1	104.8	123.0	142.4	163.4
Tree Pit	4½'	59.6	67.9	76.6	85.9	95.6	106.2	128.2	152.7	179.2	207.9	238.6
Ball		43.9	49.5	55.6	62.7	69.8	77.4	93.4	111.0	130.3	150.9	172.9
Tree Pit	4¾'	63.0	71.6	80.9	90.7	101.0	112.0	135.3	161.2	189.1	219.4	265.1
Ball		46.0	52.3	58.8	66.2	73.7	81.7	98.6	117.2	137.6	159.7	182.4
Tree Pit	5'	66.3	75.4	85.2	95.5	106.3	117.9	142.5	169.7	199.1	230.9	265.1
Ball		48.5	55.0	62.0	69.7	77.5	86.0	103.9	123.4	144.9	168.2	192.0
Tree Pit	5½'	72.9	83.0	93.6	105.2	116.9	129.6	156.8	186.7	219.0	254.0	291.6
Ball		53.2	60.5	68.3	76.6	85.2	94.6	114.2	135.9	159.6	184.6	211.0
Tree Pit	6'	79.5	90.5	102.1	114.5	127.5	141.5	171.0	203.6	238.9	277.1	318.1
Ball		58.0	66.0	74.5	83.5	93.0	103.1	124.7	148.5	174.2	202.0	230.0

PLANTING & WEATHER

Recommendations for New Grass Seeding

1. If soil is compacted, loosen by tilling to at least 6".
2. Level the area and remove all debris and large stones.
3. Spread fertilizer as recommended.
4. Spread lime as determined by pH test.
5. Rake in lime and fertilizer.
6. Spread seed by type, rate and method prescribed.
7. Lightly rake in seed if needed.
8. Apply mulch if needed.
9. Commence watering keeping surface moist until at least 2 leaves have developed on new seedlings. After this, allow to dry off, watering 2 to 3 times per week.
10. Additional fertilizer and lime may be applied after second cutting.

The type of grass seed mixture is determined by sun exposure, shade, soil type, temperature range, moisture range, and intended use of the seeded area. Fertilizer and lime should be disked 4" to 6" into the seed bed. For steep slopes, some type of erosion control method should be used. Hay or straw can be lightly disked in or spread on the surface. Geotextile fabrics, wood fibers, and recycled paper fibers are also frequently used. These can be staked, stapled or anchored with sprayed tar emulsion. Strips of sod between seeded areas and hemp blankets containing seed and fertilizer are also good erosion control materials. Late fall seeding tends to have less weeds, but may need some reseeding in the spring. Depending on the quantity and conditions, seeding can be done by broadcasting, drop seeding, rotary seeding, hydro or hydraulic seeding, or aerial blowers.

Plant Spacing Chart

This chart may be used when plants are to be placed equidistant from each other, staggering their position in each row.

Plant Spacing (Inches)	Row Spacing (Inches)	Plants Per (CSF)	Plant Spacing (Feet)	Row Spacing (Feet)	Plants Per (MSF)
			4	3.46	72
6	5.20	462	5	4.33	46
8	6.93	260	6	5.20	32
10	8.66	166	8	6.93	18
12	10.39	115	10	8.66	12
15	12.99	74	12	10.39	8
18	15.59	51.32	15	12.99	5.13
21	18.19	37.70	20	17.32	2.89
24	20.78	28.87	25	21.65	1.85
30	25.98	18.48	30	25.98	1.28
36	31.18	12.83	40	34.64	0.72

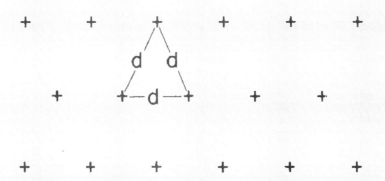

MAJOR TREES

Silhouettes indicate specimens of natural form, but varieties or forced forms possessing compact, spreading, columnar or pyramidal characteristics are available. The height at the ten year stage of development is given as an architectural design factor to be considered in the selection of tree sizes.

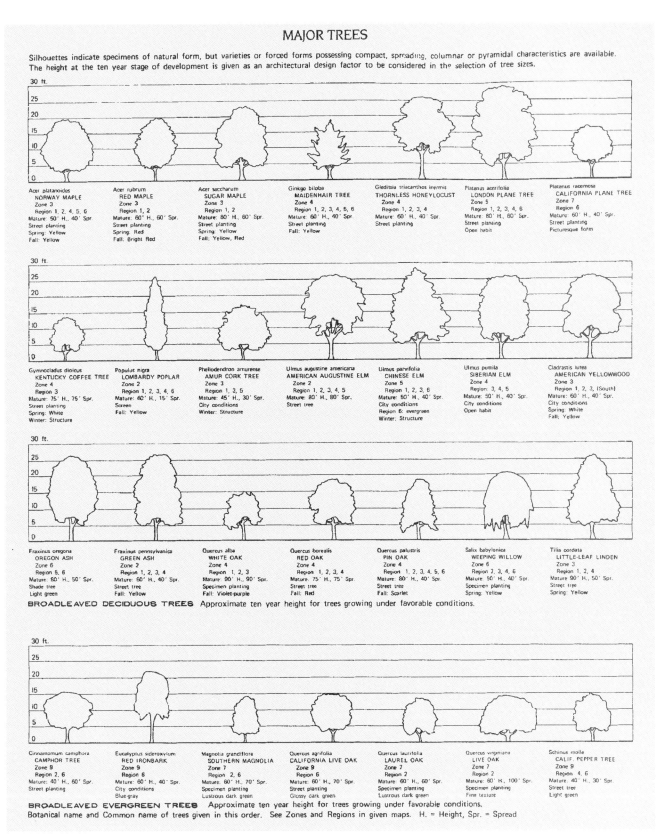

Acer platanoides
NORWAY MAPLE
Zone 3
Region 1, 2, 4, 5, 6
Mature: 50' H., 40' Spr.
Street planting
Spring: Yellow
Fall: Yellow

Acer rubrum
RED MAPLE
Zone 3
Region 1, 2
Mature: 60' H., 60' Spr.
Street planting
Spring: Red
Fall: Bright Red

Acer saccharum
SUGAR MAPLE
Zone 3
Region 1, 2
Mature: 80' H., 60' Spr.
Street planting
Spring: Yellow
Fall: Yellow, Red

Ginkgo biloba
MAIDENHAIR TREE
Zone 4
Region 1, 2, 3, 4, 5, 6
Mature: 60' H., 40' Spr.
Street planting
Fall: Yellow

Gleditsia triacanthos inermis
THORNLESS HONEYLOCUST
Zone 4
Region 1, 2, 3, 4
Mature: 60' H., 40' Spr.
Street planting

Platanus acerifolia
LONDON PLANE TREE
Zone 5
Region 1, 2, 3, 4, 6
Mature: 80' H., 60' Spr.
Street planting
Open habit

Platanus racemosa
CALIFORNIA PLANE TREE
Zone 7
Region 6
Mature: 60' H., 40' Spr.
Street planting
Picturesque form

Gymnocladus dioicus
KENTUCKY COFFEE TREE
Zone 4
Region 3
Mature: 75' H., 75' Spr.
Street planting
Spring: White
Winter: Structure

Populus nigra
LOMBARDY POPLAR
Zone 2
Region 1, 2, 3, 4, 6
Mature: 60' H., 15' Spr.
Screen
Fall: Yellow

Phellodendron amurense
AMUR CORK TREE
Zone 3
Region 1, 3, 5
Mature: 45' H., 30' Spr.
City conditions
Winter: Structure

Ulmus augustine americana
AMERICAN AUGUSTINE ELM
Zone 2
Region 1, 2, 3, 4, 5
Mature: 80' H., 80' Spr.
Street tree

Ulmus parvifolia
CHINESE ELM
Zone 5
Region 1, 2, 3, 6
Mature: 50' H., 40' Spr.
City conditions
Region 6: evergreen
Winter: Structure

Ulmus pumila
SIBERIAN ELM
Zone 4
Region: 3, 4, 5
Mature: 50' H., 40' Spr.
City conditions
Open habit

Cladrastis lutea
AMERICAN YELLOWWOOD
Zone 3
Region 1, 2, 3, (South)
Mature: 60' H., 40' Spr.
City conditions
Spring: White
Fall: Yellow

Fraxinus oregona
OREGON ASH
Zone 6
Region 5, 6
Mature: 80' H., 50' Spr.
Shade tree
Light green

Fraxinus pennsylvanica
GREEN ASH
Zone 2
Region 1, 2, 3, 4
Mature: 60' H., 40' Spr.
Street tree
Fall: Yellow

Quercus alba
WHITE OAK
Zone 4
Region 1, 2, 3
Mature: 90' H., 90' Spr.
Specimen planting
Fall: Violet-purple

Quercus borealis
RED OAK
Zone 4
Region 1, 2, 3, 4
Mature: 75' H., 75' Spr.
Street tree
Fall: Red

Quercus palustris
PIN OAK
Zone 4
Region 1, 2, 3, 4, 5, 6
Mature: 80' H., 40' Spr.
Street tree
Fall: Scarlet

Salix babylonica
WEEPING WILLOW
Zone 6
Region 2, 3, 4, 6
Mature: 50' H., 40' Spr.
Specimen planting
Spring: Yellow

Tilia cordata
LITTLE-LEAF LINDEN
Zone 3
Region 1, 2, 4
Mature 90' H., 50' Spr.
Street tree
Spring: Yellow

BROADLEAVED DECIDUOUS TREES Approximate ten year height for trees growing under favorable conditions.

Cinnamomum camphora
CAMPHOR TREE
Zone 9
Region 2, 6
Mature: 40' H., 60' Spr.
Street planting

Eucalyptus sideroxylum
RED IRONBARK
Zone 9
Region 6
Mature: 60' H., 40' Spr.
City conditions
Blue-gray

Magnolia grandiflora
SOUTHERN MAGNOLIA
Zone 7
Region 2, 6
Mature: 60' H., 70' Spr.
Specimen planting
Lustrous dark green

Quercus agrifolia
CALIFORNIA LIVE OAK
Zone 9
Region 6
Mature: 60' H., 70' Spr.
Street planting
Glossy dark green

Quercus laurifolia
LAUREL OAK
Zone 7
Region 2
Mature: 60' H., 60' Spr.
Specimen planting
Lustrous dark green

Quercus virginiana
LIVE OAK
Zone 7
Region 2
Mature: 60' H., 100' Spr.
Specimen planting
Fine texture

Schinus molle
CALIF. PEPPER TREE
Zone 9
Region 4, 6
Mature: 40' H., 30' Spr.
Street tree
Light green

BROADLEAVED EVERGREEN TREES Approximate ten year height for trees growing under favorable conditions.
Botanical name and Common name of trees given in this order. See Zones and Regions in given maps. H. = Height, Spr. = Spread

(courtesy Laurence & Beatriz Coffin, Urban Planners & Landscape Architects; Washington, DC)

**PLANTING
& WEATHER**

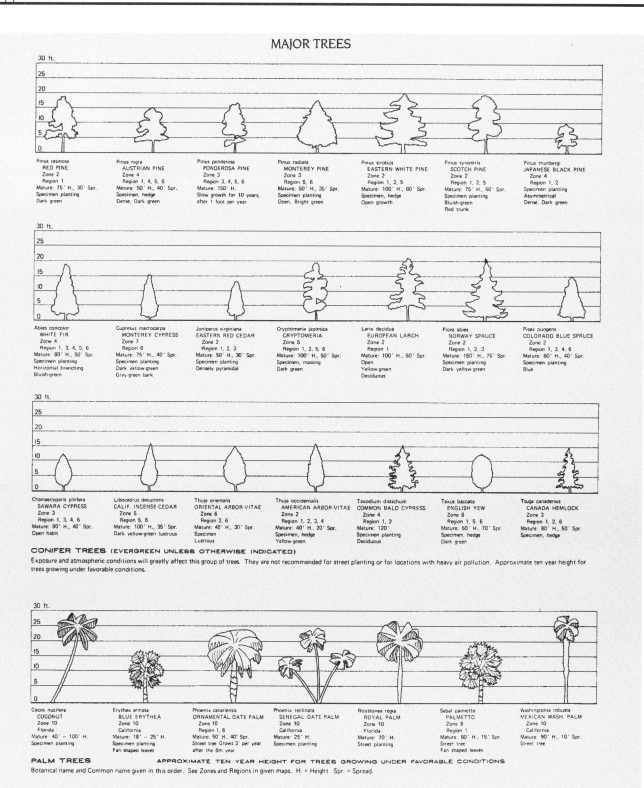

MAJOR TREES

CONIFER TREES (EVERGREEN UNLESS OTHERWISE INDICATED)

Exposure and atmospheric conditions will greatly affect this group of trees. They are not recommended for street planting or for locations with heavy air pollution. Approximate ten year height for trees growing under favorable conditions.

PALM TREES APPROXIMATE TEN YEAR HEIGHT FOR TREES GROWING UNDER FAVORABLE CONDITIONS

Botanical name and Common name given in this order. See Zones and Regions in given maps. H. = Height Spr. = Spread.

(courtesy Laurence & Beatriz Coffin, Urban Planners & Landscape Architects; Washington, DC)

MINOR TREES AND SHRUBS

Betula populifolia	Cornus florida	Cornus nutalli	Cercis canadensis	Crataegus phaenopyrum	Ilex opaca	Lagerstroemia indica
GREY BIRCH	FLOWERING DOGWOOD	PACIFIC DOGWOOD	EASTERN REDBUD	WASHINGTON HAWTHORN	AMERICAN HOLLY	CRAPE MYRTLE
Zone 2	Zone 4	Zone 7	Zone 4	Zone 4	Zone 5	Zone 7
Region 1, 2, 3, 4, 5	Region 1, 2, 3(East)	Region 5, 6	Region 1, 2, 4	Region 1, 2	Region 1, 2	Region 2, 6
Mature: 30' H., 20' Spr.	Mature: 20' H., 25' Spr.	Mature: 30' H., 30' Spr.	Mature: 30' H., 30' Spr.	Mature: 30' H., 30' Spr.	Mature: 40' H., 25' Spr.	Mature: 20' H., 20' Spr.
White bark	Spring: White or Pink	Spring: White	Spring: Purplish Pink	Spring: White	Dark green, Red fruit	Spring: Pink, Bluish
Fall: Yellow	Fall: Red	Fall: Scarlet and Yellow	Fall: Yellow	Fall: Orange	Evergreen	Dense

Acer palmatum	Delonix regia	Myrica california	Magnolia soulangeana	Malus (species)	Prunus serrulata	Photinia serrulata
JAPANESE MAPLE	FLAME TREE	CALIFORNIA BAYBERRY	SAUCER MAGNOLIA	FLOWERING CRAB	ORIENTAL CHERRY	CHINESE PHOTINIA
Zone 5	Zone 10	Zone 7	Zone 5	Zone 4	Zone 5, 6	Zone 7
Region 1, 2, 6	Florida	Region 5, 6	Region 1, 2, 6	Region 1, 2, 4	Region 1, 2, 5, 6	Region 2, 6
Spring: Red	Mature: 40' H., 40' Spr.	Mature: 30' H., 15' Spr.	Mature: 25' H., 25' Spr.	Mature: 20' H., 25' Spr.	Mature: 25' H., 25' Spr.	Mature: 36' H., 25' Spr.
Fall: Red	Summer: Red flowers	Bronze colored	Spring: White - Pink	Spring: White, Pink, Red	Spring: White, Pink	Spring: New growth Red
	Fern-like foliage	Evergreen	Coarse texture	Dense	Glossy bark	Lustrous evergreen

Botanical name and Common name of trees and shrubs given in this order. See Zones and Regions in given maps.
H. = Height   Spr. = Spread
MINOR TREES—ADAPTED TO CITY CONDITIONS, DECIDUOUS UNLESS OTHERWISE SPECIFIED.

SIZE | DECIDUOUS SHRUBS—WITHSTANDING CITY CONDITIONS   **| EVERGREEN SHRUBS—WITHSTANDING CITY CONDITIONS**

10' to 15' HIGH Scale 1" = 30'	Cornus racemosa GRAY DOGWOOD Zone 4 Region 1, 2 Red stalks Hedge	Hamamells virginiana COMMON WITCH HAZEL Zone 4 Region 1, 2, 3 Fall: Yellow	Ligustrum amurense AMUR PRIVET Zone 3 Region 1, 2, 3, 5, 6 Nearly evergreen Hedge or specimen	Syringa vulgaris COMMON LILAC Zone 3 Region 1, 4, 5 Spring: Lilac Massing	Juniperus chinensis columnaris CHINESE JUNIPER Zone 4 Region 1, 2, 3 Hedge specimen	Taxus cupidata capitata JAPANESE YEW Zone 4 Region 1, 2, 3, 4, 5, 6 Specimen Dark green	Rhododendron maximum ROSEBAY RHODODENDRON Zone 3 Region 1, 2, 5 Spring: Pink Dark green, dense
6' to 10' HIGH Scale 1" = 20'	Aronia arbutifolia RED CHOKEBERRY Zone 5 Region 1, 2 Spring: White Fall: Red	Fremontia californica FLANNEL BUSH Zone 7 California Spring: Yellow Massing	Spirea prunifolia plena BRIDALWREATH SPIREA Zone 4 Region 1, 2, 3 Spring: White	Vibornum tomentosum DOUBLEFILE VIBURNUM Zone 2 Region 1, 2, 3, 4, 5, 6 Spring: White Massing	Taxus cuspidata JAPANESE YEW Zone 4 Region 1, 2, 3, 4, 5, 6 Hedge Dark green	Myrtus communis MYRTLE Zone 8–9 Region 2, 6 Hedge, Specimen Massing	Nerium oleander NERIUM Zone 7–8 Region 2, 3, 4, 6 Bamboo-like Light green—white flower
2' to 6' HIGH Scale 1" = 20'	Berberis thunbergi JAPANESE BARBERRY Zone 5 Region 1, 2, 3, 4, 5, 6 Fall: Scarlet Hedge	Forsythia intermediaspetabilis SHOWY BORDER FORSYTHIA Zone 5 Region 1, 2, 3, 4, 5, 6 Spring: Yellow Massing	Euonymus alata WINGED EUONYMUS Zone 3 Region 1, 2, 5, 6 Fall: Scarlet Hedge: Massing	Rosa rugosa RUGOSA ROSE Zone 2 Region 1, 2 Fall: Orange Hedge	Juniperus chinensis pfitzeriana PFITZER'S JUNIPER Zone 4 Region 1, 2 Feathery texture	Buxus suffruticosa DWARF BOX Zone 5 Region 2, 3, 6 Dark lustrous	Pinus mugo mughus MUGO PINE Zone 2 Region 1, 2, 4, 5, 6 Bright green Specimen, Massing
6" to 24" HIGH Used as ground cover	Cotoneaster horizontalis ROCK SPRAY Zone 4 Region 1, 2, 3, 4, 5, 6	Cytisus albus PORTUGUESE BROOM Zone 5 Region 1, 5 White flowers	Euonymus fortunei WINTER CREEPER Zone 2 Region 1, 2, 3, 4, 5, 6	Juniperus sabina tamariscifolia TAMARIX JUNIPER Zone 4 Region 3, 4, 5, 6	Juniperus chinensis sargenti SARGENT JUNIPER Zone 4 Region 1, 2	Hedera helix vars. ENGLISH IVY Zone 4 Region 1, 2	Pachistima cambyi CAMBYI PACHISTIMA Zone 5 Region 1, 2 Fall: Bronze

Silhouettes indicate specimens of natural form. Shrubs are adaptable to different height and forms by pruning. A wide range of varieties and exotic shrubs can be found throughout the plant regions. A few shrubs commonly used are listed here.

(courtesy Laurence & Beatriz Coffin, Urban Planners & Landscape Archtects; Washington, DC)

PLANTING & WEATHER

Plant Distribution

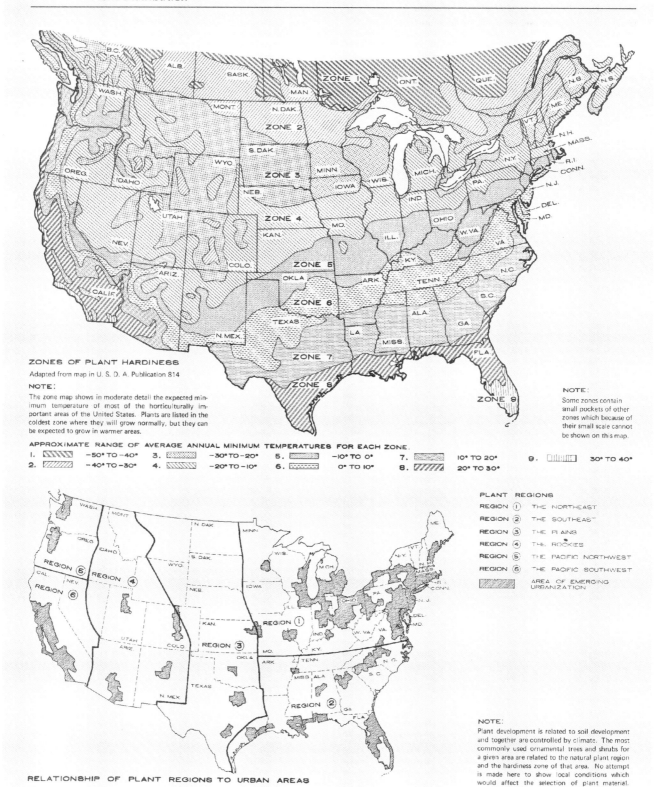

ZONES OF PLANT HARDINESS

Adapted from map in U. S. D. A. Publication 814

NOTE:

The zone map shows in moderate detail the expected minimum temperature of most of the horticulturally important areas of the United States. Plants are listed in the coldest zone where they will grow normally, but they can be expected to grow in warmer areas.

NOTE:

Some zones contain small pockets of other zones which because of their small scale cannot be shown on this map.

APPROXIMATE RANGE OF AVERAGE ANNUAL MINIMUM TEMPERATURES FOR EACH ZONE.

1.	−50° TO −40°	3.	−30° TO −20°	5.	−10° TO 0°	7.	10° TO 20°	9.	30° TO 40°
2.	−40° TO −30°	4.	−20° TO −10°	6.	0° TO 10°	8.	20° TO 30°		

PLANT REGIONS

REGION ① THE NORTHEAST
REGION ② THE SOUTHEAST
REGION ③ THE PLAINS
REGION ④ THE ROCKIES
REGION ⑤ THE PACIFIC NORTHWEST
REGION ⑥ THE PACIFIC SOUTHWEST

AREA OF EMERGING URBANIZATION

RELATIONSHIP OF PLANT REGIONS TO URBAN AREAS

NOTE:

Plant development is related to soil development and together are controlled by climate. The most commonly used ornamental trees and shrubs for a given area are related to the natural plant region and the hardiness zone of that area. No attempt is made here to show local conditions which would affect the selection of plant material.

(courtesy Laurence & Beatriz Coffin, Urban Planners & Landscape Architects, Washington, DC)

Trees and Plants by Environment and Purposes

Dry, Windy, Exposed Areas
Barberry
Junipers, all varieties
Locust
Maple
Oak
Pines, all varieties
Poplar, Hybrid
Privet
Spruce, all varieties
Sumac, Staghorn

Lightly Wooded Areas
Dogwood
Hemlock
Larch
Pine, White
Rhododendron
Spruce, Norway
Redbud

Total Shade Areas
Hemlock
Ivy, English
Myrtle
Pachysandra
Privet
Spice Bush
Yews, Japanese

Cold Temperatures of Northern U.S. and Canada
Arborvitae, American
Birch, White
Dogwood, Silky
Fir, Balsam
Fir, Douglas
Hemlock
Juniper, Andorra
Juniper, Blue Rug
Linden, Little Leaf
Maple, Sugar
Mountain Ash
Myrtle
Olive, Russian

Pine, Mugho
Pine, Ponderosa
Pine, Red
Pine, Scotch
Poplar, Hybrid
Privet
Rosa Rugosa
Spruce, Dwarf Alberta
Spruce, Black Hills
Spruce, Blue
Spruce, Norway
Spruce, White, Engelman
Yellow Wood

Wet, Swampy Areas
American Arborvitae
Birch, White
Black Gum
Hemlock
Maple, Red
Pine, White
Willow

Poor, Dry, Rocky Soil
Barberry
Crownvetch
Eastern Red Cedar
Juniper, Virginiana
Locust, Black
Locust, Bristly
Locust, Honey
Olive, Russian
Pines, all varieties
Privet
Rosa Rugosa
Sumac, Staghorn

Seashore Planting
Arborvitae, American
Juniper, Tamarix
Locust, Black
Oak, White
Olive, Russian
Pine, Austrian
Pine, Japanese Black

Pine, Mugho
Pine, Scotch
Privet, Amur River
Rosa Rugosa
Yew, Japanese

City Planting
Barberry
Fir, Concolor
Forsythia
Hemlock
Holly, Japanese
Ivy, English
Juniper, Andorra
Linden, Little Leaf
Locust, Honey
Maple, Norway, Silver
Oak, Pin, Red
Olive, Russian
Pachysandra
Pine, Austrian
Pine, White
Privet
Rosa Rugosa
Sumac, Staghorn
Yew, Japanese

Bonsai Planting
Azaleas
Birch, White
Ginkgo
Junipers
Pine, Bristlecone
Pine, Mugho
Spruce, Engleman
Spruce, Dwarf Alberta

Street Planting
Linden, Little Leaf
Oak, Pin
Ginkgo

Fast Growth
Birch, White

Crownvetch
Dogwood, Silky
Fir, Douglas
Juniper, Blue Pfitzer
Juniper, Blue Rug
Maple, Silver
Olive, Autumn
Pines, Austrian, Ponderosa, Red
    Scotch and White
Poplar, Hybrid
Privet
Spruce, Norway
Spruce, Serbian
Taxus, Cuspidata, Hicksi
Willow

Dense, Impenetrable Hedges
Field Plantings:
    Locust, Bristly,
    Olive, Autumn
    Sumac

Residential Areas:
    Barberry, Red or Green
    Juniper, Blue Pfitzer
    Rosa Rugosa

Food for Birds
Ash, Mountain
Barberry
Bittersweet
Cherry, Manchu
Dogwood, Silky
Honeysuckle, Rem Red
Hawthorn
Oaks
Olive, Autumn, Russian
Privet
Rosa Rugosa
Sumac

Erosion Control
Crownvetch
Locust, Bristly
Willow

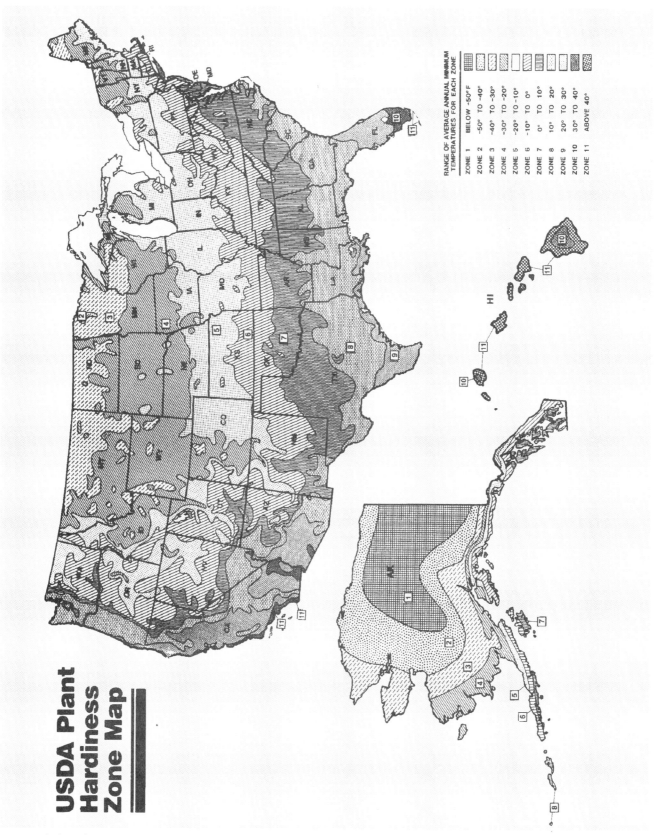

USDA Plant Hardiness Zone Map

RANGE OF AVERAGE ANNUAL MINIMUM TEMPERATURES FOR EACH ZONE

ZONE 1   BELOW -50°F
ZONE 2   -50° TO -40°
ZONE 3   -40° TO -30°
ZONE 4   -30° TO -20°
ZONE 5   -20° TO -10°
ZONE 6   -10° TO 0°
ZONE 7   0° TO 10°
ZONE 8   10° TO 20°
ZONE 9   20° TO 30°
ZONE 10   30° TO 40°
ZONE 11   ABOVE 40°

(courtesy Agricultural Research Service, USDA)

Maximum Depth of Frost Penetration in Inches

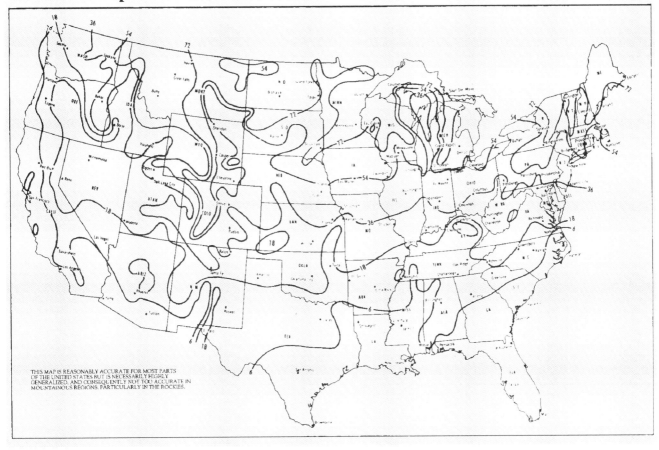

THIS MAP IS REASONABLY ACCURATE FOR MOST PARTS
OF THE UNITED STATES BUT IS NECESSARILY HIGHLY
GENERALIZED, AND CONSEQUENTLY NOT TOO ACCURATE IN
MOUNTAINOUS REGIONS, PARTICULARLY IN THE ROCKIES.

Weather Data and Design Conditions

City	Latitude (1) °	Latitude (1) 1'	Winter Temperatures (1) Med. of Annual Extremes	Winter Temperatures (1) 99%	Winter Temperatures (1) 97½%	Winter Degree Days (2)	Summer (Design Dry Bulb) Temperatures and Relative Humidity 1%	Summer (Design Dry Bulb) Temperatures and Relative Humidity 2½%	Summer (Design Dry Bulb) Temperatures and Relative Humidity 5%
UNITED STATES									
Albuquerque, NM	35	0	5.1	12	16	4,400	96/61	94/61	92/61
Atlanta, GA	33	4	11.9	17	22	3,000	94/74	92/74	90/73
Baltimore, MD	39	2	7	14	17	4,600	94/75	91/75	89/74
Birmingham, AL	33	3	13	17	21	2,600	96/74	94/75	92/74
Bismarck, ND	46	5	-32	-23	-19	8,800	95/68	91/68	88/67
Boise, ID	43	3	1	3	10	5,800	96/65	94/64	91/64
Boston, MA	42	2	-1	6	9	5,600	91/73	88/71	85/70
Burlington, VT	44	3	-17	-12	-7	8,200	88/72	85/70	82/69
Charleston, WV	38	2	3	7	11	4,400	92/74	90/73	87/72
Charlotte, NC	35	1	13	18	22	3,200	95/74	93/74	91/74
Casper, WY	42	5	-21	-11	-5	7,400	92/58	90/57	87/57
Chicago, IL	41	5	-8	-3	2	6,600	94/75	91/74	88/73
Cincinnati, OH	39	1	0	1	6	4,400	92/73	90/72	88/72
Cleveland, OH	41	2	-3	1	5	6,400	91/73	88/72	86/71
Columbia, SC	34	0	16	20	24	2,400	97/76	95/75	93/75
Dallas, TX	32	5	14	18	22	2,400	102/75	100/75	97/75
Denver, CO	39	5	-10	-5	1	6,200	93/59	91/59	89/59
Des Moines, IA	41	3	-14	-10	-5	6,600	94/75	91/74	88/73
Detroit, MI	42	2	-3	3	6	6,200	91/73	88/72	86/71
Great Falls, MT	47	3	-25	-21	-15	7,800	91/60	88/60	85/59
Hartford, CT	41	5	-4	3	7	6,200	91/74	88/73	85/72
Houston, TX	29	5	24	28	33	1,400	97/77	95/77	93/77
Indianapolis, IN	39	4	-7	-2	2	5,600	92/74	90/74	87/73
Jackson, MS	32	2	16	21	25	2,200	97/76	95/76	93/76
Kansas City, MO	39	1	4	2	6	4,800	99/75	96/74	93/74
Las Vegas, NV	36	1	18	25	28	2,800	108/66	106/65	104/65
Lexington, KY	38	0	-1	3	8	4,600	93/73	91/73	88/72
Little Rock, AR	34	4	11	15	20	3,200	99/76	96/77	94/77
Los Angeles, CA	34	0	36	41	43	2,000	93/70	89/70	86/69
Memphis, TN	35	0	10	13	18	3,200	98/77	95/76	93/76
Miami, FL	25	5	39	44	47	200	91/77	90/77	89/77
Milwaukee, WI	43	0	-11	-8	-4	7,600	90/74	87/73	84/71
Minneapolis, MN	44	5	-22	-16	-12	8,400	92/75	89/73	86/71
New Orleans, LA	30	0	28	29	33	1,400	93/78	92/77	90/77
New York, NY	40	5	6	11	15	5,000	92/74	89/73	87/72
Norfolk, VA	36	5	15	20	22	3,400	93/77	91/76	89/76
Oklahoma City, OK	35	2	4	9	13	3,200	100/74	97/74	95/73
Omaha, NE	41	2	-13	-8	-3	6,600	94/76	91/75	88/74
Philadelphia, PA	39	5	6	10	14	4,400	93/75	90/74	87/72
Phoenix, AZ	33	3	27	31	34	1,800	109/71	107/71	105/71
Pittsburgh, PA	40	3	-1	3	7	6,000	91/72	88/71	86/70
Portland, ME	43	4	-10	-6	-1	7,600	87/72	84/71	81/69
Portland, OR	45	4	18	17	23	4,600	89/68	85/67	81/65
Portsmouth, NH	43	1	-8	-2	2	7,200	89/73	85/71	83/70
Providence, RI	41	4	-1	5	9	6,000	89/73	86/72	83/70
Rochester, NY	43	1	-5	1	5	6,800	91/73	88/71	85/70
Salt Lake City, UT	40	5	0	3	8	6,000	97/62	95/62	92/61
San Francisco, CA	37	5	36	38	40	3,000	74/63	71/62	69/61
Seattle, WA	47	4	22	22	27	5,200	85/68	82/66	78/65
Sioux Falls, SD	43	4	-21	-15	-11	7,800	94/73	91/72	88/71
St. Louis, MO	38	4	-3	3	8	5,000	98/75	94/75	91/75
Tampa, FL	28	0	32	36	40	680	92/77	91/77	90/76
Trenton, NJ	40	1	4	11	14	5,000	91/75	88/74	85/73
Washington, DC	38	5	7	14	17	4,200	93/75	91/74	89/74
Wichita, KS	37	4	-3	3	7	4,600	101/72	98/73	96/73
Wilmington, DE	39	4	5	10	14	5,000	92/74	89/74	87/73
ALASKA									
Anchorage	61	1	-29	-23	-18	10,800	71/59	68/58	66/56
Fairbanks	64	5	-59	-51	-47	14,280	82/62	78/60	75/59
CANADA									
Edmonton, Alta.	53	3	-30	-29	-25	11,000	85/66	82/65	79/63
Halifax, N.S.	44	4	-4	1	5	8,000	79/66	76/65	74/64
Montreal, Que.	45	3	-20	-16	-10	9,000	88/73	85/72	83/71
Saskatoon, Sask.	52	1	-35	-35	-31	11,000	89/68	86/66	83/65
St. John, Nwf.	47	4	1	3	7	8,600	77/66	75/65	73/64
Saint John, N.B.	45	2	-15	-12	-8	8,200	80/67	77/65	75/64
Toronto, Ont.	43	4	-10	-5	-1	7,000	90/73	87/72	85/71
Vancouver, B.C.	49	1	13	15	19	6,000	79/67	77/66	74/65
Winnipeg, Man.	49	5	-31	-30	-27	10,800	89/73	86/71	84/70

(1) Handbook of Fundamentals, ASHRAE, Inc., NY 1989
(2) Local Climatological Annual Survey, USDC Env. Science Services Administration, Asheville, NC

SITE IRRIGATION

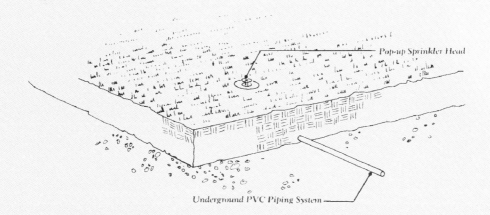

Pop-up Sprinkler Head

Underground PVC Piping System

Site irrigation is accomplished with sprinkler heads that are attached to a permanent underground piping system, usually of PVC pipe or flexible polyethylene tubing. The system may be controlled at a main valve, either manually or automatically, or at each individual sprinkler head.

Several types of sprinkler head operations are available: spray, impact, or rotary. Any of these heads may accommodate one of several types of mountings: pop-up, riser mount, or quick connect. The mountings are made of plastic or brass in both economy and heavy-duty models.

The area covered by a single sprinkler head can range in a circular or arc pattern from 10' to 100' in radius, or in a quadrilateral pattern, such as a 24' square or a 40' by 6' rectangle. Radius pattern heads can be adjusted for irrigating areas along property boundaries. Since large radius sprays require great amounts of water, the local water pressure must be sufficient. If this is not the case, then booster pumps may be required to provide the necessary pressure. Generally, the larger-coverage sprinklers provide a more economical system.

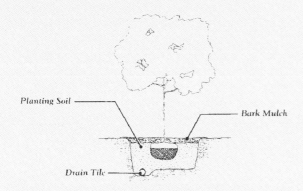

Planting Soil

Bark Mulch

Drain Tile

Tree/Shrub Irrigation and Drainage

The site served is usually divided into zones determined by the nature of the landscaping (turf or shrub), the amount of irrigation needed (sunny or shady), and the coverage of the sprinkler head (small or large). Each zone is controlled by a separate valve. In an automated system, each of these valves and the main valve from the water supply are electrically operated. The electrical service to each of these valves is connected to and controlled from a remote panel.

Man-hours

Description	m/hr	Unit
Sprinkler System, Golf Course, Fully Automatic	.600	9 holes
12' Radius Heads, 15' Spacing		
Minimum	.343	head
Maximum	.600	head
30' Radius Heads, Automatic		
Minimum	.857	head
Maximum	1.040	head
Sprinkler Heads		
Minimum	.267	head
Maximum	.320	head
Trenching, Chain Trencher, 12 hp		
4" Wide, 12" Deep	.010	lf
6" Wide, 24" Deep	.015	lf
Backfill and Compact		
4" Wide, 12" Deep	.010	lf
6" Wide, 24" Deep	.030	lf
Trenching and Backfilling, Chain Trencher, 40 hp		
6" Wide, 12" Deep	.007	lf
8" Wide, 36" Deep	.010	lf
Compaction		
6" Wide, 12" Deep	.003	lf
8" Wide, 36" Deep	.005	lf
Vibrating Plow		
8" Deep	.004	lf
12" Deep	.006	lf
Automatic Valves, Solenoid		
3/4" Diameter	.363	Ea.
2" Diameter	.500	Ea.
Automatic Controllers		
4 Station	1.500	Ea.
12 Station	2.000	Ea.

PLANTING & WEATHER

Cross Reference List of Plants by Common Names

(Courtesy of Monrovia Nursery Company)

A
African Daisy ................................OSTEOSPERMUM
African Iris ....MORAEA
African Sumac ....RHUS
Alaskan Fern ....POLYSTICHUM
Alder ....ALNUS
Arborvitae ....THUJA
Arron's Beard ....HYPERICUM
Ash ....FRAXINUS
Aspen ....POPULUS
Australian Tree Fern ....ALSOPHILA
Australian Willow ....GEIJERA
Autumn Fern ....DRYOPTERIS
B
Bamboo ....NANDINA PHYLLOSTACHYS, SASA
Bamboo Palm ....CHAMAEDOREA
Banana Shrub ....MICHELIA
Banana Tree ....ENSETE
Barberry ....BERBERIS
Beauty Bush ....KOLKWITZIA
Big Tree ..........................SEQUOIADENDRON
Birch ....BETULA
Bird of Paradise, Bird of Paradise Tree ....STRELITZIA
Bird's Eye Bush ....OCHNA
Black Gum ....NYSSA
Black Laurel ....GORDONIA
Blue Hair Grass ....KOELERIA
Blue Hibiscus ....ALYOGYNE
Bluebeard ....CARYOPTERIS
Boston Ivy ......................PARTHENOCISSUS
Bottle-brush ....CALLISTEMON
Bottle Tree ..........................BRACHYCHITON
Bower Vine ....PANDOREA
Boxwood ....BUXUS
Bridal Wreath ....SPIRAEA
Brisbane Box ....TRISTANIA
Broom ....CYTISUS, SPARTIUM
Brush Cherry ....EUGENIA (SYZGIUM)
Bunya-Bunya ....ARAUCARIA
Bush Germander ....TEUCRIUM
Buttercup Shrub ....POTENTILLA
Butterfly Bush ....BUDDLEIA
C
Cajeput Tree ....MELALEUCA
California Christmas Tree ....CEDRUS
California Lilac ....CEANOTHUS
Camphor Tree ....CINNAMOMUM
Candytuft ....IBERIS
Cape Honeysuckle ....TECOMARIA
Carob Tree ....CERATONIA
Carolina Jessamine ....GELSEMIUM
Carrotwood Tree ....CUPANIOPSIS
Cat's Claw Vine ....MACFADYENA
Cedar ....CALOCEDRUS, CEDRUS, CRYPTOMERIA
Cherry Tree (ornamental) ....PRUNUS
Chilean Jasmine ....MANDEVILLA
Chinese Gooseberry ....ACTINIDIA
Chinese Lantern ....ABUTILON
Cinquefoils ....POTENTILLA
Coast Redwood ....SEQUOIA
Confederate Jasmine ................TRACHELOSPERMUM
Confederate Rose ....(HARDY) HIBISCUS
Coral Tree ....ERYTHRINA
Coral Vine ....ANTIGONON
Cottonwood ....POPULUS
Crab Apple Tree (ornamental) ....MALUS
Crape Myrtle ..........................LAGERSTROEMIA
Crenate Chinese Croton ....EXCOECARIA
Crested Lady Fern ....ATHYRIUM
Cupid's Dart ....CATANANCHE
Cypress ..............CHAMAECYPARIS, CUPRESSOCYPARIS, CUPRESSUS
D
Date Palm ....PHOENIX
Dawn Redwood ....METASEQUOIA
Daylillies ..................................HEMEROCALLIS
Desert Willow ....CHILOPSIS
Dogwood ....CORNUS
Dracaena Palm ....CORDYLINE
Dusty Miller ....CENTRAUREA
Dwarf Keffirboom ....ERYTHRINA
Dwarf Karo ....PITTOSPORUM

E
Elm ....ULMUS
Emu Bush ....EREMOPHILA
English Fern ....POLYSTICHUM
Evergreen Wisteria ....MILLETTIA
F
False Holly ....OSMANTHUS
Ferns ...ALSOPHILA, ASPLENIUM, ATHYRIUM, CYRTOMIUM, DICKSONIA, DRYOPTERIS, NEPHROLEPIS, ONOCLEA, OSMUNDA, POLYSTICHUM, RUMOHRA
Fescue ....FESTUCA
Fig (Ornamental and Fruit Bearing) ....FICUS
Firethorn ....PYRACANTHA
Flame Bottle Tree ......................BRACHYCHITON
Floss Silk Tree ....CHORISIA
Flowering Quince ....CHAENOMELES
Flowering Maple ....ABUTILON
Flowering Willow ....CHILOPSIS
Fortnight Lily ....MORAEA
Fountain Grass ....PENNISETUM
Franklin Tree ....FRANKLINIA
G
Geraldton Wax Flower ................CHAMAELAUCIUM
Giant Sequoia ..........................SEQUOIADENRON
Gold Medallion Tree ....CASSIA
Golden Bells ....FORSYTHIA
Golden Rain Tree ..........................KOELREUTERIA
Golden Shrub Daisy ....EURYOPS
Grape (Fruiting) ....VITIS
Grape Ivy ....CISSUS
Grapefruit ....CITRUS
Grasses ....CAREX, CHONDROPETALUM, CORTADERIA, FESTUCA, KOELERIA, MISCANTHUS, PENNISETUM
Grecian Pattern Plant ....ACANTHUS
Guadalupe Palm ....BRAHEA
Guava ....FEIJOA, PSIDIUM
Guinea Gold Vine ....HIBBERTIA
Gum Tree ....EUCALYPTUS
H
Heart-leaf Flame Pea ....CHORIZEMA
Heath, Heather ....ERICA
Heavenly Bamboo ....NANDINA
Heliotrope ..............................HELIOTROPIUM
Hemlock ....TSUGA
Himalayan Sweet Box ....SARCOCOCCA
Holly ....ILEX
Holly Fern ....CYRTOMIUM
Honeysuckle ....LONICERA
Hopseed Bush ....DODONAEA
Horse Chestnut ....AESCULUS
Horsetail Reed Grass ....EQUISETUM
Hummingbird Bush ....GREVILLEA
I
Incense Cedar ....CALOCEDRUS
Indian Hawthorn ....RAPHIOLEPIS
Indian Laurel Fig ....FICUS
Indian Rhododendron ....MELASTOMA
Indigo ....INDIGOFERA
Ironbark ....EUCALYPTUS
Ivy ....HEDERA
J
Japanese Aralia ....FATSIA
Japanese Lace Fern ....POLYSTICHUM
Japanese Plum ....ERIOBOTRYA
Japanese Sedge Grass ....CAREX
Japanese Silver Grass ....MISCANTHUS
Japanese Spurge ....PACHYSANDRA
Japanese Sword Fern ....DRYOPTERIS
Japanese Umbrella Pine ....SCIADOPITYS
Jasmine ....JASMINUM, MANDEVILLA, STEPHANOTIS, TRACHELOSPERMUM
Jessamine ....CESTRUM, GELSEMIUM, MURRAYA
Juniper ....JUNIPERUS
K
Kaffir Lilly ....CLIVIA
King Plam ................................ARCHONTOPHOENIX
Kiwi Vine ....ACTINIDIA
Kumquat ....CITRUS (FORTUNELLA)
L
Lace Fern ....POLYSTICHUM
Larch ....LARIX
Laurel ....PRUNUS
Lavender ....LAVANDULA
Lavender Cotton ....SANTOLINA
Lavender Star Plant ....GREWIA

Cross Reference List of Plants by Common Names (Continued)

L	Leatherleaf Fern	RUMOHRA
	Lemon	CITRUS
	Lemon Leaf	GAULTHERIA
	Lilac	BUDDLEIA, CEANOTHUS, SYRINGA
	Lilac Hibiscus	ALYOGYNE
	Lily of the Nile	AGAPANTHUS
	Lily of the Valley Shrub	PIERIS
	Lily Turf	LIRIOPE, OPHIOPOGON
	Lime	CITRUS
	Loblolly Bay	GORDONIA
	Loquat	ERIOBOTRYA
	Loosestrife	LYTHRUM
M	Madagascar Jasmine	STEPHANOTIS
	Maiden Grass	MISCANTHUS
	Maidenhair Tree	GINKGO
	Mallet Flower	TUPIDANTHUS
	Manzanita	ARCTOSTAPHYLOS
	Maple	ACER
	Marmalade Bush	STRETOSOLEN
	Marsupial Lobelia	DAMPIERA
	Mediterranean Fan Palm	CHAMAEROPS
	Mescal Bean	SOPHORA
	Mesquite	PROSOPIS
	Mexican Fan Palm	WASHINGTONIA
	Mimosa Tree	ALBIZIA
	Mock Orange	PHILADELPHUS, PITTOSPORUM
	Mondo Grass	OPHIOPOGON
	Mother Fern	ASPLENIUM
	Mountain Ash	SORBUS
	Mulberry	MORUS
	Myrtle	MYRTUS
N	Natal Plum	CARISSA
	Neanthe Bella Palm	CHAMAEDOREA
	Night Blooming Jessamine	CESTRUM
	Nightshade	SOLANUM
	Ninebark	PHYSOCARPUS
	Norfolk Island Pine	ARAUCARIA
N	Oak	QUERCUS
	Oleander	NERIUM, THEVETIA
	Olive	OLEA
	Orange	CITRUS
	Orange Clock Vine	THUNBERGIA
	Orange Jessamine	MURRAYA
	Orchid Tree	BAUHINIA
	Oregon Grape Holly	MAHONIA
P	Palms	ARCHONTOPHOENIX, ARECASTRUM, BRAHEA, CHAMAEDOREA, CHAMAEROPS, CYCAS, PHOENIX, TRACHYCARPUS, WASHINGTONIA
	Pampas Grass	CORTADERIA
	Paraguay Nightshade	SOLANUM
	Passion Flower, Passion Vine	PASSIFLORA
	Pear (Ornamental)	PYRUS
	Pepperidge Tree	NYSSA
	Pepper Tree	SCHINUS
	Periwinkle	VINCA
	Pine	PINUS
	Pistachio	PISTACIA
	Plumbago	CERATOSTIGMA
	Pomegranate	PUNICA
	Potato Vine	SOLANUM
	Poplar	POPULUS
	Powder Puff	CALLIANDRA
	Princess Flower	TIBOUCHINA
	Privet	LIGUSTRUM
	Pussy Willow	SALIX
Q	Quaking Aspen	POPULUS
	Queen Palm	ARECASTRUM
	Queen's Wreath	ANTIGONON
R	Redbud	CERCIS
	Red Bird of Paradise Bush	CAESALPINIA
	Red Clusterberry	COTONEASTER
	Red-Leaf Plum	PRUNUS
	Red Yucca	HESPERALOB
	Redwood	METASEQUOIA, SEQUOIA
	Rock Rose	CISTUS
	Rose	ROSA

	Rose of Sharon	HIBISCUS (ALTHAEA)
	Rosemary	ROSMARINUS
	Royal Fern	OSMUNDA
	Rubber Tree	FICUS
	Ruffled Leaf Wonder	FATSHEDERA
S	Sago Palm	CYCAS
	Salal	GAULTHERIA
	Sand Cherry	PRUNUS
	Satinwood	MURRAYA
	Saxifrage	SAXIFRAGA
	Scotch Broom	CYTISUS
	Sea Lavender	LIMONIUM
	Sedge Grass	CAREX
	Senisa	LEUCOPHYLLUM
	Sensitive Fern	ONOCLEA
	Shaddock	CITRUS
	Shrimp Plant	JUSTICIA
	Siberian Gooseberry	ACTINIDIA
	Silk Oak	GREVILLEA
	Silk Tree	ALBIZIA
	Silverberry	ELAEAGNUS
	Silver Dollar Tree	EUCALYPTUS
	Silver Lace Vine	POLYGONUM
	Snail Vine	VIGNA
	Snowball	VIBURNUM
	Spanish Broom	SPARTIUM
	Spring Bouquet	VIBURNUM
	Spruce	PICEA
	Spurge	PACHYSANDRA
	St. John's Bread Tree	CERATONIA
	St. John's-Wort	HYPERICUM
	Star Jasmine	TRACHELOSPERMUM
	Star Pine	ARAUCARIA
	Stonecrop	SEDUM
	Strawberry Bush	ARBUTUS
	Summer Lilac	BUDDLEIA
	Swamp Tea Tree	MELALEUCA
	Sweet Broom	CYTISUS
	Sweet Gum	LIQUIDAMBAR
	Sweet Olive	OSMANTHUS
	Sweet Pea Shrub	POLYGALA
	Sword Fern	NEPHROLEPIS
	Sycamore	PLATANUS
T	Tangelo	CITRUS
	Tangerine	CITRUS
	Tasmanian Tree Fern	DICKSONIA
	Tea Plant	CAMELLIA
	Tea Tree	LEPTOSPERMUM
	Texas Mountain Laurel	SOPHORA
	Texas Sage	LEUCOPHYLLUM
	Thyme	THYMUS
	Trailing African Daisy	OSTEOSPERMUM
	Trailing Hop Bush	DODONAEA
	Trumpet Creeper	CAMPSIS
	Trumpet Tree	TABEBUIA
	Trumpet Vine	CAMPSIS, CLYTOSTOMA, DISTICTUS, MACFADYENA
	Tulip Tree	LIRIODENDRON
U	Umbrella Plant	SCHEFFLERA
V	Victorian Box	PITTOSPORUM
	Vine Lilac	HARDENBERGIA
	Virginia Creeper	PARTHENOCISSUS
W	Wattles	ACACIA
	Wax Leaf Privet	LIGUSTURM
	Western Sword Fern	POLYSTICHUM
	White Sapote	CASIMIROA
	Willow Leaved Peppermint	EUCALYPTUS
	Windmill Palm	TRACHYCARPUS
	Woodbine	LONICERA
	Woadwaxen	GENISTA
Y	Yarrow	ACHILLEA
	Yellow Bells, Yellow Elder	TECOMA
	Yellow Oleander	THEVETIA
	Yellow Poplar	LIRIODENDRON
	Yesterday, Today, Tomorrow	BRUNFELSIA

PLANTING & WEATHER

Horticultural References, Resources and Books

This list is made up of standard references as well as personal recommendations. All accurate planting information is site specific. Some nurseryman's catalogs are widely used as references within the industry; some of these are listed here. Your relevant and accurate sources are local suppliers.

Cooperative Extension Services
U.S. Dept. of Agriculture
Regional publications on plants, crops, weeds, lawns, pests, methods and special situations. Contact your state or local office.

Agricultural Research Service
USDA
Beltsville, MD
(301) 504-1606

Coffin & Coffin
Landscape Architects and Urban Designers
715 G Street, SE
Washington, DC 20003

The Water Resources Group in most Western states. Contact nearest water supply agency or USDA Cooperative Extension.

Xeriscape Colorado! Inc.
P.O. Box 40202
Denver, CO 80204-0202
www.xeriscape.org
Non-profit group promoting water-conserving landscapes.

Architectural Graphic Standards, 9th edition
(available on CD-ROM)
John Wiley & Sons, Inc. Publishers

Trade Journals, Magazines, Monographs published by many of the professional organizations listed in this Appendix. This is among the most timely information.

Sunset Books
Sunset Publishing Corp.
80 Willow Road
Menlo Park, CA 94025-3691
www.sunsetbooks.com
Publishes a wide variety of outdoor building and gardening books and magazines.

Time-Life Books
200 Duke Street
Alexandria, VA 22134
Publishes a wide variety of outdoor building and horticultural titles.

Hortus Third
by Staff of the L.H. Bailey Hortorium
Cornell University
Macmillan Publishing USA

Encyclopedia of Gardening
The American Horticultural Society

A-Z *Encyclopedia of Garden Plants* 1997
DK Publishers, Inc.
95 Madison Avenue
New York, NY 10016

Taylor's Guides to Gardening Series
Some regional guides, a wide range of topics.

The Ortho Problem Solver
Ortho Books

Rodale Publications
Rodale Press, Inc.
33 E. Minor Street
Emmaus, PA 18098

PROFESSIONAL REFERENCES

Bailey Nurseries, Inc.
Reference Guide and Catalog
1325 Bailey Road
St. Paul, MN 55119-6199
(612) 459-9744

Monrovia Nurseries
18331 E. Foothill Blvd.
Azusa, CA 91702-2638

Northeast Nursery, Inc.
234 Newbury Street
Peabody, MA 01960
(978) 535-6550

Oregon Assn. of Nurserymen
Directory & Buyers Guide
2780 S.E. Harrison St., Suite 102
Milwaukie, OR 97222
1-800-342-6401

The Pacific Northwest Gardener's Book of Lists
McNeilan, Ray & Jan
Taylor Publishing Co.
1550 W. Mockingbird Lane
Dallas, TX 75235

Professional Organizations and Networks

American Nursery & Landscape
Association (202) 789-2900
1250 I Street NW, Suite 500
Washington, DC 20005
www.anla.org

American Society of Landscape Architects (ASLA)
(202) 898-2444
636 I Street, NW
Washington, D.C. 20001-3736
www.asla.org
For Historic Landscape Preservation, contact
ASLA Historic Preservation Committee

Associated Landscape Contractors of America (ALCA)
(703) 736-9666
150 Elden Street, Suite 270
Herndon, VA 20170
www.alca.org

The Associated General Contractors of America
(202) 393-2040
1957 E Street, NW
Washington, DC 20006
www.agc.org

Association of Professional Landscape Designers (APLD)
(312) 201-0101
104 So. Michigan Avenue, Suite 1500
Chicago, IL 60603

Center for Irrigation Technology
(209) 278-2066
California State University Fresno
5370 N. Chestnut Ave. M/S 18
Fresno, CA 93740-8021
www.atinet.org/cati/cit

International Facility Management Association (IFMA)
(713) 623-4362
1 E. Greenway Plaza, Suite 1100
Houston, TX 77046-0194
www.ifma.org

The Irrigation Association
(703) 573-3551
8260 Willow Oaks Corporate Dr., Suite 120
Fairfax, VA 22031

Professional Lawn Care Association of America
(800) 458-3466
1000 Johnson Ferry Road NE, Suite C-135
Marietta, GA 30068
www.plcaa.org

Industry References

The Blue Book (Regional Editions)
(800) 431-2584
Contractor's Register, Inc.
P.O. Box 500
Jefferson Valley, NY 10535
www.thebluebook.com

Thomas Regional Directory Co.
(212) 629-2100
5 Penn Plaza
New York, NY 10117-0769
www.thomasregional.com

American Society for Testing and Materials (ASTM)
(610) 832-9566
100 Barr Harbor Drive
West Conshocken, PA 19428

Wood References

American Institute of Timber Construction
7012 So. Revere Pkwy, Suite 140
Englewood, CO 80112

APA–The Engineered Wood Association
(formerly American Plywood Assoc.)
P.O. Box 11700
Tacoma, WA 98411

California Redwood Association
405 Enfrente Drive, Suite 200
Novato, CA 94949

Southern Forest Products Assn.
P.O. Box 641700
Kenner, LA 70064

Western Wood Products Assn.
Yeon Building
522 SW 5th Ave.
Portland, OR 97204-2112

U.S. Forest Service
Forest Products Laboratory
1 Gifford Pinchot Drive
Madison, WI 53705-2398

Forest Service Office of Information
P.O. Box 96090
Washington, DC 20090-6090

Masonry References

Brick Industry Association
11490 Commerce Park Drive
Reston, VA 20191

Indiana Limestone Institute
Stone City Bank Bldg. S-400
Bedford, IN 47421

International Masonry Institute
823 15th Street NW, Suite 1001
Washington, DC 20005

International Union of Bricklayers and Allied Craftsmen
815 15th St., NW
Washington, DC 20005

PROFESSIONAL REFERENCES

Manufacturers

Hunter Industries Incorporated
1940 Diamond Street
San Marcos, CA 92069
(760) 744-5240

Landscape Forms, Inc.
431 Lawndale Avenue
Kalamazoo, MI 49001
(800) 521-2546

Neenah Foundry Company
Box 729
2121 Brooks Avenue
Neenah, WI 54957
(414) 725-7000

Quick Crete Products Corp.
741 West Parkridge Avenue
P.O. Box 639
Norco, CA 91760
(909) 737-6240

Abbreviations

A	Area Square Feet; Ampere	C.I.P.	Cast in Place	Fig	Figure
	Asbestos Bonded Steel	Circ.	Circuit	Fin.	Finished
A.C.	Alternating Current	C.L.	Carload Lot	Fixt.	Fixture
	Air Conditioning;	Clab.	Common Laborer	Fl. Oz.	Fluid Ounces
	Asbestos Cement	C.L.F.	Hundred Linear Feet	Flr.	Floor
Ac	Acre	cm	Centimeter	Fmg.	Framing
A.C.I.	American Concrete Institute	CMP	Corr. Metal Pipe	Fndtn.	Foundation
Addit.	Additional	C.M.U.	Concrete Masonry Unit	Fori.	Foreman, inside
Adj.	Adjustable	Col.	Column	Foro.	Foreman, outside
Agg.	Aggregate	CO₂	Carbon Dioxide	Fount.	Fountain
A hr	Ampere-hour	Comb.	Combination	4 PST	Four Pole, Single Throw
A.I.A.	American Institute of Architects	Compr.	Compressor	FPM	Feet per Minute
Allow.	Allowance	Conc.	Concrete	FPT	Female Pipe Thread
alt.	Altitude	Cont.	Continuous;	Fr.	Frame
Alum.	Aluminum		Continued	Ft.	Foot; Feet
a.m.	ante meridiem	Corr.	Corrugated	Ftng.	Fitting
Amp.	Ampere	Cov.	Cover	Ftg.	Footing
Approx.	Approximate	Cplg.	Coupling	Ft. Lb.	Foot Pound
Apt.	Apartment	C.P.M.	Critical Path Method	Furn.	Furniture
Asb.	Asbestos	CPVC	Chlorinated Polyvinyl Chloride	g	Gram
A.S.B.C.	American Standard Building Code	C. Pr.	Hundred Pair	Ga.	Gauge
Asbe.	Asbestos Worker	Creos.	Creosote	Gal.	Gallon
A.S.M.E.	American Society of	C.S.F.	Hundred Square Feet	Gal./Min.	Gallon Per Minute
	Mechanical Engineers	C.S.I.	Construction Specification	Galv.	Galvanized
A.S.T.M.	American Society for		Institute	Gen.	General
	Testing and Materials	Cu	Cubic	Glaz.	Glazier
Attchmt.	Attachment	Cu. Ft.	Cubic Foot	GPD	Gallons per Day
Avg.	Average	Cwt.	100 Pounds	GPH	Gallons per Hour
Bbl.	Barrel	C.Y.	Cubic Yard (27 cubic feet)	GPM	Gallons per Minute
	Balled & Burlapped	C.Y./Hr.	Cubic Yard per Hour	GR	Grade
BCF	Bank Cubic Foot	Cyl.	Cylinder	Gran.	Granular
BCY	Bank Cubic Yard	d	Penny (nail size)	Grnd.	Ground
B.&W.	Black and White	D	Deep; Depth, Discharge	H.D.	Heavy Duty; High Density
B.F.	Board Feet	Dis.		Hdr.	Header
Bg. Cem.	Bag of Cement	Disch.	Discharge	Hdwe.	Hardware
B.I.	Black Iron	Dbl.	Double	Help.	Helper average
Bit.		DC	Direct Current	Hg	Mercury
Bitum.	Bituminous	Demob.	Demobilization	H.O.	High Output
Bldg.	Building	Diag.	Diagonal	Horiz.	Horizontal
Blk	Block	Diam.	Diameter	H.P.	Horsepower; High Pressure
Bm	Beam	Distrib.	Distribution	H.P.F.	High Power Factor
Brg.	Bearing	Dk.	Deck	Hr.	Hour
Brhe.	Bricklayer Helper	Do.	Ditto	Hrs./Day	Hours Per Day
Bric	Bricklayer	Dp.	Depth	HSC	High Short Circuit
Brk.	Brick	D.P.S.T.	Double Pole, Single Throw	Ht.	Height
Brng.	Bearing	Dr.	Driver	Htg	Heating
Brs.	Brass	Drink.	Drinking	Htrs.	Heaters
Brz.	Bronze	Dty	Duty	HVAC	Heating, Ventilating &
Bsn.	Basin	E	Equipment Only; East		Air Conditioning
Btr.	Better	Ea.	Each	Hvy.	Heavy
BTU	British Thermal Unit	Econ.	Economy	HW	Hot Water
BTUH	BTU per Hour	EDP	Electronic Data Processing	Hyd.;	
BU	Bushel	Eq.	Equation	Hydr.	Hydraulic
BX	Interlocked Armored Cable	Elec	Electrician; Electrical	ID	Inside Diameter
c	Conductivity	Elev.	Elevator; Elevating	I.D.	Inside Dimension;
C	Hundred;		Thin Wall Conduit		Identification
	Centigrade	Eng	Engine	I.F.	Inside Frosted
C/C	Center to Center		Equip. Oper., heavy	I.M.C.	Intermediate Metal Conduit
Cair.	Air Tool Laborer	Eqhv.	Equip. Oper., light	In.	Inch
Cal.	Caliper	Eqlt	Equip. Oper., medium	Incan.	Incandescent
Calc	Calculated	Eqmd.	Equip. Oper., Master Mechanic	Incl.	Included; Including
Cap.	Capacity	Eqmm.	Equip. Oper., oilers	Int.	Interior
Carp.	Carpenter	Eqol.	Equipment	Inst.	Installation
C.B.	Circuit Breaker	Equip.	Estimated	Insul.	Insulation
C.C.F.	Hundred Cubic Feet	Est.	Each Way	I.P.	Iron Pipe
cd	Candela	E.W.	Excavation	I.P.S.	Iron Pipe Size; Inside Pipe Size
CD	Grade of Plywood Face & Back	Excav.	Fahrenheit; Female; Fill	I.P.T.	Iron Pipe Threaded
CDX	Plywood, grade C&D, exterior glue	F	Fabricated	K	Thousand; Thousand Pounds
Cefi.	Cement Finisher	Fab.	Fiberglass	K.D.A.T.	Kiln Dried After Treatment
Cem.	Cement	FBGS	Footcandles	kg	Kilogram
CF	Hundred Feet	F.C.	Compressive Stress in Concrete;	Kip.	1000 Pounds
CF	Cubic Feet	Fc.	Extreme Compressive Stress	Km	Kilometer
CFM	Cubic Feet per Minute		Flat Grain	K.L.F.	Kips per Linear Foot
c.g.	Center of Gravity	F.G.	Feet Head	K.S.F.	Kips per Square Foot
CHW	Commercial Hot Water	FH	Federal Housing Administration	K.S.I.	Kips per Square Inch
C.I.	Cast Iron	F.H.A.		KW	Kilo Watt

Abbreviations

Abbrev.	Definition	Abbrev.	Definition	Abbrev.	Definition
KWh	Kilowatt-hour	Mult.	Multi, Multiply	Sched	Schedule
L.	Labor Only; Length; Long	MYD	Thousand yards	S.C.R.	Modular Brick
Lab.	Labor	N	Natural; North	S.E.	Surfaced Edge
lat	Latitude	NA	Not Available; Not Applicable	S.F.	Square Foot
Lath.	Lather	N.B.C.	National Building Code	S.F.C.A.	Square Foot Contact Area
Lav.	Lavatory	N.L.B.	Non-Load-Bearing	S.F.G.	Square Foot of Ground
lb.; #	Pound	No.	Number	S.F. Hor.	Square Foot Horizontal
L.B.	Load Bearing, L Conduit Body	NPS	Nominal Pipe Size	Shee.	Sheet Metal Worker
L. & E.	Labor & Equipment	OC	On Center	Sin.	Sine
lb./hr.	Pounds per Hour	OD	Outside Diameter	Skwk	Skilled Worker
lb./L.F.	Pounds per Linear Foot	O.D.	Outside Dimension	S.P.	Static Pressure; Single Pole;
lbf/sq in.	Pound-force per Square Inch	O & P	Overhead and Profit		Self Propelled
LCF	Loose Cubic Foot	Oper.	Operator	Spri.	Sprinkler Installer
LCY	Loose Cubic Yard	Opng	Opening	Sq.	Square; 100 square feet
L.C.L.	Less than Carload Lot	Orna	Ornamental	S.P.D.T.	Single Pole, Double Throw
Ld.	Load	Ovhd	Overhead	S.P.S.T.	Single Pole, Single Throw
L.F.	Linear Foot	Oz.	Ounce	SPT	Standard Pipe Thread
Lg	Long, Length, Large	P	Pole; Applied Load; Projection	S.S.	Single Strength; Stainless Steel
L.J	Long Span Standard Strength	p.	Page	St. Stl.	Steel
	Bar Joist	Pc	Piece	Std	Standard
L.L.	Live Load	P.C.	Portland Cement;	Str.	Strength; Starter; Straight
L.L.D.	Lamp Lumen Depreciation		Power Connector	Struct	Structural
lm	Lumen	P.C.F.	Pounds per Cubic Foot	Sty.	Story
lm/sf	Lumber Square Foot	P.E.	Professional Engineer;	Subj.	Subject
lm/W	Lumen Per Watt		Porcelain Enamel; Polyethylene;	Subs.	Subcontractors
L.O.A.	Length Over All		Plain End	Surf.	Surface
log	Logarithm	Perf	Perforated	Sw.	Switch
L.P.	Liquefied Petroleum;	Ph.	Phase	S.Y.	Square Yard
	Low Pressure	P.I.	Pressure Injected	Sys.	System
L.P.F.	Low Power Factor	Pile.	Pile Driver	t.	Thickness
Lt.	Light	Pkg.	Package	T	Temperature; Ton
L.T.L.	Less than Truckload Lot	Pl.	Plate	T.C.	Terra Cotta
Lt. Wt.	Lightweight	PLS	Pure Live Seed	T. & G.	Tongue & Groove;
L.V.	Low Voltage	Pluh.	Plumbers Helper		Tar & Gravel
M	Thousand; Material; Male;	Plum.	Plumber	Th.; Thk.	Thick
	Light Wall Copper	Ply.	Plywood	Thn.	Thin
m/hr	Man-hour	Pord	Painter, Ordinary	Thrded	Threaded
Mach.	Machine	pp	Pages	Tilf.	Tile Layer Floor
Maint.	Maintenance	PP; PPL	Polypropylene	Tilh.	Tile Layer Helper
Marb.	Marble Setter	P.P.M.	Parts per Million	T.L.	Truckload
Mat.	Material	Pr.	Pair	T/M	Tan/Mile
Mat'l	Material	Prefab	Prefabricated	Tot.	Total
Max	Maximum	Prefin.	Prefinished	Tr.	Trade
MBF	Thousand Board Feet	PSF; psf	Pounds per Square Foot	Transf.	Transformer
M.C.F.	Thousand Cubic Feet	PSI; psi	Pounds per Square Inch	Trhv.	Truck Driver, Heavy
M.C.F.M.	Thousand Cubic Feet	PSIG	Pounds per Square Inch Gauge	Trlr.	Trailer
	per Minute	PSP	Plastic Sewer Pipe	Trlt.	Truck Driver, Light
MD	Medium Duty	Pspr.	Painter, Spray	UCI	Uniform Construction Index
Med.	Medium	P.T.	Potential Transformer	U.L.	Underwriters Laboratory
MF	Thousand Feet	P. & T.	Pressure & Temperature	Unfin.	Unfinished
M.F.B.M.	Thousand Feet Board Measure	Ptd.	Painted	V	Volt
Mfg.	Manufacturing	Ptns.	Partitions	VA	Volt/amp
Mfrs.	Manufacturers	PVC	Polyvinyl Chloride	Vent.	Ventilating
mg	Milligram	Pvmt.	Pavement	Vert.	Vertical
MH	Manhole; Metal-	Pwr.	Power	V.G.	Vertical Grain
	Halide; Man Hour	Quan.; Qty.	Quantity	Vib.	Vibrating
MHz	Megahertz	Qt.	Quart	Vol.	Volume
Mi.	Mile	R.C.P.	Reinforced Concrete Pipe	W	Wire; Watt; Wide; West
MI	Malleable Iron; Mineral Insulated	Rect.	Rectangle	w/	With
mm	Millimeter	Reg.	Regular	Wldg.	Welding
Min.	Minimum	Reinf.	Reinforced	Wrck.	Wrecker
Misc.	Miscellaneous	Req'd.	Required	W.S.P.	Water, Steam, Petroleum
M.L.F.	Thousand Linear Feet	Resi	Residential	WT; Wt	Weight
Mo.	Month	Rgh.	Rough	WWF	Welded Wire Fabric
Mobil.	Mobilization	R.H.W.	Rubber, Heat & Water Resistant	XFMR	Transformer
MPH	Miles per Hour		Residential Hot Water	XHD	Extra Heavy Duty
MPT	Male Pipe Thread	Rnd.	Round	yd	Yard
MRT	Mile Round Trip	Rodm.	Rodman	yr	Year
M.S.F.	Thousand Square Feet	R.O.W.	Right of Way	%	Percent
Mstz.	Mosaic & Terrazzo Worker	RPM	Revolutions per Minute	~	Approximately
M.S.Y.	Thousand Square Yards	R.S.	Rapid Start	∅	Phase
Mtd.	Mounted	RT	Round Trip	@	At
Mthe.	Mosaic & Terrazzo Helper	S.	Suction; Single Entrance;	#	Pound; Number
Mtng	Mounting		South	<	Less Than
		Scaf.	Scaffold	>	Greater Than
		Sch.;			

INDEX

Notes

Notes

Notes